Critical Acclaim for **Best Dives of the Western Hemisphere** and **Best Dives of the Caribbean:**

" . . . the bible of Caribbean dive-travel. . . . I highly recommend it"
Christopher Lofting, The Travel Show, WOR Network Radio

"It's super! . . . a great reference and we love it."
Dive Travel Magazine

" . . . A terrific guide."
John Clayton, The Travel Show, KABC Radio, Los Angeles

" . . . a must have. . . for divers, snorkelers or those who just love to float in liquid turquoise."
Brenda Fine, Travel Editor, The New York Law Journal

" . . . a good travel planner."
Jill Schensul, Travel Editor, The Record

"It's a trustworthy publication."
Undercurrent

" . . . opens a new world of adventure to anyone with a mask and snorkel."

Pat Reilly, travel writer, Commerce Magazine

" . . . the best coverage of the subject matter I've seen, and incredibly easy to read. . . essential for the serious or beginning diver."
Dr. Susan Cropper, DVM, Society of Aquatic Veterinarians

" . . . details more than 200 of the finest dive sites in the Caribbean."
Bill Smith, Dive Travel News

"I have bought both editions of this book [Caribbean], because the first edition got so dog-eared that I wanted a clean one for vacation last year. The book is a marvelous source for both the snorkeler and the diver."
Cindy McBride, diver

Using This Guide

Quick-reference symbols are used throughout this guide to identify diving and snorkeling areas. Each has been given a rating of from one to five starfish by prominent divemasters in the area.

☆☆☆☆☆   **Five Starfish**. Best of the best diving; best visibility, best marine life, best reef or kelp dive.

☆☆☆☆   **Four Starfish**. Fantastic dive. Outstanding marine life or visual interest.

☆☆☆   **Three Starfish**. Superb dive. Excellent visibility and marine life or wreck.

☆☆   **Two Starfish**. Good dive. Interesting fish and plant life. Good visibility.

☆   **One Starfish**. Pleasant dive. Better than average.

Map Symbols

Dive site   Shipwreck

Snorkeling area   Airport

Best Dives

of the

Western Hemisphere

Second Edition

Joyce & Jon Huber

HUNTER

Hunter Publishing, Inc.
130 Campus Drive, Edison NJ 08818
(732) 225-1900, (800) 255-0343, fax (732) 417-0482

The Boundary, Wheatley Road, Garsington
Oxford, OX44 9EJ England
01865-361122, fax 01865-361133

ISBN 1-55650-858-1

© 1999 Joyce & Jon Huber

Cover: *Antler Coral & Grunts*, Jon Huber
Maps by Joyce Huber

For complete information about the hundreds of other travel guides offered by Hunter Publishing, visit our Web site at:

www.hunterpublishing.com

Every effort has been made to ensure that the information in this book is correct, but the publishera, authors and contributors do not assume, and hereby disclaim, liability to any party for los or damage caused by errors, omissions, misleading information or potential problems caused by information in this guide, even if such errors or omissions are a result of negligence, accident or any other cause.

This publication is intended only as a guide. Additional information should be obtained prior to visiting each area. Every effort has been made to obtain accurate and up-to-date information for this publication. However, considering the sheer magnitude of the research involved, not all information could not be confirmed immediately prior to press time. All prices quoted are subject to change.

Contents

Acknowledgments

The authors thank all Best Dives' contributors, correspondents, photographers and researchers for their enormous effort in preparing material for this edition.

A special thanks to Lissa Dailey and Michael Hunter of Hunter Publishing. For work on the GALAPAGOS: Marc Bernardi of Aquatic Encounters. GRAND TURK: Cecil Ingham and Connie Rus. BAHAMAS: Michelle Landa, BSMG Marketing, Graeme Teague, Stuart Cove's Dive South Ocean, John Stewart, UNEXSO, Lynn Dixon, Nekton Cruises; Anita, Amanda, Neil and Ken Liggett, Rick and Lisa Ocklemann. BARBADOS: Nicole DiBenedetto, Ruder-Finn, Michael Young, Underwater Barbados. BRITISH VIRGIN ISLANDS: Kristen Driska and Tammy Peters of FDB, NY, JoAnn and Jonathan Pannaman, Bret Gilliam and Joe Giacinto of Dive BVI. BONAIRE, Dee Scarr, Touch the Sea, Lisa Blau and Marie Rosa of Adams Unlimited, Brenda Fine, Kathy Rothschild, Dive Safaris Worldwide. CAYMAN ISLANDS: Christopher Lofting, Maria Shaw, Mike Emmanuel, Lynda Long. BELIZE: Shakira Samuels, Belize Tourism, Bob Wescott, Mollie Tichy, Wescott Group. BERMUDA: Olivia Serafin, Porter Novelli. BRAZIL: Bill and Jeanie Smith. CURACAO: Mary Brennan, Erwin F. Eustacia, Ivan Englentina, and Eva Van Dalen, Michel Angelo Harms, Curacao Tourism. FLORIDA KEYS: Tom Mc Kelvey, Jim and Nadia Spencer, Andy Dear, Andy Newman, Stuart Newman Associates. HAWAII: Alison Young, McNeil Wilson. MEXICO: Diana Cabrals, Mexican Tourism, Myrna Bush, Club Akumal Caribe, Susan and Rick Sammon, CEDAM. SANTA CATALINA: Julien Foreman, Catalina Island Visitors Bureau. UNITED STATES VIRGIN ISLANDS: Chad Thompson, Amy Atkinson, Talia Woodard, Martin Public Relations, Lucy Portlock, Pelagic Pleasures, Luana Wheatley, Michelle Pugh, Mike Meyers, Monica Leedy. GENERAL: Dennis and Karen Sabo, Landfall Productions, Barbara Swab, Frank Holler, Holler Swab & Partners, Bob DiChiara, Dr. Susan Cropper.

Introduction

Photo ©Mary Brooks, UNEXSO

As the dive population grows, so does the diversity of vacation and destination choices. Yet, deciding which tropical picture to put yourself in can become a tough job.

Travel and dive magazines dazzle us with glorious color photos taken on the best reefs and under the best weather and sea conditions. TV commercials promise sunny skies and smiling islanders waiting with luscious, frosty drinks. And, through the magic of technology, we see fish dancing and singing beneath cruise ships. Let's face it, they all look good. Of course, if you're in a northern climate during February the fish look even friendlier, and you don't care if they can't really dance, you just want to get there. But, where?

Helping you decide where to go and what to see is what **Best Dives of the Western Hemisphere** is intended to do. We've included a wider variety of resorts, inns and even a few campgrounds. The *Resource and Travel Tip* chapter covers the certification agencies, top dive-travel tour companies, dive-travel insurance plans and tidbits that are good to consider before traveling.

And, we have the lowdown on vacation surprises... what they say and what they don't say: "The dive site is just off the beach" [if you don't mind swimming two miles over a reef shallow enough to shred your skin]; "Good for beginning divers" [on the third Wednesday of the first month with two full moons]; "Luxury resort special for a fraction of the normal rate" [per-person, sharing the room with three strangers plus a hefty room tax and resort levy]; "money-saving dive package" [unless it rains every day, then we keep your money and offer you a rain check for the next time you travel thousands of miles and spend the money to get here]. If you've taken a few dive vacations, you probably have some "vacation surprise" stories too.

Our favorite was our third weathered-out trip to the Florida Keys many years ago. The tourist board posted signs that read "Always good weather in the Keys," and in the pictures they sent us there always was . We happened to ar-

Photo ©Marc Bernardi, Aquatic Encounters

Hammerheads, Galapagos.

rive during a tropical depression. Black clouds rolled across the horizon. High winds bent the palms low enough to beat the sand. Furious winds churned the normally flat bays into a froth of whitecaps. And everyone there looked us in the eye and said, "You should have been here last week." So we made it a point to find out when "last week" happens. Be sure to note the "best time to go" in each chapter.

Have a great trip, and when you get home let us know the highs and lows of your vacation. We'll pick some to run in our next edition. Write to us care of the publisher's address listed on the copyright page or e-mail us at jonhuber@worldnet.att.net or bestdives@juno.com.

Resources & Travel Tips

Scuba Certifying Organizations

Locations for scuba instruction near your home may be obtained from one of the following organizations.

IDEA, International Diving Educators Association, PO Box 8427, Jacksonville, FL 32239-8427. ☎ 904-744-5554.

NASDS, National Association of Scuba Diving Schools, 1012 S. Yates, Memphis, TN 38119. ☎ 800-735-3483; 901-767-7265. Website: divesafe.com.

NAUI, National Association of Underwater Instructors, PO Box 14650, Montclair, CA 91763. ☎ 800-553-6284; 909-621-5801. Lost cards 909-621-6210; fax 901-621-6405. Website: www.naui.org.

PADI INTERNATIONAL, Professional Association of Diving Instructors, 1251 E. Dyer Rd., Suite 100, Santa Ana, CA 92705-5605. ☎ 800-729-7234; 714-540-7234. Website: www.padi.com.

PDIC INTERNATIONAL, Professional Diving Instructors Corporation 1554 Gardener Ave, Scranton, PA 18509. ☎ 717-342-9434; fax 717-342-1480. E-mail: info@PDIC-INTL.com. Website: www.pdic-intl.com.

SSI, Scuba Schools International, 2619 Canton Court, Fort Collins, CO 80525. ☎ 800-892-2702; 303-482-0883. E-mail: admin@ssiusa.com or ssilen@aol.com.

YMCA, National YMCA Scuba Program, Oakbrook Square, 6083-A Oakbrook Parkway, Norcross/Atlanta, GA 30093. ☎ 770-662-5172; fax 770-242-9059. E-mail: scubaymca@aol.com. Website: www.webcom.com/cscripts/-ymca/ymca.html.

Cruises & Package Tours

Package vacations may save you hundreds of dollars, but be sure to read the fine print carefully when you are comparing tours. Consider transfers, sightseeing tours, meals, auto rentals, acceptable accommodations, and taxes. Tanks and weights may or may not be included. Also ask whether extra airline weight allowances are included for dive gear.

Aquatic Encounters features live-aboard vacations to the Galapagos aboard the *Reina Silvia*, to Papau New Guinea, Thailand, Ningaloo Reef, Australia for whaleshark encounters and to the Dominican Republic for humpback whale adventures. This is a top-notch operation offering personalized service. ☎ 800-757-1365 pin code 1815 or 303-494-8384, fax 303-494-1202. Website: www.aquaticencounters.com.

Oceanic Society Expeditions, a non-profit environmental group, offers research-oriented snorkel trips and dolphin swims. ☎ 415-441-1106 or 800-326-7491 or write to the Oceanic Society, Fort Mason Center, Bldg. E, San Francisco, CA 94123. Website: www.oceanic-society.org.

Landfall Dive and Adventure Travel offers hassle-free, money-saving tours for groups and individual divers to the Bahamas, Bonaire, Belize, BVI, Cozumel, Dominica, St. Vincent & the Grenadines, Bay Islands, Honduras, St. Kitts, St. Lucia, Turks and Caicos and the Pacific. ☎ 916-563-0164, fax 916-924-1059. E-mail: landfall@pattravel.com. Website: landfallproductions. com.

CEDAM (Conservation, Ecology, Diving, Archaeology, Museums) offers programs as varied as an underwater archaeological dig on an ancient shipwreck or a mapping tour of the Galapagos. Write them at 1 Fox Rd., Croton, NY 10520. ☎ (914) 271-5365; fax (914) 271-4723. E-mail: cedamint@ aol.com. Website: www.cedam.org.

Tropical Adventures offers more than 27 destinations and live-aboards worldwide. ☎ 800-247-3483. Website: www.divetropical.com.

Handicapped Divers

Handicapped divers will find help and information by contacting the **Handicapped Scuba Association** (HSA). The association has provided scuba instruction to people with physical disabilities since 1975. Over 600 instructors in 24 countries are HSA-trained. HSA has developed the "Resort Evaluation Program" to help handicapped divers select a vacation destination. They check out facilities and work with the staff and management to ensure accessibility. Once a resort is totally accessible it is certified by HSA.

For a list of HSA-certified resorts, group-travel opportunities and more information on HSA's programs, instruction and activities, ☎ 949-498-6128. E-mail: hsahdq@compuserve.com.

Money

Most large resorts, restaurants and dive operators will accept major credit cards, although you risk being charged at a higher rate if the local currency fluctuates. Traveler's checks are accepted almost everywhere and often you'll get a better exchange rate for them than cash. It's always a good idea to have some local currency on hand for cabs, tips and small purchases.

Insurance

Many types of travel insurance are available, covering everything from lost luggage and trip cancellations tp medical expenses. Since emergency medical assistance and air ambulance fees can run into thousands of dollars, it is wise to be prepared. Trips purchased with some major credit cards include life insurance.

Divers Alert Network (DAN) offers divers' health insurance for $35 a year plus an annual membership fee of $25, $35 for a family. Any treatment required for an accident or emergency that is a direct result of diving, such as decompression sickness (the bends), arterial gas embolism or pulmonary barotrauma is covered up to $125,000. Air ambulance to the closest medical care facility, recompression chamber care and in-patient hospital care are covered. Non-diving travel-related accidents are NOT covered.

Lacking the ability to pay, a diver may be refused transport and/or treatment. For more information write to DAN, PO Box 3823, Duke University Medical Center, Durham, NC 27710. ☎ 919) 684-2948. For emergencies worldwide call collect ☎ 800-446-2671 or 919-684-4DAN (4326). E-mail: dan@ dan.ycg.org. Website: http://www.dan.ycg.org.

International SOS Assistance is a medical assistance service to travelers who are more than 100 miles from home. For just $55 per person for seven to 14 days, or $96 per couple, SOS covers air evacuation and travel-related assistance. Evacuation is to the closest medical care facility, which is determined by SOS staff doctors. Representative Michael Klein states that SOS has and will send out a private LearJet if necessary to accommodate a patient. Hospitalization is NOT covered. Standard Blue Cross and Blue Shield policies do cover medical costs while traveling. For individual and group information write to International SOS Assistance, Box 11568, Philadelphia, PA 19116. ☎ 800-523-8930 or 215-244-1500. E-mail: jfahy @intsos.com. Website: www.intsos.com.

Lost luggage insurance is available at the ticket counters of many airlines. If you have a homeowner's policy, you may already be covered. Be sure to check first with your insurance agent.

Keep a list of all your dive equipment and other valuables including the name of the manufacturer, model, date of purchase, new price and serial number, if any, on your person when traveling. Immediately report any theft or loss of baggage to the local police, hotel security people or airline and get a copy of that report. Both the list and the report of loss or theft will be needed to collect from your insurance company. Do not expect airlines to cheerfully compensate you for any loss without a lot of red tape and hassle. Regardless of the value of your gear the airline pays by the weight ($9 per pound) of what is lost. Be sure to tag your luggage with your name and address. Use a business address if possible.

Packing Checklist

___ MASK

___ SNORKEL

___ FINS

___ REGULATOR

___ DEPTH GUAGE

___ BOUYANCY
COMPENSATOR
(stab jacket)

___ WET SUIT, SHORTIE
OR LYCRA WET SKIN

___ WET SUIT BOOTS

___ MESH CATCH BAG

___ U/W DIVE LIGHTS

___ DRAMAMINE or other
seasickness preventative

___ GEAR MARKER

___ DIVER CERTIFICATION
CARD (C-card)

___ DIVER LOG BOOK

___ SUNGLASSES

___ SPARE MASK STRAP

___ DIVE KNIFE OR SHEARS

___ SPARE SNORKEL
RETAINER RING

___ SPARE STRAPS

___ SUBMERSIBLE
PRESSURE GAUGE

___ WATCH/BOTTOM TIMER

___ WEIGHT BELT
(no lead)

___ DE-FOG SOLUTION

___ REEF GLOVES
(not for use in marine parks)

___ CYALUME STICKS
(chemical light sticks)

___ U\W CAMERA AND FILM

___ FISH ID BOOK

___ DIVE TABLES

___ PASSPORT or proof of
citizenship as required

___ DIVE TABLES
(or computer)

___ SUNTAN LOTION

___ HAT (with visor or brim)

Documents

Carry your personal documents on you at all times. Be sure to keep a separate record of passport numbers, visas, or tourist cards in your luggage.

Security

Tourists flashing wads of cash and expensive jewelry are prime targets for robbers. Avoid off-the-beaten-track areas of cities, especially at night. Do not carry a lot of cash, expensive cameras or jewelry. Keep alert to what's going on around you. Stay with your luggage until it is checked in with the airlines. Jewelry should be kept in the hotel safe.

Rental cars have become a target for robbers in some areas. To avoid problems, try to rent a car without rental company markings. If someone bumps into your car, do not stop. Drive to a police station and report the incident. Do not stop for hitchhikers or to assist strangers.

Drugs

Penalties for possession of illegal drugs are very harsh and the risk you take for holding even a half-ounce of marijuana cannot be stressed enough. Punishment often entails long jail terms. In certain areas, such as Mexico, your embassy and the best lawyer won't be much help. You are guilty until proven innocent. Selling drugs is still cause for public hanging in some areas.

Cameras

Divers traveling with expensive camera gear or electronic equipment should register each item with customs *before* leaving the country.

Sundries

Suntan lotion, aspirin, antihistamines, decongestants, anti-fog solutions, or mosquito repellent should be purchased before your trip. These products are not always available and may cost quite a bit more than you pay for them at home.

First Aid

Every diver should carry a small first aid kit for minor cuts, bruises or ailments. Be sure to include a topical antihistamine ointment, antihistamine tablets, seasickness preventive, decongestant, throat lozenges, band-aids, aspirin and diarrhea treatment.

Sunburn Protection

Avoid prolonged exposure to the sun, especially during peak hours, 10 am to 3 pm. Since most dive trips occur during peak hours, whenever possible opt for trips on dive boats with sun canopies, use sunblock lotions or a sunscreen with a protection factor of at least 15, select hats with a wide brim and wear protective clothing of fabrics made to block the sun's ultraviolet rays.

Diver Identification

Most dive operations require that you hold a certification card and a logbook. A check-out dive may be required if you cannot produce a log of recent dives.

New Divers

Every dive shop in the US offers a "resort course" or introductory class. If you have not yet learned to dive and want to find out more, stop in at your local dive shop. You'll find learning the sport or deciding whether you really want to before you travel much easier than trying to do it all at a resort destination. Once you commit, it's a good idea to get certified before you go. Stretching out the certification course over a few weeks gives you more time to absorb what you're learning. Plus, you'll have ample opportunity to solve problems and ask questions in a pool rather than the ocean. You can take the open-water portion of the certification at any of the destinations in this book. You'll notice we list "referrals" under many of the resort area dive shops. That means they can complete your certification.

Additional Reading

Undercurrent, a monthly newsletter, is a must have for avid divers. Each issue packs in fascinating stories on a variety of dive subjects ranging from the Bermuda Triangle to using Mosquito Nuts as malaria prophylaxis, diving, dive resorts, live-aboards, and treasure hunting. New subscribers pay $39. ☎ 800-326-1896 or 415-5906. Website: www.undercurrent.org. Send checks to Undercurrent, PO Box 1658, Sausalito, CA 94966.

Section I

The Atlantic

Bahamas

When you say "the Bahamas," you're talking about an archipelago containing approximately 700 islands and more than 2,500 cays that stretch from 50 miles off Florida's east coast to the waters off southeastern Cuba – an area with more diving and snorkeling variety than anywhere else, from dramatic walls and dropoffs, shipwrecks and sharks to shallow reefs and dolphin encounters.

The islands vary in size too, with Andros being the largest. The most visited tourist areas include Nassau, the capital on New Providence Island; the Abacos chain, including Great Abacos, Little Abacos, Elbow Cay, Treasure Cay and others; Eleuthera/Harbour Island; the Exumas; Bimini; the Berry Islands; Cat Island; Long Island; Crooked Island; San Salvador; Grand Bahama Island; and Andros. Geographically, all are similar with low, thick pine forests sloping to mangrove swamps, lagoons and lakes. Many coastlines are rimmed with shimmering pink or white sandy beaches. The highest point in the country is Mount Alvernia, which rises 206 feet above sea level.

Dive adventures can begin almost anywhere, when you consider that the islands cap two barrier reefs (the Little and Great Bahama Banks) that wander through 500 miles of tropical ocean and cover 100,000 square miles. This dense coral reef system winds through hundreds of historic wrecks, mysterious blue holes and vacated movie sets.

A magnificent trench known as The Tongue of the Ocean (TOTO) starts off New Providence Island's south end and runs along the eastern side of Andros. TOTO offers shark encounters at the Deer Island Buoy (aka Shark Buoy), which was tethered in 6,000 ft of water by the US Navy, 12 miles offshore, as part of the Sound Surveillance System (SOSUS) for tracking submarines, whales and underwater seismic events.

Old-world charm and new world glamour combine in Nassau, the capital of the Bahamas on New Providence Island, and in its world-class resort areas, Cable Beach and Paradise Island. Grand Bahama Island has modern resorts in Freeport/Lucaya and the rustic charm of old settlements such as West End. The Out Islands offer pampered seclusion in Robinson Crusoe-style hideaways. Together, the Bahamas provide every style of dive and snorkeling vacation, from sophisticated to simple. And it's easy to get there, via frequent

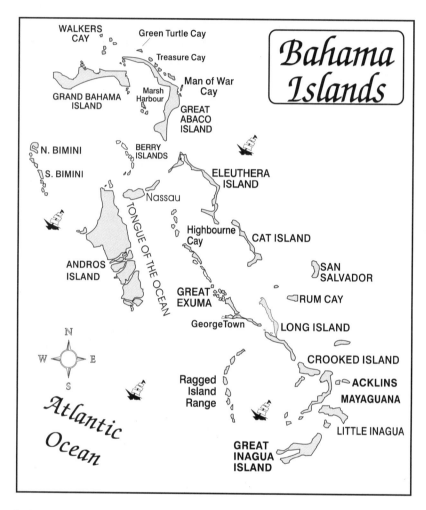

flights by major airlines or on the national flag carrier, Bahamasair. If you can't decide on one area, inter-island air services enable you to combine a visit to Nassau or Freeport with a trip to the Out Islands.

History

The Commonwealth of the Bahamas was originally settled by Lucayan Indians who paddled their way north from the Caribbean, though credit for "discovering" the islands is given to Christopher Columbus, who landed on Guanahani, now San Salvador, in 1492. Conquistadors soon followed in pursuit of gold, killing off the Lucayans with disease, enslavement and hardship. English settlers arrived in 1647 seeking religious freedom. They named the island where they landed Eleuthera – the Greek word for freedom. After years of unstable rule, the islands became a Crown Colony. Captain Woodes Rogers was the first Royal Governor. During the American Revolution, the islands fell to Spain and were not restored to Great Britain until 1783. British Loyalists soon emigrated to the islands of the Bahamas, many bringing black slaves with them. A slave-free society was declared in 1834 by the British Emancipation Act.

Many island inhabitants are descendants of British Loyalists, slaves or pirates who shipwrecked on the islands.

After nearly 250 years of British colonial rule, on July 10, 1973 the Commonwealth of the Bahamas declared its independence. The Bahamas now has a parliamentary Democracy Governor-General as head of state.

When to Go

The high season runs from mid-December through mid-April, though some divers and snorkelers prefer the warmer, and sometimes calmer, waters of late April, May and June. Hurricane season occurs from late July through mid-November with most activity in September. Seawater temperature ranges from 73°F in February to 82°F in August.

The climate of the Bahamas is idyllic, with the mean air temperature in January about 77°F and in August, 89°. The difference between the warmest and coolest months is only about 12°.

Sightseeing

In Nassau, Cable Beach, and Paradise Island you can enjoy topside scenery by taxi, bicycle or horse-drawn surrey complete with fringed top.

To get a personal view, ask for a driver who is a Bahamahost. Bahamahosts are certified by the Bahamas Ministry of Tourism and are extremely knowledgeable about native history, folklore, flora, sports and just about everything else.

People-to-People Program

One of the best ways to meet Bahamians is to sign up for the People-to-People Program. Organized by the Ministry of Tourism 20 years ago, it matches visitors with one of the more than 1,500 Bahamians of similar ages and interests for a day or evening activity that might include boating, fishing, shopping, a back-street tour or visiting Bahamians in their home for a traditional meal of peas 'n rice, fried fish, and guava duff.

The program also has a list of volunteers who are ready to assist visitors with their weddings. To sign up, ☎ 242-36-0435.

Junkanoo

This exciting parade in celebration of winter goes so far back that its origin is obscure. Some say it can be traced to a festival held on the Gold Coast of Africa and is named after an early 18th-century African prince, John Connu, who promoted revelry as a release from the oppression of slavery. Others say the name comes from the French "gens inconnus" or "unknown people," describing those who paraded in masks. In any case, the fun begins on January 1 with a raucous parade of costumed revelers dancing in the streets to the music of goatskin drums, horns, whistles, and bugles. Crowds dance and sing. Costumes are outsized extravaganzas constructed on wood and cardboard frames and covered with brightly colored designs. Junkanoo is celebrated in Nassau, Grand Bahama, Exuma, Eleuthera, Harbour Island and Freeport.

Dining

Bahamian cuisine also shares an African accent. Some dishes are simple, using ingredients such as cornmeal flour. Others are more elaborate, using tropical spices and fruits, such as soursop, tamarind, coconut or banana.

A staple of the Bahamian diet is "Johnny Cake," a rich pan-cooked bread much like cornbread. The recipe arrived with early settlers, who may have called it "Journey Cake" because it fed them during their journey.

Conch (pronounced "konk"), a mollusk whose pink-lipped shells are often heaped along Bahamian beaches, is as integral to the Bahamian diet as the hamburger is to America. Culinary variations on conch include conch fritters, cracked conch, conch burgers, conch chowder, conch salad, and scorched conch. Served with all Bahamian meals is "peas 'n rice," a satisfying combination of pigeon peas and spicy white rice. Naturally, seafood is a specialty throughout the islands. Almost every restaurant offers fresh fish: grouper, yellowtail, crab, lobster, scallops, snapper and tile fish. Several Bahamas restaurants offer haute cuisine.

Although you can enjoy the most refined Continental cuisine prepared by some of the world's finest chefs, for a genuinely Bahamian experience try the authentic local cooking. Its rich tradition and exotic ingredients make for memorable meals.

Shopping

Shopping has long been an exciting side-venture for divers visiting the Bahamas. The Bahamian dollar is equal in value to and interchangeable with the US dollar and you'll find a great selection of top quality items from all over the globe to choose from. Shoppers are sometimes surprised to find that they can buy luxury items at 20 to 40% below what they cost in the United States. Cameras, cashmere cardigans, watches and emerald jewelry head the list of items bought by tourists and "professional" shoppers alike.

In Nassau, stroll along bustling **Bay Street**, where you'll find one of the largest selections of china and crystal outside centers like Paris and New York. For less expensive gifts like handmade straw hats, handbags, dolls and straw bags, visit the **Straw Market** in the Market Plaza on Bay Street, which is open seven days a week. Here you can test your skills at bartering for many handmade creations.

In Freeport, the **International Bazaar** is an irresistible lure. There are more than 65 shops on this 10-acre site, with architectural styles reflecting the country whose merchandise is featured. Here you can go "around the world" in a matter of hours or minutes! Since it was designed by movie special effects artist Charles Drew, it not only offers a wide selection of high-quality items from five continents, but the dramatic settings are straight from Hollywood.

In the bazaar, you will find yourself treading the streets of Japan, buying embroidered silk robes, beaded bags and incense. Around the corner, in the Middle East, you may select from a stunning collection of carved ivories, shining brass work or lifelike wooden animals. The International Bazaar is a special place for the shopper who likes to explore.

Also on Grand Bahama is **Port Lucaya**'s multi-million-dollar shopping and entertainment complex, offering a vibrant cultural mix of fine shopping, Bahamian-style restaurants and entertainment, all complemented by the natural brilliance of the turquoise waterfront. The shops are housed in 12 buildings, each with its own individual design.

Other Activities

Besides the dive operations on 18 islands offering scuba and snorkeling, there are more than 200 tennis courts, including almost 100 in the Nassau/Paradise Island/Cable Beach area. There are championship golf courses, casinos, more than 30 major annual fishing tournaments, marinas for motor boating and sailing and airports for private aviators. Squash, polo, parasailing, board sailing, horseback riding, water skiing, and bicycling are some of the other things you can do. There's also shelling, softball, cricket, motor biking, volleyball, ping-pong, skeet shooting, shuffleboard, surfing, jet skiing and paddle boating. Non-diving family members looking for a unique touch can swim cheek-to-cheek with six specially trained, bottle-nosed dolphins at Port Lucaya and Blue Lagoon Island, off Paradise Island.

Bahamas

New Providence Island

New Providence Island, the site of Nassau, the capital of the Bahamas and two famous resort areas – Cable Beach and Paradise Island, offers casino gambling and a wealth of on-shore activities in addition to virgin reef diving and snorkeling. Divers know New Providence best as the sub-sea movie setting for Disney's *20,000 Leagues Under the Sea, Splash,* and *Cocoon,* the James Bond thrillers, *Thunderball, Never Say Never, For Your Eyes Only,* and *Jaws IV.* Diving around New Providence offers steep walls, drop-offs, caves, shallow reefs, ocean holes, and wrecks.

The best spots for experienced divers exist off the southwest coast.

Best Dives of New Providence

Interesting dives exist all around New Providence and adjacent Paradise Island. The north side of Paradise Island shelters a number of shipwrecks and the Lost Ocean Hole.

The southwest area which skirts the eastern rim of the Tongue of the Ocean is where you'll find the old movie sets and the best wall dives. Most diehard Bahama divers head for this area while new divers and snorkelers enjoy the special attention offered by the Cable Beach and Paradise Island operators.

☆☆☆☆ **Northwest Shipwrecks** off Paradise Island include **The Mahoney**, a steamship that went down in a hurricane near the turn of the century. She rests in 30 to 40 ft on one end and 100 ft at the other. There is also the

Courtesy Stuart Cove's Dive South Ocean

Shark Arena.

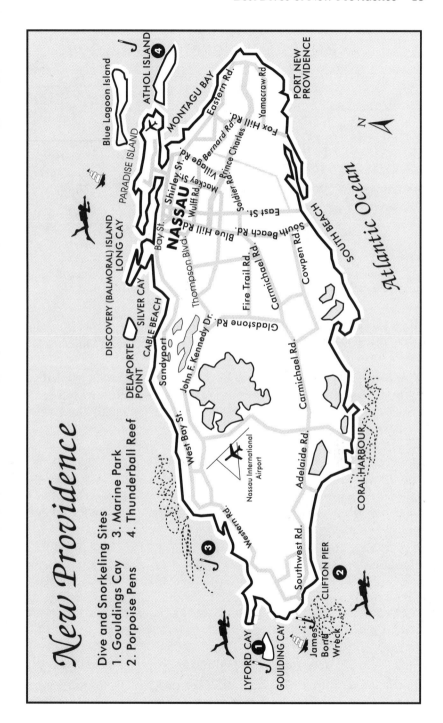

New Providence

Dive and Snorkeling Sites
1. Gouldings Cay   3. Marine Park
2. Porpoise Pens   4. Thunderball Reef

Dive Boat, Nassau.

Ana Lise, a 150 ft freighter at 90 ft, the adjacent **Bahama Shell**, a 90-ft tanker, and the **Helena C**, a 90-ft freighter. Nearby the **De La Salle**, sits upright at 70 ft.

☆☆☆☆ Southwest of New Providence, **Thunderball Reef**, named for the James Bond film, offers good visibility and a very photogenic setting for shallow water dives and snorkeling. Although small in size, this spot shelters gorgonians, staghorn, and elkhorn corals. The reef supports a dense population of tropicals, queen angels, lobsters and other small critters. Sea conditions are calm with little or no current. Depths 10 to 30 ft. Boat access.

☆☆☆ **New Providence Wrecks** off the southwest coast include the **Bahama Mama**, intentionally sunk in 1995 at 40 ft, the **Willaurie**, a 130-ft freighter at 50 ft, the **Sea Viking** a 60-ft fishing boat and the **David Tucker II** at 50 ft.

☆☆☆☆ **Gouldings Cay**, a tiny island located off the west end of New Providence, borders a very pretty coral reef that was used as a setting for the films *Cocoon, Never Say Never, 20,000 Leagues Under the Sea* and *Splash*. The area encompasses several acres and offers both shallow snorkeling sites and deeper dives. Eagle rays, turtles, old wreck sections, schools of tropicals, morays, and acres of elkhorn make this a favorite dive area.

The *Tears of Allah* wreck from the James Bond movie *Never Say Never* sits in 45 ft of water, as does the nearby *Vulcan Bomber* from *Thunderball*.

☆☆☆☆**Lost Blue Hole**, about 10 miles east of Nassau, measures more than 100 feet in diameter. Numerous grunts, Nassau groupers, eels and barracuda inhabit coral heads that surround the top of the hole at 45 ft. Light current. Boat access. Scuba.

☆☆☆ **Shark Wall**, off the southwest side of New Providence Island, is a 50-ft drop-off along the deep-water abyss known as the Tongue of the Ocean. Caribbean reef sharks, lemon and bull sharks cruise the area. The *David Tucker II* sits off the wall. Boat access. Experienced scuba divers.

☆☆☆☆ **Schoolhouse Reef**, on the south side of New Providence Island, is a super snorkeling and shallow scuba spot. Every imaginable fish and sea critter encircle two huge coral mounds. Depths average 15 ft. Boat access.

☆☆☆☆ **Southwest Reef,** a tongue-and-groove formation on the south side of New Providence bottoms at 25 ft. Lots of soft corals. Good for diving and snorkeling. Light current. Boat access.

☆☆☆ **Blue Lagoon Island**, a small watersports and picnic island located approximately one-half mile from Paradise Island, is surrounded by a three-acre marine park. It's home to grouper, moray eels, crawfish, barracuda and a group of affectionate Southern stingrays. Dolphin Encounters at Blue Lagoon offers a swim-with-the-dolphins program for snorkelers that allows you to get close up during a half-hour swim. ☎ 242-327-5066.

New Providence Dive Operators
(rates subject to change)

Dive Dive Dive Ltd. offers dive/accommodation packages in five deluxe villas on the quiet south side of New Providence Island. Newly renovated villas sleep up to four divers. Each has a kitchen, cable TV and VCR player. Dive boats visit the James Bond Wreck, the Tongue of the Ocean and several reef areas. Two dives cost $70, shark dives $115. Snorkel trips $25 (free gear). Daily pickups from all hotels. Certification and Nitrox courses. Videos, camera and gear rentals. Nitrox and Trimix blends. Friendly staff. Will pick up divers from any hotel on the island. Call for special dive/hotel packages that can save you money. ☎ 800-368-3483, 954-785-3501, fax 954-786-9356. E-mail: info@divedivedive.com. Website: www.divedivedive.com.

Stuart Cove's Dive South Ocean sits on the southwest, lee side of New Providence Island – minutes from sheltered reefs and wrecks. The shop offers shark adventures, reef, wreck and wall dives, snorkeling programs every afternoon and dive-hotel packages with neighboring South Ocean Dive, Beach and Golf Resort and the Nassau Marriott. Extreme Adventures include Wall Flying via submersible scooter, Shark Adventures and Rebreather Adventures. Pick-up service for divers is provided from any resort. Two-tank, à la carte dives cost $70, full day $115, shark dives $115, snorkel trip, $30. Tanks, weights and belt included for divers; mask, fins, snorkel, and vest for snorkelers. Reduced-rate multiple-dive packages are available. Friendly,

Bahamas

helpful service. ☎ 800-879-9832 or 954-524-5755, fax 954-524-5925. E-mail: scove1045@aol.com. Website: www.stuart cove.com.

Nassau Scuba Centre offers shark and shark chainmail suit dives, rebreathers, Nitrox and PADI instruction. Two-tank dives include tanks, weights and belt for $65. Day trips to Andros or Chub Cay cost $115. Lost Blue Hole Dive Trip (minimum 10 divers) costs $85. Hotel packages are offered with Casuarinas of Cable Beach, Orange Hill Beach Inn and the Nassau Beach Hotel. ☎ 888-962-7728, 800-327-8150, 954-462-3400, 809-362-1964 or 809-362-1379. Fax 954-462-4100. Write to: PO Box 21766, Ft Lauderdale, FL 33335. E-mail: dive@nassau-scubacentre.com. Website: www.nassau-scubacentre.com.

Bahama Divers serves hotels on Paradise Island with three boats and nine instructors. Packages with all hotels on Paradise Island and Cable Beach. Resort courses. ☎ 800-398-DIVE or 954-351-5644, fax 954-351-9740. Write to PO Box SS 5004, Nassau, Bahamas.

Sun Divers, Ltd has three boats, offers pick-up at all hotels on Paradise Island. Resort courses. ☎ 800-258-4786 or 954-489-7725, fax 242-393-1630. Write to PO Box N 10728, Nassau, Bahamas.

Divers Haven sells gear, sundries, resort courses, dive trips. Hotel packages with Comfort Suites, Red Carpet Inn, Radisson Cable Beach. ☎ 242-393-0869 or 242-393-3285, fax 242-393-3695. Write to: PO Box N 1658, Nassau, Bahamas.

New Providence Island Accommodations

South Ocean Golf, Beach & Dive Resort, on the southwest side of New Providence Island, features 250 guest rooms in two categories – standard or deluxe oceanfront, two freshwater pools, a 1,500-ft natural beach, 18-hole golf course, tennis courts, two restaurants, beach bar and golf bars. Babysitting, tour desk, watersports center with snorkeling, board sailing and sailing. Stuart Cove Dive shop on premises. The resort is just four miles from the airport, 10 miles from Nassau. Oceanfront rooms are closest to the dive shop. Standard rooms (lovely) are around the golf course, a seven-minute walk to the dive shop docks. All rooms have phones, A/C, color cable TV. High-season rates for a standard room, double occupancy, are from $705 for five nights, three two-tank dives. Non-divers pay $480. Oceanfront rooms – five nights, three dives – cost $787 for a diver, $562 for non-diver. Summer rates (April 13 to Dec 23) for the standard room drop to $551 for the diver and $351 for the non-diver. Summer rates for oceanfront, five nights/three dives, drop to $638 for the diver and $438 for the non-diver. Airport transfers are not included. ☎ 800-879-9832 or 954-524-5755, fax 954-524-5924.

Dive Dive Dive offers lovely villas on the quiet south side of New Providence. Dive boats are docked outside. Each villa has a kitchen, A/C, TV, VCR, patio with barbecue. Packages with Dive Dive Dive include airport transfers, diving, continental breakfast, trip to shopping center. Each villa accommodates four. Winter rates for a double are from $655 for five nights with four dives. Tanks, weights and belts included. ☎ 800-368-3483, fax 242-362-1994. Website: www.divedivedive.com.

Nassau Marriott Resort and Crystal Palace Casino offers 860 guest rooms and suites with phones, air-conditioning, satellite TV. Amenities include an 800-seat theater with Las Vegas-style shows, a private lagoon bordered by two acres of beach, a swimming pool with water slide and pool bar, fitness center, 18 tennis courts lighted for night play, four racquetball courts, two squash courts, casino gambling, and numerous dining options, including a pizzeria, New York-style deli open 24 hours, a seaside buffet, a snack shop, Chinese and seafood restaurants, plus a dinner theater.

If you want the glitz, glamour and gambling opportunities of Nassau and Cable Beach, this is the place, but expect a 25-minute ride to the dive shop docks. Room rates in winter start at $310 per night. Package rates vary depending on whether day of arrival and departure fall on a weekend or weekday. Rates with Stuart Cove for five nights and four dives in winter start at $1,248 per diver, $1,023 per non-diver. Summer rates are from $800 for five nights/four dives and $575 for a non-diver. Complimentary transfers to the dive shop are included. ☎ 800-879-9832 or 954-524-5755, fax 954-524-5925. Hotel direct, 800-331-6358 or 800-222-7466.

Casuarinas of Cable Beach, also a 25-minute ride to dive-shop docks, is a family-owned 78-room hotel. All rooms have TV, air-conditioning, phone and private bath. The resort features a small beach, two restaurants, two pools. Some oceanfront rooms. Packages with Nassau Scuba Centre during winter start at $538 for five nights. Package includes two boat dives daily, tanks, weights and belts, complimentary transportation to the dive shop. Non-divers deduct $65 per dive day. Summer rates drop to $483 for five nights/three dives. ☎ 888-962-7728, or 954-462-3400, fax 954-462-4100.

Orange Hill Beach Inn is a quiet 320-room inn four miles from the Cable Beach hotels and casinos, 100 yards from the beach. Rooms have TV, A/C, kitchen facilities, private bath. Pool. Packages with Nassau Scuba Centre start at $543 for five nights, two boat dives daily – three days of diving, tanks, weights and belts, transportation to dive shop. Low season rates for five nights are from $490. Travel time to dive shop about 15 minutes. Local bus service to downtown and the Straw Market. ☎ 888-962-7728 or 954-462-3400. Hotel direct 800-805-5485 or 242-327-7157.

Bahamas

Nassau Beach Hotel offers all-inclusive or SuperSaver packages. The 411-room resort sits on Cable Beach, five minutes from the center of town, 20 minutes from south side dive boat docks. Rooms have safes, a balcony, A/C, hair dryers, phone, cable TV. Free non-motorized watersports. Six restaurants, four bars, pool. Golf course and casino next door. All-inclusive packages through Nassau Scuba Centre during the high season range from $1,095 for five nights. Includes meals, daily transportation to the Nassau Scuba Centre, all taxes and gratuities, wine or soft drink with lunch and dinner, upgraded room. The SuperSaver Package booked through Nassau Scuba Centre does not include meals. For five nights with three two-tank dives, rates are from $669. ☎ 888-962-7728 or 954-462-3400, fax 954-4100. Hotel direct: 800-331-6538 or 242-327-7711, fax 242-327-8829.

Atlantis, Paradise Island is a wonderful resort for snorkelers headed to nearby Blue Lagoon Island. This gigantic 1,147-room property includes a 14-acre waterscape, four lagoons with waterfalls, an underwater grill and bar, the largest open-air aquarium in the world, two free-form pools, and 12 restaurants – one with an underwater view. Dive shop on premises visits wrecks around Paradise Island. Winter rates start at $350 per room, per day. ☎ 800-321-3000 or 242-363-3000, fax 242-363-3524.

Sandals Royal Bahamian Resort & Spa on Cable Beach features eight gourmet restaurants, seven pools, 406 guest rooms, 240 suites, a private offshore island, a water sports complex, and The Spa, featuring facials, hydrotherapy, mud baths and massages. Diving and snorkeling are part of their all-inclusive rates, which vary greatly depending on the accommodations. Winter rates for six nights in a premium room run from $1,840 per person. Summer rates drop to $1,710. Spa services are extra. Call or visit their Website for a complete list of rates for suites and rooms. ☎ 800-SANDALS or 242-327-6400, fax 242-327-6961. Write to: PO Box 39-CB-13005, Cable Beach, Nassau Bahamas. Website: www.sandals.com.

Grand Bahama Island

Grand Bahama Island, the fourth largest in the Bahamas chain, lies about 60 miles east of Florida, a 30-minute flight from Fort Lauderdale or Miami. Whether diving for the first time, or the hundredth, you'll find Grand Bahama Island an easy spot to enjoy coral reefs, ancient caves, mysterious shipwrecks combined with every type of marine life from dolphins to angelfish. It is also home to UNEXSO, the Underwater Explorers Society.

Tourist activity centers around Freeport/Lucaya, the capital of Grand Bahama and the second largest city in the Bahamas. It is the site of many tourist beaches and activities as well as the International Bazaar and Port Lucaya Marketplace.

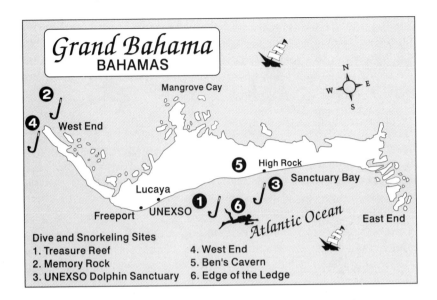

West End, a picturesque fishing village on the western tip of the island, is the oldest city and a popular sightseeing spot. It is known for its history as a liquor smuggling town during Prohibition. Driving the coast road from West End to town brings you past Deadman's Reef and Paradise Cove, where you can swim out to some terrific snorkeling reefs.

The Blue Holes

The Islands of the Bahamas were once joined together as a huge underwater mountain range. However, during the Ice Age, giant glaciers built up. Water levels dropped and the land began to protrude above the water's surface. As the glaciers melted, the "sponge-like" surface caused holes to form, along with an intricate labyrinth of underground caverns. **Gold Rock Blue Hole**, Grand Bahama Island, has fascinated geologists and researchers for years. **Ben's Cavern** (see *Best Dives of Grand Bahama*) offers divers a look at an inland sinkhole. Others may be seen offshore.

Diving

More than 60 identified and buoyed dive sites exist along the South shore of Grand Bahama Island, including two huge wrecks sunk as artificial reefs. Shallow reefs, such as Rainbow Reef and the Fish Farm, range from four to 15 ft deep and feature forests of elkhorn and staghorn coral interspersed with hard coral, gorgonians and seafans. Thousands of reef fish inhabit this area, including large schools of grunt, snapper, goatfish and sergeant majors.

Bahamas

Depths on the medium reef average about 40 ft. This area is typified by large mushroom-shaped coral heads scattered across a soft sandy bottom. The heads rise about 10 ft from the sea bottom. Angel's Camp and Eden Banks are two nice areas. Larger pelagic fish are often seen here.

The reef averages 75 ft in depth and is riddled with undersea canyons and caves. Divers are flanked by massive coral buttresses as they swim down perpendicular surge channels. Larger groupers and turtles inhabit the depths.

Less than a mile out from the Lucaya beach, the continental shelf abruptly drops off from a depth of 80 ft to more than 2,000. The face of this wall is deeply pocketed with coral overhangs and is covered with fuzzy sea whips and blood-red sponges. This is an aura of beauty and mystery as one hangs suspended over the indigo blue abyss.

Overall, the reefs are healthy with good displays of soft corals, sponges and tropicals, but the big attractions here are the dolphin and shark dives. Alternate dive attractions include caverns and blue holes, both in the ocean and inland.

The Gulf Stream passes through many of the best dive sites around the island, providing visibility that can exceed 200 ft. Dive sites are close (most less than 15 minutes from shore).

Best Dives of Grand Bahama

Most sites are within a 15-minute boat ride. Sea conditions are usually calm, but can kick up with storms or high winds.

☆☆☆☆☆ **Dolphin Dives**, created by UNEXSO (Underwater Explorers Society), allows divers to swim alongside trained dolphins in the open ocean. Non-diving partners can meet the dolphins at a holding facility in Sanctuary Bay, a 20-minute ferry ride from UNEXSO's dock. Participants first sit on a dock with their feet in the water while dolphins swim around. They later move into waist-deep water and interact with the dolphins.

A **Dolphin Assistant Trainer Program** allows snorkeling, feeding and training sessions. Assistant trainers must be at least 16 years old and speak English.

☆☆☆☆☆ **Shark Dives** offered by UNEXSO and Xanadu Undersea Adventures enable you to observe a number of sharks at close range. Exciting, but not for the timid.

☆☆☆☆☆ **Theo's Wreck** is the favorite dive on Grand Bahama. This 230-ft steel freighter sits in 100 ft of water and is dramatically perched on a ledge that drops off to 2,000 ft.

✰✰ **The José**, a 60-ft tugboat, was intentionally sunk to serve as an artificial reef and dive attraction. She rests at 45 ft and shelters a number of small fish. Boat access.

✰✰ **Poppa Doc**, a 50-ft cargo boat sunk during a storm, offers divers a fun site at 60 ft. Boat access.

✰✰✰ The **Ethridge Wreck**, nearby at 60 ft, is another favorite.

✰✰✰✰✰ **Edge of the Ledge** sits less than a mile out from the Lucaya beach. Here the continental shelf abruptly drops off from a depth of 80 ft to more than 2,000 ft. The face of this wall is deeply pocketed with coral overhangs and covered with fuzzy sea whips and blood-red sponges. Good for novice and experienced divers. Seas vary with wind conditions. Often calm. Boat access.

✰✰✰✰ **Ben's Cavern** offers an opportunity to go cave diving without going into a cave. Located within a 40-acre national park, this inland cavern developed centuries ago when the level of the sea was much lower than it is now. Giant stalactites grew down from the ceilings and stalagmites grew up from the floors. Eons later, the level of the ocean rose, flooding the cavern. Eventually the ceiling of Ben's Cavern collapsed, resulting in a crystal clear inland pool. Divers entering this 50-ft-deep pool are able to explore the cave without losing quick access to the cavern opening above.

At approximately 35 ft (sea level), divers swim through a halocline (a transition zone of cool fresh water to warmer saltwater) where vision is blurred for a few feet.

Certified guides take visiting divers on a tour of the "breakdown pile" (a large pile of stones from the collapsed ceiling), drapery-like "flowstones" (which look like moving water frozen into positions), a number of types of fossils (shells, corals, conchs, sand dollars, and chrinoids), "Table Rock" (a large column broken from the ceiling), stalagmites, stalactites, and "soda straws" (baby stalactites).

Ben's Cavern lies in the Bahamian "bush" about 20 miles east of UNEXSO. There is a parking area close to the cavern opening, and a spiral staircase leads down to a dock-like entry point at the side of the pool. Guided dive shop trips must be arranged on a custom basis with UNEXSO, who supervise a limited number of diver permits for the Bahamas National Trust. Reservations should be made well in advance.

Snorkeling Grand Bahama

✰✰✰ **Treasure Reef** is the site where more than $2.4 million in Spanish Treasure was discovered in the 1960s. Thousands of reef fish inhabit this area, including large schools of grunt, snapper, goatfish, and sergeant majors.

Bahamas

UNEXSO diver wearing chain mail suit hand-feeds shark, Grand Bahama.

Photo ©UNEXSO

Depths range from four to 15 feet. Elkhorn and staghorn corals, gorgonians, and colorful seafans decorate the bottom. Boat access.

☆☆☆ **Memory Rock** offers a look at spectacular brain, pillar and star coral formations. Friendly fish and usually calm seas make this a favorite snorkeling and photo spot. Boat access.

☆☆ **Paradise Cove** is the best spot to snorkel over a reef from the shore. To reach this spot from Freeport/Lucaya, drive the main highway west toward West End. Turn off at Deadman's Reef where you'll find Paradise Cove. Usually calm.

Grand Bahama Dive Operators

UNEXSO, short for the **Underwater Explorers Society**, is world re-nowned for expert diver training and unusual underwater activities like the Dolphin Experience and Marine Identification Workshops, during which the resident naturalist will put you on a "first name basis" with dozens of marine

*Snorkeling
Bahamas Out Islands.*

Photo by Michael Lawrence
©Jean Michel Cousteau's Out
Islands Snorkeling Adventures

creatures. Their dive sites are close-in, yet so varied they can accommodate both novice and experienced divers as well as snorkelers. UNEXSO's dive facility is world class, with two pools, a well-stocked dive shop and boutique, a fully equipped photo/video center, the largest professional scuba training staff in the Bahamas, and a lively après-dive restaurant and pub. Their unique chain mail suit shark-feeding course costs $2,500 at press time. Reliable dive gear rentals are available, as are reef tours, video and still camera rentals, E-6 processing, and multiple dive packages. ☎ 800-992-DIVE for further information or write UNEXSO, Box F-2433, Freeport, Bahamas.

Xanadu Undersea Adventures, located at the Xanadu Beach Resort, offers resort, certification, rescue, first aid, deep dive, wreck dive, Dive Master and Scuba Instructor courses, open-water and rusty diver checkouts. A two-tank dive costs $55. Packages up to 20 tanks for $394 are available. Add $15 for a night dive, $30 for a shark dive. Non-diving companions pay $15 to ride on the boat, snorkelers pay $20, which includes use of a mask, fins, and snorkel. The shop operates on a schedule with boats leaving at 8 am, 10:30 am and 1 pm. The early dive is 60 to 100 ft, the mid-morning dive usually shallow and the afternoon dive from 40 to 60 ft. All dives have guided tours and divemaster assistance. Dives include the use of weights, weight belt, tank and air fills. Hotel packages with Xanadu Beach resort, Royal Islander Hotel, Royal Palm Resort and Running Mon Resort. ☎ 800-327-8150 or 954-462-3400, fax 954-4100. E-mail: xanadu@nealwatson.com. Website:

nealwatson.com/xanadu.htm. Write to PO Box 21766, Fort Lauderdale FL
33335-1766.

Grand Bahama Accommodations

Room rates are subject to a $12 per person, per night tax unless stated other-
wise. All rates subject to change. Websites: www.grand-bahama.com/ho-
tels.html or www.grandbahamavacations.com.

Grand Bahama Beach Hotel is on the beach across from the Port Lucaya
Marketplace within walking distance to UNEXSO. The recently renovated resort features 250 rooms, a huge pool, lounge and snack bar. Near a variety of
restaurants. Shuttle to the Arawak restaurant. ☎ 800-622-6770 or 305-592-
5757, fax 242-373-8662. Room rates are from $129 per day. Packages with
UNEXSO for five nights/six dives in winter (12/21-4/18) range upward from
$450, low season from $400. ☎ 800-992 DIVE or 954-351-9889.

Xanadu Beach Resort & Marina, once the home of Howard Hughes, offers two restaurants, lounge, three tennis courts, one lighted, on-site dive center, 77-slip marina, tour desk, babysitting, gift shop, beauty salon, bike and
scooter rental, and private beach with its own straw market. Each of the 186
guest rooms and suites have a balcony or patio. Room rates start at $140.
Packages with Xanadu Undersea Adventures start from $498 for five nights/
four dives, $464 during the low season (4/16 -12/14). Includes room taxes,
service charges, tanks, weights and belts. ☎ 800-327-8150 or 954-462-3400,
fax 954-462-4100. E-mail: xanadu@nealwatson.com. Write to: PO Box
21766, Ft Lauderdale, FL 33335. Hotel direct: ☎ 242-352-6782, fax 242-
352-5799.

Port Lucaya Resort & Yacht Club, adjacent to the Port Lucaya Marketplace, offers 160 rooms, an Olympic pool, jacuzzi, restaurant two bars and 50-
slip marina. This resort juts out into the bay, like a peninsula with hotel buildings positioned in a circle around the pool and grounds. Built in 1993.
Walking distance to UNEXSO. Room rates are from $135 for a single, each
person add $25, children under 12 free. ☎ 800-582-2921 or 800-LUCAYA-
1, fax 242-373-6652. Dive packages with UNEXSO for five nights, six dives
are from $450. Snorkelers from $370. ☎ 800-992-DIVE or 954-351-9889.

Club Fortuna Beach, a 204-room low-rise resort sits on 1,200 ft of white
sandy beach away from the hustle and bustle. Amenities include a large pool,
restaurant, lounge, tennis, exercise room and shopping arcade. A short drive
from UNEXSO and Port Lucaya. All-inclusive rates with three meals per day
are from $300 per person, per day in winter, from $240 in summer. ☎ 800-
847-4502 or 242-373-4000, fax 242-373-5555. E-mail: maxcar@
batelnet.bs. Packages with UNEXSO for five nights/six dives are from $785
for a diver, $705 for a snorkeler. ☎ 800-992-DIVE.

Royal Islander Hotel features 100 air-conditioned rooms with cable TV, phone and a choice of two doubles or a king-size bed. Non-smoking rooms available. No beach. Pool, restaurant open for three meals a day, children's playground, gift shop, complimentary shuttle to Xanadu Beach. Short drive or walk to Princess Casino and the International Bazaar. Room rates for a double start at $104. Hotel direct: ☎ 242-351-6000, fax 242-351-3546. Packages with Xanadu Undersea Adventures for five nights and four dives start at $498 in winter, $464 in summer. ☎ 800-327-8150. Includes transport to dive shop, taxes, tanks, weights and belts.

Bahamas Princess Resort & Casino, the island's largest deluxe resort with 965 room and suites sits on 100 lush acres adjacent to the International Bazaar and Princess Casino. The resort offers nine restaurants and bars, two pools and a beach club. Near UNEXSO. Rooms per day are from $135, from $200 for a suite. ☎ 800-545-1300, fax 954-359-9585. Website: www.grandbahamavacations.com. Packages with UNEXSO for five nights, six dives are from $460 in winter, $395 summer. ☎ 800-992-DIVE or 954-351-9889.

Royal Palm Resort is located five minutes from the airport and a half mile from downtown. The property consists of 48 rooms with TV, freshwater pool, restaurant and bar. Rates are from $120 per day.☎ 242-352-3462, fax 242-352-5759. E-mail: royal@batelnet.bs. Packages with Xanadu Undersea Adventures for four nights/three dives are from $328 in winter, $312 in summer. Includes free transport to the beach and International Bazaar, room taxes, service charges, tanks, weights and belts.

Running Mon Resort, on Freeport's south shore features air-conditioned rooms with TV and phones. Pool, waterfront restaurant and lounge. No beach. Room rates are from $110 per day for a double. ☎ 242-352-6833, fax 242-352-6835. Packages with Xanadu for five nights, four dives are from $404 in winter, $378 in summer. They include diving, tanks, weights, belts, daily transportation to the dive shop, complimentary transportation to the beach and International Bazaar, room, service charges. ☎ 800-327-8150.

Pelican Bay, on the waterfront adjacent to the shops and restaurants of Port Lucaya Marketplace, features 48 large rooms, pool, Jacuzzi, pool bar next to the Underwater Explorer's Society. Packages with UNEXSO for five nights, six divers are from $460 in winter. ☎ 800-992-DIVE.

The Out Islands

Bahama Out Islands offer pristine reefs for diving and snorkeling. Twenty six out-island resorts offer a special program just for snorkelers. The Bahama Out

Bahamas

Islands Snorkeling Adventures, created by Jean-Michel Cousteau, combines guided reef excursions by professionally trained instructors. Participating resorts are noted under each island description.

The Abaco Islands

The Abaco Islands are the northernmost group in the Bahamas stretching roughly 130 miles from Walker's Cay to Great Abaco. Most of the diving activity takes place around Marsh Harbour, Walker's Cay, and Treasure Cay.

The history of this special island group explains its New England-style villages. Many of the residents are descendants of the British Loyalists who left New York, New England and the Carolinas following the Revolutionary War. Some became fishermen, some became wreckers and others learned boat building.

The **Albert Lowe Museum**, a 150-year-old former residence on Green Turtle Cay, is devoted to showcasing the history of the Abacos and its shipbuilding traditions. It was created by Alton Lowe in honor of his father, who was a noted carver of ship models.

Getting to the Abacos

Bahamasair from Nassau to Marsh Harbour. Charter to Walker's Cay from Ft. Lauderdale (see *Walker's Cay* below).

Best Dives of the Abacos

☆☆☆☆☆**Pelican Cay National Park**, a 2,000-acre national underwater preserve offers endless mazes of coral tunnels, walls, pinnacles and remains of modern and ancient wrecks.

The park is shallow and ranges in depth from breaking the surface to about 30 ft. The marine life is spectacular, with eagle rays, jacks, angels, critters, huge groupers, and colorful sponges to be seen. Pelican Park offers the underwater photographer and video enthusiast an abundance of beautiful subseascapes.

☆☆☆☆☆ **Fowl Cays National Park**, an underwater preserve, features more than 20 sites. Coral sea mounts and pinnacles provide great snorkeling in the shallows and fine scuba sites with large grouper, nurse shark and tropical fish. Currents are very light. Depths are from the surface at low tide to 60 ft. Underwater terrain is rocky with many caverns. During summer numerous copper sweepers and silversides crowd the shadows.

☆☆☆☆ **Shark Rodeo**, off Walker's Cay, whirls with adventure as more than 100 sharks circle a frozen barrelful of fishheads affectionately known as the "chumsicle." The sharks take turns feeding in groups of a half-dozen at once while their buddies investigate the surroundings. This attraction is put on by Walker's Cay Undersea Adventures for intrepid divers. The site is a short boat ride from shore.

☆☆☆☆ *USS Adirondack*, a Federal-era battleship resting in 30 ft of water, offers both snorkelers and scuba divers a look at the remains of the superstructure and some interesting antique cannons. A host of colorful reef fish inhabit the area around it. Boat access.

☆☆☆ *Deborah K*, a 165-ft light cargo ship, was used as a mail boat by the Bahamian government until Independence Day, 1998 when she was stripped of hazards to the environment and scuttled off Fowl Cay. She sits upright facing east at 100 ft. Residents include a huge grouper, horse-eyed jacks, angelfish and yellowtails. Top of the mast reaches up to 35 feet. Cargo holds are open. Good visibility. Boat access. Experienced divers only.

☆☆☆☆ **Spiral Cavern**, off Walker's Cay, features walls of fish in caverns and around monster-size coral heads with a maximum depth of 45 ft. Boat access. Experienced divers.

Additional favorite sites, all less than a 10-minute boat ride, are **The Tower**, a 60-ft-tall coral pinnacle, **Grouper Alley**, home to several Nassau grouper, **Shark Alley**, a valley of non-aggressive nurse and reef sharks, **Tutts Reef** and **Cathedral**, a bright cavern densely packed with tropical fish and turtles.

Snorkeling the Abacos

The best shore snorkeling sites lie off Guana Cay, where the reef sits less than 50 ft from the beach at the Guana Beach Resort and Hopetown Harbour Lodge, which has a section of beautiful barrier reef just 30 ft from their lovely two-mile-long beach. Excellent shallow reefs exist less than a mile off Green Turtle Cay and Spanish Cay.

Abaco Dive Operators

Abaco Beach Resort Dive Centre. Located in Marsh Harbour, this upbeat shop offers resort courses and all levels of training, reef trips and equipment rentals. Nitrox. The shop's 36-ft custom dive boat carries a maximum of 20 divers. PADI, YMCA, ANDI, NASDA, CMAS and BSAC training in English, French or Spanish. Rates are $45 for a one-tank dive, $70 for two tanks. Equipment rental. Most dives are about 100 ft. Visits the Tower, Shark Alley, Tutts Reef, Cathedral and the *Deborah K*. Equipment storage at the dive shop. ☎ 800-838-4189 or 242-367-4646. Website: dive@greatabaco.com.

Dive Abaco, at the town marina in Marsh Harbour, offers easy diving inside the Barrier Reef at the Tunnels, where trained grouper and snapper pose for photos or the Towers at 60 ft and the Caves at 45 ft, both with spectacular coral formations and marine life. The owner of the dive shop is also the boat captain

*Candy-Striped
Lighthouse on
Elbow Cay,
Abaco.*

© Bahamas Tourist
Board

and dive master. Dive Abaco uses a 30-ft custom dive boat with a full-width dive platform, open transom and easy-access ladder. Oxygen is on board. This is a nice operation. Hotel/dive packages are available with Abaco Towns by the Sea, the Conch Inn resort, Island Breezes, Lofty Fig Villas and Pelican Beach Villas. Write to: PO Box AB 20555, Marsh Harbour, Abaco, Bahamas. ☎ 800-247-5338 or 242-367-2787, fax 242-367-4779. E-mail: dive.abaco@internetfl.com. Website: www.internetfl.com/abaco.

Brendal's Dive Shop, on Green Turtle Cay at the Green Turtle Club and Marina, caters to novices as well as experienced divers. Tours explore Pelican Park and the Coral Catacombs, both teeming with moray eels, turtles, rays, schools of grunts and porpoises. Resort courses are offered and equipment rentals are available. Dive packages with lodging at the Green Turtle and Bluff House are available. Write to: Brendal Stevens, Green Turtle Cay, Green Turtle Club and Marina, Bahamas. ☎ (US) 800-780-9941 or 242-365-4411.

Divers Down at the Treasure Cay Marina offers two-tank dives to the reefs and wrecks. Snorkelers welcome. Resort and certification courses. Gear rentals. Retail store sells snorkel gear. ☎ 800-327-1584 or 242-365-8465, fax 242-365-8508. E-mail: jic@oii.net.

Walker's Cay Undersea Adventures has a staff of six with four instructors, two boats that carry 16 to 25 passengers and a retail shop selling gear and accessories. Rentals. Dive groups can arranges for special tours and cookouts. Packages with Walker's Cay Hotel and Marina on property. ☎ 800-327-8150 or 954-462-3400, fax 954-462-4100. On island 242-353-1252.

Abaco Islands Accommodations
Rates subject to change

Elbow Cay

The **Abaco Inn** on Elbow Cay features 15 guests rooms and suites, each with a private patio and hammock. On-site Clubhouse Lounge serves beachfront tropical meals. Short walk to Hope Town and the Elbow Cay Lighthouse. Winter rates for a double are from $135. From $195 for s suite. Summer from $100. ☎ 800-468-8799 or 242-366-0133, fax 242-366-0113. E-mail: abacoinn@batelnet.bs. Website: www.oii.net/AbacoInn. Participant in the Jean-Michel Cousteau Out Island Snorkeling Adventures program.

Hope Town Harbour Lodge features a nice, shallow coral reef 30 feet off the beach. The Lodge offers 20 remodeled rooms. AC and ceiling fans. Overlooks Hope Town Harbour. To reach this resort take a ferry from Marsh Harbour. Rates for a double are from $130. Butterfly House from $1,250 weekly. ☎ 800-316-7844 or 242-366-0095, fax 242-366-0286. E-mail: harbourlodge@batelnet.bs. Participant in the Snorkeling Adventures program.

Great Abaco

To reach Great Abaco, fly into Marsh Harbour Airport and take a taxi to the resort.

Abaco Beach Resort & Boat Harbour features spacious, air-conditioned rooms, TV, phones, mini-fridges, and patios. Two-bedroom, two-bath villas are also available. Rates are from $145 for a deluxe oceanfront room between September 2 and December 21. From $185 between December 22 and September 1. Villas (104 persons) are from $300 during the low season, from $400 in the high season. ☎ 800-468-4799 or 242-367-2158, fax 242-367-2819.

Conch Inn Hotel & Marina offers nine recently renovated, air-conditioned rooms, each with a single and double bed overlooking Marsh Harbour. Pool, cable TV, mini market. Good restaurant. Full-service marina offers sailboat charters and rentals. The Moorings is on-premises. ☎ 800-688-4752 or 242-367-4000, fax 242-367-4004. Write to PO Box AB-20469, Marsh Harbour, Abaco, Bahamas. Packages with Dive Abaco.

The Lofty Fig has six nice rooms, each with air-conditioning, a queen-size bed, sofa, small dinette, kitchen and porch. Pool, bicycle, scooter, car and boat rentals. Close to restaurants, bars, and dive shop. Packages with Dive Abaco. ☎ 800-688-4752 or 242-367-2681. Write to PO Box AB 20437.

Pelican Beach Villas, on Pelican Shores on Marsh Harbour, features beachfront villas that sleep six, with kitchen, refrigerator, microwave. Near to

Bahamas

restaurants, shops and activities. Safe dockage for small boats. Mermaid Reef, a shallow snorkeling area, is nearby. Weekly rates for a double are from $1,045. For a triple from $1,145. $50 each extra person. ☎ 800-642-4752 or 242-367-3600. Write to Pelican Beach Villas, Marsh Harbour, Abaco, Bahamas.

Great Guana Cay

To reach Guana Cay, fly into Marsh Harbour, taxi to the Conch Inn Marina where the Guana Cay ferry picks up at 11 am and 3:30 pm. Or take the AIT ferry at Triple J Marina at 12 noon and 4 pm. Boat ride takes 20 minutes.

Guana Beach Resort & Marina offers eight rooms and seven suites with kitchens. Newly renovated bar and restaurant open for breakfast, lunch and dinner. Terrific snorkeling off their seven-mile beach. A 50-ft swim brings you over a lovely reef with healthy seafans and corals. Friendly service. Winter (December 16 to May 31)rates are from $140 for a room, from $210 for a two-bedroom suite. ☎ 800-227-3366 or 242-365-5133, fax 242-365-5134. E-mail: guanabeach@guanabeach.com.

Guana Seaside Village, a new, romantic, beachfront resort, has eight lovely rooms, one suite with kitchenette and a long sandy beach with great snorkeling just 50 ft offshore. Beachside restaurant. Winter (December 15 to April 15) rates are from $145 per day for a double. Suites are $160 for up to four. Summer per day rates are from $130 for a beachfront room, $145 for the suite. ☎ 800-242-0942 or 242-365-5146. E-mail: guanaseaside@oii.net. Website: www.oii.net/GreatGuana.

Green Turtle Cay

To reach this island, fly into Treasure Cay airport. Taxi to the ferry dock and ferry to Bluff House's or the Green Turtle Inn's docks.

Rates subject to change.

Bluff House Club & Marina is a plush resort with a very attentive staff. Each of the 28 air-conditioned rooms and suites have refrigerators, coffee makers and hair dryers. Restaurant and Beach Club. Room rates in winter are from $110, $135 for a split level, $140 for a studio, $215 for a suite. Villas are from $385 per day. ☎ 800-688-4752 or 242-365-4247, fax 242-365-4248. E-mail: BluffHouse@oii.net. Website: www.oii.net/BluffHouse.

Green Turtle Club & Marina features 34 enormous air-conditioned rooms and cottages on a small island surrounded by white sand beaches. Rooms and villas each have a private patio or deck, paddle fans, and refrigerator. Pool, snorkeling, boat rentals, 35-slip marina. Brendal's Dive shop on premises. Fabulous restaurant. Winter rates (January 2 to April 14) are $165 per room, $185 for a suite, $269 for a one-bedroom villa, $379 for a two-bedroom villa (one-six persons) ☎ 800-688-4752 or 242-365-4271, fax 242-365-4272. E-mail: greenturtle@batelnet.bs. Website: www.greenturtle club.com.

Spanish Cay

Reach this one-resort island by flying into Spanish Cay. The hotel will pick you up. Or taxi to the government dock at Cooperstown. The Spanish Cay ferry will bring you to Spanish Cay. For private pilots, the island also has a 5,000-ft runway with customs service on Saturday and Sunday. On-island transportation is via bicycle or golf cart.

Rates subject to change.

Spanish Cay Resort & Marina has five newly renovated suites, seven one- and two-bedroom apartments and a 70-slip marina. There is no longer a dive shop and no scuba diving services are available, but snorkelers will find a nice reef about 50 yards off the beach. Boat rentals available from the marina. This lovely resort appeals to an older crowd. Year-round rates are from $150 for suites, from $225 for apartments. ☎ 888-722-6474 or 242-365-0083, fax 561-655-0172.

Treasure Cay

To reach Treasure Cay, fly into Treasure Cay International Airport, then take a taxi to the resort. The island has an 18-hole golf course, 150-slip marina, restaurants and shops.

Rates subject to change.

Banyan Beach Club arranges diving and offshore snorkeling with nearby Divers Down. Snorkelers will find beautiful corals upon entering the water to the left of the resort property. The resort offers two- and three-bedroom condos. Each unit has an all-electric kitchen, cable TV, air-conditioning, phone. Golf carts are rented for transportation. Rates for the two-bedroom year-round are $200 for one night, $540 for three nights, $1,050 for seven nights. Beachfront units are $225, $600, and $1,250. Three-bedroom condos start at $675 for three nights. ☎ 888-625-3060 or 242-365-8111, fax 561-625-5301.

Treasure Cay Hotel Resort & Marina has a fabulous 3.5-mile beach, a modern 150-slip marina and an 18-hole golf course. Diver Down Dive Shop is on premises. Winter rates (December 18 to April 27): Standard rooms start at $130 for a double, suites from $175. Villas from $385 per day. Summer rates (April 28-December 17): From $95 for a standard room, $155 for deluxe, $130 for a suite, $315 for villas. Meal plans are $44 per day, per person. ☎ 800-327-1584 or 954-525-7711, fax 954-525-1699. E-mail: abaco@ gate.net. Website: www.treasurecay.com.

Bahamas

Walker's Cay

Walker's Cay Undersea Adventures. Located at the northern end of the Abacos, this resort and dive center, the only one on the island, offers guests private air charters to and from Ft. Lauderdale. Walker's Cay Undersea Adventures dive shop is well equipped and offers a resort course, which includes a short introductory scuba lesson in a pool followed by a closely supervised shallow dive. Open water dives for a PADI certification are available. Access to most of the dives, which are at the upper end of Barrier Reef, is by boat. Choose from a scattering of lovely villas and cottages for your stay. ☎ 800-327-8150 or 954-462-3400. Local 242-353-1252, fax 954-462-4100. E-mail: nealwatson@aol.com. Website: www.nealwatson.com/walkers.htm.

Andros Island

Andros, the largest of the Bahama islands, yet the least populated, fringes the second largest barrier reef in the Western Hemisphere. Dive sites sit within 10 minutes from the Small Hope Bay Lodge on the northeastern coast. Superb visibility and calm seas, ranging from flat during summer months to two to three feet during the winter are the norm.

Folklore buffs might want to pack some flowery bits of fabric for the legendary Chick Charnies of Andros. These are half-bird, half-man creatures that build their nests by bending the tops of two pine trees together. Legend has it the creatures drive away evil spirits and protect the good from the bad. Legend also says visitors to Andros should explore the island carrying flowers and bright bits of fabric to leave for the Chick Charnies, all of which will be returned to the giver in riches.

Getting to Andros

Andros has three airports: at centrally located San Andros, at Andros Town, and at Congo Town in the south. Air service is by Island Express from Fort Lauderdale, Bahamasair from Nassau and several private charters – Small Hope Bay Charter, Southern Outbound Air, Miami Air Charter and Air Link.

Best Dives of Andros

☆☆☆☆☆ **Brad's Mountain**, a favorite spot for scuba divers of all skill levels, features a huge coral mountain rising from a 50-ft depth to a peak at 20 ft, carved into wonderful arches, caves and crevices loaded with silversides

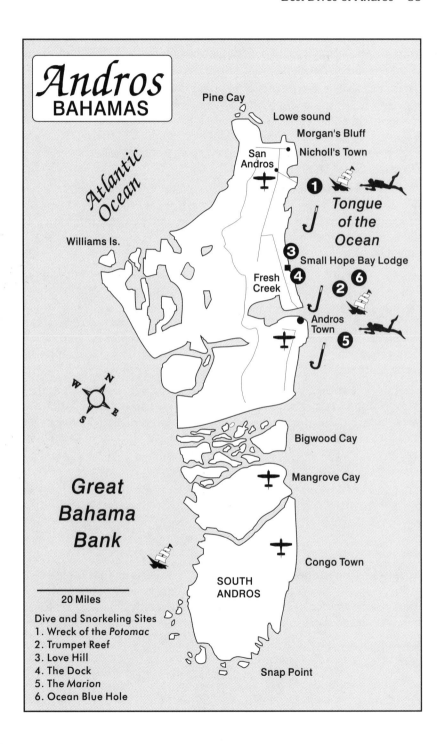

Andros
BAHAMAS

Pine Cay

Lowe sound

Morgan's Bluff

Nicholl's Town

San Andros

Atlantic Ocean

1

Tongue of the Ocean

Williams Is.

3

Small Hope Bay Lodge

Fresh Creek

4

6

2

Andros Town

5

Bigwood Cay

Mangrove Cay

Great Bahama Bank

Congo Town

SOUTH ANDROS

Snap Point

20 Miles

Dive and Snorkeling Sites
1. Wreck of the *Potomac*
2. Trumpet Reef
3. Love Hill
4. The Dock
5. The *Marion*
6. Ocean Blue Hole

and armies of mini-critters. Festive sea fan, sponge, and coral displays kaleidoscope into a blaze of color. Spade fish, Bermuda chub, parrot fish, grunts and French and Queen angelfish crowd the area. Boat access.

☆☆☆☆☆ **The Blue Hole** is a huge bell-shaped crater, perhaps 300 ft across, which drops off to great depths. It opens at 50 ft in the center of a coral garden. Divers who circle its perimeter at a depth of 100 ft find huge rock pillars and deep shafts. Huge stingrays glide by amidst super-sized midnight parrot fish, snapper and large crabs. This dive is not recommended for beginners. Do not enter the shafts. Boat access.

☆☆☆☆ **The Barge,** an LC landing craft that sank in 1963, is a delight for a novice diver with a new camera. Sitting in 70 ft of water the wreck is home to a bevy of friendly morays and grouper. They will greet you at the anchor line, eat from your hand and offer you a tour. Pretty coral formations are found here also. Boat access.

☆☆☆☆ **Giant's Staircase**. Advanced divers will enjoy exploring this wall, which slopes at irregular angles and, as the name implies, looks much like a giant's staircase with the final step dropping off 6,000 ft into the Tongue of the Ocean. The wall starts at 90 ft. A variety of corals surrounding a huge sand patch adorn the top of the wall where garden eels peer up from time to time. (They retreat back into the sand when you get too close) Experienced divers. Boat access.

☆☆☆☆ **Turnbull's Gut**, a fascinating wall dive, starts at 80 ft, then plunges into a wide canyon (the "gut"), which extends laterally 100 ft to a spectacular 6,000-ft drop in the Tongue of the Ocean. The wall shelters lettuce corals, black coral, vibrant sea fans and sponges. The "gut," plentiful with fish, often belches large rays. This dive is recommended for those with some experience. Boat access.

☆☆☆ **The Marion**, a sunken barge 100 ft long and 40 ft wide, presents a fun dive for all skill levels. With a huge tractor and a crane nearby, the wreckage lies in a large sand patch surrounded by a really pretty coral garden. Residents include spotted grouper, parrot fish, southern sting rays, garden eels, and nurse sharks.

☆☆☆☆ **The Dungeons** are a series of caves weaving in and out of the wall at the Tongue of the Ocean. Some, formed by interconnecting pillars of coral, wind into the wall for 100 ft. Groupers, silversides, rays and sharks are found here. Advanced divers only. Depth range is from 70 to 90 ft. Boat access.

Snorkeling Andros

☆☆☆☆☆ **Trumpet Reef** displays healthy elkhorn, staghorn, brain and soft corals. Trumpet fish are everywhere, joined by beautiful queen and French angels, schools of grunts and yellowtail. Snorkelers and beginning divers get hooked by the bounty and beauty of marine life here. Depths range from two to 15 ft. Boat access.

☆☆☆☆ **Love Hill** rises from a shimmering white sand bottom into huge thickets of elkhorn and staghorn corals. Soft corals and gorgonians hug the hillside. A full range of tropical fish and marine animals inhabit the area. Depths are two to 15 ft. Boat access.

☆☆☆ **The Dock at Small Hope Bay Lodge** is a terrific spot for a night snorkel. Fish are abundant and varied amidst 35 years of stuff that's fallen off the dock, including ruins of the previous dock. Sea life includes snappers, blue tangs, parrot fish, barracuda, angelfish, flounder, puffer fish, eagle rays, and octopus. An occasional dolphin breezes by.

Andros Dive Operators & Accommodations

Rates subject to change.

Small Hope Bay Lodge has been hosting divers since 1960. Guests stay in one of 20 one- and two-bedroom cottages at the water's edge and are invited to soothe themselves in a hot tub on the beach or meet with the resident masseuse. Guest cabins feature handmade batik Androsian fabrics and ceiling fans. Excellent meals include Bahamian specialties such as conch chowder, red snapper and lobster.

Besides diving and snorkeling, the resort offers Sunfish sailing, wind surfing and fishing. Small Hope Bay also has Coakley House, a three-bedroom, three-bath oceanfront villa, fully equipped with a dock, beach, patio and bikes. Guests are offered free introductory scuba and snorkeling lessons. Experienced divers are brought to walls and blue holes to dive. Winter rates for a diver are from $220 per day, which includes all meals, help-yourself bar, hors d'oeuvres, airport transfers, and use of snorkel gear, sailboat, kayaks, board surfers and hot tub. For reservations or information, ☎ (US) 800-223-6961 or 242-368-2014, fax 242-368-2015. Write to PO Box 21667, Fort Lauderdale, FL 33335-1667.   E-mail: SHBinfo@SmallHope.com.   Website: www.SmallHope.com.

Andros Lighthouse Yacht Club & Marina features an 18-slip marina. Onshore, they have 20 luxurious, air-conditioned rooms with private baths, king size beds or two double beds. Rates for a double in winter range from $150 per day. M.A.P. add $40. Maid service is $2.50 extra per day. Andros Undersea Adventures on premises operates fast custom dive boats, offers package vacations, rentals, instruction, still and video camera rentals. Diving costs $70 for a two-tank dive (same day). ☎ 800-327-8150 or 954-462-3400, fax   954-462-4100.   E-mail: nealwatson@aol.com.   Website: www.nealwatson.com. Write to PO Box 21766, Ft. Lauderdale, FL 33335.

Bahamas

The Berry Islands

The Berry Islands, a group of small islands and cays, many privately owned lie just north of New Providence. The best dive and snorkeling areas are along the barrier reef at the northern end of the "Tongue of the Ocean" at Chub Cay.

Best Dives of the Berry Islands

☆☆☆☆ **The Fishbowl**, a wall dive, takes its name for the throngs of fish and marine animals that adorn the area's valleys and ridges. Thriving shallow reefs rich with huge sponges, corals, sea fans and critters welcome snorkelers. Deep dramatic coral cliff drop-offs lure scuba fans. This reef is excellent for underwater photography.

☆☆☆ **Angelfish Reef**, as the name implies, provides shelter to numerous French and queen angels, many of which will pose for a video or still photo. Grunts, rays, turtles, eels, and barracudas are found swimming among the staghorn, elkhorn and brain corals. The average depth is 50 ft and visibility is usually good.

Snorkeling the Berry Islands

☆☆☆ **Moma Rhoda's Reef** delights snorkelers and scuba divers with masses of bright sponges, critters, coral mounds and crevices. Walls of sergeant majors, rays, grunts, hogfish, groupers, jacks, yellowtail and every imaginable critter hang out here. Snorkelers are advised to take care that wave action does not toss them into the shallow areas of the reef. Boat access.

☆☆ **The Reef at Chub Cay** sits off the western coast about 15 ft from the shoreline with depths from three to 60 ft. Undersea Adventures recently installed a concrete pad and steps over the ironshore to allow snorkelers and divers easy entry to the shallow elkhorn gardens. Beach dive.

Berry Islands Dive Operator & Accommodations

The Chub Cay Resort on Chub Cay is a well-planned, self-contained dive resort that caters to the special needs of the underwater photographer with a full service photo lab and custom dive boats. Guests enjoy modern, comfortable rooms, the Flying Bridge restaurant, pool, and gift shop. Divemaster Bill Whaley has 20 sites within a few minutes of the marina. Rates are from $444 for five days, four nights, with three boat dives daily, tanks, weights, and belts, airport transfers, air-conditioned room, ☎ 800-327-8150. E-mail: chub@ nealwatson.com. Website: www.chubcaydive.com. Write Undersea Adventures, PO Box 21766, Fort Lauderdale, FL 33335.

Getting to the Berry Islands

The Berry islands are reached by private charters. **Island Express** serves Great Harbour Cay from Fort Lauderdale. **Southern Pride Aviation**, ☎ 954-938- 8991, provides transportation from Fort Lauderdale Executive Airport to Chub Cay for guests of the Chub Cay Resort and for divers who book a package tour with **Chub Cay Undersea Adventures**. ☎ 800-327-8150. Allow at least 2½ hours between flights if you are arriving at Fort Lauderdale International. You'll need to take a taxi from there to Executive Airport at 1625 W. Commercial Blvd.

Bimini

Bimini divides into two islands, North and South Bimini, separated by a shallow, narrow channel. Alice Town, North Bimini, the hub of tourism and commerce, centers around one main road, King's Highway, where you'll find a half-dozen local restaurants and hometown bars. During fishing tournaments the entire town comes to life. Over 50 world records have been set here. Bimini was also the inspiration for Ernest Hemingway's *Islands in the Stream*. South Bimini is very rural and quiet, with just two small hotels and a small airstrip.

Lying 50 miles east of Miami, Bimini edges the warm currents of the Gulf Stream, which nurture and preserve diverse corals, white sand beaches and marine animals.

For the experienced diver, drift dives on the Bimini Wall offer some nice sights; for the novice or snorkeler, Rainbow Reef is the favorite. A playful crowd of fish awaits divers at the shallow freighter wreck *Sapona*.

Overall, Bimini is best known as the one-time stomping ground for Ernest Hemingway and Adam Clayton Powell. What visitors may not know about is Bimini's legend of the **Lost City of Atlantis**. For years, curious scientists have come to Bimini to investigate its mysteries.

According to Greek philosopher Plato, Atlantis was a vast land with an ideal government, advanced agriculture, an elaborate system of canals and bridges and luxurious temples. The kingdom, which was ruled by Poseidon and his 10 sons, threatened to overpower Europe. However, the people became corrupt and the culture was destroyed by volcanoes.

Plato's Mediterranean depiction of Atlantis has since been revived to include the Islands of the Bahamas. American clairvoyant Edgar Cayce, otherwise known as the "Sleeping Prophet," claimed he could foretell the future during hypnotic trances. In 1934, he predicted that the sunken portion of Atlantis lay

Bahamas

near Bimini, off the coast of Florida and would be discovered between 1968-and 1969.

In 1968, after Bimini fisherman reported they saw large flat rocks on the ocean floor in Bimini, marine technology expert Dimitri Rebikoff investigated the site and discovered what is now known as the Bimini Road. According to Rebikoff, "The Road," covered by 15 feet of water, was made of hundreds of flat rocks laid out in two straight parallel rows. He felt the right angles of the rocks were not possible in nature and must be from a buried civilization. A few later scientists have disputed this, saying that the placement of the rocks may have resulted from erosion, but their story isn't nearly as interesting!

In 1974, Dr. David Zink, archeological director for the Bahamas, determined the profile of the structure was horizontal, unlike the normal sloped ocean floor. Zink also found two ancient artifacts, a tongue-and-groove building block and a stylized marble head near the sunken road that had to have been imported. Most recently, in 1997, an extensive aerial survey of the site and further sampling was completed. Bill Donato, American anthropologist and archeologist, found unnatural features on the stones, such as a perpendicular cut from top to bottom. After weighing all the pros and cons, we don't know if the road is part of Atlantis, but we can guarantee it to be a fun snorkel trail.

The **Sand Mounds of Bimini** offer more mystery. Large sand dunes that appear in the shape of a shark, a cat and a sea horse lie in North Bimini, and are so vast they can only be recognized from the air. The mounds appear on early maps of the island that were drawn by natives. However, these natives did not have the capability to fly over the island, so they never actually saw the mounds. The origin of these formations remains unknown.

Bimini north end features an intricate labyrinth of narrow tunnels, one of which is connected to a creek that has earned the name the **Healing Hole**. At high tide, the tunnels fill with water rich in mineral content and empty into the creek. This water is said to have mystical healing powers.

Getting to Bimini

Bimini lies just 60 miles off Florida's coast and may easily be reached by boat or plane. From Miami, fly into North Bimini Airport via the Chalk's International Airlines (☎ 305-653-5572, 800-348-4644), a popular seaplane service. From there take a water taxi or the Bimini Bus to your hotel. A short ferry ride connects North and South Bimini.

Best Dives of Bimini

Reefs along Bimini's shore range from 35 to 100 ft, with healthy fish populations and vibrant corals. A nice shore-entry snorkeling reef sits off the beach at the **Bimini Beach Club & Marina** (☎ 242-359-8228, fax 954-725-0918) on the south end of North Bimini.

☆☆☆ **The Nodules** are a fascinating web of coral structures: ledges, tunnels, overhangs, caverns, swim-through chimneys, and towering coral heads, all lavish with gorgonians, sea fans, sponges and invertebrates. Schools of copper sweepers, sergeant majors, grunts, groupers, snappers and lobster inhabit this reef. Average depth 70 ft. For experienced divers. Boat access.

☆☆☆ **Tuna Alley** is a special coral passageway frequented by migrating tuna along with large groupers, angelfish, and stingrays. Fabulous visibility. Average depth is 50 ft. Boat access.

Best Snorkeling Sites of Bimini

☆☆☆ **Sunshine Reef** hosts crowds of butterfly fish, angels, parrot fish, lobsters, moray eels, grunts. At noon, the sun's rays sparkle waves of pinks and ruby light across the corals. This is a good spot for photos. Average depth runs 15 ft. Boat access.

☆☆☆☆ **The Road to Atlantis** at 15-ft depths offers fun snorkeling adventure. Located at the north end of Bimini, it makes for endless après-dive, tale-swapping opportunities. Boat access. (See details above.)

Dive Operators of Bimini

Bill and Nowdla Keefe's Bimini Undersea has complete dive/accommodation packages with the Bimini Big Game Fishing Club, Blue Water Resort, Seacrest and Diver's Dorm. PADI, NAUI affiliations. All are within a five-minute walk of the dive shop. This operation has been around for 17 years and offers a variety of dive and snorkeling trips, including one to a wild spotted dolphin pod. Retail shop sells snorkel gear, clothing accessories. Rental gear too. ☎ 800-348-4644 or 305-653-5572, fax 305-652-9148. E-mail: info@ biminiunderseaadventures.com. Website: www.biminiundersea.com. PO Box 693515, Miami, FL 33269.

Scuba Bimini at the South Bimini Yacht Club & Marina features wreck dives, wall and reef dives. No special trips for snorkelers; although they may join the dive trips, many spots are too deep. Complete vacation packages available with the Yacht Club (see resort listing below). ☎ 800-848-4073 or 954-359-2705, fax 954-462-4100. E-mail: beth@nealwatson.com. Write to 1043 S.E. 17th Street, Fort Lauderdale, FL 33316.

Bimini Accommodations

Rates subject to change. Call for current rates.

The South Bimini Yacht Club features 25 spacious rooms with two queen beds, private bath and air-conditioning. There is a full-service water taxi to

Bahamas

North Bimini for nighttime activities. Scuba Bimini on property. Resort restaurant serves breakfast, lunch and dinner daily. Rates for divers are from $493 for five days, four nights, including three boat dives each dive day (not day of arrival or departure), room, taxes and service charges, parking at the Ft. Lauderdale Executive Airport, night dives Wednesday or Saturday. Nondivers pay from $175. Airfare supplement $110, plus US departure taxes. ☎ 800-848-4073 or 954-359-2705, fax 954-462-4100. E-mail: beth@ nealwatson.com.

Bimini Big Game Fishing Club & Hotel has 49 air-conditioned rooms, cottages and penthouses that cater to fishermen. Restaurant. Diving and snorkeling trips are arranged with Bill and Nowdla Keefe's Bimini Undersea Shop. Many shops and island bars nearby. Resort rates year-round for a room are from $154 per day, cottages from $200 per day. Packages. ☎ 800-737-1007 or 242-347-3391 or 3393, fax 242-347-3392. Website: www.bimini-big-game-club.com.

Cat Island

Cat Island is a sparsely populated, hilly and largely undeveloped 50-mile-long island just south of Eleuthera. An impressive line of pink and white sand beaches rim its perimeter. For centuries Cat Island was called San Salvador and some believe this is where Columbus first landed. However in 1926 a nearby island was designated San Salvador (as it is know today) and the name Cat Island was revived here.

A single road runs the island's length, making it difficult to get lost while exploring. Appropriately called Main Road, it begins at Arthur's Town in the north and ends at Port Howe in the south. Along the way, visitors will spot residents engaged in traditional activities such as straw plaiting (weaving) hats and bags.

The island's historical sites are easily accessible from the Main Road too. At Port Howe, one can see the ruins of the **Deveaux Mansion**, a two-story, whitewashed building formerly used as a cotton plantation and now overrun with wild vegetation. The mansion was once the home of Col. Andrew Deveaux of the US Navy and was given to him as a reward for recapturing Nassau from the Spaniards in 1783.

Mt. Alvernia, the highest point on Cat Island and in all the Bahamas, rises up 206 feet through a thick pine forest. The **Hermitage**, a small monastery built by Father Jerome, an Anglican seminarian turned Catholic priest, sits at the summit.

Many Cat Island residents lead a primitive existence without electricity or stoves. Obeah, a counterpart of Voodoo from Haiti, is still practiced here. Practitioners believe that one can interact with the spirit world, and those using the power of Obeah can protect their property and cast or prevent a spell from being cast on other people. Island inhabitants hang bottles from trees with salt minerals sprinkled below to protect them and their families from evil spirits (don't touch them).

For divers and snorkelers seeking total seclusion and who want to explore miles of underwater wilderness, this is a terrific spot. Twelve miles of wall diving sites lie along the southern coast with depths starting at 50 feet. Shallow reefs off the Greenwood Resort beach range from 15 to 40 ft. Up-to-date facilities exist for both private pilots and boaters.

Cat Island Accommodations

Greenwood Beach Resort offers 20 rooms on eight miles of pink beach. Rooms feature private baths, king-size beds and patios. Ceiling fans and sea breezes keep you cool. Their oceanfront restaurant and lounge has satellite TV and provides a nice spot to swap fish tales. Good food. Diving and snorkeling off the beach. On-premises Cat Island Dive Center offers full scuba services. Room rates are $85 from May 15th to November 1, $99 in winter plus service charges. Dive packages for five nights are $482 in summer, $780 in winter including, room, meals and diving. ☎ 800-688-4752 or 242-342-3053. Website: www.hotelgreenwoodinn.com.

Fernandez Bay Village is a small, family-run resort offering six lovely beachfront villas with kitchens and six cottages. Great hospitality. Good restaurant serves native seafood specialties, fresh fruit. Terrific snorkeling exists off the resort beach in three to six feet of water. Good for children. Scuba trips are arranged with the nearby Greenwood Beach Resort. Winter rates start at $220 per day, summer from $215 per day. Includes two meals per day. ☎ 800-940-1905, or 954-474-4821, fax 954-474-4864. E-mail: fbv@batelnet.bs. Website: www.fernandezbayvillage.com.

Hawk's Nest Resort & Marina features a marina and an airstrip. They rent 10 guest rooms with ceiling fans, new king size beds, private baths, and patios. Fridges available. Clubhouse restaurant and bar offers food and drinks. Nice snorkeling beach. They do not have a full-service dive shop, but they do have a compressor and will take guests out to the reef or rent you a dinghy. Informal, but fun. Rates year-round start at $270 per night for two and include con-

Bahamas

tinental breakfast and dinner. They also rent a two-bedroom house, which sleeps six for $370 per day or $2,200 per week. ☎ 800-688-4752, direct 242-342-7050.

Crooked Island

This remote islet, 380 nautical miles from Ft. Lauderdale, offers unexplored reefs and spectacular beaches where you can walk for miles without seeing another soul. It is fabulous for snorkeling and diving. The reef starts at the shoreline, slopes to 40 ft, then plunges steeply to 600 ft in the Crooked Island Passage. Snorkelers can walk in just about anywhere on the island. Divers opt for the wall dives, which start about 300 yards offshore with the top at 45 ft. The sole resort, Pittstown Point Landing accommodates all watersports.

Crooked Island Dive Operator & Accommodations

Pittstown Point Landing, a comfortable 12-room beachfront resort, overlooks Bird Rock Lighthouse. Its close proximity to neighboring Colonel Hill Airport makes it a popular spot for private pilots. It offers personalized service to snorkelers and experienced divers. ☎ 800-752-2322 or 242-344-2507, fax 704-881-0771. Website: www.pittstown.com.

Getting to Crooked Island

Bahamasair has two flights per week to Crooked Island. The one resort provides transportation from the airport. Private pilots can land at either Colonel Hill Airport or Pittstown Point Landing Strip.

Eleuthera Island

Eleuthera, a long, narrow arc, stretches from New Providence for 110 miles to Cat Island. Spanish Wells, tiny Harbour Island, and a small cay called Current are considered part of Eleuthera. Together they offer some of the most famous and interesting shallow wrecks and dive sites in all of the Bahamas.

The name Eleuthera, which means freedom in Greek, was bestowed by British Puritans who settled the island in 1648. Seeking religious freedom, they lived in caves and developed the land for farming. Their fine produce became known throughout the islands and coastal US as far as New England. Even today, despite a coral and limestone surface, the land they tilled is considered one of the prime agricultural areas in the Bahamas. Hilly farmlands in the center of the island have a rich, red soil that is ideal for producing pineapples, tomatoes and vegetables. In the late 1800s Eleuthera dominated the world's pineapple market with its sweet fruit.

Best Dives of Eleuthera

✰✰✰✰✰ **Current Cut**, a narrow ocean channel between Eleuthera and Current Island, serves as the major link between Eleuthera Sound and the open sea. Tide changes cause millions of gallons of seawater to whip through this narrow gap at speeds of seven to 10 knots with visibility ranging from 50 to 80 ft. Divers "shooting the cut" can join schools of horse-eye jacks, eagle rays and barracuda as they sail by at exhilarating speeds. Depth in the center is 65 ft, with sharp, smooth, vertical walls on both sides and large potholes lining the bottom. Not for the timid! Boat access. Experienced divers.

✰✰✰**Egg Island Lighthouse Reef**, located due west of Egg Island in 60 ft of water, features 35-ft coral heads rising from a sandy bottom. Reef regulars include grouper, squirrel fish, glasseye snappers, crevalle jacks, amberjacks, blue chromis, wrasse, parrot fish, and surgeon fish. The reef is pretty, with varied corals, pastel sponges and good visibility. A photographer's paradise.

✰✰✰✰**The Gardens**, a favorite reef for photographers, sits about one mile west of the Cut. Diverse corals and sponges provide a home to large schools of surgeon fish, parrot fish, blue chromis, queen and French angels, butterfly fish, goatfish, porgies, margates and snappers. Crabs, shrimp and lobster are abundant and giant manta rays are frequently sighted here.

✰✰✰ **Miller's Reef**, off the east coast of Harbour Island, forms a maze of coral archways, canyons, caves and pinnacles at depths from 50 to 100 ft. Schools of grunts, hogfish, turtles, angels, barracuda, lobsters, chubs, and jacks along with mini-critters reside in the reef.

Snorkeling & Shallow Dives of Eleuthera

Five shore-entry sites exist off the **Cove Eleuthera Beach**, a nice reef parallels the shore just 20 yards off the beach side of the island in **Governor's Harbour**, **Hachet Bay** and **Palmetto Point**. **Rock Sound** also has some nice shore snorkeling.

✰✰ **Mystery Reef**, located three miles outside of Current Cut, in the direction of Egg Island, has six coral heads in 25 ft of water. The heads, which sit in the middle of a sprawling sand patch, are 10 to 20 ft high. Swarms of small fish provide endless entertainment and can be hand fed. Great photo opportunities. Visibility 70 ft.

✰✰✰ **Freighter Wreck**. Approximately five miles from Current Cut lies the rusting hull of a 250-ft Lebanese freighter that caught fire and was purposely run aground. The wreck sits perfectly upright in 20 ft of water with most of her structure above the surface. Her keel is broken at mid-ship, making salvage an unlikely prospect. Although the propeller was removed by scrap-metal salvors, furnishings and ship's parts are scattered around the hull. Large parrot fish, glasseye snappers, and watchful angels are attracted to the wreck.

Bahamas

☆☆☆ **Devil's Backbone**, north of Spanish Wells island, is a long stretch of shallow coral reefs. Great clumps of razor-sharp elkhorn coral rise to the surface and are often awash at low tide. This treacherous barrier reef is a graveyard for ships, but a paradise for divers and snorkelers. Boat access.

☆☆☆☆ **Train Wreck**. Perhaps the most unusual shipwreck in all the Bahamas is the remains of a steam locomotive lying in 15 ft of water. Still in the barge, which sank during a storm in 1865, it was part of a Union train believed captured by the Confederacy and sold to a Cuban sugar plantation. The wreck site also contains three sets of wheel trucks believed to be part of the same locomotive, and wood beams half-buried in the sandy sea floor. The wreckage, which is slowly settling in a garden of elkhorn and brain coral formations, offers some great opportunities for wide-angle photography.

☆☆☆☆ *Cienfuegos* **Wreck**. Just a few hundred yards away from the Train Wreck lies the *Cienfuegos* wreck, the twisted remains of a passenger steamer that sank in 1895. Part of the Ward Line of New York, this 200-ft-long steel-hulled ship crashed into the reef during a bad storm. All passengers on board survived and her cargo of rice was salvaged. The remaining wreckage lies in 35 ft of water with some sections at a mere 10 ft. Prominent features are two giant heat exchangers, a big boiler and the main drive shaft. The wreck, looking much like an undersea junk yard with jumbled steel plates, broken ribs and twisted steel beams, makes for a fascinating dive.

☆☆☆ **Potato & Onion Wreck**. The ***Vanaheim***, an 86-ft coastal freighter, was carrying a cargo of potatoes and onions when she crashed into Devil's Backbone in February, 1969. The force of the heavy seas during the storm pushed her over the barrier reef into 15 ft of water – an easy dive. Surrounding the wreck are very pretty reefs. Boat access.

Eleuthera Dive Operators & Accommodations

The Cove Eleuthera sprawls across 28 beachfront acres with two beautiful ocean coves. Guests select from 24 ocean- or garden-view rooms. Their main dining room serves Bahamian and continental favorites. Friendly staff. Terrific close-in snorkeling exists off the beach. Scuba is arranged with Valentine's Dive shop. There is a charge for the 30-minute cab ride each way, but the dive shop waives the gear rental fees for guests. Winter (December 18 to April 28) rates for a double start at $129. Summer rates are from $109. ☎ 800-552-5960 or 242-335-5338, fax 242-335-5338. E-mail: george@ thecoveleuthera.com. Website: www.thecoveleuthera.com.

Cambridge Villas, located in Gregory Town, provides free transportation to and from the beach for snorkelers. Diving is arranged with Valentine's, requiring a cab ride to and from the dive shop. Accommodations are apartments with fully- equipped kitchenettes, standard and superior double, triple and quad rooms with private baths. Air-conditioned. Saltwater pool. Winter weekly rates for a two-bedroom are from $950 for a superior double; in summer, rates are $913.50. Includes taxes, gratuities and M.A.P. ☎ 800-688-4752 or 242-335-5080, fax 242-335-5308. The resort has a five-passenger airplane for island hopping.

Rainbow Inn offers miles of deserted beaches, great snorkeling from the shore and rooms with refrigerators, microwave ovens, coffee makers, air-conditioning and sundecks. They also offer one- , two- , and three-bedroom villas. (Closed from September through November 15.) A full-service marina is two miles away. Near to shops. ☎ 800-688-0047 or 242-335- 0294, fax 242-335-0294.

Harbour Island

Getting to Harbour Island

Fly into North Eleuthera Airport, then take a taxi to the water taxi for Harbour Island. It docks at Valentine's Yacht Club.

Harbour Island Dive Operator & Accommodations

Valentine's Yacht Club and Dive Center features a complete dive shop, scuba and snorkeling tours, fishing charters and 21 air-conditioned rooms, convenient to Dunmore Town. They also offer 39 boat slips for craft up to 160 ft in their deep-water facility. Closed from Sept through December 3.

The resort's English-style pub and an outdoor bar serve fresh seafood and local produce. Their dive shop offers free snorkel lessons every day with a video show, booklet and pool practice. A nice reef outside the dive shop is good for all levels of snorkelers.

Winter rates (December 21 to April 13) for six days, five nights are from $592 per person for a double with three boat dives per day except days of arrival and departure. Boat night dives and trips to Current Cut are extra. No credit or refunds for unused package features. Summer (April 27 to December 19) dive package rates for six days, five nights start at $520 per person for a double. M.A.P. add $35 per adult, $20 per child under 12 per day. ☎ 800-323-565, 502-897-6481 or 242-333-2309. Hotel direct: ☎ 242-333-2142, fax 242-333-2135.

The Exumas

Three hundred sixty-five islands and cays strung out over 120 miles of ocean from New Providence to Long Island make up the Exumas. Exuma's 3,600

Bahamas

residents live on Great Exuma or Little Exuma, the two largest islands that connect by a short bridge. They earn a living by fishing or by farming onions, tomatoes, pigeon peas, guavas, papayas and mangoes.

Some of the fields still have wild cotton growing, a testament to the islands' history. Lord John Rolle, who imported the first cottonseeds in the 18th century, had more than 300 slaves on Great Exuma. The slaves, following the custom of the day, adopted their master's surname. When cotton proved to be a failure and the prospect of emancipation loomed, he deeded 2,300 acres of land to his former slaves. This land, in turn, has been passed on to each new generation and can never be sold to outsiders. Today almost half of the residents go by the name Rolle.

In the heart of the Exuma Cays lies the **Exuma Cays Land and Sea Park**, a 176-square-mile nature preserve that is home to coral reefs, exotic marine life and the Bahamian iguana – some of which grow over two feet long.

Renowned as a cruising spot for live-aboard dive boats and private yachts, the Exumas boast 200 miles of robust coral reefs. Depths average 35 ft, making them ideal for divers of all skill levels as well as underwater photo enthusiasts. Snorkelers will find many shallow spots, especially around Stocking Island.

History buffs will enjoy a tour to the "**Hermitage**" plantation house at Williams Town, Little Exuma. The plantation house is from the Loyalist years (1783-1834). Cotton plantations flourished on Exuma during this period, sending regular cargo ships directly from Elizabeth Harbor to England. The "Hermitage" is one of the few, if not the only, reasonably preserved houses from this period. Cotton was profitable for about 15 good years before poor management and the chenille bug laid waste to the industry. The "cotton" islands are Exuma, Long and Cat islands where you can still see the wild cotton growing.

Getting to the Exumas

Fly into Exuma International Airport. Taxi to the hotel.

Best Dives of the Exumas

☆☆☆☆ **Coral Reef** and **Sting Ray Reef**, off Uly Cay, lie just north of Stocking Island. Elkhorn and soft coral patches shelter hordes of trumpet fish, barracuda, turtles, large schools of grunts and yellowtail. Depths range from 20 to 40 ft. Boat access. Good for scuba and snorkeling.

☆☆☆ **Conch Cay** is a northern dive area offering shallow walls and wide ledges for easy exploration with scuba or just a mask and snorkel. Marine life is the big attraction here – huge turtles, rays and occasional sharks. The shallow reef's depths range from six to 20 ft. Boat access.

☆☆ **Long Reef**, sitting at the southern tip of Stocking Island, encompasses a maze of staghorn and elkhorn coral thickets. Residents include queen triggerfish, grey and French angelfish, grunts, hogfish and turtles. Depths are 25 to 60 ft. Snorkel or scuba. Boat access.

☆ **Lobster Reef**, situated in the Eastern Channel just north of Man of War Cay, features huge coral masses teeming with lobster, hogfish, snapper, angels, sergeant majors and morays. Scuba. Boat access.

☆☆☆ **Crab Cay Blue Hole** (aka Crab Cay Crevasse) lies south of George Town. Starting at a depth of 35 ft, this mysterious blue hole provides a sensual diving experience. The unusual current in the area creates a twirling drift dive with fish and critters racing by. Scuba. Boat access.

Exuma Dive Operators

Exuma Dive Center tours all the best dive sites of Exuma and Stocking Island and has packages in conjunction with the Peace and Plenty Hotel, Coconut Cove, Two Turtles and Regatta Point. Friendly, experienced staff. They also offer bonefishing, deep sea fishing, boat and motoscooter rentals. Dive trips start at $60, including tank and weight belt. Snorkel trips $35. Rental of a 17-ft Polar Craft with Bimini top is $80 per day plus a $100 security deposit. NAUI, IDEA, IANTD instruction. Equipment rentals. ☎ 800-874-7213 or 242-336-2390, fax 242-336-2391. E-mail: exumadive@bahamasvg.com. Website: www.webcom.com/cdk/exumadive.html.

Exuma Accommodations

In 1783, Lord Denys Rolle sailed to Exuma on the the English trading ship *Peace and Plenty*. The name passed on to a cotton plantation, to a sponge warehouse and then to a huge resort complex.

Club Peace and Plenty in George Town on Great Exuma offers 35 recently renovated accommodations, an indoor-outdoor dining room, tropical gardens, private balconies, and a wealth of water sports. The resort shuttles guests twice daily to nearby Stocking Island, where you can snorkel surrounding reefs, sunbathe or explore the island's caves. Snack bar service. Dive trips are arranged with nearby Exuma Divers who will arrange transportation to and from the resort. Their Eco-Dive package includes round-trip air from Ft Lauderdale or Miami, two dives per day, weights and tanks, transfers from the airport, daily ferry to Stocking Island, air-conditioned suite, gratuities and resort tax. For six days and five nights (eight tanks) $750 per person. Room only starts at $155 per day for a double. ☎ 800-525-2210. E-mail pandp@ peaceandplenty.com. Website: www.peaceandplenty.com.

Coconut Cove Hotel features 11 beachfront or beach-view rooms with terraces. Two are air-conditioned. All have ceiling fans and queen-sized beds. Meals are prepared to the diner's specifications. Pool. Dive and snorkeling trips with nearby Exuma Dive Center. Year-round rates range from $140 to $250 for a double. ☎ 800-688-4752 or 242-336-2659, fax 242-336-2658.

Regatta Point has six spacious apartments on a beautiful, small island near George Town's shops and restaurants. Dive and snorkeling trips with Exuma Dive Center. Winter room rates are from $128 per day for a one-bedroom apartment, double occupancy. Summer from $104 per day. ☎ 800-310-8125 or 242-336-2206, fax 242-336-2046.

Two Turtles Inn features 14 rooms overlooking George Town shops and restaurants. Guest rooms are all air-conditioned with TV. Some have kitchenettes. Diving and snorkeling with Exuma Dive Center. Winter rates start at $98 per day for a double. Summer from $78. ☎ 800-688-4752 or 242-336-2545, fax 242-336-2528.

Long Island

Long Island, home of the Stella Maris dive community, is world-renowned as a mecca for reef explorers. At 80-miles long and four miles wide, Long Island is also one of the most scenic hideaways in the Bahamas. The island is divided by the Tropic of Cancer and is bordered on each side by two contrasting coasts, one with a soft white beach, the other with rocky cliffs that plunge into the sea. Inland, the island varies from sloping hills in the northeast to low hillsides and swampland in the south.

Snorkelers can bike, hike or boat to the dive sites. Divers find walls, reefs and wrecks within a short distance of the Stella Maris docks.

No one is quite certain when the name Long Island took hold. The island was originally named "Yuma" by the Lucayan Indians, then renamed "Fernandina" by Christopher Columbus upon his third landfall in the New World. In 1790, Fernandina was settled by Loyalists from the Carolinas and their slaves. They built large plantations and produced sea island cotton until the abolition of slavery, which made them unprofitable.

Today, the plantations are overgrown and non-productive, though agriculture is still a very important part of life. Pothole farming, which is a method that uses fertile holes in the limestone where top-soil collects, yields much of the food supply for the other islands, including peas, corn, pineapples and bananas. Raising sheep, goats and pigs is also popular among islanders.

Their pace of life has not changed much from the past. A carriage road, built more than a century ago, connects the island's major settlements of Burnt Ground, Simms, Wood Hill, Clarence Town, Roses and South Point, all situated around the island's harbours and anchorages. Snorkelers can bicycle from spot to spot.

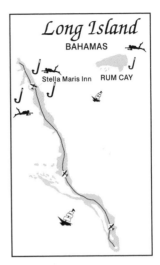

Getting to Long Island

Fly into Stella Maris Airport. Take a taxi to either hotel. ($40 for two to Cape Santa Maria Beach Resort, $3.50 per person to Stella Maris. Stella Maris offers its own commuter service from Nassau, George Town and other destinations.)

Best Dives of Long Island

☆☆☆☆☆ **Stella Maris Shark Reef** was the first shark dive in the Bahamas and it is still one of the best with dependable shark appearances. Upon entering the water, divers are greeted by seven to 14 sharks, who stay with the divers for the entire dive. Among them are gray tipped reef sharks, bull sharks and a very tame nurse shark. A single hammerhead makes an occasional appearance. The drill is simply to sit still on the ocean floor and watch Stella Maris divemasters feed the sharks. The sharks stay in the "circus ring" but there are unmatched photo and video opportunities for the viewers. Divers are warned not to travel about during the dive nor visit the reef without the guides. Sea conditions are sometimes choppy. The depth is about 30 ft. The boat trip takes roughly 30 minutes. Suggested for experienced ocean divers.

☆☆☆☆☆ **Cape Santa Maria Ship's Grave Yard.** This is a deep reef with a drop-off where the prime attraction is the wreck of **M.S. Comberbach**, a 103-ft steel freighter at 100 ft that was especially prepared for safe diving before it was sunk. The hull is intact and sits upright on its keel so the interior can be easily explored. Divers enter through the front hatch, swim through the freight hold into the engine room to the control stand, with escape outlets open in every section. The wreck itself offers fantastic still and video possibilities. Super visibility. Divers are greeted by extremely tame oversized groupers. The reef, which spreads over three-quarters of a mile with a 50-ft wall drop-off to another 50 ft wall, is covered with enormous sponges of all types and colors. The seas are generally calm. Located just one mile from shore. Recommended for experienced divers. Boat access.

☆☆☆☆☆ **Conception Island Wall** is one of the most beautiful reefs in the Bahamas. Gigantic coral heads climb from a depth of 90 ft to 55 ft and the

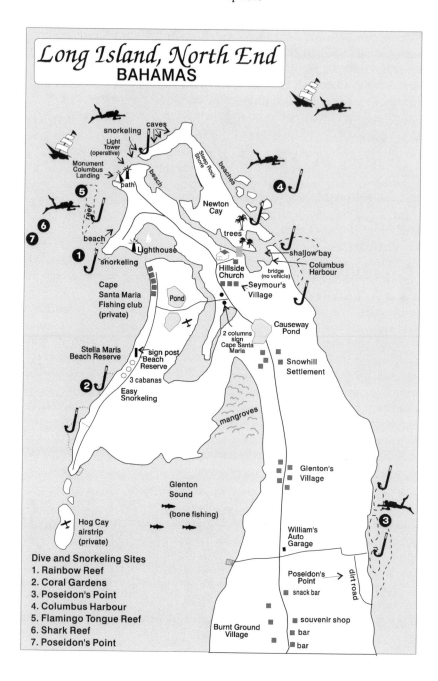

Long Island, North End
BAHAMAS

snorkeling

caves

Light
Tower
(operative)

Monument
Columbus
Landing

path

beach

Steep Rock Shore

beaches

Newton
Cay

trees

reef

beach

Lighthouse

snorkeling

Cape
Santa Maria
Fishing club
(private)

Pond

shallow bay

Hillside
Church

bridge
(no vehicle)

Columbus
Harbour

Seymour's
Village

2 columns
sign
Cape Santa
Maria

Causeway
Pond

Stella Maris
Beach Reserve

sign post
Beach
Reserve

3 cabanas

Snowhill
Settlement

Easy
Snorkeling

mangroves

Glenton
Sound

(bone fishing)

Glenton's
Village

Hog Cay
airstrip
(private)

William's
Auto
Garage

Poseidon's
Point

dirt road

snack bar

souvenir shop

bar

bar

Burnt Ground
Village

Dive and Snorkeling Sites
1. Rainbow Reef
2. Coral Gardens
3. Poseidon's Point
4. Columbus Harbour
5. Flamingo Tongue Reef
6. Shark Reef
7. Poseidon's Point

wall, which drops in straight ladder-steps, is covered with a lush carpet of corals and fantastic sponges. Caves and tunnels invite novice and experienced divers alike. The site sits just 300 ft from the beach with depths from 45 ft to bottomless. Conception Island, off the northeast tip of Long Island is an underwater park and a bird and turtle breeding area. Boat access.

☆☆☆ **Flamingo Tongue Reef** takes its name from the thousands of flamingo tongue shells along its bottom. It's located six miles from Stella Maris Marina within a half-mile of the shore – a 15-minute boat ride. It is a great spot for beginners since the reef is only 25 ft below the surface and the seas are almost always calm. Large moray eels, groupers, and schooling fish abound. Caves and cuts add a touch of mystery. Good snorkeling.

Snorkeling Long Island

☆☆☆ **West Bar Reef**, a lovely, pristine coral garden in the shape of a bar some 600 ft long and 300 ft wide, lies within half a mile of two beautiful beaches. The reef has a superb variety of brain and staghorn corals along with soft corals and towering pillar corals, all at a depth of 15 ft. It is in the lee of the island, protected from wind, waves, and strong currents. Visibility is excellent. Boat access.

☆☆☆☆ **Southampton Reef** is the site of a wrecked ocean freighter that sank some 80 years ago. The 300-ft hull has been flattened by time and the ebb and flow of water, yet it still offers dramatic photo possibilities. Prominent are huge engine boilers, the shaft, propellers, and anchors and lots of ship's debris. Thickets of elkhorn and staghorn surround the wreck, providing refuge for huge grouper, sleeping nurse sharks, and large parrot fish. Depths range from five ft to 100 ft with the average about 25 ft. Sea conditions range from dead calm to rough. One major drawback to this dive is the three-hour boat ride from Long Island (Stella Maris dock).

☆☆☆☆ **Coral Gardens** and **Poseidon's Pint** are two beautiful snorkeling reefs accessible from the beach or by boat (a three- or four-minute ride from the Stella Maris docks). Access depends on the weather. The gardens sparkle with dramatic displays of massive brain, elkhorn, and staghorn coral. Eagle rays, sand rays, tarpon and crawfish are in residence here. Depths range from three to 30 ft.

☆☆ **Rainbow Reef**, terrific for snorkeling, has three easy entries from Cape Santa Maria Beach. It lies 20 yards from shore and is completely protected in most weather situations except northwest winds. Encrusting corals and sponges cover the rocky bottom, which is inhabited by a good mix of reef fish. Passing eagle rays are frequently sighted. Some large stingrays bury themselves in the sand. Beach or boat access.

Bahamas

Dive Operators & Accommodations

Stella Maris Inn, a dive and snorkeling plantation-style resort offers rooms, cottages and luxury villas all situated high atop the hillcrest of the island's east shoreline and featuring breathtaking views of the ocean. The dive operation is top-notch, offering guided reef and wreck tours. Non-divers and snorkelers get special attention too with a wide choice of beaches, cycling, cruises, and even a glass bottom boat. Guided day and night snorkeling tours. Complimentary shuttle bus service to different shore-entry snorkeling spots. Great dive packages available. Reef, bone and deep-sea fishing. Winter dive package rates for eight days and seven nights start at $860 per person, double occupancy. Included are deluxe hotel room, welcome drink, six days of scuba diving (two-three dives per day), weekly cave party, slide shows. Add $45 per person, per day, for breakfast and dinner. ☎ 800-426-0466 or 954-359-8236 or 242-338-2050, fax 954-359-8238. E-mail: smrc@stellamarisresort.com. Website: www.stellamarisresort.com.

Cape Santa Maria Beach Resort offers only snorkeling tours aboard their catamaran. Guests stay in beachfront cottages overlooking four miles of white sand beach. Snorkeling reef off the beach. Fly fishing off the flats. Winter rates are from $245 for a one-bedroom villa. For three meals per day add $65 per person, per day, $35 per child. ☎ 800-663-7090 or 250-338-3366, fax 250-598-1361. E-mail: obmg@pinc.com. Expect the cab ride to cost $40 for two to this resort from the Stella Maris Airport.

San Salvador Island

Miles of virgin shallow reefs, walls and new wrecks are yet to be explored in the waters around San Salvador, truly one of the diving jewels of the Bahamas. It is so remote that the Riding Rock Inn feels they must point out in their promotional material that it is *not in south america* . On the shore, visitors delight in miles of white sand beaches, including the site where Christopher Columbus first set foot in the New World.

The island's several name changes reflect its checkered past. The Lucayan Indians initially named the island "Guanahani." Then, in 1492, Columbus made his first landfall in the New World on the island. He named it San Salvador or "Holy Saviour," and noted in his travel journal that "the beauty of these islands surpasses that of any other and as much as the day surpasses the night in Splendor." Today, four separate monuments mark the spots where he came ashore, although it is generally thought that he landed at Long Bay where a large stone cross stands. Centuries later British pirate Captain George Watling took over the island, making it his headquarters and naming it

*Monument to Columbus,
San Salvador, Bahamas.*

© Bahamas Tourist Board

"Watling Island" after himself. The island retained this name until 1925, when it was then renamed San Salvador.

Besides diving and snorkeling, visitors to the island enjoy touring the plantation ruins, climbing to the top of the old kerosene-operated lighthouse and exploring the archeological sites of the Lucayan Indians.

Getting to San Salvador

Regularly scheduled Riding Rock Inn charter flights depart from Ft. Lauderdale each Saturday morning at 10 am (☎ 800-272-1492). Bahamasair flies from Nassau and Miami to the island. The marina can accommodate large vessels.

Best Dives of San Salvador

Most of San Salvador's dive sites are off the leeward side of the island, sheltered from wind and high waves. Dives are along a cliff and there is usually no current. Depths range from shallow to 130 ft. You can dive at your own skill level.

☆☆☆☆ **Hole in the Wall** at the end of Gardiners Reef, on the southwest side of the island, offers dramatic topography. Two deep crevices inhabited by king crabs and big lobsters cut through the wall from 50 to 110-120 ft. Resident schoolmaster snappers hover around a big black coral tree at 90 ft. Large pillar corals crown the rim of both crevices. Locals include schools of horse-eyed jacks. Occasional hammerhead sharks and manta rays spin by the blue water off the wall.

Riding Rock Inn, San Salvador, Bahamas.

☆☆☆☆ **Telephone Pole** is the classic San Salvador wall dive. It starts on a sand bottom at 40 ft, then slopes off into a large "well lit" cave. Swimming near the roof you can pop out on the face of a straight drop-off at 70 ft. Turn right to see a magnificent large purple tube sponge usually inhabited by several brittle starfish.

☆☆☆☆☆ **Dolittle's Grottos**, located off the southwest corner of the island, is popular for its big barrel sponges, variety of corals, caves and grottos. Three main caves cut into the wall at 50 ft come out at 80-90 ft. These are not true caves, but more like tunnels or chutes with holes in the roofs.

South of the caves, a sand "causeway" starts at 70 ft, rises to 60 ft, then gently plunges to great depths. Coral walls 15 to 20 ft high flank the causeway on both sides. The top of the wall is shallow, 30 to 35 ft, with large stands of pillar coral and lots of micro subjects. Boat access.

☆☆☆☆☆ **Double Caves** in French Bay is locally known as the "wall to end all walls." A constant current washes the area with nutrients that feed a huge variety of soft and hard corals. Every inch of wall is splashed with vibrant color. The big attraction is two "well lit" caves. The first is entered from a large crevice that cuts through the wall beginning on sand at 60 ft. Like Dolittle's, they are really chutes or tunnels with big holes in the roofs rather than actual caves.

Coral walls tower above the diver by 25 to 30 ft. As you follow the line of the crevice, you come to a large hole where you can swim through an A-shaped cave that opens up at 110 ft. Leaving the cave, you see two big black coral

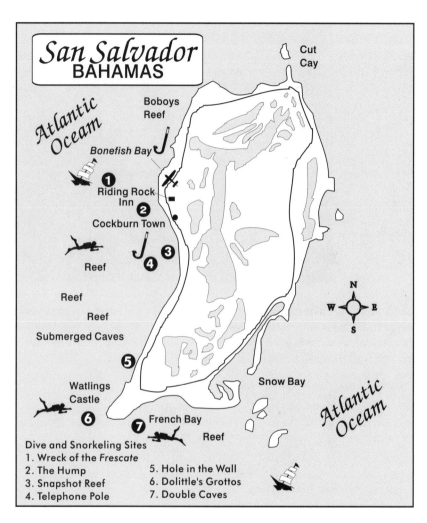

San Salvador
BAHAMAS

Atlantic
Ocean

Cut
Cay

Boboys
Reef

Bonefish Bay

1
Riding Rock
Inn
2
Cockburn Town

Reef

3

4

Reef

Reef

Submerged Caves

5

Watlings
Castle

6

7 French Bay

Snow Bay

Atlantic
Ocean

N
W E
S

Reef

Dive and Snorkeling Sites
1. Wreck of the *Frescate*
2. The Hump
3. Snapshot Reef
4. Telephone Pole
5. Hole in the Wall
6. Dolittle's Grottos
7. Double Caves

Bahamas

trees. Schools of hammerheads, eagle rays and manta rays are frequently sighted along the wall.

Enter the second cave through an arch at 110 ft, then up the wall to a sand hole at 60 ft. From here, you can ascend to the top of the wall at 40 ft or go through another crevice that leads back to the wall. Good for experienced ocean divers. Boat access.

☆☆☆☆ **The Hump**, a large mound of coral 80 ft long, 40 ft wide and 20 ft high, lies just two minutes by boat from the Guanahani Dive boat docks. A favorite spot for night dives, the Hump shelters thousands of critters in its many cracks and crevices. Big spiny lobsters and Caribbean King Crabs hang out

The Nekton
*floating dive
resort.*

Courtesy
Nekton Diving
Cruises

under the ledges. A spotted moray eel or chain moray eel might be seen peeking from a hole. Flamingo tongues graze the sea fans. Beware the scorpion fish. At night hundreds of red shrimp emerge, small octopus cruise the top of the reef and the rare orange ball anemone appears.

Snorkeling San Salvador

Snapshot Reef, a short ride from the resort, packs in schools of angelfish, groupers, parrot fish, trumpetfish, damsels, blue chromis, tangs, tarpon, and invertebrates – all waiting for a handout. Boat access.

The Frescate, a 261-ft freighter resting at 20 ft, hit the reefs in 1902 and its wreck has since attracted throngs of lobster, silversides and barracuda. Outstanding visibility. Boat access.

The prettiest beach-entry sites lie about three miles south of the resort. You can reach them by bicycle or rental car. There is also nice snorkeling off the end of the runway. Climb down a small slope to get there or swim north from the Riding Rock Inn Beach.

Dive Operator & Accommodations
Rates subject to change.

Riding Rock Inn offers divers all the comforts of home in a relaxed, casual atmosphere. This plush resort has 12 standard air-conditioned rooms and 30 deluxe oceanfront rooms, conference center, pool, restaurant, and marina. Standard rooms, single or double, are from $110, deluxe from $136. Children under 12 (one per adult) free. Meals are about $55 per person per day, about $35 per child per day. Bike and car rentals available. Drivers must be 25 years or older. ☎ 800-272-1492, 954-359-8353, fax 954-359-8254. E-mail: ridingrock@aol.com. Website: www.ridingrock.com. Write to: Out Island Service Company, Inc., 1170 Lee Wagener Blvd., Suite 103, Ft Lauderdale FL 33315-3561.

Club Med on Columbus Isle offers all-inclusive dive vacations starting at $1,120. ☎ 800-CLUBMED. You can book direct, but it might be easiest to book through your travel agent.

Guanahani Divers Ltd., based at the Riding Rock Inn, is well equipped with a large photo center featuring daily E-6 film processing, camera and video rentals and a resident pro skilled in both video and still photography. They operate three fast V-hulled boats that have a sun deck, camera work area with freshwater rinse, and large swim platform with ladder and safety gear. Snorkeling available. Rental gear. Two dives on the morning trip costs $60, one dive, $40. Beginners' resort course (gear/dive included) $105, snorkel trip $20, finish-up scuba course with dives $100, refresher course $65. ☎ 800-272-1492 or 954-359-8353. On-island 331-2631.

Bahamas Live-Aboards

Note: passport needed.

Touring the Bahamas by boat offers access to remote reefs and wrecks normally out of cruising area for land-based dive operations. The downside of is the trade-off of living space for being on the water. Snorkelers are welcome but pay the same price and will find some areas too deep.

Blackbeard's Cruises offer a relaxing week of sailing, snorkeling and diving through the Bahama islands, including one night ashore. Three 65-ft passenger monohulls are available, each crewed by two captains, a first mate, dive instructors, cook and crew. Guests choose single- or double-space bunks. Cabins are fully air-conditioned. Shared heads. Trips include all meals, beverages, bedding, fishing tackle, tanks, back packs and weight belts for certified divers. Main divng areas are Bimini, Victories, Cat Cay, shark areas, Grand Bahama, Nassau, Exuma and the Berries. Topside excursions. Cost is $729 per person, plus $55 port tax. Recommended for diehard divers and sailing fans. Snorkelers welcome. Dress is casual. Boarding in Miami. ☎ 1-800-327-9600 or 305-888-1226, fax 305-884-4214 or write to PO Box 66-1091, Miami Springs FL 33266. E-mail: sales@blackbeard-cruises.com. Website: www.blackbeard-cruises.com.

Sea Fever Diving Cruises tour remote Bahama areas – Cay Sal Banks, Shark Blue Hole, Exuma Cays, Berries, Little Bahama Bank and Dolphin

Grounds. Captain Tom Guarino, one of the best in the islands, has 26 years' experience navigating these areas.

The 90-ft aluminum-hulled **Sea Fever** has air-conditioning throughout. Passengers share two heads. Rates for a six-day, five-night trip run from $1,099 per person, seven days from $1,299 plus port taxes. Tanks, weights and belts supplied. Drinks extra. E-6 processing, video editing, shore excursions, waterskiing, Nitrox, Nitrox instruction. ☎ 800-44-FEVER or 305-531-DIVE. Write: Captain Tom Guarino, PO Box 21725, Ft. Lauderdale, FL 33335. E-mail: seafevr@gate.net. Website: www.seafever.com.

Bottom Time Adventures operates a first-class floating dive resort, **The Bottom Time II**. This 86-ft luxury catamaran tours remote out-island destinations as well as familiar dive spots around the Exuma Cays, Cat Cay, and Eleuthera. ☎ 800-234-8464 or 954-921-7798. Website: www.bottom time2.com.

Nekton Diving Cruises caters to scuba divers and snorkelers. Their staff of 11 includes seven instructors who offer guided reef or wreck tours daily. A special 17-ft tender on board the 78-ft yacht is dedicated to carrying snorkeling guests to the best shallow spots.

The unique twin-hulled design of the yacht eliminates the rocking that causes most seasickness. Cabins are nice rooms. E-6 processing, complete audio/visual capabilities, spa, private baths and elevating dive platform. Departs from Ft. Lauderdale, Georgetown and Great Exuma. Tours include Cay Sal Banks and snorkeling with wild spotted dolphins.

The boat tours alternate between Belize and the Bahamas. Rates for seven nights, six dive days range from $1,295 to $1,495 plus taxes. Call for current schedules. ☎ 800-899-6753 or 954-463-9324, fax 954-463-8938. Website: www.nektoncruises.com.

MV Ballymena transports dive and snorkeling groups from reef to wrecks in pure luxury. The 124-ft modern yacht features roomy air-conditioned cabins with CD players. Higher-priced staterooms have TV and VCR. Two custom tenders – 22 ft and 31 ft – take divers and snorkelers to all the top spots, which are listed on their Website. The main diving areas are Exumas, Andros, Cat Island, San Salvador, Conception, Long Island and Crooked Island. E-6 processing, A/V, kayaks, Sailfish, Sunfish. Capacity 20 passengers. Whole-boat, all-inclusive charters are offered at $6,000 per day for up to eight passengers; $6,250 for 10; $6,500 for 12; $7,500 for 13 to 20. ☎ 800-241-4591 or 242-394-0951, fax 242-394-0948. E-mail: balymena@bahamas.net.bs. Website: www.ballymenacruise.com.

Cruise Ships' Private Island Retreats

Several cruise lines operating in the Caribbean, including the **Disney Cruise Line, Holland-America Cruise Line, Norwegian Cruise Line, Premier Cruises, Princess Cruises** and **Royal Caribbean**, call at their own private islands.

Each island is equipped with snorkeling facilities, Bahamian craft shops, food pavilions, at least one local bar and miles of white-sand beach. Most of the ships anchor offshore and shuttle passengers via small boats, or "tenders," to the island.

Disney Cruise Line's Bahamian retreat, **Castaway Cay**, is 1,000 acres of sand and sun. There are separate activities for children and adults. This is the only island cruise retreat that is equipped with a cruise ship pier. Diving is arranged with Nassau shops. Snorkeling is possible at the island.

Princess Cruises's home-away-from-home, **Princess Cay**, lies on the southwest coast of Eleuthera. Princess Cay touts 1.5 miles of lovely beach. Their New Waves program with PADI offers instruction, dive and snorkeling excursions.

Holland Cruises' **Half Moon Cay**, near Eleuthera, is a 2,400-acre island with fine snorkeling beaches, nature trails, bone fishing, water sports center and even a wedding chapel.

Norwegian Cruise Lines' **Great Stirrup Cay** was the first private island to be developed by a cruise line. The island is part of the Berry Islands, between Nassau and Freeport. Great Stirrup Cay boasts six beaches, two of which are maintained. Snorkeling around the island is superb.

Royal Caribbean International's **Coco Cay** is adjacent to Great Stirrup Cay and is a 140-acre island in the Berry Islands. The island's most unusual attraction, especially to divers, is the underwater sunken airplane, a nice coral reef and a sunken replica of Bluebeard's flagship, *Queen Anne's Revenge*, waiting to be explored.

Premier Cruise's **Salt Cay** lies three miles northeast of Paradise Island and can be reached by tender from Prince George's Dock in Nassau. The destination has earned fame as the filming location for *Gilligan's Island*. Diving and snorkeling excursions are arranged with Nassau shops.

Facts

Recompression Chamber: Located on Lyford Key in Nassau. The chamber in Nassau is privately owned by Bahamas Hyperbaric Center Limited, ☎ 242-362-

5765, fax 242-362-5766. A second chamber operated by UNEXSO on Grand Bahama Island was not operational at press time (☎ 242-373-1244). Dr. John Clements, based at the Lucayan Medical Center (☎ 242-373-7400) on Grand Bahama, specializes in dive-related injuries. UNEXSO transports divers to Florida if necessary. The trip is two-three hours. A third chamber is operated by Club Med on San Salvador for their guests.

Getting There: Daily flights service Nassau International Airport and Freeport from most US gateway cities. Freeport and the Out Islands are scheduled daily from South Florida by Bahamasair, ☎ 800-222-4262; American Eagle, ☎ 800-433-7300 and Chalk's International Airlines, ☎ 305-653-5572, 800-346-4644. Some of the Out Island resorts arrange their own charters from Fort Lauderdale or Nassau. Check with individual resorts for details.

Private Planes: More than 50 airstrips serving light planes are scattered throughout the Bahamas. Some are paved and lighted with instrument approaches, some are no more than patches of crushed coral along a beach. Private aircraft pilots are required to obtain a cruising permit before entering Bahamas airspace and should contact the Bahamas Private Pilot Briefing Center at ☎ 800-32-SPORT-USA. Excellent plotting services and charts are also available through AOPA, ☎ 800-USA-AOPA.

A 500-page, annually updated book, *The Pilot's Bahamas and Caribbean Aviation Guide* published by Pilot Publications, PO Box 88, Pauma Valley, CA 92061 (☎ 800-521-2120) contains every airport in the Bahamas, Turks & Caicos, Hispaniola, Puerto Rico, USVI, Jamaica and the Eastern Caribbean islands, plus Cancun and Cozumel, Belize and Roatan, Honduras. The flight guide also includes aerial photos, charts, maps, customs and other information on island flights. Cost is $44.95 plus $6.00 shipping.

Driving: On the left. You may drive on your own license for up to three months. Those staying longer must obtain a Bahamian license. If you drive a motor scooter a helmet is required.

Documents: United States law now requires citizens to carry a current passport to re-enter the US. To enter the Bahamas, US citizens and Canadians need proof of citizenship and a return ticket.

Customs: Under current (United States) regulations, each visitor is allowed to return home with up to $600 worth of merchandise duty-free, provided the resident has been out of the United States for at least 48 hours and has not claimed the exemption within 30 days. Each adult may bring back two liters of spirits, but one must be a product of the Bahamas or another Caribbean Basin country. Up to $1,000 beyond the $600 will be assessed at 10%. If you carry expensive cameras, electronics or dive gear, it is best to register them with customs before your trip.

Canadians may take home US $100 worth of purchases duty-free after 48 hours and up to $300 worth of goods after seven days.

Each person leaving the Bahamas must pay a $15 departure tax.

Vaccinations: Certifications for smallpox and cholera shots are needed for persons coming from an endemic area.

Currency: The Bahamian dollar is the monetary equivalent of the US dollar. The $3 Bahamian bill, square 15¢ pieces and fluted 10¢ pieces are popular among souvenir hunters.

The US dollar is also considered legal tender, but Canadian dollars are not widely accepted. Travelers checks and major credit cards are widely accepted.

Climate: Average year-round temperatures range from 70 to 85°F. The rainy season lasts from early June through late October. Islands toward the south end of the arc have warmer weather.

Clothing: Casual. A light jacket or sweater is needed in the evening, especially during winter months. You may want to dress up in the evening for some hotels, restaurants, and casinos in Nassau and Freeport. The Out Islands are very casual.

For diving, a light wetsuit or lycra wetskin is desirable in winter.

Time Zone: The Bahamas are on Eastern Standard Time (EST) (GMT+5) from the last Sunday in October to the last Saturday in April, and Eastern Daylight Time (GMT+1) from the first Sunday in April to the last Saturday in October.

Electricity: 120 volts, 60 cycles. No adaptors necessary for US electrical products.

Service Charges: The standard tip is 15%. Some hotels and resorts add a service charge to cover gratuities.

Religious Services: Houses of worship for many faiths minister to visitors in Nassau. Check with your hotel for individual island services.

Weddings: Couples wishing to marry in the Bahamas may now do so after only one day. Marriage license $40. ☎ 888-NUPTIALS or 800-BAHAMAS.

For Additional Information: For general information about all the Bahama Islands, ☎ 800-4-BAHAMAS. Website: www.gobahamas.com.

For Nassau and Paradise Island, ☎ 800-327-9019, 800-866-DIVE (3483) or 305-931-1555, fax 305-931-3005. Or write to Bahamas Tourist Offices in the US at 150 E. 52nd St, 28th Fl, New York, NY 10022 or at 19495 Biscayne Blvd, Suite 809, Aventura, FL 33180.

For Grand Bahama, ☎ 800-448-3386. Website: www.grand-bahama.com.

Out Island Promotion Board, ☎ 800-688-4752 or 954-359-8099, fax 954-359-8098. E-mail: boipb@ix.netcom.com. Website: www.bahama-out-islands.com.

Bahamas

Turks & Caicos

Despite a rapid and huge growth in dive tourism during the past 10 years, the Turks & Caicos remain one of the last great diving frontiers, with miles of vast reefs and wrecks yet to be explored. In fact, some of the finest and oldest coral communities in the Western Hemisphere fringe the shores.

Located well off the beaten path, at the southeastern tip of the Great Bahama Bank, most of these islands are sparsely populated. Topside, the terrain and vegetation resembles the Bahamas – flat with scrub brush and tall cactus, edged by pink and white sand beaches.

The Turks consist of two main islands: Grand Turk and Salt Cay, which are separated from the Caicos by a 22-mile-wide deep-water channel, the Turks Island Passage. The Caicos group consists of six principal islands: West Caicos, Providenciales, North Caicos, Grand Caicos, East Caicos and South Caicos. All are flanked by small uninhabited cays.

Providenciales' posh hotels, casino gambling and direct flights from Miami attract most dive tourists. Grand Turk, on the other hand, has fabulous diving too, but lacks the posh resorts and takes a little more effort to get to.

History

Soon after Ponce de Leon discovered the Turks & Caicos during the 1500s, word of the islands' vast salt flats spread quickly. Bermudians came first to rake salt and stayed to become the first European occupants of the islands. They converted salinas (salt ponds) on Grand Turk, Salt Cay and South Caicos into workable salt mines and developed an export trade of salt and slaves to the American colonies. Fortunes were made from this "white gold." Lavish houses and churches that they built can still be seen in the islands.

As demand for the sea salt grew, so grew governments' interest in the islands. After a few hostile bouts, the islands went to Spain, then France, then the Brits, who governed the islands until the 1700s, when the Turks & Caicos were declared an extension of the Bahamas. Between 1848 and 1962, Jamaica ruled. Presently they are a British dependency. Through all these power shifts, the islands' peaceful waters churned into a haven for pirates who preyed on the West Indies merchant ships.

The Great Depression and World War II ruined the salt industry. By the 1960s salt sales had severely diminished. All the islands suffered and many islanders migrated to the Bahamas, Miami and New York. British Government aid provided a substandard economy for those who remained.

Fortunately, the advent of flights to the islands, the Cold War and Space Exploration rejuvenated the national economy and enabled the introduction of tourism. The American Navy, NASA and the Coast Guard built bases that caused an economic, social and cultural revolution. The first tourists were private pilots en route to the West Indies during the 1960s who fell in love with the islands. They invested in three small hotels and established a domestic air service which linked all the inhabited islands to each other and the US.

Their efforts paid off. By the 1970s the islands were growing in popularity with scuba divers and leisure travelers. In 1978 scheduled jet service was introduced from Miami and the 1980s, following construction of the Club Med village on Providenciales, was a decade of continued tourism investment and growth.

When to Go

A substantial annual rainfall during the late summer and early fall almost dictates that you visit the Turks and Caicos in late winter, spring or early summer. Generally, the high season runs a week later than most Caribbean islands and at many establishments lower hotel prices prevail until mid-December.

Grand Turk

Grand Turk, the seat of the Turks & Caicos government, has about 4,300 permanent residents, not counting street chickens or the dive-tourist crowd. Aside from Front Street, the main road along the western coast, most of the island's streets are fairly narrow, bordered by low stone walls. Grand Turk is home to the **National Museum**, where exhibits of the oldest European shipwreck are displayed.

Cockburn Town, the main municipality, reflects the islands' history in its colorful homes. Some, over 100 years old, are either brightly painted wood frame construction or made from Bermudian stone brought in as ballast by ships seeking salt. Donkey carts clatter through the streets.

Best Dives of Grand Turk

Superb diving and snorkeling exist all along Grand Turk's western coast. The reef starts shallow just 300 yards off shore, then drops to about 35 ft for a quarter-mile. Then the wall drops 7,000 ft into the Turks Island Passage, an expressway for every imaginable creature in the sea. Schools of manta rays come in to feed on the shallow reefs during spring, a period when the waters are rich with a bloom of plankton – free-swimming micro-organisms that are a food source for many species of marine life. Bottlenose dolphins pass through the dive areas and, occasionally in late winter, humpback whales do as well.

Photo ©Cecil Ingham, Sea Eye Diving

Dolphin Dive off Grand Turk.

Several shallow areas entice snorkelers. Good shore diving exists off Governor's Beach on the south end.

⭐⭐⭐⭐ **The Gardens** start at 35 ft, then slope off to channel depths. Marine life is so abundant along this section of the Grand Turk wall that the magnificence of the animals often overshadows the reef's exquisite beauty. Residents include giant Nassau grouper, oversized parrots, rock beauties, and Spanish hogfish, as well as schools of large barracuda. During springtime, manta rays come in to feed. Tiny cleaner shrimp and octopi inhabit the crevices. Mini-critters hide in the vase sponges and gorgonians that grow from the wall. Farther down you'll find immense barrel sponges and black corals. Visibility is usually excellent except during the plankton "blooms," which create a soupy cloud over parts of the reef.

⭐⭐⭐⭐⭐ **The Tunnels**, just south of the Gardens, are swim-through chutes between 50 and 75 ft. Reef life is similar to the Gardens. Six-ft mantas arrive during spring migration. At 60 ft there's a big sandy bowl where our researchers surprised a number of spotted and Nassau groupers. Big and small jacks, trunk fish and enormous file fish sway with the light current. Spotted and green morays poke their heads out from the crevices.

⭐⭐⭐⭐ **The Anchor**, one of the prettiest sections of the Grand Turk wall, features huge pastel sea fans, dense thickets of soft and hard corals, and some huge tube and barrel sponges. Black coral is found in the deeper sections. Like

Turks & Caicos

most of the wall, the reef starts at about 40 ft and drops off to channel depths. Unusual coral sculptures provide superb photo compositions.

Snorkeling Grand Turk

Good beach snorkeling is found off the **Sitting Pretty Hotel** (formerly the Kittina), the **Arawak Hotel, Guanahani Beach Resort** and the **Salt Raker Inn**, where juvenile reef fish (angels, barracudas) shells, and small turtles blast by shallow coral heads.

☆☆**South Dock** at the south end of Grand Turk is a virtual junkyard of lost cargo from ships inhabited by a flirty community of frog fish, sea horses, batfish, eels, and shrimp and crabs. Sponges cover the pilings. Check with the dockmaster before entering the water.

☆☆☆☆ Snorkeling trips take off to **Round Cay** and **Gibbs Cay**, two out islands surrounded by elkhorn reefs. Bright sponges and colorful gorgonians abound. At Gibbs, friendly stingrays greet you in the shallows off the beach. They will pose for your pictures while you pet and handfeed them.

Dive Operators of Grand Turk
Rates subject to change.

Sea Eye Diving, in Cockburn, picks up from most Grand Turk resorts. Owner Cecil Ingham has been diving Grand Turk for many years and is a trustworthy dive operator and superb underwater photographer. The shop offers PADI and NAUI courses from resort to instructor, including Nitrox training. Sea Eye boats tour the wall and reefs with special trips to the *HMS Endymion Wreck*. Rate for a single dive is $30, two-tank dive $50, night dive $35. Gibbs Cay snorkeling beach barbecue and stingray encounter $40. Six skiffs carry eight to 10 divers. Average trip time is 10 minutes. The shop's 41-ft dive boat visits areas out of the immediate cruising range. ☎ 649-946-1408, fax 649-946-1407. E-mail: ci@tciway.tc. Website: www.reefnet.on.ca/grandturk. Write to: PO Box 67, Duke Street, Grand Turk, Turks & Caicos Islands, BWI.

Blue Water Divers in Cockburn Town at the Salt Raker Inn, offers guided reef trips to the Grand Turk Wall as well as to some of the small uninhabited cays south of Grand Turk. The shop offers a complete line of rental gear including 35mm cameras. Open year-round, they offer terrific hotel-dive packages with the Salt Raker Inn. Single-tank dives cost $30, two-tanks $55, night dive $35. Dive packages drop the cost per dive down to $25. Snorkelers are welcome to join the dive boat for $10 with their own gear or for $15 with rental equipment. Snorkel-sightseeing trips to the cays cost $20. ☎ 649-946-1226. E-mail: mrolling@tciway.tc. Website: www.microplan.com/bluerake.htm.

Write to: Blue Water Divers, PO Box 124, Grand Turk, Turks & Caicos Islands, BWI. Complete dive/accommodation packages available.

Oasis Divers offer wall and reef tours, a full line of rental gear, dive computers, cameras and video recorders. They also have E-6 processing. PADI certifications and training through Divemaster. Nitrox courses. The PADI shop provides towels and refreshments on board and does complete gear handling and set up. They offer daily afternoon and night dives. One-tank dive $30, two-tank dive $50, snorkel trip $20. Whale watching trips with Captain Everette Freites are offered during January, February and March.

Hotel-dive packages with Arawak Inn for seven nights start at $685 per person with unlimited beach diving, tanks and weights, airport transfers, six days of two single-tank divers per day and continental breakfast. Similar packages with the new eight-room Island House are from $682 to $829; with Turks Head Inn from $682 to $929 per person; Salt Raker Inn from $670 to $855; Guanahani Beach Resort or Sitting Pretty from $665 per person. ☎ 800-892-3995 or 649-946-1128. E-mail: oasisdiv@tciway.tc. Website: www.oasisdivers.com. Write to PO Box 137, Grand Turk, BWI.

Grand Turk Accommodations

For additional resorts and accommodations contact the Turks & Caicos Tourism Office, ☎ 800-241-0824. E-mail: tci.tourism@tciway.tc. Website: www.turksandcaicostourism.

The Arawak Inn & Beach Club has the best beach snorkeling on Grand Turk. Numerous coral heads buzzing with fish dot the shallows, all close to the shore. The resort features 15 air-conditioned rooms, a restaurant, phones, TV and pool. Room rates start at $125 per night. ☎ 800-725-2822, 800-577-3872. Direct: 649-946-2277, fax 649-946-2279.

Guanahani Beach Resort offers 16 spacious, oceanfront rooms with air-conditioning, TV, phones, a gift shop and convenient dive facility with storage and rinse area on the beach. Snorkeling off the beach. Excellent restaurant. Room rates start at $137. (Undergoing renovation at press time.) ☎ 800-725-2822, 800-577-3872 or 649-946-1459, fax 649-946-1460.

The Sitting Pretty Hotel has 24 simple, beachfront rooms with air-conditioning, some with kitchenettes. TV and phones. Diving with Sea Eye. Native restaurant, beach bar, sand beach, and freshwater pool. $137. (Undergoing renovation at press time.) ☎ 800-577-3872 or 649-946-2232, fax 649-946-2668.

The Salt Raker Inn, a 150-year-old Bermudian shipwright's home, features 10 lovely guest rooms and three suites that open onto the sea or gardens. Air-conditioning and ceiling fans. Good restaurant. ☎ 800-548-8462 or 649-946-2260, fax 649-946-2817. E-mail: blueraker@aol.com.

Turks & Caicos

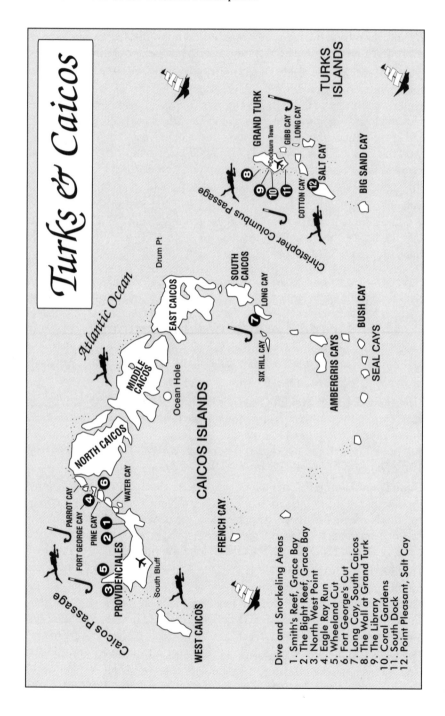

Turks & Caicos

Atlantic Ocean

Caicos Passage

Christopher Columbus Passage

Dive and Snorkeling Areas

1. Smith's Reef, Grace Bay
2. The Bight Reef, Grace Bay
3. North West Point
4. Eagle Ray Run
5. Wheeland Cut
6. Fort George's Cut
7. Long Cay, South Caicos
8. The Wall at Grand Turk
9. The Library
10. Coral Gardens
11. South Dock
12. Point Pleasant, Salt Cay

TURKS ISLANDS

GRAND TURK

Cockburn Town

GIBB CAY
LONG CAY
COTTON CAY
SALT CAY

BIG SAND CAY

Drum Pt

EAST CAICOS

MIDDLE CAICOS

NORTH CAICOS

WATER CAY

PARROT CAY
FORT GEORGE CAY
PINE CAY

PROVIDENCIALES

South Bluff

WEST CAICOS

Ocean Hole

SOUTH CAICOS

LONG CAY

SIX HILL CAY

CAICOS ISLANDS

FRENCH CAY

AMBERGRIS CAYS

SEAL CAYS

BUSH CAY

Turks Head Inn, an 1860s mansion, once served as a US consulate, then a governor's private guest house. Seven rooms all have original antique furnishings (four-poster beds, rocking chairs), air-conditioning, TV and balconies. One apartment has a kitchenette. Outstanding restaurant features local and European specialties. Expensive. ☎ 649-946-2466, fax 649-946-2825, or book through your travel agent.

Salt Cay

Salt Cay, the most remote of the inhabited islands, lies seven miles southeast of Grand Turk. It features 101 friendly residents, one dive shop, outstanding diving and a rich heritage dating back to the 1700s when Salt Cay flourished as one of the world's largest salt exporters. The salt industry died during the 1960s, but you can still tour the Salinas (salt ponds) and windmills where the salt was mined and stored. Lovely churches and grand plantation homes – many converted to inns – attest to the prosperity of those days.

Today's wealth lies in Salt Cay's magnificent diving and snorkeling. Pristine walls packed with fish, spectacular corals and sponges bathe in the rush of sea water passing through the outlying channel. Because the island is remote and tricky to reach few divers make the trek, but those who do are rewarded with fine diving. Topside, miles of deserted beaches make for terrific shelling and bird watching.

During January, February and March, Salt Cay transforms into Humpback Whale Headquarters, as the island sits directly in the Columbus Passage, the byway for whales migrating to Silver Banks.

Nightlife is limited to stargazing and moonlight dives. Two restaurants and one café provide fresh-caught seafood and steaks.

Best Dives of Salt Cay

The wall dives start at 35 feet, dropping to 7,000 ft. Salt Cay Divers tour the Grand Turk sites as well.

☆☆☆☆ *The HMS Endymion* is a favorite shallow wreck at depths from 15 to 30 feet. There's actually not much left of the wreck, just the cannons and anchors, but it's worth a trip for the abundant fish life. The trip from Salt Cay takes between 40 and 50 minutes. Sea conditions vary.

☆☆☆☆ **Point Pleasant**, the Turks and Caicos' best snorkeling and shallow-dive spot off the northern tip of Salt Cay, will leave you in awe with massive vertical brain corals, giant elkhorn and staghorn gardens – all in 15 ft of water. You can swim side-by-side with big turtles, stoplight parrot fish, pompano, and eagle rays. This fabulous spot is always calm with no currents. Visibility exceeds 100 ft. Beach or boat access.

Turks & Caicos

Salt Cay Dive Operator

Debbie Manos at **Salt Cay Divers** will handle your entire Salt Cay dive vacation with stays at a choice of inns converted from the old plantation homes or in the Castaways Beach House cottages. If you pass up their sumptuous meal and plan to cook for yourself, they will stock your cottage with foods from your own pre-arranged menu. The fully-equipped PADI dive shop runs skiffs to the walls. Most sites are a few minutes from shore. The dive shop also rents kayaks and offers sailing cruises. ☎ 649-946-6906, fax 649-946-6940. E-mail: scdivers@tciway.tc. Website: www.saltcaydivers.tc.

Salt Cay Accommodations

Castaways Beach House offers six simple beachfront guest rooms at moderate rates. ☎ 315-536-7061, fax 315-536-0737; direct 649-946-6921, fax 649-946-6922.

Mount Pleasant Guest House has eight comfortable, beachfront rooms with TV. ☎ 649-946-6927 for voice and fax.

For a list of 20 guest houses and dive-package rates (from $974 to $1,114 per person for a week), contact Salt Cay Divers at ☎ 649-946-6906, fax 649-946-6940. E-mail: scdivers@tciway.tc. Website: www.saltcaydivers.tc.

The Caicos

The Caicos' six principal islands and their surrounding small cays offer superb wall diving. Along the barrier reef surrounding them you'll find iridescent sea anemones, huge basket sponges and dense gardens of elkhorn coral. Closer to shore are patches of coral swarming with reef tropicals. Miles of beautiful swimming beaches attract families and non-divers as well.

All island activities center around the resorts. Most Provo (short for Providenciales) dive sites require a 35-minute boat ride from the dive shops.

Best Dives of Providenciales Island & North Caicos

☆☆☆☆☆ **West Wall** comprises hundreds of sites along a vertical edge of the continental shelf. A few favorites are Grand Canyon, Black Coral Forest and Carol's Wall. Drop-offs begin at 25 ft and bottom at 6,000 ft. Divers exploring this ledge encounter huge fish, schooling eagle and manta rays, shark and dolphin. During winter months, humpback whales pass by.

Spectacular gigantic barrel sponges, tube sponges and anemones grow from the ledges, providing cover for arrow and spider crabs, sea cucumbers, Spanish lobster, barber shrimp, green and spotted moray eels. Forests of black coral start as shallow as 60 ft.

Visibility is always excellent, with sea conditions dependent on the winds and weather. Recommended for experienced divers.

☆☆☆☆ **The Pinnacles** on the northeast coast of Provo near Grace Bay, range in depth from 35 to 60 ft. This spur and groove reef shelters Nassau grouper, sea turtles, snapper, sergeant majors, basslets, and schooling grunts. Clump plate corals dotted with purple and orange sponges make bright homes for moray eels that surprise divers by emerging during daylight hours. Visibility is exceptional. Usually calm, though seas vary with the winds.

☆☆☆ **Southwind Shipwreck**, an 80-ft freighter off Provo's north coast, provides dramatic backgrounds for fish and diver portraits. Sunk during 1985, the wreck's denizens include several tame grouper and barracuda, Spanish hogfish, French angels, horse-eye jacks, damsels, schools of sergeant majors and yellowtail. The wreck sits on the sand at 60 ft. Visibility is usually good. Seas vary, usually light chop.

☆☆☆ **Grouper Hole**, off the north shore, is a wide sand hole encircling a large coral head. Mammoth grouper and jewfish circle the area. Seas are generally calm. Light current may occasionally be encountered.

Snorkeling Provo

The Turks and Caicos National Trust has established snorkeling trails on Smith's Reef and Bight Reef in Providenciales' Grace Bay. Both are close to the shoreline. The marked trails display 24 tile signs with directions and tips on reef preservation. Beach signs direct visitors to points of entry.

☆☆☆ **Smith's Reef**, located north of Turtle Cove off Bridge Road at the beginning of Grace Bay, has a reef trail that runs along a shallow shelf through flourishing elkhorn and staghorn corals, vase sponges and pink-tipped anemones. Depths run from eight to 25 ft, with the majority eight to 10 ft. Residents include three turtles, parrot fish, yellow and blue-headed wrasses, queen angels and lots of juvenile fish. There is also a *huge* green moray who pops his head out from the coral now and then, as well as stingrays, small eagle rays and nurse sharks. A large barracuda hangs out and adores getting close to snorkelers. Beach access. If you can't find the entry point, stop in at Provo Turtle Divers in Turtle Cove for directions.

☆☆☆ **The Bight Reef** is in the Grace Bay area known as the Bight, just offshore from a large white house. A public footpath leads to the beach and two marker buoys indicate both ends of the snorkel trail. This trail has 11 signs that describe corals and how they grow. Depths range from three to 15 ft. Daily denizens are yellow-tailed snappers, big jolthead porgies and sand sifting mojarras. Calm. Beach entry.

☆☆☆ **Eagle Ray Run**, off Fort George Cay, features sun-splashed elkhorn corals, large eagle rays, turtles, spotted groupers and crustaceans. The reef pierces the surface in some spots with deeper areas to about 20 ft. Good Visibility. Beach entry.

☆☆☆☆ **Wheeland Cut**, on the northwest point just off Navigation Light, shelters schools of grunts and sergeant majors, turtles, barracuda, an occasional small shark and a host of critters amidst a dense elkhorn reef. Vase sponges and gorgonians thrive in the light current. Boat access.

☆ **Fort George's Cut**, on the northeastern end of Provo just off Fort George Cay, is very shallow and a good place for beginning divers. The bottom is strewn with patches of coral and some old cannons inhabited by juvenile barracuda that peek out from the shadows.

Caicos Islands Dive Operators

Art Pickering's Provo Turtle Divers offers reef trips from their Ocean Club location. Use of gear included. Friendly and helpful service. Cost for a one-tank dive is $40, two-tank dive $70. Average boat trip is 45 minutes. Hotel pick-up service available. Snorkeling trips. Hotel-dive packages with Comfort Suites (from $891 for six nights, five dive days), Erebus Inn (from $975 for seven nights, five dive days), Ocean Club (from $1,285 for seven nights, five dive days) and Turtle Cove Inn (from $707 for seven nights, five dive days). ☎ 800- 833-1341 or 649-946-4232, fax 649-941-5296. Write to Box 219, Providenciales, Turks & Caicos, B.W.I. E-mail: Provoturtle divers@ provo.net. Website: www.provoturtledivers.com.

Caicos Adventures specializes in diving West Caicos and French Cay. Maximum 12 divers. Day trips include lunch, sodas, water and snacks. Dive-hotel packages available. ☎ 800-513-5822 or 649-941-3346, fax 649-941-3346. E-mail: divucrzy. Website:www.caicosadventures.tc.

Flamingo Divers offers guided reef trips aboard two 29-ft custom Delta dive boats, NAUI and YMCA instruction, resort courses and rental gear. Hotel-dive packages available. They also offer cheaper hostel-style rooms and stays at Provo Marine Biology Centre. One-tank dives cost $40, two-tank, $70. ☎ 800- 204-9282 or 649-946-4193, fax 649-946-4193. E-mail: flamingo@ provo.net. Website: www.provo.net/flamingo. Write to: PO Box 322, Providenciales, Turks & Caicos, B.W.I.

Dive Provo provides a complete range of services including a full-service, photo-video operation. Besides dive gear, they rent ocean kayaks, Laser sailboats and Windsurfers. Snorkeling tours. Dive Provo offers complete vacation packages. Winter rates are for seven nights, five dive days. Hotel-dive packages with the Allegro Resort (from $1,739 pp), Comfort Suites Hotel (from $1,011 pp), Le Deck Hotel (from $1,081 pp), Crystal Bay Resort Condominiums (from $1,466 pp), Erebus Inn (from $941 pp) and Ocean Club ($1,264 pp). Two-tank dives cost $75. Dive areas include Grace Bay, Northwest Point, Pine Cay and West Caicos. ☎ 800-234-7768 or 649-946-5029. E-mail: diveprov@gate.net. Website: www.diveprovo.com. Write to: PO Box 350, Providenciales, Turks and Caicos Islands, B.W.I.

Photo Service

Fish Frames photo service rents a wide variety of cameras and offers one- or two-day photo courses, E-6 processing, personalized video or stills of your snorkeling or dive tour. ☎ 649-946-5841.

Providenciales Accommodations

Note: The all-inclusive resorts are easiest to book through a travel agent. A few Turks and Caicos' hotels close during summer months. For additional information, contact the tourist board. ☎ 800-241-0824 or 649-946-2321/2, fax 649-946-2733.

Allegro Resort Turks & Caicos recently completed a major renovation. The 400-room property on Grace Bay offers two restaurants, two pools, bar and a children's (four-12)activity program and indoor club. PADI five-star facility on premises. Dive packages. Room rates for two are from $390 ($195 per person). Rate does not include scuba trips. ☎ 800-858-2258, Website: www.allegroresorts.com.

Beaches Turks & Caicos, an all-inclusive luxury resort on Grace Bay, features 390 rooms with satellite TV, air-conditioning, minibar, coffee maker, hair dryer and in-room safe. Two free-form pools, a childrens' pool and a scuba training pool ensure sufficient wetness between dives. The resort dive shop has fast boats and visits the best dive and snorkeling spots. Winter rates start at $1,790 per person for six nights. ☎ 800-BEACHES. Website: www.beaches.com.

Erebus Inn, one of Provo's first hotels, sits on Turtle Cove with 28 rooms overlooking the Turtle Cove Marina. All have air-conditioning, cable TV, mini-bars and direct-dial phones. The resort, in walking distance of snorkeling sites, offers a free shuttle or boat to a private beach. The inn features a pool, tennis, miniature golf, a bar, restaurant, and sun deck. Room rates are from $115. ☎ 649-946-4240, fax 649-946-4704.

Turtle Cove Inn features a dive center and marina, 32 guest rooms and one suite. Each room has a porch or balcony, air-conditioning, cable TV and phones. Pool with waterfall. Two restaurants feature indoor or outdoor seating and a nice selection of Caribbean lobster dishes, pastas and sauces. Swim or snorkel to Smiths Reef off the beach. The resort also has a beach shuttle, fresh-water pool, cycle, jeep and scooter rental. More restaurants within easy walking distance. Winter room rates are from $120 per night. Dive packages include accommodations, airport transfers, tanks, weights, belt, guide boat. They start at $328 per person for two two-tank dives, $581 for four two-tank dives, $834 for six two-tank dives. ☎ 800-887-0477, direct 649-946-4203, fax 649-946-4141. Website: www.provo.net/turtlecoveinn.

Club Med Turkoise, on Grace Bay Beach features all-inclusive packages from $1,299 per person for seven days. Diving costs from $160 for five days. If you haven't stayed at Club Med before, they charge a $30 initiation fee and a $50 annual membership fee. The 298-room resort offers all water sports, lounge, disco and restaurant. Golf nearby. ☎ 800-258-2633, direct 649-946-5500, fax 649-946-5501. Website: www.clubmed.com.

Treasure Beach Villas offers 18 deluxe beachfront suites. Near beach snorkeling sites. ☎ 649-464-4325, fax 649-946-4108.

Ledeck Hotel & Beach Club, a 25-room hotel on a lovely stretch of Grace Bay beach, features a Creole restaurant and freshwater pool. Air-conditioned guest rooms have color TV. Diving arranged with nearby Dive Provo. ☎ 800-528-1905 or 649-946-5547, fax 649-946-5770. Write to Box 144, Grace Bay, Providenciales.

Grace Bay Club, a posh, all-suite resort features 22 air-conditioned suites and penthouses. Balconies overlook the sea. All have cable TV, ceiling fans, safes, washer/dryer. Daily rates run $355 to $1,255. ☎ 800-946-5757.

The Comfort Suites Turks & Caicos Islands, adjacent to the Ports of Call shopping Village and across the street from Grace Bay Beach, offers 99 junior suites with either a king size bed or two twin beds, sofa bed and fridge. Winter room rates from $190 per day. Off-season, from $135. Dive packages with Provo Turtle Divers. ☎ 800-992-2015 or 305-992-2015; direct 649-946-8888, fax 649-946-5444.

The Sands at Grace Bay features 39 luxurious one-, two- and three-bedroom suites. All have air-conditioning, floor-to-ceiling windows and contemporary furnishings. They also have fax and Internet access, cable TV, kitchenettes with microwave, in-room safe and direct-dial phones. Oceanfront cabana restaurant and bar, dune deck, easy beach access, free-form pool, tour desk and vehicle rentals. Dive packages that include tanks, weights, transfers, taxes and accommodations are with Calypso Adventures. Package rates start at $495 for three nights, $1,230 for seven nights. ☎ toll free 877-77-SANDS. Website: www.thesandsresort.com.

The Prospect of Whitby Hotel, on North Caicos, neighbor island to Providenciales, features a secluded beachfront location, spacious, air-conditioned rooms with phones and TV. Restaurant, bar and lounge, dive shop, baby-sitting, travel services. Dive-hotel packages. Room rates range from $120 to $205 per day. ☎ 649-946-7119, fax 649-946-7114.

South Caicos

Countless snorkeling coves and miles of shell-lined beaches make this island a beachcomber's paradise. It is also ideal for those wishing a quiet escape from telephones, television and newspapers. A herd of wild horses roams the Eastern Ridge.

Diving and snorkeling on the nearby reefs and uninhabited cays is magnificent. There is excellent snorkeling on the western shores.

Best Dives of South Caicos

☆☆☆☆☆ **The Arches Reef**, beautiful by day, is also a favorite choice for night dives. On one evening exploration, BDWH diver, Dr. Susan Cropper made friends with two enormous angel fish and saw many large sleeping parrot fish. Glass-eyed snappers, brittle stars, blue tangs, big puffers, banded butterflies and a bevy of critters line a huge coral-encrusted arch which itself is covered with finger corals, gorgonians, and red and orange sponges. Stands of elkhorn and brain corals offer a nice photo background.

☆☆☆☆ **The Plane**, actually the remains of a *Convair 340,* houses six-ft nurse sharks, eagle rays, huge coral crabs, schools of grunts and some big barracudas that like to follow divers around. The fuselage sits on the edge of a wall and makes an interesting video subject. Seas are generally calm.

☆☆☆☆ **Amos' Wall** dive centers around a huge cut in the wall between 65 and 130 ft. This spot shelters many "cleaning stations" where barracuda and other fish line up to have "barber" or "cleaning" shrimp pick parasites from their teeth and scales. Both lavender and clear shrimp have also been observed. Huge eagle rays, sea turtles, big grouper, queen angels, and Spanish hogfish abound. A super dive.

☆☆☆ **Anchor Alley**, a junkyard for lost anchors, is also a byway for huge spotted gray angels, a number of Nassau grouper, spotted morays, and king-size jacks. The coral heads rise from the sand at 70 ft to within 40 ft of the surface. Abundant sea cucumbers. Seas vary with wind conditions.

☆☆☆ **The Point**, a favorite night dive, sits off the south end of South Caicos. Numerous lobsters, butterfly fish, crabs, spotted cowfish, morays and parrots rove the reef. Shrimp and sea cucumbers comb the ledges.

South Caicos Accommodations

Club Carib Harbour & Beach Resorts has two locations, one overlooking Cockburn Harbour and one at the Beach. The Harbour is good for scuba divers, while the Club Carib Beach Resort is the choice of snorkelers. Choose from eight rooms cooled by ceiling fans (no air-conditioning) or a two-room, air-conditioned villa with a kitchen. During high tide the water ranges from three ft inshore to six ft 200 yards offshore. There are small reefs in this area with plenty of marine life. A two-minute boat ride from the harbour will take you to the marine park. The 16-room resort features a restaurant and bar. Horseback riding. Color TV. Dive shop on premises operates four boats. ☎ 800-241-0824 or 649-946-3444, fax 649-946-3446.

Live-Aboards
(rates subject to change)

Peter Hughes Diving operates the 120-ft luxury dive yacht **Wind Dancer** between April 10 and December 31 and 110-ft **Sea Dancer**, which departs Providenciales every Saturday. Seven nights aboard **Wind Dancer** or **Sea Dancer** costs between $1,195 and $1,495, varying with your choice of stateroom. The lower-end rooms have upper and lower bunks, the more expensive master stateroom has a queen bed, private head/shower, TV, VCR and porthole view. Both vessels have air-conditioning to all areas, E-6 processing, Nitrox, video and camera rental, photo instruction, an accommodating crew, good food and up-to-date navigation and safety equipment. ☎ 800-932-6237 or 305-669-9391, fax 305-669-9475.

Newly refurbished **Turks & Caicos Aggressor** accommodates 14 divers in six staterooms, five with double and single berths and private baths. The sixth cabin is a roomy quad for four divers with private head and shower outside the door. There is also a new Nitrox system. January through March, this yacht offers humpback whale watching charters from Grand Turk. April through December, she offers scuba charter from Providenciales. The yacht provides breakfast to order, maid service, all meals, on-board film development, a video lounge. Week-long stays are from $995 for the quad, from $1,495 pp, double occupancy for the stateroom. ☎ 800-348-2628 or 504-385-2628, fax 504-384-0817. E-mail: diveboat@aol.com or diveboat@compuserve.com. Website: www.aggressor.com.

Facts

Recompression Chamber: Providenciales.

Getting There: American Airlines (☎ 800-433-7300) provides twice-daily service from Miami to Providenciales. Beaches Champagne Express offers nonstop service Sundays from New York and Philadelphia to Providenciales.

Bahamasair (☎ 800-222-4262) flies from Miami to Grand Turk Thursdays and Mondays. Service between the islands is available on Turks & Caicos Airways (☎ 649-

946-4255), Inter-Island Airways (☎ 649-941-5481), and SkyKing (☎ 649-941-KING). Flying time from Miami to Providenciales is 80 minutes.

Island Transportation: Taxis. Car rentals available on Grand Turk and Providenciales.

Driving: Traffic moves on the left side of the roads.

Documents: US and Canadian residents require proof of citizenship such as a passport, birth certificate or voter registrations car and photo identification, plus a return ticket.

Customs: Cameras and personal dive equipment do not require any special paperwork. No spear guns are allowed on the islands.

Currency: The US dollar is legal tender.

Climate: 70 to 90°F year-round. Water temperature never below 74°F. Possibility of storms and heavy rainfall July through November. Credit cards and personal checks are not welcome in some Turks and Caicos establishments.

Clothing: Lightweight, casual. A lightweight lycra wetskin is a good idea for winter snorkeling or to prevent coral abrasion.

Diving: All divers must present a valid C-card before they will be allowed to dive. Spearguns and Hawaiian slings are not permitted in the Turks and Caicos. Treasure hunting is forbidden.

Electricity: 110 volt, 60 cycle.

Time: Eastern Standard Time.

Language: English.

Tax: There is a $15 departure tax. Hotels may add a 15% service charge and a 7% government accommodation tax.

Religious Services: Roman Catholic, Anglican, Baptist, Methodist, Seventh Day Adventist, Church of God.

For Additional Information: Turks and Caicos Tourist Board, PO Box 128, Grand Turk, Turks and Caicos Islands, ☎ 800-241-0824, 649-946-2321, fax 649-946-2733. E-mail: tci.tourism@tciway.tc. Website: www.turksandcaicostourism.com.

Bermuda

Sitting hundreds of miles from anywhere, or more precisely 650 miles off the coast of North Carolina, Britain's oldest colony is known for its natural beauty. Everyone who's been to Bermuda understands why Mark Twain once said: "You go to heaven if you want – I'd rather stay here in Bermuda."

Geographically, Bermuda consists of 181 hilly islands and countless cayes that swing from northwest to southwest in a fish-hook shape. Its 21-mile stretch of islands is connected by several bridges and causeways. Town Hill, the highest point, rises 260 feet above sea level. There are no rivers or fresh-water lakes. Residents depend solely on rainfall for drinking water.

Bermuda is divided into nine parishes – once known as tribes. The boundaries still remain as they were drawn on the original maps in 1622, and the original names from the principal shareholders have been retained: Hamilton, Smith, Devonshire, Paget, Warwick, Sandys and St. Georges. About 58,460 people live on 20 of the islands.

Surrounding Bermuda is one of the largest fringing reef systems in the entire world. Despite a continuous influx of tour boats, the dive operators' installation and use of 20 permanent moorings, along with adherence to smart buoyancy control measures, has kept the reefs in pristine condition.

History

Though the islands were first discovered in 1503 by Juan de Bermudez, a Spaniard who left his name and sailed away, the first visitors to stay in Bermuda were British travelers shipwrecked when Admiral Sir George Somers' flagship *Sea Venture* came to grief on Bermuda's reefs in 1609. Enroute to the Jamestown Colony, they ran aground on the shallow reefs that ring the island.

Bermuda Today

The natural beauty of this tiny island, both above and below the sea is well guarded by preservation laws. Visitors are often surprised to find a noticeable lack of neon signs, skyscrapers or strip malls. Many areas of the island have been kept exactly the same as when the first shipwrecked settlers arrived. The quality of life is high in Bermuda – no pollution, no unemployment and no illiteracy.

When to Go

March through December are prime months for divers to visit Bermuda, though some operators dive all year. Annual rainfall is 57.6 inches, with October being the wettest month. Snorkeling is best during summer when the waters of the Gulf Stream reach 85°F. In winter, the main flow of warm water moves away from Bermuda, causing local temperatures to drop as low as 60°F. This annual cold spell prohibits the growth of delicate corals and sponges, but heartier corals, such as brain, star, sea fans, soft corals, pillar corals and some long purple tube sponges thrive. Overall, Bermuda's reefs are very lush with marine growth. The predominant soft corals swaying in the surges impart a garden-like quality to the reefs.

Although Bermuda is an undisputed paradise for shallow-water wreck diving, coral formations along Bermuda's south shore offer divers another amazing treat. Nature has provided a coral architecture of canyons, caves, grottoes, labyrinths, and tunnels – which may make you entirely forget about Bermuda's singular claim to fame, her hundreds of shipwrecks.

In Peter Benchley's story, *The Deep*, two vacationing divers enlist the aid of a seasoned Bermuda treasure hunter, supposedly modeled after real life treasure-hunting celebrity, Teddy Tucker, and they find a cache of golden artifacts from a lost treasure galleon. Experts agree that many of Bermuda's treasure galleons are yet to be found.

 Bermuda law requires that all diving be done with a government-licensed guide. Most dive operations will pick you up at your hotel and transport you and your equipment to and from the dive boat. No car rentals exist on Bermuda and the taxi and horse-drawn carriage operators have not yet demonstrated any fondness for divers piling loads of dripping gear in the back seat.

The Shipwrecks of Bermuda

Three centuries of sunken ships lie at rest in Bermuda's briny deeps. To protect them while still allowing recreational and commercial access, the Bermuda Government has created a special department – "The Receiver of Wrecks." This agency is responsible for issuing licenses to individuals for the excavation of newly discovered shipwreck sites in Bermuda waters. Despite modern navigational aids and numerous safety precautions ships still wreck occasionally on Bermuda's reefs.

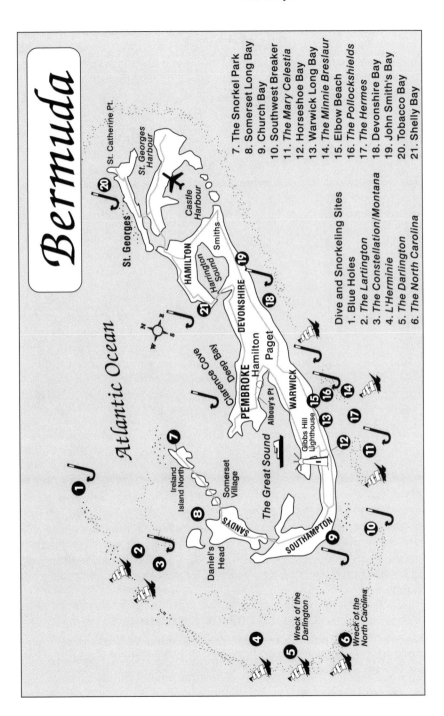

Bermuda

Atlantic Ocean

Dive and Snorkeling Sites

1. Blue Holes
2. *The Lartington*
3. *The Constellation/Montana*
4. *L'Herminie*
5. *The Darlington*
6. *The North Carolina*
7. The Snorkel Park
8. Somerset Long Bay
9. Church Bay
10. Southwest Breaker
11. *The Mary Celestia*
12. Horseshoe Bay
13. Warwick Long Bay
14. *The Minnie Breslaur*
15. Elbow Beach
16. *The Pollockshields*
17. *The Hermes*
18. Devonshire Bay
19. John Smith's Bay
20. Tobacco Bay
21. Shelly Bay

The Government officially acknowledges the existence of as many as 400 wrecks. These have been charted, more or less identified, properly worked, and most of them left alone. Some of the older and more historically important wrecks are protected sites, and divers are forbidden to visit these wrecks.

Robert Marx, in one of his books, remarks that there are at least 1,500 shipwrecks and possibly 2,000 in Bermuda waters. His estimates come from personal research, including original photographs of ships that sank in the past 100 years or so and drawings of older ships or their sister ships. Local divers agree that figure may not be an exaggeration.

The waters around Bermuda have given up a great deal of what most call treasure to eager and diligent treasure hunters. Most notable of the Bermudian treasure hunters would certainly be Mr. Teddy Tucker. Teddy has developed numerous innovative methods to search for wrecks, including riding in a hot air balloon towed behind a power boat. His innovations have proved to be very successful and he has recovered more than any other Bermudian treasure hunter.

The greatest single find from Bermuda waters must be the "Tucker Treasure," discovered after many years of working the same site. This find produced numerous gold bars, gold cakes, pearl-studded golden buttons, and a magnificent emerald cross. It also netted numerous artifacts depicting life at the time of the wreck (1595), which is often called one of the most important finds of the century. Others of Teddy's wrecks have yielded considerable gold and silver and, even though he is now getting on in years, he is still out in the reefs looking for new wrecks or working on those he has already registered.

Another legendary Bermuda treasure hunter is Mr. Harry Cox, who has found a nice-sized collection, as he prefers to call it. It consists of a quantity of gold coins, bars and circlets, a pearl cross and a gold ring with a space for a large stone. Ironically, almost one year from the day of discovering the ring, one of Harry's crew came up with a three-karat emerald. It fit perfectly into the space in the ring. But the best find of this particular collection must be the 15-ft-long double-braided gold chain. Each link is gold soldered with the lost wax process common in the Middle Ages, but unknown to modern jewelers and goldsmiths until recently. Harry believes this collection to be the personal property of a merchant who may have fallen overboard or been cast off a ship in sight of Bermuda.

Best Dives of Bermuda

Unless otherwise noted, Bermuda's wreck dives are all boat access.

☆☆☆☆☆ The *Constellation/Montana*, a few miles off the northwestern coast of Bermuda, consists of two ships that sank on exactly the same reef, although 80 years apart. The *Montana* was an English paddlewheel steamer on her maiden voyage as a Confederate blockade runner during the American Civil War. She was a very sleek vessel, 236 ft in length and with a beam of 25 ft. Her steam engines and twin paddlewheels were capable of turning out some 260 hp. She ground to a halt in shallow reefs 5½ miles from the Western end of Bermuda on December 30, 1863. As she was an iron-hulled ship, a great deal of her hull and boilers are remarkably intact and make for an excellent dive. Numerous reef fish and some rather large schools of barracuda make the *Montana*, also known as the *Nola*, *Gloria* and *Paramount,* their home. Literally overlapping the *Montana* is the remains of the *Constellation*. This four-masted, wooden-hulled schooner sank on the Bermuda reefs en route from New York to Venezuela on July 31, 1943. Hers was a general cargo, but on her deck she carried 700 cases of Scotch whiskey, an assortment of drugs and hundreds of bags of cement which, when washed with seawater, solidified into concrete and so remain to this very day. The *Constellation* is often referred to as the "Dime Store" or "Woolworth" wreck because of the wide variety of artifacts that can be seen. After perusing the *Constellation*, a diver might think he had been diving at Woolworth's. She was carrying all sorts of goods to be sold in Venezuela, including red glass, cut glass, china, glasses, tea and coffee cups and saucers, tickets to Coney Island (in Spanish), Yo Yos, 78 rpm records by RCA (with labels in Spanish), cases of pistachio nuts, radios, parts for radios, religious artifacts, devotion altars of pewter, crucifixes, cosmetic supplies by Mennen and Elizabeth Arden, cold cream, Vaseline, and pharmaceutical products, including at least eight different types of drug ampules, which provided Peter Benchley with the premise for *The Deep*. This is a very enjoyable dive and all in 30 ft of water. The site is about five miles offshore and is recommended for both snorkelers and divers. Some areas of the reef are as shallow as eight feet. The sea conditions vary with the wind direction and speed. Dive boat captains vigorously discourage taking bottles and artifacts from the *Constellation*.

☆☆ **The *Cristobal Colon*,** a 480-ft, three-story Spanish luxury liner is Bermuda's largest known shipwreck. She ran aground on October 25, 1936 after hitting a reef between North Rock and North Breaker. The ship sat on the reef for some time while furniture, art and other valuables were salvaged. The following year Captain Stephensen of the Norwegian steamer *Aristo* mistook the stationary wreck of the *Colon* as a ship under way and "followed" her onto the reefs. Following that tragedy the Bermuda government dismantled the *Colon's* mast and funnel to prevent other ships from mistaking her for an active vessel. Today, the *Cristobal Colon* lies in 15 ft (at the bow) to 80 ft (at the stern) with her remains scattered across 100,000 square ft of seafloor. Divers and snorkelers will find plenty of fish hiding beneath the propellers, drive shafts and boilers lying on the bottom.

Bermuda

☆☆ The 250-ft steamship **Aristo** (aka *Iristo*) sank under tow during a rescue effort. Her general cargo included a vintage fire truck that sits off the forward deck, gasoline drums and a steamroller. Rocks and coral rubble surround the hull. Visibility varies. Seas calm. Depths to 50 ft with the bow coming to within 18 ft of the surface.

☆☆☆☆ *Lartington*. Long listed on the Bermuda wreck chart as an unidentified 19th-century wreck, the *Lartington* was often referred to as the *Nola*, until one of Blue Water Divers' young divemasters discovered her name under the port side of her partially intact bow. After writing to Harland & Wolf, a builder of this type of vessel during the 1800s, we learned that this sort of ship, a sailing steamer, was very common in the late 1800s.

The Lartington *gave rise to the expression, "tramp steamer," because every time the coal burning engines were fired up, she belched out a cloud of coal dust, liberally coating everything and everyone aboard with black soot. Then everyone resembled railroad hoboes, or tramps, and the name stuck!*

The *Lartington's* saturation steam boilers are visible amidships and, at the stern, the driveshaft and propeller. The steering controls located on the fantail are now encrusted with over 100 years of coral growth. The bow, partially destroyed, lies a few feet above the 30-ft-deep sand bottom. There is an air pocket inside the bow, but it is oxygen-poor, so breathing in is definitely a bad idea.

The surrounding reef is very nice, honeycombed with small caves and some tunnelsn. In many places it comes to within 10 ft of the surface. The entire length of the wreck is visible from the surface, although it's too long for snorkeling. She lies facing almost due south, as if heading into Bermuda. This site is recommended for snorkelers and divers, both novice and expert. Sea conditions vary with the wind.

☆☆☆☆ **Southwest Breaker**. This massive breaking reef, the cause of at least one wreck along Bermuda's south shore, rises from a 30-ft bottom and actually protrudes above the surface, casting up considerable whitewater even on the calmest days. Through the center of the breaker is a massive tunnel, large enough to drive a boat through. The tunnel is often occupied by two to four black grouper and a resident barracuda who is none too shy of photographers. In early summer, clouds of fry or glass eye minnows feed in the nutrient-rich and oxygenated waters here. They draw others and then more still until the breaker is home to more fish than you can count. The surrounding reef is very colorful and appears quite lush, with many smaller non-breaking heads known locally as "blindbreakers." These are carved with numerous ledges and caves. This area, a favorite for night dives, is excellent for snorkelers and novice and experienced scuba divers. It is particularly interesting to photograph. Surface swells are encountered here.

☆☆☆ *Mary Celestia*. After making at least five round trips to Wilmington, NC successfully, running the Northern blockade of Confederate ports, the *Mary Celestia* ran aground on the "Blind Breakers" and sank on September 13, 1864, only nine months after her sister ship, the *Montana*, was wrecked on the Northern reefs. The story, as reported in the Royal Gazette a week later, states that her captain, knowing the waters of Bermuda, warned the navigator about the breakers. The navigator remarked with a certain surety, "I know these waters like I know my own house!" He apparently hadn't spent much time at home, for within minutes the *Mary Celestia* struck bottom. She was towed off the reef the next morning and reportedly sank within 10 minutes, the seas rushing in through a great hole torn in her underside.

The only loss of life on the Mary Celestia *was the ship's cook, who returned to salvage his frying pan or some piece of personal equipment. The remainder of the crew made it to shore, where most of them died of the yellow fever that was ravaging Bermuda at the time.*

Today, the *Mary* sits quietly in just under 60 ft of water as if she were still steaming along. More than 120 years' accumulation of sand covers most of her hull, but her two rectangular steam boilers and engine machinery lie upright and perfectly visible. Both of her paddle wheels stand upright. The entire wreck is surrounded by a high reef, honeycombed with caverns, canyons and cuts that open onto the sand bottom. Dive boats normally anchor on the shallow top of the reef, allowing for a gradual descent onto the sand hole housing the wreck, and spend part of the dive moving about the cuts and tunnels. The anchor of the wreck lies in about 30 ft of water, just on the edge of the drop-off from the shallow to the deeper sand pocket.

Very large schools of parrot fish are are frequently sighted here. The reef, which starts at 15 ft and drops off to 60 ft, is lush with hard and soft corals. Surface swells are common to this area, visibility varies. Large black grouper inhabit the wreck during spring, fall and winter. It's a terrific night dive site when visibility is good.

☆☆☆ The British merchant ship **Minnie Breslaur** sank in the 1870s after striking the Southwest Breaker reef. Her stern lies in a sand pocket at 70 ft, her bow, totally collapsed on a flat coral reef at 40 ft, points out to sea. Her midships section, steam boilers and engine mechanism lie angled upward from a sandy bottom at 70 ft to the flat reef top at 40 ft. Several old torpedo-shaped bottles, Belfast and marble bottles (made by pinching the neck around a clear marble) have been recovered from her hull, and several small black coral trees can be found on the site, with one growing right above the propeller on the stern of the wreck. The adjacent reef consists of numerous small caves and tunnels and in the mounds of high reef just inshore of the stern a honeycomb of tunnels works its way through the reef formation. It is not uncommon to see schools of large jacks or several large barracudas on this dive. Where she rests, near deep water, visibility is often incredible, sometimes exceeding 150 ft. Sea fans and small brain corals surround the wreck. Visiting the *Minnie Breslaur* requires some previous diving experience. Large surface swells are generally encountered at this location.

☆☆☆☆ **The *Hermes***, a Disney-like shipwreck, was intentionally sunk in May, 1985, by the Bermuda Diving Association. Much of the work that had gone into her cleaning and final sinking was performed by Ross Menses, a Bermuda's dive tour operator. Her sinking was perfect; she sits on the bottom as if she were still steaming along. Her stern is wedged between two large coral mounds at 80 ft, her deck at 50 ft and her mast structure in less than 30 ft of water. Since her sinking, the powerful swells have moved her slightly closer to shore, but this has helped to better secure her position into the reef. Visibility is often exceptional on this site. The *Hermes* is 167 ft long, yet visibility is so good that you might see past the stern while standing on the bow. A surface swell is to be expected here, but generally does not affect underwater conditions. Some scuba experience recommended.

☆☆ **The *Xing Da* Wreck**, a 325-ft freighter, was confiscated off Bermuda by a US Marine patrol in 1996 when they discovered a cargo of illegal immigrants. The immigrants were deported and the ship was given to the Bermuda government for use as an artificial reef. She now lies at depths from 40 to 110 ft. Visibility is excellent. Residents include grouper, lobsters, barracudas and grunts. Expect a stiff surface current. For experienced divers.

☆☆☆ **L'Herminie**, a huge French ship carrying 495 crew members, sank on a flat calm day in 1838. En route back to France after seeing action against Maxmillian in Mexico, she ground to a halt on the shallow flats of Bermuda's western ledge. The reef in this area is rather bland, visibility is rarely in excess of 60 to 80 ft, and the water always has a slightly greenish tone, but it is a very exciting dive! Even though this site was thoroughly worked by three of Bermuda's finest wreck hunters, it still boasts over 40 cannons, easily visible atop the sand or reef. There were originally 60 of these huge 12 pounders but the others lie beneath the sand.

The wreckage is scattered over a vast area, indicative of the immense size of the ship. Her anchor and armory section lie at one end of the sand flat, the anchor standing straight up, flukes spread across the bottom and rising at least

15 ft from the bottom. The armory section has yielded numerous 12- and 32-pound cannon balls, chain shot, bar shot, musket balls, ball molds, canister shot with cotton wadding still intact, numerous copper sheathing nails and many more interesting artifacts. In the middle of the sand flat lie the crossed cannons and two large guns just touching each other. Her windlass, capstan and several other cannon are also visible around the sand flat. Across a low piece of reef lies the galley section and stern, where large square iron boxes thought to be water casks can be found. Also visible are bricks from the oven, many still in the original formation, numerous cannon in neat rows along the reef, piles of cannon balls and bits and pieces of glass fragments, pottery and copper nails and sheathing.

Divers occasionally discover very valuable artifacts from *L'Herminie.* One example is a pair of matching black glass rum bottles, embossed across the bottom "H. Ricketts Bristol," a major bottle maker of that time. Another amazing find was a clear glass figural bottle in the form of a maiden with a water jug above her head. Still another diver found a perfectly intact pewter mug with handle still in place. Weights for measuring scales, olive oil bottles and embossed labels are found as well. Dive depths average 30 ft. Fabulous for snorkeling too.

☆☆☆ **The *North Carolina*,** a late 19th-century wreck, sits off the south shore of Southampton. Although broken into two distinct sections, she remains pretty much intact. The bow section is perhaps one of the eeriest pieces of wreckage in the sea. Her bowsprit looms rather menacingly, covered with algae and rustcicles; the sides of her hull hold the riggings for her sail fittings, called dead-eyes due to their resemblance to the death's head – two holes for the eye sockets and a third that represents the mouth. Given the silt and murkiness of the water in that area, the *North Carolina* is a little spooky. The reef here is storm-damaged and not terribly prolific, fish life tends to be a bit mundane, but as a very photogenic wreck, the *North Carolina* ranks high on the list. Maximum depth 45 ft.

☆☆☆ **The *Darlington*,** located off the western end of Southampton, sank in the 1870s, running straight into Long Bar, one of the most shallow stretches of reef in Bermuda. This long, shallow flat is now marked by channel stakes and the Chub Head Beacon, which warns ships of the reefs.

The *Darlington* was a sailing steamer. Her huge cylindrical steam boilers lie amidships with the stern pulpit rising to within three ft of the surface, making for an impressive photo in late afternoon. Ironically, right next to the *Darlington* lies an ancient bit of wreckage unknown as to date of origin. She has given up several bronze hull spikes, copper sheathing that is very brittle and almost crumbles upon touch, lots of old wood and numerous copper sheathing nails much smaller than those found on other early 1800s wrecks. Contributor

Bermuda

John Buckley found a section of an amphora or pottery jug complete with handle, which has been tentatively dated to the late 1700s in style. But there are no large timbers, cannon or riggings around to aid in further definition of this "Ghost Wreck." The *Darlington* lies in no more than 25 ft of water and is often done as a second dive with the *North Carolina* on a two-tank dive trip.

☆☆☆ ***Rita Zovetta***, a 360-ft Italian cargo steamship piloted by Captain Fortunato de Gregant, ran aground during a hurricane on February 11, 1924. The ship, en route to Baltimore with a cargo of manganese ore, went down near St. David's Island off Bermuda's east end. The hull rests between 20 and 70 ft. Semi-penetrable with some nice swim-throughs. Good visibility. Expect some surface swells.

Other notable reef and wreck sites include **The Caves**, **Kevin's Wreck** (probably the **Lord Donegal**, 1822, and featured in a Jacques Cousteau special); **Tarpon Hole**, a coral reef dive near Elbow Beach off the south shore, **The Catacombs** (the reefs behind the *Virginia Merchant* site, 1620, located off Warwick Long Bay on the South Shores), **Smuggler's Notch** and **Champagne Breaker**. These sites are similar in nature, all having a common high reef that starts at the surface and drops down to depths of 45-50 ft. The reef is honeycombed with caves, caverns, tunnels, cuts, canyons, crevices and labyrinths. Divers find 50-ft pinnacles breaking the surface here and huge cathedral arches of coral with myriads of snapper and other reef fish.

☆☆ **The *Taunton***, a 228-ft Norwegian cargo steamer, hit Bermuda's northeast reefs during fog on November 24, 1920. Her remains are widely scattered, but her boilers and engine compartment lie intact and upright. The Gibb's Hill Lighthouse Museum displays the ship's bell. The *Taunton* rests in 20-ft depths; her bow comes to within 10 feet of the surface.

☆☆☆ **Blue Holes**. Not to be confused with the real blue holes of the Bahamas or Belize, these are deep sand pockets surrounded by exceptionally shallow reef – in some places as shallow as four ft – which drop straight down into an iridescent teal blue, reaching a maximum depth of nearly 70 ft. The reef here is incredibly lush with sea fans, soft corals and black coral bushes. There are two holes directly adjacent to each other that are joined at the bottom by a series of tunnels where one can often find a school of huge tarpon. An occasional enormous (150-200 lb) grouper can also be found on the reefs. There are many of the colorful reef fish that inhabit all of Bermuda's dive sites. Exceptional visibility. The Blue Holes area offers five different dive sites at depths from 30 to 70 ft. When conditions are right, this is a must-see spot for every diver. Terrific snorkeling exists in the shallows.

Additional good sites frequented by the shops are the ***Caraquet***, a 200-ft British mail steamer at 40 ft, the ***Madiana***, a 160-ft passenger liner that ran aground in 1923, depth 40 ft, and the "**Airplane Wreck**," a B-29 bomber that took off from Bermuda and went down due to a fuel problem, with no injuries to the pilot or crew.

Beach Snorkeling

Snorkeling tours to the offshore wrecks and reefs are offered at every hotel desk. New swimmers and beginning snorkelers should test their skills at sheltered Devonshire Bay, Jobson's Cove or Shelly Bay before heading offshore.

☆☆ **The Snorkel Park** at The Royal Naval Dockyard (fort) is adjacent to the Maritime Museum, a short walk from the cruise ship dock, ferry and bus stops. It's open daily from 10:30 am to 6 pm.

The park, a protected coral reef preserve, has well marked reef trails, floating rest stations and a helpful staff, including experienced life guards. Depths are shallow and the seas calm. Bottom terrain consists of plate corals and gorgonians. Schools of grunts, doctor fish and parrot fish roam about. Several historic cannons dating back to the 1500s are marked off. Look along the base of the fort for ceramic shards, musket miniballs and insulators dating from the fort's use as a radio station in WWII.

Rental equipment is available on-site, including flotation vests, masks and snorkels. ☎ 444-234-1006, fax 441-292-5193. E-mail: bic@ibl.bm

☆☆☆ The reef at **Elbow Beach** starts 10 yards from the shoreline, then stretches seaward for a mile. If you are not staying at the Elbow Beach Hotel, be sure to enter the water from the public beach to the west of the resort and swim east toward the restaurant.

☆☆☆ A 300-yard swim from Elbow Beach seaward takes you over the wreck of the **Pollockshields**, a 323-ft German-built steamer. The swim out takes 10 to 15 minutes. A strong surge makes this a bad choice on windy or choppy days. For advanced snorkelers only.

☆☆☆ **Church Bay**, a terrific spot when seas are calm, may be entered anywhere along the beach. Park along the road above the beach and climb down the steep stairway.

☆☆☆ **John Smith's Bay**, on the beautiful south shore, is handicapped accessible and has a lifeguard from April through October. A 50-yard swim brings you over a shallow reef. Usually calm with exceptional visibility.

☆☆ **Tobacco Bay's** grassy terrain shelters soft corals and schools of juvenile fish. A rocky breakwater separating the bay from the ocean keeps this area calm. Depths run from three to 10 ft.

☆**Somerset Long Bay**, on Bermuda's southwest end, appeals to first time snorkelers with calm, shallow water and a wealth of marine life. Nice spot for a picnic.

Bermuda

The rocks encircling **Devonshire Bay**, on the south shore, harbor an abundance of fish and invertebrates.

☆ On a calm day, **Shelly Bay**, on the north shore, features easy access and impressive marine life. Avoid this spot on windy days unless you want to go board sailing. The parking lot and surrounding area are accessible to people with disabilities.

Dive Operators of Bermuda

One-tank dives average $50, two-tanks $70, snorkeling $40 with gear. Tanks and weights are included, but additional scuba equipment rental is extra. Night dives are $60, excluding equipment. Resort courses cost about $100.

Blue Water Divers & Watersports, Bermuda's oldest full-service dive center now has three shops, located at Somerset Bridge, Marriott's Castle Harbour Hotel and Elbow Beach Hotel. Their fast boats visit all the best wrecks plus the Airplane Wreck and the *Pollockshields*, a shore dive off Elbow Beach that is explored with underwater scooters (DPVs).

For those not certified, they offer beginner/resort instruction and great snorkeling from the dive boat.

Trips depart at 9 am for 16 to 18 scuba divers and 1:30 pm with a mix of 20-22 certified and beginner divers and snorkelers. The shop's three boats are outfitted with a dive platform, ladder, tank racks, oxygen, toilets and showers. Instructors and guides are on all excursions.

The Elbow Beach location offers shore diving and pool instruction. One night dive per week is scheduled. PADI courses, CPR and first aid.

During March, April and May they offer full- and half-day whale watch charters. ☎ 441-234-1034, fax 441-234-3561. E-mail: bwdivers@ibl.bm. Website: www.divebermuda.com. Write to: PO Box SN 165, Southampton, SN BX, Bermuda.

Fantasea Diving & Snorkelling Ltd., a five-star PADI facility, can be reached by a 10-minute ferry, taxi or scooter ride from the city of Hamilton, the cruise ship terminal or the central hotels.

The shop employs internationally qualified PADI and NAUI instructors. Two custom dive boats carry 18 and 30 divers to the favorite wrecks and reefs. Snorkelers welcome. Large snorkeling groups travel aboard a custom 55-ft catamaran *Aristocat*. The shop offers whale watching in April, parasailing, sunset and dinner cruises aboard the catamaran, gear and camera rentals, all levels of instruction. Accommodation-dive packages, ☎ 800-637-4116. Dive and snorkel reservations and information, ☎ 888-DO-A-DIVE or 441- 236-6339, fax 441-236-8926. E-mail: info@fantasea.bm. Website: www. fantasea.bm.

Nautilus Diving Ltd. Located at the Southampton Princess Hotel, this PADI five-star IDC Center offers one-tank reef dives in the morning and a shallow wreck dive in the afternoon. The 40-ft *Cracklin Rosie* cruises at 15 knots, has a dive platform, ladder and carries up to 30 divers. Snorkelers welcome, with gear provided. Resort courses in hotel pool followed by an ocean dive on a shallow reef. Certification courses, referrals and Discover Scuba courses are conducted daily. Referrals. Rental gear including kayaks, floats, dive and snorkeling equipment. ☎ 441-238-2332 or 295-9485, fax 441-234-5180. E-mail: nautilus@ibl.bm. Website: www.bermuda.bm/nautilus.

Nautilus Diving Ltd. In Hamilton at the Princess Hotel, they carry up to 20 divers to favorite sites off the west, north and east side of the island. Their 40-ft custom dive boat, *Cante Libra*, has a dive platform and ladder. Rental gear. PADI five-star facility, IDC. ☎ 441-295-9485 or 441-238-2332 ext 4371, fax 441-234-5180. E-mail: nautilus@ibl.bm. Website: www.Bermuda.bm/ nautilus.

South Side Scuba, at the Sonesta Beach Hotel, Southampton, offers a resort course in the hotel pool, then a shallow dive on the reefs. Includes all dive gear. Scuba excursions to the south shore reefs. Packages available. Local, ☎ 441-238-1833, fax 441-238-3199. Accommodations, 800-SONESTA. E-mail: sonetab@ibl.bm.

Scuba Look, located at the Grotto Bay Beach Hotel, Hamilton Parish, visits the reefs on the east end and south shores of Bermuda. Snorkelers welcome. Resort course in hotel pool. Open March through November. All equipment provided. Local, ☎ 441-292-1717 or 441-235-1427, fax 441-295-2421. E-mail: scubluk@ibl.com. Website: www.diveguideint.com/p0078.htm.

Snorkeling Tours & Rentals

Snorkeling cruises cost from $25 for a short tour to $50 for a half-day.

Blue Water Divers and Watersports offers a Guided Snorkel Certificate Program for all ages and abilities. They teach mask defogging, clearing and adjustment, removing and replacing the mask on the surface, swimming in waves and surf, surface exit and entry techniques, surface breathing, clearing the snorkel, submerging, exploring, resurfacing and regaining position, use of a snorkel vest, first aid, free dive techniques, use of weight belt, basic knowledge of marine life, fish and coral identifying. ☎ 441-234-1034, fax 234-3561. E-mail: bwdivers@ibl.bm Website: www.divebermuda.com.

Bermuda Barefoot Cruises Ltd. departs Darrell's Wharf, Devonshire for snorkeling and sightseeing aboard the 32-ft *Minnow*. Equipment and instruction provided. Complimentary refreshments on return trip. ☎ 441-236-3498.

Bermuda

M.V. Bermuda Longtail Party Boat operates a 65-ft motor catamaran that carries 200 people. Tours depart Flag Pole, Front Street, Hamilton. Snacks and drinks sold on board. ☎ 441-292-0282, fax 441-295-6459.

Bermuda Water Tours offers both glass-bottom and snorkeling cruises aboard the 50-ft, 75-passenger *Bottom Peeper*. Tours depart near the Ferry Terminal, Hamilton. Gear provided. Full bar and changing facilities on board. Refreshments on return trip. Operates from the end of April 1 to November 30. ☎ 441-236-1500, fax 441-292-0801.

Bermuda Water Sports departs St. Georges for half-day snorkel cruises aboard the 100-passenger glass-bottom boat, *Sun Deck Too*. Anchors in waist-high water on an island beach. Guides feed and identify fish and corals. Instruction and equipment provided. Full bar and snack bar on board. May to November. ☎ 441-293-2640 or 441-293-8333 ext. 1938.

Fantasea Diving and Snorkeling, at Darrell's Wharf on the Warwick Ferry Route, takes snorkelers with scuba divers to the favorite wrecks and reefs. ☎ 441-236-6339, fax 441-236-8926, 888-DO-A-DIVE. E-mail: fantasea@ibl.bm. Website: www.bermuda.com/scuba.

Hayward's Cruises' 54-ft, 35-passenger snorkeling and glass-bottom boat, *Explorer*, departs next to the Ferry Terminal in Hamilton. Bring swim suit and towels. Snorkeling gear provided. Instruction. Changing facilities on board. Cameras available for rent. Complimentary swizzle on return trip. May to November. ☎ 441-292-8652.

Jessie James Cruises aboard the 57 ft., 40-passenger *Rambler* and 48-ft, 75-passenger *Consort* depart Albouy's Point, Hamilton. Pick-ups at Darrell's and Belmont wharves. ☎ 441-236-4804, fax 441-236-9208.

Pitman Boat Tours' snorkeling and glass-bottom boat trip departs Somerset Bridge Hotel dock and cruises five miles northwest to the perimeter reef. Snorkeling instruction on ancient shipwrecks and coral reefs. Gear supplied. Changing facilities on board. No children under five years. ☎ 441-234-0700.

Salt Kettle Boat Rentals Ltd., Salt Kettle, Paget, offers snorkeling cruises to the western barrier reef and shipwrecks. Refreshments. ☎ 441-236-4863 or 441-236-3612, fax 441-236-2427.

Sand Dollar Cruises are aboard the 40-ft, 189-passenger, Bristol Sloop *Sand Dollar*, departing Marriott's Castle Harbour dock, Hamilton. Gear provided. This boat may be chartered. ☎ 441-236-1967 or 234-8218.

Nautilus Diving Ltd., at the Southampton Princess Hotel, offers morning and afternoon reef and wreck tours. All equipment provided. Snorkeling is from a 40-ft boat to reefs within 10 minutes of shore. Group charters available. ☎ 441-238-2332 or 441-238-8000 ext. 6073.

St. Peter's Church, St. George's.

Tobacco Bay Beach House on Tobacco Bay, St. George's. Snorkeling and underwater cameras for rent. Ideal for beginners. ☎ 441-293-9711.

Other Activities

Helmet Diving is fun for all ages. No lessons needed. Depth 10 to 14 ft. Does not get your hair wet. Available at **Hartley's Helmet**, Flatt's Village Smith's, ☎ 441-292-4434, or **Greg Hartley's Under Sea Adventure**, Village Inn dock, Somerset. ☎ 441-234-2861.

Horseback Riding along scenic beach and shore trails is available year-round. Law requires that all rides be supervised. Both experienced or inexperienced riders are welcome at **Lee Bow Riding Centre**, Tribe Road # 1, Devonshire, ☎ 441-236-4181, or **Spicelands Riding Centre**, Middle Road, Warwick. ☎ 441-238-8212 or 238-8246.

Golf is one of Bermuda's most popular year-round attractions. Golf courses are located at **Belmont Golf Club**, Warwick (☎ 441-236-6400, fax 441-236-0120); **Castle Harbour Golf Club**, Hamilton Parish (☎ 441-298-6959, fax 441-293-1051); **Mid Ocean Club**, Tucker's Town (☎ 441-293-0330, fax 441-293-8837); **Ocean View Golf & Country Club**, Devonshire (☎ 441-295-9093, 295-6500, fax 441-295- 9097); **Port Royal Golf Course**, Southampton (☎ 441-234-0974, 295-6500, fax 441-234-3562); **Southampton Princess Golf Club**, Southampton (☎ 441-239-6952, fax 441-238-8479), **Riddells Bay Golf & Country Club**, Warwick (☎ 441-238-1060, 238-3225, fax 441-238- 8785); and **St. George's Golf**

By Bill Garrett, Bermuda Dept of Tourism

Bermuda

Club, St. George's Parish (☎ 441-297-8353, 295-6500, fax 441-297-2273).

Para-Sailing can be arranged at the **Bermuda Island Parasail Co**, Darrell's Wharf (☎ 232-2871 or 297-1789, **St. George's Parasail**, Somers Wharf (☎ 297-1542), St. George's, or **Skyrider Bermuda** at the Royal Naval Dockyard (☎ 234-3091).

Nature Walks at Spittal Pond, Smith's Parish, take you through a 64-acre reserve and park. The sanctuary is a major habitat for waterfowl and shorebirds and is situated along the rugged coastline bordering the Atlantic Ocean to the south. Here visitors can see Bermuda's only two wild flamingoes.

Sightseeing

Taxis sporting blue flags are driven by qualified tour guides who know all about the island and usually throw in a few local anecdotes for good measure. Particularly interesting visits include **Hamilton**, the island's capital, **Flatts Village** for a tour of the **Government Aquarium, Natural History Museum and Zoo** with its superb collection of marine life, gaily colored exotic birds and relics of Bermuda's history.

While in Hamilton, don't miss a stop at the **Underwater Exploration Institute** on East Broadway, which features interactive exhibits including a simulated journey to the bottom of the ocean, films, treasures from the sea, a neat gift shop and restaurant. Open daily from 10 am to 6 pm. ☎ 441-292-7219, fax 441-236-6141.

St. George's, the historic former capital, is another must-see with the pillory and stocks in King's Square, as is **St. Peter's Church,** with its glistening white facade and Bermuda cedar interior. It is the oldest Anglican church in the Western Hemisphere.

In Southampton, stop in at **Bermuda Triangle Brewing** on Industrial Park Road for a microbrewery tour. Tours start at 4 pm, Monday-Friday between March and October, on Saturdays from November to March. ☎ 441-238-2430, fax 441-238-1759.

Several reminders of both American and Bermudian history are found in St. George's, notably the replica of the ***Deliverance***, the tiny ship that Sir George Somers and his shipwrecked crew built from natural Bermuda cedar and what could be salvaged from the shipwreck of the *Sea Venture*. Nearby **Fort St. Catherine**, at Bermuda's eastern end, houses dioramas of the colony's history and replicas of the Crown Jewels. The fortification lends itself to exploration. Other notable sites include the **Crystal Caves** or **Leamington Caves,** with their superb stalactite and stalagmite formations and impressive illuminations.

Dolphin Quest at Southampton Princess.

For a more leisurely look at the islands, try a horse-drawn carriage tour (sans wetsuits) through the blossom-lined streets and lanes. Helicopter tours are offered by **Bermuda Helicopters, Ltd.**, Southampton. ☎ 293-4800, 295-1180 or 238-0551.

Shopping

Bermuda shopping offers great savings on imports from Great Britain and Europe. Most large shops are in the City of Hamilton with branches in St. George's, Somerset, Royal Naval Dockyard and several major hotels.

Local "buys" include island-made sherry peppers, black rum and local liqueurs, rum cakes, jams, jellies, soups and dressings as well as cookbooks featuring island recipes. Lilies, passion flowers, cedar, allspice, bay laurel and island limes go into locally produced perfumes and fragrances.

Accommodations

All room rates fluctuate and are subject to 7.25% Bermuda Government Hotel Occupancy Tax, service charges and a resort levy. Contact individual properties or dive shops for dive-accommodation packages. Prices below are for summer – the high season on Bermuda. They are per room for a double and do not include taxes or service charges. Rates are subject to change.

Bermuda

Accommodations range from ultra-luxurious resorts to inexpensive house-keeping cottages and charming small hotels. Call ☎ 800-223-6106 (US), 416-923-9600 (Canada) or 071-734-8813 (England) for a list.

Elbow Beach, on the south shore in Paget Parish, has Blue Water Divers on-site. The hotel features an immense, pink sand beach, three restaurants, a heated pool, shopping arcade, tennis courts and 50 acres of lush gardens. Guests stay in the main hotel or suites in the out buildings. Rooms have telephone, radio, remote 25-channel TV, safe, robes, slippers, hairdryer and air-conditioning. Rooms are from $385 per night, suites from $485. Rates drop between November and March. ☎ 800-344-3526 or 441-236-3535, fax 441-236-8043. Write to PO Box HM 455, Hamilton, HM BX, Bermuda.

Southampton Princess Hotel features a three-acre lagoon in East Whale Bay that houses several friendly dolphins. The lagoon opens to the sea and has an underwater fence. Marine mammal specialists offer several interactive "Dolphin Quest" programs for children and adults. Southampton guests get priority bookings, but non-guests may sign up on a space-available basis. Packages for the dolphin encounter are available.

The resort sits on one of the highest points in Bermuda, with panoramic views from all 600 rooms. Air-conditioned. Nautilus Diving on premises. Amenities include six restaurants, two pools, private beach and beach club, 18-hole par-three golf course, 11 tennis courts, health club, game room, shops and beauty salon. Room rates per day in summer run from $329 to $629 for a petite suite. ☎ 800-223-1818 (US) or 441-238-3000, 800-268-7176, fax 441-238-8968. Write to PO Box HM 1379, Hamilton HM FX, Bermuda.

The Reefs sits on a cliff overlooking Christian Bay, Southampton. Built around the ruins of a 1680 farmhouse, this luxury resort features 67 rooms and suites plus eight two- and three-bedroom cottages, two bars, three terrific restaurants, two tennis courts and a fitness center. Good snorkeling for all skill levels exists over the patch reefs just off the beach. Dive trips are arranged with Blue Water Divers. MAP Summer rates which include breakfast and lunch or dinner start at $358 for a room (double), $398 for a cottage, $658 for a two-bedroom cottage plus a service charge of $17 per day. The Reefs participates in a carousel dining program with other hotels that gives guests an opportunity to try other restaurants. ☎ 800-742-2008 or 441-238-0222, fax 441-742-8372. E-mail: reefsbda@ibl.bm. Website: www.bermuda.bm. Write: South Road, Southampton SN 02, Bermuda.

Sonesta Beach Hotel & Spa is a modern luxury resort hotel with 25 acres of picturesque grounds. SouthSide Scuba and Snorkelling, Inc. on premises. Summer room rates are from $340 to $440 per night. ☎ 441-238-8122 or 800-SONESTA (US), fax 441-238-8463. Write to PO Box HM 1070, Hamilton HM EX, Bermuda.

Grotto Bay Beach Hotel & Tennis Club sits on 21 acres of beachfront gardens in Hamilton Parish with two underground grottos, deep-water dock, a freshwater pool with swim-up bar, and outdoor hot tub. Bus stop at door. Scuba Look dive shop on premises offers dive and snorkeling tours. A private beach features two small coves in an enclosed bay and a 500,000-year-old cave to explore. Deep water dock. All rooms have private balconies and panoramic sea views, cable TV, phone, coffeemaker, safe, mini-fridge and hairdryer. Air-conditioned. All-inclusive packages available. Summer room rates start at $205. ☎ 800-582-3190 (US) or 441-293-8333, fax 441-293-2306. E-mail: gro@bspl.bm. Write to: 11 Blue Hole Hill, Hamilton Parish CR 04, Bermuda.

Marriott's Castle Harbour Resort, adjacent to the world-renowned Castle Harbour Golf Club, now features Blue Water Divers & Watersports on their property. This classic Bermuda resort sits on a hilltop amidst 250 manicured acres and touts two private beaches, one being the largest resort beach in Bermuda. Guest rooms overlook the gardens, fairways, pool or Castle Harbour and Harrington Sound, many with balconies or terraces. All have individual climate control, ironing board and iron, hairdryer. The resort is convenient to the airport. Room rates start at $289 per night. ☎ 800-223-6388 or 441-293-2040, fax 441-293-8288.

Dining

Bermuda menus cater to every taste and pocketbook with more than 100 restaurants and fast-food eateries. Prices for two range from $10 at a fast-food restaurant to more than $200 for gourmet cuisine. Traditional dishes of Bermuda are mussel pie, fish chowder laced with black rum and sherry peppers, spiny Bermuda lobster (September to April), Hoppin' John (blackeyed peas and rice) and a Sunday morning breakfast of codfish and potatoes. The island drinks are a Rum Swizzle, a mixture of four colors of rum and fruit juices, and "dark and stormy," an interesting blend of black rum and ginger beer. The small eateries may offer delicacies such as conch stew, fritters or hashed fish. A 15% gratuity charge is added to the bill at most restaurants. Most accept Amex, Visa and MC.

For informal dining in Hamilton Parish, try the **Landfall Restaurant** on North Shore Road. Open Monday from 9 am to 9 pm seven days a week, this restaurant serves lunch and dinner and offers salads, appetizers and sandwiches starting at $3. Dinner entrées include sweet & sour chicken, filet mignon and barbecued spare ribs. ☎ 293-1322.

Local favorites and fine coffees are found at **Kathy's Kaffee**, on Front Street in Hamilton. Kathy's serves fish chowder, curry chicken, codfish cakes and

Bermuda

hamburgers in a café-style atmosphere. From $4.00. Monday-Friday, 7:30 to 4 am. Saturday, 8:30 to 4 am. ☎ 295-5203.

The Pubs of Hamilton are popular for rehashing the day's dive and enjoying island dinner specialties. Try **The Hog Penny**, Bermuda's oldest English style pub and restaurant at 5 Burnaby Hill, Hamilton ☎ 292-2524, the **White Horse Tavern**, at 8 King's Square, St. George, ☎ 297-1838, **North Rock Brewing Co.** at 10 South Road, Smiths Parish, ☎ 236-6633, **The Swizzle Inn** on Blue Hole Hill, Bailey's Bay, or **The Frog & Onion** on Freeport Road at the Royal Naval Dockyard for creative entrées. Meals start at $20.

Bouchées Waterfront Bistro on 36 Water Street, St. Georges serves French and Mediterranean cuisine. Open for lunch and dinner. Entrées average $40. ☎ 297-2951.

Pasta Basta at 1 Elliott Street, Hamilton (☎ 295-9785) and 14 York St (☎ 297-2927), St. George, offers Italian lunch and dinner specialties from $10. No credit cards.

Tuscany Restaurant, Bermuda House, 95 Front Street, Hamilton (☎ 292-4507), **Tio Pepe** at 117 South Road, Southampton (☎ 238-1897) and **La Trattoria** on 22 Washington Lane, Hamilton (☎ 295-1877), feature formal Italian entrées from $25.

Mediterranean and Continental haute cuisine are offered by **The Harbourfront,** 21 Front Street West, Hamilton (☎ 295-4207, closed Sundays), **Ascot's** at the Royal Palms, 24 Rosemont Ave, Pembroke,(☎ 295-9644) and the **Waterlot Inn** at the Southampton Princess, Southampton (☎ 239-6967). All from $50.

Most large hotels offer elegant dining as well as nightly entertainment with steel bands, limbo and calypso groups or international stars. There is no gambling in Bermuda.

Be sure to stop for tea at the **Gibbs Hill Lighthouse Tea Room** on Lighthouse Road Southampton (☎ 238-0524).

Facts

Recompression Chamber: Located at King Edward Memorial Hospital, Point Finger Road, Paget. Drs. Charles Schultz and Carol Ferris. ☎ 236-2345 ext 1592.

Getting There. Daily direct flights leave from most US east coast gateway cities aboard American (☎ 800-433-7300), Continental, USAir, Air Canada, or British Airways.

Island Transportation: There are no rental cars available to visitors. Taxis, pink buses, ferries, bicycles or mopeds offer a variety of transportation methods. Traffic is on the left side of the roads at a speed limit of only 20 mph. Moped drivers must be at least 16 years of age and wear safety helmets.

Documents: Passports are the preferred documents when entering Bermuda. Visitors from the United States are required to have one of the following: a passport, or a birth certificate with a raised seal along with a photo ID. Canadians need either a valid Canadian passport, a Canadian certificate of citizenship, proof of their landed immigrant status or a birth certificate and photo ID.

Currency: Legal tender is the Bermuda dollar which is equal to $1 US. Travelers' checks and major credit cards accepted in most establishments.

Climate: Bermuda is a semi-tropical island. Rainfall is distributed evenly throughout the year. Average temperature during the period April to November ranges from the mid-70s to mid-80s. Cool months: December-March, 65-70°F.

Clothing: Conservative. Bathing suits, abbreviated tops and short shorts are not acceptable except at beaches and pools. In public, beach wear must be covered. Casual sportswear is acceptable in restaurants at lunch time and in fast-food restaurants any time, but some upscale restaurants require gentlemen to wear a jacket and tie in the evenings.

Electricity: 110 volts, 60 cycles AC throughout the island.

Time: Atlantic Standard (Eastern standard + 1 hr.)

Tax: A 7.25% hotel tax is payable upon checkout. Airport departure tax, $20.

For Additional Information: *US,* Suite 201, 310 Madison Avenue, New York, NY 10017. ☎ 800-BERMUDA, 800-223-6106 or 416-923-9600. *United Kingdom,* Bermuda Tourism, BCB Ltd., 1 Battersea Church Road, London SW11 3LY, England. ☎ 071-734-8813. Websites: www.bermudatourism.com or www.bermuda.bm.

Bermuda

The Florida Keys

Once a favorite hunting ground of ruthless pirates like Black Caesar and Blackbeard, the Florida Keys now attract scuba divers and snorkelers from around the world.

A necklace of islands that begin just south of Miami, the Florida Keys are connected by the Overseas Highway's 42 bridges – one seven miles long – over the Atlantic Ocean and Gulf of Mexico. The area is divided into five regions: Key Largo, Islamorada, Marathon, Big Pine Key and Key West. Most dive and snorkeling vacations center around Key Largo, Big Pine Key and Key West.

The entire 125-mile chain, including its shallow water flats, mangrove islets and coral reefs, has been designated the Florida Keys National Marine Sanctuary.

Key Largo, the jumping-off point to the Florida Keys and the area's most popular diving, lies 42 miles south-southwest of Miami. The largest of the island chain, Key Largo's star attraction is **John Pennekamp Coral Reef State Park** – the first underwater preserve in the United States – and the adjacent **Key Largo National Marine Sanctuary**. These two refuges, part of the Keys Marine Sanctuary, feature 55 varieties of delicate corals and almost 500 different species of fish.

Islamorada is the centerpiece of the "purple isles." Spanish explorers named the area "morada" (purple) either for the lovely violet sea snail, *janthina janthina*, found on the seashore here, or for the purple bougainvillea flowers found in the area.

Known as the Sportfishing Capital of the World, Islamorada features the Keys' largest fleet of offshore charter boats and shallow-water "back country" boats.

Marathon, home to the Seven Mile Bridge, is the heart of the Florida Keys, centrally located between Key Largo and Key West. It features the **Dolphin Research Center**, one of four Keys facilities that provide visitors an opportunity to swim and interact with the playful mammals.

Big Pine Key and the Lower Keys straddle the **Looe Key National Marine Sanctuary**, a terrific shallow-water dive spot also popular for kayak-snorkeling trips.

Just west of Looe Key, the 210-foot island freighter ***Adolphus Busch Senior*** rests on the sea floor as an artificial reef. Endangered miniature Key deer and a few alligators rove Big Pine's wooded areas.

Key West, the nation's southernmost city, marks the final stop on the Overseas Highway. Situated closer to Havana than Miami, Key West exerts a charm all its own, with quaint, palm-studded streets, century-old gingerbread mansions and a relaxed citizenry of self-styled "Conchs." Offshore lies *Stargazer*, an undersea living work of cosmic art created by sculptor Ann Labriola.

Key West's legendary treasure hunter Mel Fisher, who died in December 1998, recovered more than $400 million in gold and silver from the ship Nuestra Señora de Atocha, *a 17th-century Spanish galleon that sank 45 miles west of Key West. Fisher, who spent 16 years of his life searching for the booty, established the* **Mel Fisher Maritime Heritage Society Museum**, *where visitors may view, touch and even buy some of the riches of the* Atocha *and the* Santa Margarita.

Plush resorts, mom and pop motels, marinas, restaurants and shopping areas pave the route from Key Largo to Key West.

Diving

Spectacular coral reefs, offshore from Florida's Keys, attract nearly a million sport divers each year. Patches of finger-like spur and groove reefs parallel the islands from Key Biscayne to Key West and are inhabited by over 500 varieties of fish and corals. Shallow depths, ideal for underwater video and still photography, range from just below the surface to an average maximum of 40 feet. All the sites require a 15- to 25-minute boat ride.

Snorkeling trips depart from Pennekamp Park, the Holiday Inn docks in Key Largo and from booths along the main streets in Key West. Many dive boats will carry snorkelers if space permits.

During summer, water temperatures climb to 85°F, making a wetsuit unnecessary. A safe-second regulator is encouraged, but not mandatory. Standard gear – buoyancy compensators, weight belts, weights, mask, knife, snorkel, camera and video equipment – may all be rented at most dive shops. Boaters will find small craft for rent at the marinas.

Weather

Good diving on the Florida Keys shallow reefs (most 45 ft or less) depends on good weather conditions. High winds that churn up surface swells also stir up the sandy bottom. You might plan a dive the morning after a storm and find visibility as low as 25 ft, yet return in the afternoon to calm seas and visibility in

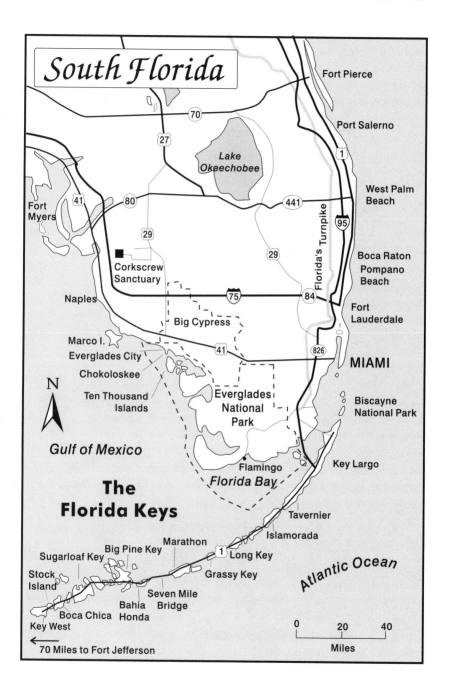

excess of 100 ft. October through June offer the best weather conditions. Because the reefs are fairly shallow, winds that churn up the seas may cause lowered visibility.

When storms rule out trips to the outer reefs, visit the Content Keys, a sheltered area which is almost always calm, located on the Gulf side of Marathon.

The Florida Keys National Marine Sanctuary

After three freighters grounded on the reefs in 1989, destroying acres of the tiny coral reef organisms, President Bush signed into law a bill designed to protect a 3,000-square-mile stretch of Florida Keys land and sea. The area, known as The Florida Keys National Marine Sanctuary, contains the entire strand of Keys barrier reefs on the Atlantic and Gulf sides of the islands. Freighter traffic close to shore is prohibited, providing a safe "cushion" area between keels and corals.

The sanctuary, managed by the National Oceanographic and Atmospheric Administration, also encompasses, and dwarfs, two previous federal preserves in the Keys, the Looe Key National Marine Sanctuary and the Key Largo National Marine Sanctuary. In contrast to the new 3,500-square-mile sanctuary, the Looe Key Sanctuary is 5.32 square miles and the Key Largo Sanctuary is 100 square miles. Within the sanctuaries, spear fishing, wearing gloves and anchoring on the coral are prohibited.

On the ocean reefs, replenishment reserves are being set up to protect and enhance the spawning, nursery or permanent resident areas of fish and other marine life. Some sections will restrict fishing, will allow diving, but will be "no-take" areas. Prime areas are shallow, heavily used reefs. Check with local dive or bait shops for current information before diving on your own.

Dive shop signs and billboards offering reef trips line the highway throughout Key Largo. Boat trips to the best dive sites takes from 15-30 minutes, depending on sea and wind conditions.

Best Dives of Key Largo & the Upper Keys

☆☆ The park's most popular dive, underwater wedding site and perhaps the one which symbolizes the area is "the statue," a nine-foot bronze replica of **Christ of the Abyss**, created by sculptor Guido Galletti for placement in the Mediterranean Sea. The statue was given to the Underwater Society of American in 1961 by industrialist Egidi Cressi.

The top of the statue is in 10 feet of water and can be seen easily from the surface. The base rests on a sandy bottom, 20 feet down, and is surrounded by huge brain corals and elkhorn formations. Stingrays and barracuda inhabit the site. A buoy marks the statue's location, but small swells make it difficult to pinpoint. If you are unfamiliar with navigating in the park, join one of the com-

Reef Etiquette

• Do not allow your hands, knees, tank or fins to contact the coral. Just touching coral causes damage to the fragile polyps.

• Spearfishing in the sanctuary is not allowed. This is one reason the fish are so friendly that you can almost reach out and touch them.

• Hand-feeding of fish is discouraged, especially with food unnatural to them. Besides the risk of bodily injury, such activity changes the natural behavior of the fish.

• Hook and line fishing is allowed. Applicable size, catch limits and seasons must be observed.

• Spiny lobsters may be captured during the season except in the Core Area of the Looe Key Sanctuary. Number and size regulations must be followed.

• Corals, shells, starfish and other animals cannot be removed from the Sanctuary.

• Regulations prohibiting littering and discharge of any substances except chum are strictly enforced.

• Fines are imposed for running aground or damaging coral. Historical artifacts are protected.

• The red and white dive flag must be flown while diving or snorkeling. Boats must go slow enough to leave no wake within 100 yards of a dive flag.

mercial dive trips. Extreme shallows in the area provide outstanding snorkeling areas, but make running aground a threat.

☆☆ More easily found is **Molasses Reef**, marked by a huge, lighted steel tower in the southeast corner of the park. Noted as the area's most popular reef dive, it carries the distinction of having had two shiploads of molasses run aground on its shallows.

The reef provides several dives, depending on where your boat is moored. Moorings M21 through M23 are for diving. M1 through M20 are shallow and better for snorkeling.

High profile coral ridges form the perimeter of a series of coral ridges, grooves, overhangs, ledges and swim-through tunnels. In one area, divers see huge silver tarpon, walls of grunts, snappers, squirrel fish and Spanish

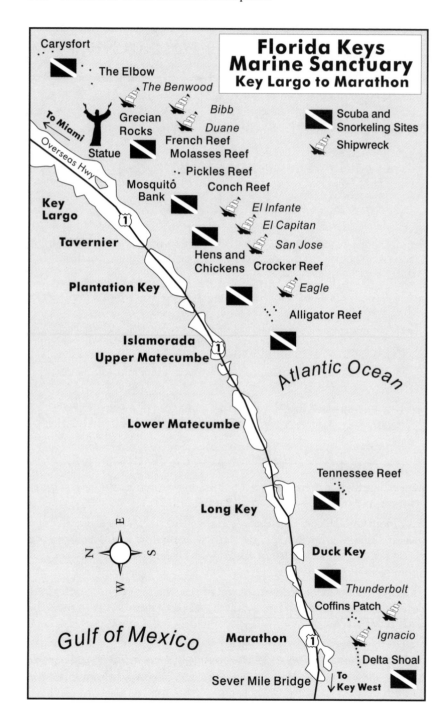

Carysfort

The Elbow

The Benwood

**Florida Keys
Marine Sanctuary
Key Largo to Marathon**

Scuba and
Snorkeling Sites

Shipwreck

Grecian
Rocks

Bibb

Duane

French Reef
Molasses Reef

Statue

To Miami

Overseas Hwy

Pickles Reef

Mosquito
Bank

Conch Reef

El Infante

**Key
Largo**

El Capitan

San Jose

Tavernier

Hens and
Chickens

Crocker Reef

Plantation Key

Eagle

Alligator Reef

**Islamorada
Upper Matecumbe**

Atlantic Ocean

Lower Matecumbe

Tennessee Reef

N
E
S
W

Long Key

Duck Key

Thunderbolt

Coffins Patch

Ignacio

Gulf of Mexico

Marathon

Delta Shoal

To
Key West

Sever Mile Bridge

Florida Keys Marine Sanctuary
Bahia Honda to Key West

■ Scuba and Snorkeling Sites

🚢 Shipwreck

Content Keys

Sugarloaf

Alexander's Wreck

Ramrod Key

Summerland

Bahia Honda

Key West   Maryland Shoal

Sambos

Dry Rocks

Looe Key   Big Pine Shoal

American Shoal

Rock Key   Aquanaut

Sand Key

U.S.S. Wilkes Barre

hogfish. In another, divers swim over an ancient Spanish anchor. Visibility often exceeds 100 ft.

Be sure to check the current at Molasses before entering the water since an occasional strong flow makes the area undiveable. Depths vary from very shallow to approximately 40 ft.

☆ Slightly northeast of Molasses stands **French Reef**, an area many consider the prettiest in the park, with swim-through tunnels, caves, and ledges carpeted in pink and lavender sea fans, tube sponges, soft corals and anemones. Shallow depths range from the surface down to 45 ft.

☆ North of French Reef lies the wreck of the **Benwood**, a 300-ft freighter hit by a German submarine during World War II and later sunk by the Coast Guard when it became a navigational hazard.

Presently under guard by throngs of sergeant majors, grunts, and yellowtails, the wreck sits on a sandy bottom at 45 ft. Lobsters, huge morays and sting rays peek out from beneath the hull as huge grouper and turtles blast by. During summer, swirls of glass minnows hover over the wreck.

☆☆☆ Despite pristine reefs and a robust fish population, a long boat ride prevents most dive operators from frequenting **Carysfort Reef**, located in the northeast corner of the park.

If you are fortunate enough to catch a trip out there, expect a good display of fish and the possibility of one huge, resident barracuda, tamed by a local divemaster, swimming up to within an inch of your mask. This unique, engaging plea for a handout makes the toothy guy tough to ignore, but sanctuary officials greatly discourage fish feeding, so try to resist sharing your lunch.

Instead, explore the reef's healthy display of staghorn, elkhorn and star corals at depths varying from very shallow to 65 feet. Normally calm waters make Carysfort a good choice for novice and experienced divers, but beware the dramatic overhangs that top the walls. We discovered some the hard way – by surfacing without first looking up.

☆☆☆ Just south of Carysfort Reef lies **The Elbow**, a crescent-shaped, spur-and-groove reef littered with the twisted remains of two steamers – the *City of Washington*, and the *Tonawanda*. Near the wrecks lie ballast and the frail remains of a wooden ship known as the Civil War wreck. Depths average 40 feet. Visibility is usually good, with an occasional strong current. Friendly barracuda and tame moray eels await.

Key Largo's Artificial Reef

In November, 1987, two vintage Coast Guard cutters were sunk off Key Largo by a team of Navy divers. The 1930s-era sister cutters **Bibb** and **Duane**, whose careers took them from the Caribbean and Cape Cod to duties in the North Atlantic, Pacific and Mediterranean, were towed to their final resting site following cleaning and removal of potential hazards for divers.

The *Bibb* sits on her side in 125 ft of water, while the *Duane* sits upright at 130 ft. The top of the *Duane* can be viewed at 75 ft. They rest seven miles offshore and one mile south of Molasses Reef. This area is a buffer zone around the Key Largo National Marine Sanctuary. Both ships have attracted huge grouper, schooling tropicals, barracudas, eels and rays. An occasional hammerhead or nurse shark makes an appearance.

The ships, now camouflaged with a thin layer of coral, were part of a seven-vessel "Secretary" class built by the Coast Guard in the late 1930s, with their original role as long-range rescue ships, according to Dr. Robert Scheina, a Coast Guard historian. "The vessels were also built to prevent poaching by Japanese fishing vessels in Alaskan waters. And there was a third purpose – one quite familiar to today's Coast Guard. There was a problem with opium smuggling from the Orient to various outlets on the West Coast of the United States. The vessels were utilized for drug interdiction back then."

*John Pennekamp
State Park, Key
Largo.*

Courtesy Monroe
County Tourism

With spare parts for the *Bibb* and *Duane* difficult to obtain and with excessive maintenance costs, the Coast Guard decommissioned the ships in 1985 and turned them over to the US Maritime Administration for disposal.

The **Speigel Grove**, Key Largo's newest dive site and artificial reef, measures a whopping 510 ft. The wreck of this amphibious boat transport sits at 124 ft, the top at 40 ft.

☆☆ South of Pennekamp Park lies **Pickles Reef**, a shallow area rich with marine life, sea fans and boulder corals. Near Pickles is **Conch Reef**, a wall dive that drops off to more than 100 feet, and the wreck of the *Eagle*, a 287-foot freighter, sunk intentionally to create an artificial reef. Residents of the wreck include parrot fish, schools of grunt, sergent majors, moray eels and angels.

☆☆ Another popular site frequented by Islamorada dive shops is **Alligator Reef**, home to walls of grunts, parrot fish and groupers and an occasional nurse shark. There are some nice stands of elkhorn and brain corals.

More spectacular, though, are the reefs surrounding the **Marquesas Islands**, 30 miles from Key West and the Dry Tortugas, 70 miles off Key West.

Key Largo & Upper Keys Dive Operators

The following operators provide guided reef and wreck trips. Prices include tanks and weights, unless otherwise stated (all subject to change). Many offer dive and accommodation packages, though some will not refund unused dives, even if they cancelled the trip. Check with the individual dive shop's cancellation policy before buying a package.

Admiral Dive Center, a full-service PADI shop operating since 1985, offers dive and snorkeling trips to the best sites in Pennekamp and the marine sanctuary. Divers and snorkelers ride on the same boats. Two-tank dives cost $50, snorkeling $30. Nitrox and Nitrox instruction available.

Owners, Captains Susan and Bill Gordon also offer three-, five- and seven-night live-aboard dive and fishing trips aboard the 65-ft *Admiral I*, which sleeps 12 (two heads). Destinations include the Keys, Cay Sal Banks and Bahamas. ☎ 800-346-3483 or 305-451-1114, fax 305-451-2731. E-mail: info@admiralcenter.com. Website: www.Admiralcenter.com. Write to: MM 103.2, Key Largo FL 33037.

American Diving Headquarters, the Keys' oldest dive shop, operates three fast, custom dive boats. They visit the best sites in Pennekamp Park and the marine sanctuary. Gear rentals. Snorkelers welcome. ☎ 800-634-8464, fax 305-451-9291. E-mail: amdiving@aol.com. Write to: MM 105.5, Bayside, Key Largo FL 33037.

Amy Slate's Amoray Dive Center, Inc., at the Amoray Dive Resort, operates a fast dive/snorkel boat to Pennekamp and the marine sanctuary. The resort, bayside, is conveniently located next to a cut from the bay to the ocean that leads to Pennekamp Park. Dive trips cost $54.50, snorkeling $25 without equipment. Accommodation packages. ☎ 800-AMORAY or 305-451-3595, fax 305-453-9516. E-mail: amoraydive@aol.com. Website: www.amoray.com. Write to: 04250 Overseas Highway, MM 104, Bayside, Key Largo, FL 33037.

Aqua Nut Divers, at Kelly's Motel, offers dive and snorkeling tours aboard two 42-ft custom dive boats. Dive trips cost $54.50. Night dives. Nitrox. E-6 processing. Courses. NAUI, PADI, SSI. and equipment rentals. ☎ 800-226-0415 or 305-451-1622, fax 305-451-4623. E-mail: kellysmo@aol.com. Website: www florida-keys.fl.us/kellys.htm.

Captain Slate's Atlantis Dive Center has three 40-ft dive boats with showers, camera tables, new heads and decks. The shop offers dive and snorkeling tours of Pennekamp Park and the marine sanctuary. Dives cost $55 with tanks and weights, $39.50 without. Snorkelers join the trips for $26.50, equipment included. Night dives. E-6 processing. Nitrox. Courses and referrals – CMAS, NASE, NAUI, PADI, SSI, YMCA. ☎ 800-331-3483, fax 305-451-9240.

Captain Slate is pictured on many Keys postcards feeding a barracuda a piece of fish from his mouth.

Caribbean Water Sports at the Sheraton Resort offers a variety of watersports, including scuba and snorkeling trips. Divers pay $40 for a one-tank dive, $60 for two-tanks. Snorkelers pay $30; $25 for children. Stop in at the beach shack behind the Sheraton Resort. ☎ 800-223-6728 or 305-852-4707, fax 305-852-5160.

Conch Republic Divers offers dive and snorkeling trips. ☎ 800-274-3483 or 305-852-1655, fax 305-853-0031. Write to: 90311 Overseas Highway, Tavernier, FL 33070.

Ocean Divers at the Marina Del Mar Resort operates two 48-ft dive boats. Reef trips cost $55 for two tanks. Snorkelers pay $35, with equipment $39. Nitrox. Night dives. E-6 processing. ☎ 800-451-1113, 305-451-1113, fax 305-451-5765. E-mail: info@oceandivers.com. Website: www.oceandivers.com. Write to: 522 Caribean Drive, Key Largo, FL 33037.

Quiescence Diving Services, Inc., on the Bay at MM 103.5, offers personalized service with no more than six divers on a boat. They visit the popular sites and some off-the-beaten-track areas. Trips cost $38, with tanks and weights $55; snorkelers pay $30, $35 with equipment supplied. The shop operates three fast boats, has Nitrox and Nitrox training, underwater photo courses, referrals. PADI, SSI, PDIC, NASDS, and IDA. The shop is next to the cut that leads to Pennekamp. ☎ 305-451-2440, fax 305-451-6440. E-mail: info@keylargodiving.com. Website: keylargodiving.com. Write to: MM 103.5, Key Largo, FL 33037.

Sea Dwellers Dive Center, Inc. operates a custom dive boat from the Holiday Inn docks. They offer resort through dive master courses. Referrals for most agencies. Rates for a two-tank dive are $39.50, with tanks and weights $57.50. Snorkelers pay $25, $33 with equipment supplied. ☎ 800-451-3640 or 305-451-3640, fax 305-451-1935. E-mail: sdwellers@aol.com. Website: www.sea-dwellers.com.

Seafarer Dive Resort runs snorkeling and scuba tours for their resort guests. The PADI shop offers courses and referrals for most agencies. ☎ 800-

*Wreck Dive,
Key Largo.*

Courtesy Florida
Keys Tourism

599-7712 or 305-852-5349, fax 852-2265. E-mail: seafarer@terranova.net. Website: www.keysdirectory.com/seafarer. Write to: PO Box 185, Key Largo, FL 33037.

Sharky's Dive Center operates both a scuba and snorkeling boat from the Holiday Inn docks. Stop by their booth to sign up or ☎ 305-451-5533. For schedules call 800-935-DIVE, fax 451-0124. Write to: 106240 Overseas Highway, Key Largo, FL 33037.

Sun Divers is an all snorkeling operation. Great for new snorkelers, they offer trips for $24.95 and equipment rentals for $5. Dry snorkels available. Sign up at the Best Western Resort in Key Largo or ☎ 800-4-KEY FUN, fax 305-451-1211.

Pennekamp State Park Dive Center operates a 16-passenger dive boat and three snorkeling boats – the *Sea Garden, El Capitan* and the *Snorkel Ex-*

press. They also offer sail- snorkel cruises aboard the catamaran *Sea Dancer*. Rentals and certifications. ☎ 305-451-1621. For information about the park in general ☎ 305-451-1621 or 305-451-1202.

Islamorada & Lower Key Largo Dive Operators

Bud 'n Mary's Dive Center operates a glass-bottom dive/snorkel boat. Their morning dives are for scuba only and visit 40- to 60-ft reefs, deeper wrecks. Afternoon tours visit shallow areas for scuba, snorkeling and glass-bottom viewing. Scuba trips cost $48.50, sometimes less if more divers are on board. Snorkelers pay $25 without equipment, $35 with. They also offer fishing trips. ☎ 800-344-7352 or 305-664-2211, fax 305-664-5592.

Caribbean Water Sports at Cheeca Lodge, offers scuba, snorkeling and parasailing. Two-tank dive trips with lead and tanks cost $60. Snorkelers join the dive trips for $30; add $6 for equipment . ☎ 888-SEA REEF or 305-664-9547, fax 305-852-5160. E-mail: divecws@aol.com.

Florida Keys Dive Center offers two-tank morning and afternoon dives aboard a 36- or 42-ft dive boat. Cost for a reef or wreck tour with weights and tanks is $59. They dive the outer reefs, the *Duane,* the *Bibb* and the *Eagle.* Packages drop the per-trip cost down to $45. Hotel packages with Ocean Pointe Suites. Freshwater showers and refreshments offered after the dive. Friendly service, night dives, Nitrox training and fills. E-6 processing. Referrals. CMAS, NAUI, PADI, PDIC, SSI, YMCA. ☎ 800-433-8946 or 305-852-4599, fax 305-852-1293. E- mail: scuba@floridakeysdivectr.com. Website: www.floridakeysdivectr.com. Write to: 90500 Overseas Hwy, MM 90.5,Plantation Key, FL 33070.

Tavernier Dive Center operates two 42-ft dive boats to the ledges, reefs and wrecks. If you are staying at an affiliated hotel, the tours cost $45, $50 if not. Snorkelers join the dive boat for $30, all equipment supplied. E-mail through their website: tavernierdivecenter.com. ☎ 800-787-9797 or 305-852-4007, fax 305-852-0869. Write to the shop at: MM 90.7, Tavernier, FL 33070.

Lady Cyana Divers offers ocean reef and wreck tours, all level PADI courses. Referrals for PADI, CMAS, NASDS, CMAS, NAUI, SSI, IANTD, YMCA, NASE. Two fast custom dive boats carry 19 and 28 passengers. Dive trips costs $52 with tanks and weights. Snorkelers pay $25 to join the trips, plus $10 for equipment use. Nitrox. E-6 processing. ☎ 800-433-8946 or 305-852-4599, fax 305-852-1293. E-mail through the website: www.ladycyana.com. Write to PO Box 1157, Mile Marker 85.9, Islamorada, FL 33036.

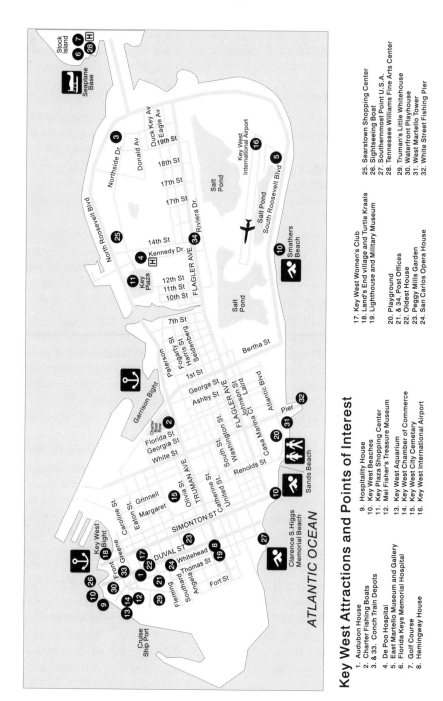

Key West Attractions and Points of Interest

1. Audubon House
2. Charter Fishing Boats
3. & 33. Conch Train Depots
4. De Poo Hospital
5. East Martello Museum and Gallery
6. Florida Keys Memorial Hospital
7. Golf Course
8. Hemingway House
9. Hospitality House
10. Key West Beaches
11. Key Plaza Shopping Center
12. Mel Fisher's Treasure Museum
13. Key West Aquarium
14. Key West Chamber of Commerce
15. Key West City Cemetary
16. Key West International Airport
17. Key West Women's Club
18. Land's End village and Turtle Kraals
19. Lighthouse and Military Museum
20. Playground
21. & 34. Post Offices
22. Oldest House
23. Peggy Mills Garden
24. San Carlos Opera House
25. Searstown Shopping Center
26. Sightseeing Boat
27. Southernmost Point U.S.A.
28. Tennessee Williams Fine Arts Center
29. Truman's Little Whitehouse
30. Waterfront Playhouse
31. West Martello Tower
32. White Street Fishing Pier

Rainbow Reef Dive Center offers reef and wreck trips, courses and hotel packages. ☎ 800-457-4354 or 305-664-4600. Website: rainbowreefdivecenter.com. Write to: 84977 Overseas Highway, Islamorada, FL 33036.

Key Largo & Upper Keys Accommodations

Keys accommodations range from informal housekeeping cottages, simply furnished bayside motels and spacious condo and house rentals to luxurious resort villages, houseboats, and campgrounds, most of which are packed tight with RVs. All accommodations are air-conditioned and most have cable TV and a refrigerator in the room.

Some of the older mom-and-pop motels on the Bay have been updated and offer a certain island charm that is hard to duplicate in the large resorts. A few are badly in need of renovation and also are parking areas for RV's. Send for current brochures.

Rates listed are per room, per night, for winter and spring. Subject to change. For a complete list of home rental agencies Contact the Key Largo Chamber of Commerce, 106000 Overseas Hwy., Key Largo FL 33037. ☎ 305-451-1414, US 800-822-1088, fax 305-451-4726.

Amy Slate's Amoray Lodge on Florida Bay offers 16 ultra-clean, attractive, modern one and two-bedroom apartments with full kitchens. Air-conditioned and ceiling fans. Sundeck. Scuba, snorkel and boat trips leave for Pennekamp Park from the resort dock aboard luxurious catamaran, *Amoray Dive*. Walking distance to several good restaurants. A great choice for Pennekamp divers. Winter suite rates $80 to $235. No pets. ☎ 800-426-6729 or 305-451-3595, fax 305-453-9516.

Best Western Suites, MM 100 oceanside, rents canalside apartments with kitchens and screened patios. Boat docking. Group discounts and dive packages available. No pets. Winter rates from $130. Write MM 100, 201 Ocean Drive, Key Largo, FL 33037. ☎ 800-462-6079 or 305-451-5081.

Holiday Inn Key Largo Resort, MM 99.7 oceanside, is adjacent to a large marina with a boat ramp and docking for all size craft. The resort features 132 suites, restaurant, gift shop, freshwater pool with waterfall and fast access to diving and recreation facilities. It is also the home of the *African Queen,* used in the 1951 movie starring Humphrey Bogart and Katharine Hepburn. No pets. Winter room rates from $129 to $189. Moderate to deluxe. Write MM 100, 99701 Overseas Hwy, Key Largo FL 33037. ☎ 800-THE-KEYS or 305-451-2121.

Howard Johnson's Resort, MM102.3 Bayside, features modern rooms, swimming in the pool or Bay, sand beach, restaurant, pool, balconies, beach bar, dock, dive and other packages. Cable TV. Refrigerators and microwaves. Some small pets are allowed. Call first. Winter rates $95 to $245. Group rates available. Write MM 102, PO Box 1024, Key Largo, FL 33037. ☎ 800-654-2000 or 305-451-1400.

Manatees are often spotted behind this resort in winter.

Island Bay Resort, Bayside at MM 92.5, features eight rooms with kitchen facilities, boat dock and ramp, sandy beach and cable TV. No pets. $65 to $125. Write PO Box 573, Tavernier, FL 33037. ☎ 305-852-4087 or 800-654-KEYS.

Kelly's Motel, MM 104.5, sits in a sheltered cove. Boat dock and ramp. Dive trips. Sandy beach. Cooking facilities. Some pets. Rooms $75 to $150. Write 104220 Overseas Hwy, Key Largo, FL 33037. ☎ 305-451-1622 or 800-226-0415.

Kona Kai Resort, at MM 97.8, is a nine-unit motel on the Bay. Cable TV, phones, fishing pier. Boat dock and ramp. No pets. Rooms $141 to $397. Write 97802 Overseas Highway, Key Largo, FL 33037. ☎ 305-852-7200 or 800-365-STAY.

Largo Lodge, at MM 101.5, is a charming, Bayside complex offering six apartments – all in a tropical garden setting. Guests must be at least 16 years old. Swimming. Small boat dock. Ramp. No pets. Rooms from $105. Write 101740 Overseas Highway, Key Largo, FL 33037. ☎ 800-IN-THE-SUN (468-4378) or 305-451-0424.

Marriott Key Largo Bay Beach Resort, MM 103.8 Bayside, features luxury accommodations, pool, sand beach, dive shop, watersports, two fine restaurants and three bars. Packages available. Rooms from $149 to $500. ☎ 800-932-9332 or 305-453-0000, fax 305-453-0093.

Marina Del Mar Bayside, MM 99.5, offers 56 comfortable rooms, freshwater pool and dock. Rooms $99 to $159. ☎ 800-242-5229, fax 305-451-9650.

Marina Del Mar, MM 100, oceanside, is a luxury dive resort on a deepwater marina in the heart of Key Largo. There are 130 rooms, suites and villas. Refrigerators in all rooms. The suites have complete kitchens. Rooms overlook the yacht basin or ocean. Dive shop on premises. Fishing charters. Meeting facilities. Waterfront restaurant. Rates $99 to $330. Write PO Box 1050, Key Largo, FL 33037. ☎ 305-451-4107, US 800-451-3483, FL 800-253-3483, Canada 800-638-3483, fax 305-451-1891.

Ocean Pointe, MM 92.5, oceanside, features one- and two-bedroom suites with Jacuzzi tubs and fully equipped kitchens, private balconies, heated swimming pool with whirlpool spa, lighted tennis courts, marina with boat ramp and rental slips, waterfront café and lounge, white sandy suntan beach, watersports equipment. Money-saving packages. No pets. Suites $170 to $210. ☎ 800-882-9464 or 305-3000, fax 305-853-3007.

Popps Motel, on the Bay at MM 95.5, has 10 units with cooking facilities, a small beach, boat dock and ramp. No pets. Rates $79 to $89. Write PO Box 43, Key Largo, FL 33037. ☎ 305-852-5201, fax 852-5200. E-mail: popps@ix.netcom.com.

Rock Reef Resort, at MM 98, offers clean, comfortable cottages and apartments on the Bay with one, two, or three bedrooms. Playground, tropical gardens. Boat dock and ramp. Sandy beach. No pets. Rates $88 to $175. Write PO Box 73, Key Largo, FL. ☎ 800-477-2343 or 305-852-2401, fax 305-852-5355. E-mail: rockreefr@aol.com. Website: http://florida-keys.fl.us/rockreef.htm.

Stone Ledge Resort, MM 95.3 Bayside, offers 19 conch-style motel rooms, sandy beach, boat dock. Ten of the units have kitchens. Refrigerators in all rooms. TV. No pets. Rooms $68 to $78. Write PO Box 50, Key Largo FL 33037. ☎ 305-852-8114.

Tropic Vista Motel, at MM 90.5, sits on an oceanside canal. Dive shop on premises. Dock. Pets allowed in some rooms. Call first. Rates $53 to $90. Write PO Box 88, Tavernier, FL 33070. ☎ 800-537-3253 or 305-852-8799.

Westin Beach Resort Key Largo, MM 97 Bayside, a splendid watersports resort, features 200 luxury rooms, two restaurants, lounge, nature trails, two pools with waterfall, pool bar and a large dock on the Bay. Private beach. Caribbean Watersports at the beach shack. Meeting facilities. No pets. Rooms $179 to $239. Write 97000 Overseas Hwy, Key Largo, FL 33037. ☎ 305-852-5553; worldwide 800-539-5274, fax 305-852-3530.

Key Largo RV & Tent Campgrounds

America Outdoors. MM 97.5. Sandy beach, laundry, bath houses. Boat dock, ramp and marina. RV sites. Pets allowed. Write 97450 Overseas Hwy, Key Largo, FL 33037. ☎ 305-852-8054, fax 305-853-0509.

Blue Lagoon Resort & Marina, MM 99.6, Bayside, rents and parks RVs. A couple of simple efficiencies for rent also. Parking is tight, but you are in the heart of Key Largo. Boat dock. Swimming. No pets. Write 99096 US Hwy 1, Key Largo, FL 33037. ☎ 305-451-2908.

Calusa Camp Resort. MM 101.5. Bayside RV park. Boat dock, ramp, marina, bait shop, camp store. Rentals. Pets allowed. Write 325 Calusa, Key Largo, FL 33037. ☎ 800-457-2267 or 305-451-0232.

Florida Keys RV Resort, MM 106, oceanside, has cable on all sites, water, electric. Good Sam Park. Pets OK. Near dive shops. ☎ 800-252-6090, fax 451-5996.

Key Largo Kampground. MM 101.5. Oceanfront RV and tent sites, boat dock, ramp, laundry and bath house. Write PO Box 118-A, Key Largo, FL 33037. ☎ 305-451-1431, US 800-KAMP-OUT.

Key Largo Dining

Key Largo is fast-food heaven, with popular chain restaurants everywhere. For all-day diving or fishing excursions there are grocery stores and even gas stations that offer packaged lunches and cold beverages to go. **Miami Subs**, MM 100, Bayside, has subs, and packaged goods to go. ☎ 451-3111. **Tower of Pizza**, MM 100, oceanside, delivers fabulous New York-style pizza, sit-down service too. ☎ 451-1461. Or try **Domino's Pizza**, Key Largo. ☎ 451-4951.

For a unique tropical atmosphere and superb gourmet cuisine, try the **Quay Restaurant**, MM 102.5, Bayside (☎ 451-0943). Indoor or garden seating. Moderate to expensive. Adjacent is the **Quay Mesquite Grill**, which serves excellent fried or broiled fish sandwiches. The complex also features a freshwater pool, boat docks, beachside bar and entertainment. Sunset cruises. Romantic, starlight seating and gourmet seafood are also found at **Snooks Bayside Club**, MM 99.9 (behind Largo Honda). ☎ 453-3799. Moderate to expensive. Garden patio or indoor dining.

Frank Keys Café offers romantic seating and decent Italian and seafood cuisine. MM 100.2. ☎ 453-0310.

The Fish House, oceanside at MM 102.4, serves excellent fresh fish, steaks and chicken for lunch or dinner. It is always packed, with a long waiting list after 6 pm. Moderate prices. Casual. ☎ 461-4665.

Ballyhoo's Seafood Grille is set in a 1930s conch house at MM 97.8 on the median strip. Fresh seafood specialties. Open daily. ☎ 852-0822.

Or try the **Cracked Conch**, MM 105, oceanside (☎ 305-451-0732) for conch fritters and fried alligator, 90 different beers and honey biscuits. Inexpensive to moderate. ☎ 451-0732.

Rick & Debbie's Tugboat, oceanside at Seagate Blvd and Ocean Drive off MM 100, is a locals' favorite. Specials are fried or broiled fish. Inexpensive to moderate. Opens 11 am weekdays, weekends at 7am. ☎ 453-9010.

Holiday Casino Cruises, MM 100 depart the Holiday Inn docks. Features casino gambling in international waters. Complimentary hors d'oeuvres. Open bar and sandwiches & burgers available. Sunday brunch with fine catered food. Overnight packages. Sign up in the Holiday Inn lobby. ☎ 451-0000.

The Italian Fisherman offers dining on a waterfront terrace. Mile Marker 104, Bayside, Key Largo. 11 am-10 pm. ☎ 451-4471.

The Marlin Restaurant, MM 102.7, is the favorite après-dive, story-swapping eatery. Open daily. ☎ 451-9555.

Señor Frijoles, MM 103.9, Bayside, offers sizzling fajitas, seafood nachos, Mexican pizza, Cancun chili fish, enchiladas and chicken specials. ☎ 451-1592.

Sundowners on the Bay at MM 104 specializes in seafood, chicken, steaks and pasta. Daily 11 am-10 pm. ☎ 451-4502.

Early breakfasts are served at **Howard Johnson**, MM 102.5, ☎ 451-2032; **Harriets**, MM 95.7, ☎ 852-8689; **Holiday Inn**, MM 100; **Gilberts**, MM 107.9, ☎ 451-1133; and **Ganim's Kountry Kitchen**, MM 102, ☎ 451-3337 and MM 99.6 across from Holiday Inn. Turn off Hwy 1 northbound at MM 103.5, onto Transylvania Ave., then head toward the ocean to find the **Hideout**, a local favorite for breakfast and lunch.

Islamorada Accommodations

Plantation Key to Long Key

For a complete list of home rental agencies, contact the Islamorada Chamber of Commerce, PO Box 915, Islamorada, FL 33036. ☎ 305-664-4503 or 1-800-FABKEYS.

Bud & Mary's Fishing Marina, MM 79.8, oceanside, consists of six motel units. Charter boats, backcountry guides, rental boats, dive boat and party fishing. No pets. Rooms $75. ☎ 800-742-7945 or 305-664-2461, fax 305-664-2461. E-mail: Budnmary@budge.net.

Breezy Palms Resort, MM 80, on the ocean, offers one-, two- and three-room villas, beach cottages or studio efficiencies. All with well-equipped kitchens and attractive furnishings. Maid service. Large swimming beach. Fresh water pool, boat harbor and ramp with a light dock for night fishing. No pets. Write PO Box 767, Islamorada, FL 33036. Rates $75 to $210. ☎ 305-664-2361, fax 305-664-2572. E-mail: breezypalms@msn.com. Website: www.breezypalms.com.

Caloosa Cove Resort, MM 73.8, offers 30 deluxe, oceanfront condos, one or two bedroom, with modern kitchens. Pool, lounge, restaurant, tennis, boat rentals, free breakfast and activities. Full-service marina with dockage. No pets. Rooms $125 to $175. Write 73801 US Hwy 1, Islamorada, FL 33036. ☎ 888-297-3208 or 305-664-8811, fax 305-664-8856.

Cheeca Lodge offers pampered seclusion, oceanside, at MM 82. Well described as being in "its own neighborhood," the resort offers guests a wealth of activities including dive and snorkeling trips, a nine-hole golf course, sailing, fishing, tennis, parasailing, windsurfing – complete with a staff of expert instructors, captains or pros. Features include oversized guestrooms and villas, most with private balconies and paddle fans, a children's recreational camp, shops, gourmet dining, entertainment, palm-lined swimming/snorkeling beach, pool, 525-foot lighted fishing pier. Dockage and marina. Conference center. On-site dive shop. No pets. $240 to $1,100. Deluxe. Write PO Box 527, Islamorada, FL 33036. ☎ 305-664-4651 or 800-327-2888, fax 305-664-2893. E-mail: Cheecalodg@aol.com.

Chesapeake of Whale Harbor, adjacent to the Whale Harbor Restaurant and Islamorada docks, sprawls across six oceanfront acres at MM 83.5. The modern resort offers motel or efficiency units, a sand beach and deep water lagoon. Walk to fishing charter boat docks. No pets. Write PO Box 909, Islamorada, FL 33036. Rates: $130-520. ☎ 800-338-3395 or 305-664-4662, fax 305-664-8595. Website: http://florida-keys.fl.us/chesapea.html.

El Capitan Resort, MM 84, offers efficiencies for two to six people in the Holiday Isle complex. Oceanside lagoon and beach. Boat dockage. No pets. Rates $120 to $240. Write MM 84, Islamorada, FL 33036. ☎ 305-664-2321, US 800-327-7070, fax 305-664-2703.

Holiday Isle Resort encompasses an entire beach club community, with every imaginable watersport and activity. Guests choose from rooms, efficiencies or suites. The beach vibrates with reggae music. Vendors offer parasailing, fishing and diving charters, sailing, windsurfing, jetskiing, inflatable-island rentals, sun lounges and dancing. Fast food stands serving barbecued dishes, pizza, ice cream, drinks and more are scattered about the grounds. There is a lovely rooftop restaurant and a unique cook-it-yourself-on-slabs-of-granite place in the parking lot. Rooms are luxurious. The beach is open to everyone and is packed early during the high season. No pets. Rates $85 to $425. Write 84001 US Hwy 1, Islamorada, FL. ☎ 305-664-2321, US 800-327-7070, fax 305-664-2703.

Harbor Lights Motel, oceanfront, MM 85, is part of the Holiday Isle beach complex, offering efficiencies, rooms and cottages. Write 84001 US Hwy 1, Islamorada, FL. Rates $65 to $110. ☎ 800-327-7070 or 305-664-3611, fax 305-664-2703. Website: www.theisle.com.

Howard Johnson Resort ,oceanside at MM 84.5 adjacent to Holiday Isle, features a soft sand beach. Guests wander back and forth to Holiday Isle beach. Boat dock and ramp. Restaurant. No pets. Write 84001 US Hwy 1, Islamorada, FL 33036. Rooms $135 to $165. ☎ US 800-6327-7070 or 305-664-2711, fax 305-664-2703. Moderate to deluxe.

La Jolla Motel, MM 82.3, Bayside, has a quiet, tropical garden atmosphere. Kitchen units are comfortable. Boat dock and ramp. Small swimming beach, grills. Rooms $59 to $125. Write Box 51, Islamorada, FL 33036. ☎ 305-664-9213. Inexpensive to moderate.

Lime Tree Bay Resort, at MM 68.5, is an older motel, but comfortable, with beautiful grounds and terrific sunset views. Kitchen units available. There is a restaurant, tennis court, boat dock and beach as well as a freshwater pool. No pets. Rates $95 to $225. Write PO Box 839, Long Key, FL 33001. ☎ 305-664-4740 or 800-723-4519. Inexpensive to moderate.

Plantation Yacht Harbor Resort, MM 87, Bayside, features tennis courts, private beach, jet skis and a huge marina with protected docking for large and small craft. A dive shop and lovely restaurant overlook the bay. No pets. Write 87000 US Hwy 1, Plantation Key, Islamorada, FL 33036. Rooms $78 to $135. ☎ 800-356-3215 or 305-852-2381, fax 853-5357. E-mail: fun@ pyh.com. Website: www.pyh.com.

Ragged Edge MM86.5 oceanside, has one- and two-bedroom air-conditioned suites and motel rooms, color TV, laundry room, guest boat harbor, marina dockage, ramps, deep water channel, fishing pier. Nice. Rates $69 to $169. ☎ 305-852-5389.

Islamorada Campgrounds

Fiesta Key KOA, MM70, Bayside, sits on a 28-acre tropical island surrounded by warm gulf waters. 350 sites. Marina, docks and ramp. ☎ 305-664-4922.

Long Key State Recreation Area, MM66, Bayside, features two nature trails, bike and canoe rental, picnic area, observation tower, guided walks. No pets. ☎ 305-664-4815.

Islamorada Dining

Islamorada's grills sizzle with fresh seafood and the most unusual dining experiences in the Keys. You'll find the hot spot for fast food on the shores of Holiday Isle, MM 84, oceanside. Food stands line this sprawling beach complex with barbecued everything. Ice cream and pretzel vendors crowd in alongside the Keys' most dazzling display of string bikinis. Or take the elevator to the sixth-floor restaurant for a quieter view of the sea. Prices rise with the elevation.

Rip's Island Ribs 'N Chicken, within the same complex, features do-it-your-way meals. Diners prepare their entrées on thick granite slabs that are heated to 600° and brought to your table. Your waitress supplies hot garlic bread, fresh, ready-to-cook vegetables and a choice of sirloin, chicken, shrimp or a combination. Just toss a little salt on your rock and give your food a turn or two until it looks right. A choice of sauces adds the finishing touch. It's easy. Or... try the ribs. They're served already cooked. Expect a long waiting line on weekends, especially in season. ☎ 664-5300.

Enjoy sunset views and fresh seafood at **The Lorelei Restaurant**, MM 82, Bayside. Sun.-Thurs., 5-10 pm. The outdoor Cabana Bar features burgers, fish sandwiches, breakfasts, lunches, dinners and a raw bar. 7 am-12 pm. Entertainment on weekends. Drive or boat to it. ☎ 664-4656.

Marker 88 offers exotic fish and steak entrées in a romantic setting. Choose from expertly prepared Scampi Mozambique, Snapper Rangoon, Lobster Marco Polo and a host of other gourmet creations. Closed Mondays. Reservations a must (☎ 305-852-9315). MM 88, Plantation Key. Moderate to expensive

Whale Harbor Restaurant features an all-you-can-eat seafood buffet nightly. Huge selection. Lovely setting in the old Islamorada lighthouse, adjacent to the Islamorada docks at MM 83.5. Moderate. ☎ 664-4959.

Try a hand-tossed pizza or pasta at **Woody's**, MM 82. Family dining in the early evening. Late night food with adult entertainment every night but Monday. Inexpensive. ☎ 664- 4335.

Cheeca Lodge offers casual dining at the **Ocean Terrace Grill**, MM 81.5. Moderate to expensive. ☎ 664-4651.

The Coral Grill, MM 83.5, Bayside, features a nightly buffet. Great strawberry daiquiris! Sun. 12 pm-9 pm, weekdays 4:30-10 pm. ☎ 664-4803.

The Green Turtle Inn, MM 81.5, has an old time Keys atmosphere and excellent cuisine. Wood-paneled walls are covered with celebrity photos. Leave room for their rum pie. Gets crowded after 6 pm. 5 pm-10 pm. Closed Mondays. ☎ 664-9031.

Plantation Yacht Harbor, MM87. Live bands. Lobster, stone crab, oysters and clams. Sunday brunch with omelette and waffle bar. Daily 11am-9 pm. ☎ 852-2381.

Squid Row, MM 81.9, oceanside, offers excellent fish dishes and fine service. Open for lunch or dinner. ☎ 664-9865.

For a quick meal try a pita sandwich at the **Ice Cream Stoppe**, MM 80.5. ☎ 664-5026.

Best Dives of the Middle Keys

Dive sites in the Middle Keys – from Long Key Bridge Key to the Seven Mile Bridge – are similar to, but often less crowded than those in Key Largo and the Upper Keys. Besides the offshore reefs and wrecks, the Marathon area has a number of sunken vessels around the new and old bridges, which serve as artificial reefs for fishing. When currents are mild you can dive a few of these spots which abound with fish, sponges and soft corals.

☆☆ **Sombrero Reef**, Marathon's most popular ocean dive and snorkeling spot offers good visibility and a wide depth range, from the shallows to 40 feet.

Cracks and crevices shot through the coral canyons that comprise the reef overflow with lobster, arrow crabs, octopi, anemones, and resident fish. A huge light tower marks the area. Boaters must tie up to the mooring buoys on the reef.

☆ Slightly north of Sombrero lies the wreck of the **Thunderbolt**, an intentionally scuttled, 188-foot freighter lying upright in 110 feet of water with the top of its wheelhouse at 70 feet. Resident fish include big barracuda, swarms of sergeant majors, queen and grey angelfish, blue tangs and moray eels.

☆ **Coffins Patch**, just north of the *Thunderbolt,* provides good snorkeling areas with mounds of pillar, elkhorn, and brain corals at depths averaging 20- to 30 ft.

Marathon & the Middle Keys Dive Operators

Abyss Pro Dive Center, behind the Holiday Inn at MM 54, oceanside offers reef and wreck trips to popular sites aboard their 34-ft dive boat. Snorkelers may join the trip if it is to a shallow site. Divers pay $54 for a trip, including tanks and weights. Snorkelers pay $35, equipment included. ☎ 800-457-0134 or 305-743-2126, fax 305-743-7081. E-mail: info@abyssdive.com. Website: www.abyssdive.com. Write to: 13175 Overseas Highway, Marathon, FL 33050.

Captain Hook's Dive Center operates a slick 30-ft dive boat and 26-ft catamaran. They offer all level PADI instruction and certification for all agencies. Two-tank dive trips with tanks and weights cost $49. Snorkelers pay $35 with equipment. Friendly service. ☎ 305-743-2444, fax 305-289-1374. E-mail: cpthooks@bellsouth.net. Website: www.thefloridakeys.com/captainhooks. Write to: 11833 Overseas Highway, Marathon, FL 33050.

Hall's Dive Center and Career Institute offers all level of instruction, trips and referral checkouts. ☎ 800-331-4255 or 305-743-5929, fax 305-743-8168. E-mail: hallsdive@aol.com. Website: www.hallsdiving.com. Write to 1994 Overseas Highway, Marathon, FL 33050.

Hurricane Aqua Center (dba Discount Divers) & Two Conchs Dive & Charters at MM 48. This PADI shop offers courses, referral checkouts and trips. A two-tank dive with tanks and weights costs $59. Snorkelers join for $43, equipment included. Maximum six divers aboard their 26-ft boat. ☎ 305-743-2400, fax 305-743-2221. Write to: 10800 Overseas Hwy, Marathon, FL 33050.

Middle Keys Scuba Center visits all sites from Sombrero Reef to Duck Key. Divers and snorkelers mix aboard their 30-ft custom dive boat. NAUI and PADI certification courses and check-out dives for all agencies. Photo and video rental equipment and courses. Divers pay $50 for a two-tank dive, including tanks and weights. Snorkelers pay $35. ☎ 305-743-2902. Friendly service. E-mail: rdoileau.aol.com. Website: www.divingdiscovery.com. Write to: 11511 Overseas Highway, Marathon, FL 33050.

The Diving Site is the only DOT hydrostatic facility in the area. This PADI shop offers resort courses through divemaster courses, PADI referrals, dive and snorkeling trips. They operate a 40-ft custom dive boat that carries up to 24 divers and a 25 ft boat that carries four divers. Nitrox courses and fills. Morning dives are to the deeper reefs and the wreck of the *Thunderbolt*. Afternoon trips are to the shallow reefs. Two-tank dives with tanks and weights cost $52.50; snorkeling trips cost $32 with equipment. Write to: 12399 Overseas Hwy, Marathon, FL 33050.

Marathon Accommodations

Rates listed are for winter and spring, per night, per room or suite.

For a complete list of rental units, condos and villas contact the **Greater Marathon Chamber of Commerce**, 12222 Overseas Hwy, Marathon, FL 33050. ☎ 305-743-5417 or 800-842-9580.

Buccaneer Resort, MM 48.5, Bayside, has 76 units, beach, café, tennis, boat dock and charters. Dive shop on premises. Some kitchen units. Waterfront restaurant and tiki bar, sandy beach, fishing docks, wave runners. Write 2600 Overseas Hwy, Marathon, FL 33050. Rooms $59 to $249. ☎ US 800-237-3329 or 305-743-9071. E-mail: buccaneer@floridakey.com. Website: www.florida.com.

Conch Key Cottages, MM 62.3, oceanside, are situated on a secluded, private island which until recently could only be reached by boat. New owners have built a landfill roadway so you can drive the short distance from US 1. Rustic, 50s-style wooden cottages have screened-in porches and huge ceiling fans. Pool. All air-conditioned with cable TV, hammock and barbecue. Coin washers and dryers on premises. Boat dock and ramp. Rates $100 to $249. Call first. Write Box 424, Marathon, FL 33050. ☎ 800-330-1877 or 305-289-1377, fax 305-743-8207.

Holiday Inn of Marathon, MM 54, oceanside, has 134 rooms, restaurant, and bar. Abyss Dives shop on property. Boat ramp and marina. No beach. pets OK. Write 13201 US Hwy 1, Marathon, FL 33050. Rates $139 to $200. ☎ 305-289-0222. For dive/hotel packages, 800-457-0134.

Faro Blanco Marine Resort, MM 48, spreads over two shores with the most diverse selection of facilities on the Atlantic and the Gulf. Choose from houseboat suites, condos, garden cottages, or an apartment in the Faro Blanco lighthouse for a special treat. There is a full-service marina if you are arriving by yacht and wish to tie up for a stay. Dockmaster stands by on VHF Channel 16. Convenient to fine restaurants and diving. Pets allowed in the houseboats and cottages, but not the condos. Children under 18 not allowed in the condos. Good for boaters. Rates $89 to $233. Write 1996 US Hwy 1, Marathon, FL 33050. ☎ 800-759-3276.

Hawks Cay Resort and Marina offers 177 spacious rooms and suites. Heated pool, saltwater lagoon with sandy beach, 18-hole golf course nearby, marine-mammal training center featuring dolphin shows for guests. Charter fishing and diving boats leave from the marina. Protected boat slips for large and small craft. Rooms $220 to $450. No pets. Write MM 61, Duck Key, FL 33050. ☎ 305-743-7000, FL 800-432-2242, fax 305-743-5215.

Howard Johnsons Resort, MM 51, oceanside, has a private beach, dive shop, dock and marina, restaurant. Good boardsailing off the beach. Pets OK. Write 13351 US Hwy 1, Marathon, FL 33050. Rooms $125 to $375. ☎ 800-321-3496 or 305-743-8550, fax 305-743-8832.

Kingsail Resort Motel, MM 50. Bayside accommodations range from modern, attractive rooms to well-equipped efficiencies and one-bedroom apartments. There is a boat ramp, dock, grocer, pool, shaded tiki. No pets. Fishing and diving charters. Rates $75 to $125. Write PO Box 986, Marathon, FL 33050. ☎ 305-743-5246, FL 800-423-7474, fax 305-743-8896.

Ocean Beach Club MM 53.5, oceanside, features 38 guest rooms, sandy white beach, hot tub and fishing pier. No pets. Rooms $100 to $170. ☎ 305-289-0525 or 800-321-7213, fax 305-289-9703. Write to PO Box 510009 KCB, Marathon, FL 33050.

Rainbow Bend Fishing Resort, oceanside at MM 58, offers free use of a motorboat or sailboat with every room plus complimentary breakfast daily. There is a wide sandy beach, pool, fishing pier, tackle shop. Dive and fishing charters. Rooms and efficiencies $135 to $225. Café. Pets OK. Write PO Box 2447, Grassy Key, FL 33050. ☎ 800-929-1505 or 305-289-1505, fax 305-743-0257. E-mail: Rainbowbend@fla-keys.com. Website: fla-keys.com/marathon/accom/rainbowbend.htm.

The **Seahorse Motel**, at MM 51, bayside, offers protected dock space, a playground, pool, barbecue patio, quiet rooms and efficiencies. Write 7196 US Hwy 1, Marathon, FL 33050. $59 to $85. ☎ 305-743-6571 or 800-874-1115, fax 305-743-0775.

Additional and varied Marathon accommodations are offered through **AA Accommodation Center, Inc.**, ☎ 800-732-2006 or 305-296-7707.

Middle Keys Dining

Long Key

Little Italy Restaurant at MM 68.5 serves early breakfasts, lunch and dinner. Italian specialties, fresh seafood and steaks in a cozy atmosphere. Open 6:30 am-2 pm, 5 pm-10 pm. Low to moderate. ☎ 664-4472.

Duck Key

Hawk's Cay Resort and Marina, MM61, features the **Cantina** for poolside lunch and dinners, **Porto Cayo** for elegant dining Tues.-Sun. 6 pm-10 pm, **The Palm Terrace** for buffet style breakfast 7 am-10:30 am and **WaterEdge** for dinner 5:30-10 pm. ☎ 743-7000.

Marathon

Marathon is a heavily populated residential community with a wide choice of restaurants.

Key Colony Inn, MM 54 at Key Colony Beach, features well-prepared seafood specialties. ☎ 743-0100.

Enjoy indoor or outdoor patio dining at the **Quay** of Marathon, MM 54. Lunch and dinner. ☎ 289-1810.

Fast, take-out food at low prices is featured at **Porky's Too** on the Marathon side of the Seven Mile Bridge. ☎ 289- 2065.

Enjoy natural foods, vegetarian delights or grilled seafood on the porch of a charming 1935 stone house at **Mangrove Mama's**, MM 20. Open for lunch and dinner. Full take-out menu too. Moderate. ☎ 745-3030.

Best Dives of the Lower Keys & Key West

Dive trips from the Lower Keys – Big Pine Key, Sugar Loaf Key, Summerland Key, Ramrod Key, Cudjoe Key and Torch Key – take off to reefs surrounding **American Shoal** and **Looe Key National Marine Sanctuary**.

☆☆ The **Looe Key** reef tract, named for the **HMS Looe**, a British frigate that ran aground on the shallow reefs in 1744, offers vibrant elkhorn and staghorn coral thickets, an abundance of sponges, soft corals and fish. Constant residents include Cuban hogfish, queen parrot fish, huge barracuda, and long snout butterfly fish. A favorite dive site of the Lower Keys, Looe Key bottoms out at 35 feet. Extreme shallow patches of sea grass and coral rubble provide a calm habitat for juvenile fish and invertebrates.

☆☆ Diving off Key West includes offshore wreck dives and tours of **Cotrell Key, Sand Key** and the **Western Dry Marks**. Huge pelagic fish and graceful rays lure divers to this area.

☆☆☆ **Stargazer**, the world's largest underwater sculptured reef, sits five miles off Key West between Sand Key and Rock Key. This magnificent steel wonder, completed in 1992 by artist Ann Labriola, is 200 feet long, 70 feet wide and stands 10 feet high in 25 ft of water. Each of its 10 sections are perforated in the pattern of different star constellations, once used to navigate the seas. Divers and snorkelers become a living part of this mystical artificial reef as they locate the positions of the constellations in its surface. Corals are beginning to grow on the structure, which shelters a small community of reef fish. Good for diving and snorkeling, with depths from the surface to 25 ft.

☆☆ **Sand Key**, marked by a lighthouse, lures snorkelers and novice divers to explore its fields of staghorn coral. Depths range from the surface to 45 ft.

☆☆☆ **Cosgrove Reef**, noted for its big heads of boulder and brain coral, attracts a number of large fish and rays.

☆☆ Advanced divers may want to tour the *Cayman Salvage Master*, at 90 feet. This 180-ft vessel was purposely sunk to form an artificial reef.

☆ **Joe's Tug** sits upright in 65 ft of water, a scenic backdrop for schools of jacks, barracuda and grunts.

☆☆ Seldom visited, though pristine for diving, are the **Marquesa Islands**, 30 miles off Key West. Extreme shallows both en route and surrounding the islands make the boat trip difficult in all but the calmest seas and docking is impossible for all but shallow draft cats and trimarans. Check with **Lost Reef Adventures** (☎ 305-296-9737) for trip availability.

Fort Jefferson National Monument

Almost 70 miles west of Key West lies a cluster of seven islands called the Dry Tortugas, which, along with surrounding coral reefs, shoals and waters, make up Fort Jefferson National Monument. Visitors to the national monument enjoy good fishing, snorkeling and touring the ruins of the historic fort. Famous for bird and marine life, as well as for its legends of pirates and sunken gold, the central feature is Fort Jefferson itself, largest of the 19th-century American coastal forts. High-speed ferries and seaplanes offer snorkeling excursions to the fort.

Big Pine & Lower Keys Dive Operators

The Lower Keys

Because all the reefs in the Looe Key Marine Sanctuary are shallow, dive shops group divers and snorkelers on the same boats. Trips to the deep wrecks are reserved for scuba divers.

Looe Key Dive Center, at the Looe Key Reef Resort (MM 27.5), takes divers and snorkelers to the best reef and wreck sites in the Looe Key Marine Sanctuary, including the wreck of the *Adolphus Busch Sr.*, aboard a fast 49-ft catamaran. A two-tank dive with tanks and weights costs $60. Snorkelers pay $25 to join the trip; add $7 for equipment. Certification courses. ☎ 800-942-5397 or 305-872-2215, fax 305-872-3786. E-mail: looekeydiv.com. Website: diveflakeys.com. Write to: PO Box 509, MM 27.5, Ramrod Key, FL 33042.

Underseas Inc., a PADI five-star center, features reef and wreck tours for divers and snorkelers to Looe Key Marine Sanctuary aboard their 50-ft catamaran or 35-ft custom dive boat. They also offer wreck dives, night dives, Nitrox and training. Still camera rentals. A two-tank dive costs $50 with weights and tanks. Snorkelers pay $25 . Universal referrals. ☎ 800-446-5663 or 305-872-2700, fax 305-872-0080. E-mail: diveuseas@aol.com.

Key West

Dive Key West, Inc. offers a large retail shop, two fast dive boats, one 36-ft, one 26 ft, that carry six to 12 divers. Snorkelers join the dive boats for reef dives. The shop visits Western Sambo, Marker I, Joe's Tug and the *Cayman* wreck. NAUI, NASDS, PADI and YMCA referrals. Two-tank dive costs $59 with weights and tanks. C-courses. ☎ 800-426-0707 or 305-296-3823, 305-296-0607. Website: www.divekeywest.com. Write to: 3128 North Roosevelt Blvd, Key West, FL 33040.

Lost Reef Adventures, Inc. takes divers and snorkelers aboard their 40-ft custom dive boat . The shop visits the Sambos, Dry Rocks, Sand Key and the wrecks. PADI and NAUI instruction. Universal referrals. A two-tank dive costs $56. Snorkelers pay $30 for the trip and equipment. ☎ 800-952-2749 or 305-296-9737, fax 305-296-6660. E-mail: lostreefkw@aol.com. Website: paradise.com. Write to: 261 Margaret Street, Key West, FL 33040.

Subtropic Dive Center, at Garrison Bight, has PADI and SSI training, Nitrox training and service, universal referrals. They operate three boats, a 42-ft BurPee, a 28-ft dive boat, and a 48-ft catamaran used for snorkeling trips. Two-tank trips cost $55, snorkelers pay $30 with full gear included. ☎ 888-461-3483, fax 305-296-9918. E-mail: info@subtropic.com. Website: subtropic.com. Write to: 1605 North Roosevelt Blvd., Key West, FL 33040.

Southpoint Divers offers tours and courses. ☎ 800-891-DIVE, 305-296-6888. Write to: 714 Duval St., Key West, FL 33040.

Lower Keys Accommodations

Big Pine Key

Big Pine is centered between Marathon and Key West. A 20-minute drive will get you to either. For a complete list of Lower Keys accommodations call, write or visit: **Lower Keys Chamber of Commerce**, PO Box 430511, Big Pine Key, FL 33043. ☎ 800-872-3722 or 305-872-2411.

Big Pine Resort Motel, located at MM 30.5, Bayside, offers nearby proximity to Looe Key Marine Sanctuary. The motel has 32 rooms, efficiencies and apartments. Parking for trailers, trucks and buses. Adjacent restaurant. No pets. Rates $59 to $69. Gay-friendly. Write to: Rt 5, Box 796, Big Pine Key, FL 33043. ☎ 800-801-8394 or 305-872-9090, fax 305-872-9090.

Dolphin Marina Resort, MM 28.5, oceanside, is at the closest marina to Looe Key Marine Sanctuary. Twelve simple motel rooms. No pets. Snorkel and sunset cruises daily. $99 to $149. ☎ 800-553-0308 or 305-872-2685, fax 305-872-0927. Website: http://thefloridakeys.com/dolphinmarina.

Parmer's Place Resort Motel, MM 28.5, Bayside, features 38 furnished efficiencies and one handicapped unit. Quiet. No pets. Rooms $77 to $293. E-mail: parmers@juno.com. Website: http://parmersplace.com. ☎ 305-872-2157, fax 305-872-2014.

Little Torch Key

Little Palm Island. Located on an out island, this luxurious resort offers all recreational facilities. Suites include private balcony, king-size bed, ceiling fans, air-conditioning, coffee maker, refrigerator, data-link line, wet bar and whirlpool. Dive shop on premises. Seaplane service. Launch transfers to the island are provided. No TV or phones. Two-night minimum stay on weekends. Rates: January 15 to March 31, $600 to $850; April 1 to May 31, $500 to $750; June 1 to December 16, $350 to $650. Meals add $140 per person, per day. No refunds on unused packages or meal plans. Write to Overseas Hwy 1, MM 28.5, Route 4, Box 1036, Little Torch Key, FL 33042. ☎ 1-800-GET LOST (343-8567) or 305-872-2524, fax 305-872-4843. E-mail: getlost@ littlepalmisland.com. Website: littlepalmisland.com.

Sugarloaf Key

Sugarloaf Lodge, at MM 17, Bayside, is a complete resort with miniature golf, airstrip, restaurant, boat rentals, fishing charters, tennis, pool and marina. Skydiving and airplane rides. Rooms $115 to $130 in winter, $75 to $90 in summer (May to December). Write to: PO Box 148, Sugarloaf Key, FL 33044. ☎ 800-553-6097 or 305-745-3211, fax 305-745-3389.

Lower Keys Campgrounds

Sugarloaf Key KOA, MM20, oceanside, offers 184 sites on 14 acres, full-service marina with canoe and boat rentals, game room, pool, hot tub, sandy beach, restaurant, laundry facilities and full-service store. ☎ 305-745-3549. Write to: PO Box 469, Summerland Key, FL 33044.

Key West

Key West has three main resort areas – **Old Town**, the center of activity and where you'll find the island's most posh, oceanfront resort complexes, **South Roosevelt Blvd**, which runs along the south shore parallel to the Atlantic Ocean, and **North Roosevelt Blvd**, the commercial strip packed with fast food joints and strip malls that runs along the island's northern, Gulf shores. Because the island is just two miles wide and four miles long, no matter where you stay, you can travel to any point within a matter of minutes.

For a complete list of Key West accommodations, including guest houses, condominiums, apartments and vacation homes, contact the **Greater Key West Chamber of Commerce**, Mallory Square, 402 Wall St., Key West, FL 33040. ☎ 800-LAST KEY or 305-294-2587.

Best Western Hibiscus Motel, 1313 Simonton St., offers 61 rooms in a tropical park-like setting. Two queen beds and refrigerator in each room, heated pool. Gay-friendly. $99 to $139. Some kitchen units. No pets. ☎ 305-296-6711.

Best Western Key Ambassador Resort Inn, 3755 S. Roosevelt Blvd. Airport pick-up. Pool, balconies, in-room fridge. Close to beach. 101 units. Rates $89 to $219. ☎ 305-296-3500, US 800-432-4315. Deluxe.

Comfort Inn, 3824 N. Roosevelt Blvd. Features 100 guest rooms. Family plans, Olympic pool. Rates $120 to $360; includes continental breakfast. ☎ 800-695-5150 or 305-294-3773, fax 305-294-3773.

Curry Mansion Inn, 511 Caroline St. Nestled alongside the original 1899 Curry Mansion, the Inn offers 15 elegant romantic rooms, each opening onto a sparkling pool and surrounded by the lush foliage of the Curry Estate. Private baths and phones, wet bars, air-conditioning, ceiling fans and TV. Rates $160 to $275. ☎ 800-253-3466 or 305-294-5349, fax 305-294-4093. E-mail: frontdesk@currymansion.com. Website: wwwcurrymansion.com.

Econo Lodge Resort of Key West, 3820 N Roosevelt Blvd., Key West, FL 33040. This 134-room family resort features tiki bar, off-street parking, 24-hour Dennys. Rooms $115 to $355. No pets. ☎ 800-766-7584 or 305-294-5511, fax 305-296-1939.

Fairfield Inn by Marriot, 2400 N. Roosevelt Blvd., Key West, FL 33040. 100 rooms, heated pool, tiki bar, cable TV, free local calls. Closest hotel to the Wharf. Some kitchen units. No pets. Handicapped accessible. Rooms $89 to $199. ☎ US 800-228-2800 or 305-296-5700.

Holiday Inn La Concha Hotel, 430 Duval St., Key West, FL 33040. This historic hotel towers over the center of Old Town and features 160 romantic rooms, a restaurant, fitness room, whirlpool spa, shops and the best view of the city from the rooftop lounge. Walk to all attractions, fishing and sightseeing. Meetings and receptions for up to 200 people. Rates $179 to $315. ☎ 800-745-2191 or 305-296-2991, fax 305-294-3283. Handicapped accessible. Website: www.keywest.com/laconcha/html.

Holiday Inn Beachside, 1111 N. Roosevelt Blvd., Key West, FL 33040. Located directly on the Gulf of Mexico, this resort offers 222 lovely rooms, 79 with water views. Amenities include large freshwater pool, whirlpool, on-site watersports and dive trips, gift ship, full service restaurant and bar, two lighted tennis courts and full catering facilities. Soft sand beach, wave runners.

Oceanfront and poolside rooms. Diving and snorkeling tours. Convenient to both sides of the island and Stock Island. Rooms $119 to $160. No pets. ☎ 800-292-7706 or 305-294-2571, fax 305-292-7252. E-mail: db_wright@msn.com.

Hampton Inn, 2801 N. Roosevelt Blvd., Key West, FL 33040. Located on the Gulf, Hampton Inn features 157 units, island decor, freshwater pool, cable TV, Showtime, heated jacuzzi, tiki bar, sundeck. Handicapped accessible. Some pets OK. Rooms from $74 (summer and winter), with much higher priced rooms available during both seasons. ☎ 305-294-2917, US 800-HAMPTON.

Howard Johnson Resort, 3031 N. Roosevelt Blvd. Key West, FL 33040. Adjacent to recreation center and Key Plaza shopping center. Pool, restaurant. Rates $159+. ☎ 800-942-0913 or 305-296-6595, fax 305-296-8351. Website: www.tarbray-hojo@travelbase.com.

Hyatt Key West Resort and Marina, 601 Front St, Key West, FL 33040. Oceanfront, this stunning, 120-room landmark resort sits two short blocks from Duval and the heart of Old Town. Pool, three fine restaurants, private sandy beach and marina. Rooms $285 to $385. ☎ US 800-233-1234 or 305-296-9900.

Key Wester Resort, 3675 S. Roosevelt Blvd., Key West, FL 33040. Sprawled across nine acres on the Atlantic, the 100-room resort features an Olympic pool, tiki bar and café at poolside, two tennis courts. A half-mile to beach, 2½ miles to town. No pets. Rates $128 to $355. ☎ 800-477-8888 or 305-296-5671, fax 305- 294-9909.

Marriott's Casa Marina Resort, MM 00, 1500 Reynolds St., Key West, FL 33040, is the island's largest oceanfront resort, featuring 314 rooms, tennis, bicycles, water sports, private beach, two pools, whirlpool and sauna. Complete health club on premises. Lovely mahogany pool bar with barbecue services. Lounge. Handicapped accessible. Rates $309 to $795. ☎ US 800-626-0777, FL or 305-296-3535, fax 305-296-3008. E-mail: Casa@keywest.com. Website: www.keywestparadise.com/casam.html.

Marriot Reach Resort, 1435 Simonton St., Key West, FL 33040. Elegant resort located on a natural sand beach. Features 149 rooms (80 suites) each with a veranda, most with ocean view, ceiling fans, wet bar, two restaurants, oceanside dining, watersports, food store, library, five bars, entertainment. Health center, lap pool. Handicapped accessible. No pets. Rates $309 to $419. ☎ US 800-874-4118 or 305-296-5000. E-mail: Reach@keywest.com. Website: www.keywestparadise.com/thereach.html.

Ocean Key House Suite Resort & Marina on Mallory Square at Zero Duval St., Key West, FL 33040, offers deluxe suites on the Gulf of Mexico.

Fully-equipped kitchens. Jacuzzi. Private balcony with water and sunset views. VCR and movie rentals. No pets. Rates $169 to $700. ☎ US 800-328-9815 or 305-296-7701. W-mail: info@oceankeyhouse.com. Website: www.keywest.com/okh.

Old Town Resorts, Inc., at 1319 Duval St., Key West, FL 33040, includes the southernmost motel in the US, the **South Beach Oceanfront Motel**, and the **La Mer Hotel**. Offers three pools, jacuzzi, tiki bar, sunning pier on the Atlantic, gift shop, dive shop, concierge. Walking distance to beach, shops, nightlife and dining. No pets. Call for rates. ☎ 305-296-6577, FL 800-354-4455, fax 294-8272.

Pegasus International Motel, 501 Southard St., Key West, FL 33040. Art Deco hotel with old-world service in Old Town at reasonable rates. 23 units. No pets. TV, private bath, air-conditioning. ☎ 800-397-8148 or 305-294-9323, fax 294-4741.

Pelican Landing Resort & Marina, 915 Eisenhower Drive, Key West, FL 33040. Marina suites sleep two to eight people. No pets. Full kitchens, heated pool, barbecue grills, cable TV, docks, fish cleaning station, barbecue grill, HBO. Two penthouses with jacuzzi. ☎ 800-527-8108 or 305-296-7583.

Pier House Resort & Caribbean Spa, One Duval St., Key West, FL 33040. In the heart of Old Town. Offers 142 eclectic, romantic guest rooms and suites with private terraces. Private beach, full-service spa, heated pool. Five restaurants, five bars, beachside entertainment. No pets. Rates $275 to $795. ☎ US 800-327-8340 or 305-296-4600, fax 305-296-7568. E-mail: pierhouse@conch.net. Website: http://pierhouse.com.

Quality Inn of Key West, 3850 N Roosevelt Blvd., Key West, FL 33040. Typical large chain features include pool, kitchen units, free coffee makers and coffee in each room. Free HBO. Rates $114 to $260. ☎ 800-553-5024 or 305-294-6681, fax 305-294-5618. E-mail: qualityikw@aol.com.

Ramada Inn Key West, 3420 N. Roosevelt Blvd., Key West, FL 33040. On the commercial strip across highway from the Gulf of Mexico. Air-conditioned, color TV, pool, tennis. Pets welcome. Handicapped accessible. Rates $120 to $260. ☎ 800-330-5541 or 305-294-5541, fax 305-294-7932.

Sheraton Suites Key West, 2001 S Roosevelt Blvd., Key West, FL 33040. 180 suites just 1/4 mile from Key West AirPort. All suites have a fridge, microwave, remote TV, complimentary breakfast. Large pool, free shuttle to and from Key West Airport and Old Town. Large meeting rooms. Rates $295 to $495. ☎ 800-425-3224 or 305-292-9800, fax 294-6009. Website: www.sheraton.com.

Southernmost Motel in the USA, 1319 Duval, Key West, FL 33040. Features two pools, jacuzzi, tiki bar poolside. Walking distance to ships, nightlife, attractions, across from beach with pier on ocean. Rates $120 to $199. ☎ 800-354-4455 or 305-296-6577. E-mail: Lamer508@aol.com. Website: www.oldtownresorts.com.

Key West Campgrounds

Boyd's Campground, Maloney Ave., Stock Island, FL 33040. ☎ 305-294-1465. Southernmost campground in the US. On the Atlantic Ocean at Key West city limits. Features all watersports, showers, restrooms, laundry, store, ice, city bus, telephone, dump station, bottle gas, electric, water, sewer hook-ups. Twenty boat slips and launching ramps. Pets OK. Pool.

Jabour's Trailer Court, 223 Elizabeth, St., Key West, FL 33040. Water-front campground in Old Town. Walking distance to everything. Tent and RVs welcome. Efficiencies. ☎ 305-294-5723.

Leo's Campground & RV Park, 5236 Suncrest Rd., Key West, FL 33040. Features 36 shady sites. Electric hookups, hot & cold showers, laundry, dump station. Security seven days a week. Barbecues. ☎ 296-5260.

Key West Dining

Key West

You'll find the locals' favorite watering hole at **The Half Shell Raw Bar** in Lands End Village. Menu features are fried or broiled fish, shrimp and conch; raw oysters and clams. Friendly service. Try for a table on the back porch, overlooking the docks, where you'll spot six or seven huge silver tarpon. Open for lunch and dinner. Moderate. ☎ 294-7496.

Across the wharf sits **Turtle Kraals Bar and Restaurant** serving fresh fish, hamburgers and the largest selection of imported beers in Key West. The restaurant is what remains of the days when turtles were brought in by the boat load from as far away as the Cayman Islands and Nicaragua. ☎ 294-2640.

Kraal is an Afrikans word meaning holding pen or enclosure. It refers to the concrete pilings that were driven into the ocean bottom to form a holding pen for the turtles until they could be shipped to the Northeast or slaughtered and made into soup at the cannery.

Pepe's Café, 806 Caroline St., serves the best breakfasts in the Keys. Frosted glasses of fresh orange juice and artfully prepared French toast or egg dishes are served indoors or outside under a canopy of flowering vines. Pub-style fare for lunch and dinner. Outdoor decor includes a white picket fence with peepholes for passersby at two levels – one for people and one for their pets. ☎ 294-7192.

The rooftop lounge at Holiday Inn's **La Concha** on Duval St. serves exotic island drinks and is the best spot in town for sunset viewing.

Mallory Market is the center of the Historic Key West waterfront and offers every imaginable fast-food outlet, plus a few you may not have imagined. One particularly good one is the conch fritter stand outside the Shipwreck Historeum, across from the Key West Aquarium.

Duval Street is lined with wonderful cafés and restaurants featuring varied, ethnic dishes. **Hooters** and the **Hard Rock Café** offer tasty, fast food.

Bagatelle, 115 Duval St., features indoor or outdoor gourmet dining in a magnificent Victorian mansion. Lunch and dinner daily. Moderate to expensive. ☎ 296-6609.

The Cheese Board at 1075 Duval St. has 52 varieties of cheese, coffees and wines. ☎ 294-0072.

Chops, at the Holiday Inn La Concha, 430 Duval St., features venison chops, duck breast, rabbit, and seafood. 5:30-10:30 pm. ☎ 296-2991.

Kelly's Caribbean Bar, Grill & Brewery, 301 Whitehead St., serves lunch, dinner or cocktails. Decent Caribbean cuisine in a tropical garden setting. Try one of their micro-brew beers. Original home of Pan American Airways. ☎ 293-8484.

Exotic dishes from Southeast Asia are found at **Dim Sum**, 613 Duval St (rear). Dinner. ☎ 294-6230.

Yo Sake at 722 Duval (☎ 294-2288) and **Kyushu** (☎ 294-2995) at 921 Truman Avenue feature Japanese cuisine and sushi bars. Lunch and dinner.

The Banana Café, 1211 Duval St. French restaurant and crêperie. Open daily except Tues. for breakfast and lunch from 8 am to 3 pm. Dinner from 7 pm-10:30 pm. ☎ 294-7227.

Hog's Breath Saloon packs guests into its bustling open-air restaurant and raw bar. Nightly entertainment from sunset to 2 am. "Hog's breath is better than no breath at all!" ☎ 296-4222.

Louie's Back Yard, at the corner of Vernon and Waddell Streets, is one of Key West's finest waterfront restaurants. American cuisine highlights the menu for lunch, dinner and Sunday brunch. Expensive. Louie's delightful patio bar sits over the sea. ☎ 294-1061.

Strip malls along N. Roosevelt Blvd. feature most fast food chain restaurants.

Other Activities

Florida Keys

Historic tours, parasailing, sailing charters, seaplane rides, and golf are available. Visit **Mel Fisher's Treasure Museum**, **Key West Aquarium**, **Ernest Hemingway's House**, the **Audubon House and Gardens**. There are also trolley tours and shopping for Haitian art, island jewelry, hand print fabrics, handcrafted hats, masks, sandals, and hammocks.

Facts

Recompression Chamber: Paradis Hyperbarics, Marathon, ☎ 305-743-9891; Mariners Hospital, Tavernier, MM 91.5, ☎ 888-506-3638.

Handicap Facilities: Most large resorts feature full handicap facilities. State and national parks have wheelchair-accessible trails, tour boats, accommodations, restaurants.

Getting There: All major national and international airlines fly into Miami Airport. Connecting scheduled flights land in Marathon and Key West.

Driving from Miami International Airport, take LeJeune Road south to 836 West. Then take the Turnpike Extension to US 1 south, which runs the length of the Keys to Key West.

Driving from the North, take Florida Turnpike to Exit 4 (Homestead-Key West). From Tampa, take 1-75 south to Naples, then east to Miami and the Turnpike Extension; or take 41 south to the Florida Turnpike, then east to the Turnpike Extension, then south to US 1.

Airlines serving Key West International Airport: American Eagle, ☎ 800-433-7300; Cape Air, ☎ 305-293-0603; Delta/Comair, ☎ 800-354-9822; Gulf Stream, ☎ 800-992-8532; USAir Express, ☎ 800-428-4322. General flight information, ☎ 305-296-5439.

Airlines serving Marathon Airport: American Eagle, ☎ 800-433-7300; Gulf stream, ☎ 800-992-8532; USAir Express, ☎ 800-4284322.

Mile Markers: Mile Markers (MM) appear on the right shoulder of the road (US 1) as small green signs with white numbers and are posted each mile beginning with number 126, just south of Florida City. They end with the zero marker at the corner of Fleming and Whitehead streets in Key West.

Awareness of these markers is useful as Keys' residents use them continually. When asking for directions in the Keys, your answer will likely be a reference to the nearest Mile Marker number.

Rental Cars: At Miami Airport, Avis, Budget, Hertz, National and Value. If possible, book rental cars in advance of your trip. In season you may be forced to rent a more expensive car than you planned.

Buses: Greyhound buses leave three times daily (7 am, noon and 6 pm) from the airport-vicinity bus station at 4111 NW 27th Street, Miami. Travel time to Key West is 4½ hrs. ☎ (in FL) 800-410-5397, 305-876-7123 or in Key West, 305-296-9072.

Clothing: During winter pack a light jacket, long-sleeved shirts and pants. Temperatures occasionally drop to the 50s. More usually, shorts and tee shirts cover most fashion needs, though one change of dressy attire may prove useful.

Scuba divers visiting the Keys between December and March will find a shortie, or lightweight wet suit appropriate. Water temperatures drop to the 70s. Winter snorkelers will be most comfortable with a lycra wetskin or light wet suit.

Hospitals: Mariners Hospital, MM 89, ☎ 305-852-4418; Fisherman's Hospital, MM 48.5, ☎ 305-743-5533; Florida Keys Health Systems, MM 5, turn right , ☎ 305- 294-5531.

Weather: ☎ 305-296-2741.

Marine Patrol: ☎ 305-743-6542.

For Additional Information: ☎ 800-FLA-KEYS. Florida Keys & Key West Visitors Bureau, PO Box 1147, Key West FL 33041. Website: www.fla-keys.com.

Part II

The Caribbean

Barbados

Barbados, a tiny island just 21 miles long and 14 miles wide, offers remarkable contrasts between its boulder-strewn northern coast and serene Caribbean shores. Inland, hilly forests slope down to golden fields of sugarcane, corn, sweet potatoes, and yams. Stunning white sand beaches rim the island.

The easternmost island of the Lesser Antilles, Barbados boasts a unique range of natural and historic attractions, from its exquisite plantation "great houses" to vast caves filled with prehistoric formations. Its quaint colonial capital, Bridgetown, surprises visitors with upscale shopping and gourmet dining.

Despite 30 years of independence from Great Britain, Barbados still exudes a British atmosphere. A statue of Admiral Nelson graces Bridgetown's Trafalgar Square, and afternoon tea remains a custom for many hotels. Good diving and snorkeling exists off the southwestern shores. Gorgeous reefs flank the rocky east coast, but pounding seas and strong currents usually limit access to this area.

When to Go

Divers, both novice and experienced, are advised to visit Barbados between April and November, when they can expect fabulous visibility on the barrier reef and calm seas. This changes from December through March, when a "North Swell" decreases visibility near shore and on the outer reefs.

During spring, summer and fall the island's shallow shipwrecks offer a variety of dive experiences. The best wrecks are found on the offshore barrier reef that extends along Barbados' western coast. The wrecks are camouflaged by soft corals, sea fans, and sponges, home to thriving communities of fish and other marine animals. Barbados presents snorkelers with miles of white-powder sand beaches and shore-access coves with a wide range of corals and friendly fish.

Best Dive & Snorkeling Sites

☆☆☆☆☆ **Dottins Reef**, a half-mile off the coast of St. James Parish on the west coast, drifts along the shore from St James to Bridgetown. It is the prettiest reef in Barbados, with visibility at 100 ft or better. Basket sponges, sea fans, gorgonians and thickets of staghorn and brain coral adorn the reef's canyons and walls. Depths start at 65 ft, with some drop-offs to 130 ft. Reef residents include rays, turtles, barracudas, parrot fish, snapper and large grouper. Seas are generally calm.

☆☆☆ **Sandy Lane**, a deeper area off Dottin's Reef, is usually a drift dive. The walls, dotted with sponges and vibrant clump corals, drop to 90 ft. Superb marine life abounds. A good spot for video photography. For experienced divers only.

☆☆☆ **Wreck of the *Pamir***, located just 200 yds offshore, is easily accessible from the beach and is very open and uncluttered. This 150-ft ship was sunk in 30 ft of water by the Barbados dive shop operators to form an artificial reef. The ship's superstructure breaks the usually calm surface, making it perfect for snorkelers and snorkel-swimmers. Swarms of sergeant majors and butterfly fish inhabit the wreck. Nearby, about 60 yds out, is a small reef. Although visibility varies, seas are always calm. Dive operators request no spearfishing or collecting. An excellent dive for novices.

☆☆☆ **Bright Ledge Reef** is a narrow reef that wraps around the island's northern tip. Depths average 60 ft, with deep drop-offs on either side. Unsuitable for novices but generally a safe dive and particularly good for photography. Encounters with gigantic pelagics, turtles and rays are frequent, with dependable sightings of parrot fish, snapper, grouper, porgy, grunts, and glass-eye snapper. The sea is generally calm unless there is a stiff wind or storm.

☆☆☆ ***The Stavronikita***, a 360-ft freighter, was gutted by a fire at sea 14 years ago. After towing the sinking ship closer to shore, the government of Barbados sunk the smoldering mass where it would benefit divers and fishermen as an artificial reef. The wreck sits in 130 ft of water, the deck at 80 ft. Although the depth discourages most novice explorers, the ship is one of the island's most interesting dives. Its hull, covered with a colorful patchwork of small sponges and clinging corals, attracts schools of silversides and large pelagics. Very appealing to photographers.

☆☆ Nearby in shallow water lie the **Conimara,** an old PT boat, and the **Lord Combermere**, an old tug – both in 30-40 ft of water. Visibility varies. Good photo opportunities abound here as well. The wrecks can be reached from the shore after a 600-yd swim.

☆☆ **Friar's Craig** is a good dive for the novice, although strong current may be occasionally encountered. This is another purposely sunken wreck. It lies in just 60 ft of water with the bridge at 30 ft, making it more accessible than the *Stavronikita*. Nearby, **Asta Reef**, a shelter for throngs of fish, is often combined with a Friar's Craig dive. A short 600-yd swim from the southwest corner of Christ Church Parish will put you over the wreck and an adjacent

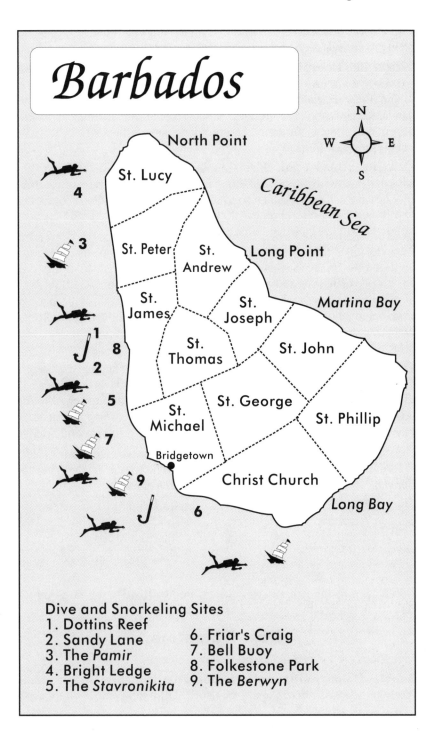

Barbados

North Point

St. Lucy

Caribbean Sea

St. Peter

St. Andrew

Long Point

St. James

St. Joseph

Martina Bay

St. Thomas

St. John

St. George

St. Michael

St. Phillip

Bridgetown

Christ Church

Long Bay

N / W E / S

4

3

1

8

2

5

7

9

6

Dive and Snorkeling Sites
1. Dottins Reef
2. Sandy Lane
3. The *Pamir*
4. Bright Ledge
5. The *Stavronikita*
6. Friar's Craig
7. Bell Buoy
8. Folkestone Park
9. The *Berwyn*

reef, **Castle Bank.** Exercise extreme caution and check the current before diving. Numerous fish and usually great visibility.

☆☆☆ **Bell Buoy Reef,** off St. Michael's Parish on the island's southwestern side, is a wall dive with a shelf at 40 ft, dropping off to a sandy bottom at 70 ft. The reef is alive with small critters amidst the shadows of large brain coral heads, sea fans, and vase sponges. Schools of small reef fish, turtles, and an occasional ray are in residence. During windy periods this spot can be wiped out by strong currents.

☆☆☆ **Caribbee Reef**, off the Caribbee Hotel is a section of the fringing reefs that parallel the southwest shore. Lots of fish, giant barrel sponges, tube sponges and sea fans. Usually good visibility. Light surge. Good for experienced divers. Depths are 60 to 120 ft. This is a boat dive.

☆☆☆ **Folkestone Park** is the favorite beach/snorkeling site in Barbados. An underwater trail has been marked around the inshore reef. It is also the favorite area for boaters and jet skiers, so the swimming and snorkeling area has been roped off to insure safety. Snorkel with or near a group. A 200-yd swim from the sandy beach will take you to a raft anchored over the wreckage of a small barge sitting in 20 ft of water. During winter when the North Swell rises, visibility can drop drastically for as long as two days. During the rest of the year, Folkestone is the number one snorkeling choice.

☆☆ The **Wreck of the *Berwyn*** is a 45-ft-long French tugboat that sank in the early 1900s. It sits at the bottom of Carlisle Bay, 200 yds off the island's southwest shore at a depth of 25 ft. Encrusted with plate corals, the wreck is host to seahorses, frogfish, wrasses, arrow crabs and other small creatures. It is a favored snorkeling photo site with good visibility and calm sea conditions.

☆☆ The **Wreck of the *Eillion*,** a former drug boat, was sunk June 8, 1996 to form part of the Carlisle Bay Marine Park. The wreck, located near the *Berwyn*, sits at 110 ft, with the top at 55 ft. Lots of fish.

***The Ce-Trek*,** an old cement-constructed boat at a depth of 40 ft, sits near the *Berwyn*. A favorite of re-entry divers, the *Ce-Trek* has attracted hordes of fish and invertebrates since its sinking in 1986. She sits 300 yds offshore.

The *Berwyn, Eillion, Ce-Trek* and the *Fox* (a small wreck) can be seen on one dive.

Two nice spots for beginning snorkelers are **Mullins Beach** and **Paynes Bay**. Both offer calm waters and ample parking.

Dive Operators

Dive shops are located along the southwest shores.

Bubbles Galore Barbados Dive Shop at the Sandy Beach Island Resort, Worthing, Christ Church, offers all levels of PADI training, with two-tank dives every morning and afternoon. Complimentary drinks served on board their custom 31-ft Bertam dive boat. Night dives upon request. Specialty courses in DAN O2 Provider, basic Nitrox, underwater photography, and navigation. All are offered in English, German, Italian, Spanish, French, Swedish, Norwegian and Russian. ☎ 246-430-0354, fax 246-430-8806. E-mail: bubbles@ caribsurf.com.

The Dive Shop Ltd., celebrating its 30th year on the island, offers daily trips at 10 am and noon with night dives twice a week. All staff members are certified by PADI, NAUI and/or ACUC. They are also DAN O2 certified. All levels of certification courses are taught. Shipwrecks *Berwyn* and *Ce-Trek* sit 300 yds from the shop. Rates are $55 for a one-tank dive, $90 for a two-tank dive. A 10-dive package costs $300 with equipment, $260 with your own equipment. Hotel/dive packages are available at the Blythwood Beach Apartments and Cacrabank Beach Apartments. For information write or call Haroon Degia, The Dive Shop Ltd. Aquatic Gap, Bay Street, St. Michael, Barbados, WI. ☎ 800-348-3756 or 246-426-9947, fax 246-426-2031. Website: www.barbados.org/diving/diveshop/diveshop.html. E-mail: hardive@caribnet. net.

Underwater Barbados, a PADI five-star dive shop in Carlisle Bay Centre, visits all the best sites aboard a 31-ft pirogue boat. Staff are medic first-aid trained and are experienced dive instructors and guides. All levels of instruction. Demonstrations and instruction are offered at the Carlisle Bay Centre on Bay Street in St. Michaels's Parish, Coconut Court Beach Hotel, Asta Beach Hotel, Long Beach Club, Sam Lords, Welcome Inn Beach Hotel. ☎ 246-426-0655, fax 246-426-0655. Write to: Michael Young, Underwater Barbados, Carlisle Bay Centre, St. Michael, Barbados, WI. E-mail: myoung@ndl.net. Website: www.ndl.net/~uwb/.

Coral Isle Divers, on Cavans Lane at the Careenage in Bridgetown, operates a custom 40-ft power catamaran dive boat with a changing room, onboard washroom and shower, dry storage areas and plenty of deck space. They offer PADI and NAUI instruction. Complimentary soft drinks. ☎ 246-434-8377, fax 246-432-1212. E-mail: coralis@caribnet.net.

Blue Reef Water Sports, St. James, runs reef and wreck trips, resort and certification courses. Their 28-ft boat carries 12 divers. ☎ 246-422-3133, fax 246-422-3133.

Hightide Watersports touts a new custom-built 30-ft dive boat, *Flyin' High*. This PADI shop offers one- and two-tank dives, night dives, snorkeling trips, and PADI instruction. Equipment sales and rentals, video camera. Gear storage. ☎ 246-432-0931.

WestSide Scuba Centre, next to The Sunset Crest Beach Club, Holetown, St. James, offers PADI courses, dive and snorkeling tours. Free transportation to and from your hotel. ☎ and fax 246-432-2558.

Beginning and advanced dive tours and certification courses are also offered at **Willies Watersports**, St Michael, ☎ 246-425-1060 or 246-422-4900; at **Dive Boat Safari** at the Barbados Hilton, St. Michael, ☎ 246-427-4350; and at **Scotch & Soda**, ☎ 246-435-7375.

Hazell's Water World Inc., in the Sandy Bank complex, Hastings, Christ Church, sells a wide range of scuba and snorkeling equipment. Repair service for dive equipment. ☎ 246-426-4043.

Atlantis Submarine dives to 150 ft, exploring the reefs and wrecks for 90 minutes. Divers on scooters outside the sub interact with the surroundings and can communicate with submarine guests. Located in Bridgetown. ☎ 246-436-8929.

Atlantis' 65-ft glass-hulled *Seatrec* (Sea Tracking and Reef Exploration Craft) features advanced glass-bottom viewing with in-cabin video monitors.

Reserve sail-snorkeling, sunset, lunch and dinner tours through **Jolly Roger Cruises**, Bridgetown, ☎ 436-6424, fax 429-8500; **Tiami Catamaran Sailing Cruises**, Bridgetown, ☎ 427-7245, fax 431-0538; **Secret Love**, ☎ 432-1972; or **Irish Mist**, ☎ 436-9201. Mask and snorkel included.

Accommodations

Most hotels and nightlife exist on the south and central western coast of the island. There are no dedicated dive resorts, but all will arrange for diving. Several guest houses, cottages and apartments may be rented for $30 per night and up. A list with current rates is available from the Barbados Board of Tourism. In the US, ☎ 800-221-9831; in Canada, ☎ 800-268-9122 or 416-512-6569, fax 416-512-6581. In Barbados, ☎ 246-427-2623/4, fax 246-426-4080. Website: www.barbados.org.

To book on the Internet, go to the www.barbados.org, then click on hotels. Click on E-mail to book reservations with the hotel of your choice.

Before booking on your own, check the travel section of your Sunday newspaper. Money-saving packages, including airfare and choice hotels, in Barbados are frequently featured by the large travel companies.

Divi Southwinds Beach Hotel sits on a half-mile of white sand beach near the St. Lawrence Gap. It is surrounded by 20 acres of tropical gardens and features 166 guest rooms and air-conditioned suites, all having a patio and pool or ocean views. Beachside restaurants offer local and international dishes. Pool-side bar and snackery. You are within walking distance of restaurants and nightlife. Room rates start at $210 in season. ☎ 800-367-3484, 607-277-

3484 or write Divi Resorts, 6340 Quadrangle Drive, Suite 300, Chapel Hill, NC 27514-8900.

Almond Beach Club, an all-inclusive resort, features 131 air-conditioned guest rooms and suites with ocean or pool views. Gourmet meals are served at the elegant beachside restaurant; refreshments at a swim-up bar adjacent to the twin pools. Dive trips are arranged with the Blue Reef Dive shop. All-inclusive rates per couple, per day, include meals, drinks, snorkeling, fishing, windsurfing, kayaking. Winter (December 18 to March 31) rates per day, per couple, start at $550 for a standard room; summer rates start at $440. ☎ 800-4ALMOND.

Grand Barbados Beach Resort is a luxury beachfront resort with scuba facilities on the premises. Located in Carlisle Bay, one mile from Bridgetown, the resort is just minutes from reef and wreck dives. Features are a fitness center, shopping arcade, coffee shop, two restaurants and bars, satellite TV, hairdryers, mini-safes, radio, phone, balconies, and meeting facilities. Mistral Windsurfing School. Room rates in winter start at $265 per night. ☎ 246-426-4000, fax 246-429-2400.

Coral Reef Club, a small, luxury beachfront resort with its own dive shop (Les Wooten's Watersports) sits in 12 acres of gardens adjacent to a superb, white sand beach. All 70 lovely, air-conditioned cottages and rooms feature secluded patios or balconies. Activities available to guests include cruises on the club's own 30-ft catamaran. Amenities include tennis court, pool, and shops. Alfresco restaurant overlooks the sea. Special nights including Bajan

Independence Arch, Bridgetown.

buffets and barbecue dinner with steel band, flaming limbo and exotic calypso dancers. Winter rates start from $370 per night. ☎ 246-422-2372, fax 246-422-1776.

Asta Beach Hotel in Christ Church, 1½ miles from Bridgetown, offers 67 beachfront rooms and suites. Diving with Underwater Barbados. All rooms are air-conditioned with private bath, kitchen, TV and telephone. Restaurant and bar, two pools. Free bus to city on weekdays. Rates are from $130 in winter. ☎ 246-427-2541, fax 246-426-9566. Book through your travel agent or the Internet.

Coconut Court, a family-owned hotel two miles from Bridgetown, features ocean views, gift shop, restaurant. TV in rooms. Rates start at $105 in winter. ☎ 246-427-1655.

Crane Beach Hotel sits on four acres overlooking a half-mile of beautiful coral sand beach. A gourmet restaurant, refreshment bar and four tennis courts are on the estate. Rates start at $160 per day. ☎ 246-423-6220, fax 246-423-5343.

Long Beach Club on Chancery Lane in Christ Church features 24 rooms. Rates are from $118 per day. ☎ 246-428-6890, fax 246-428-4957.

Sandy Beach Island Resort, Worthing, Christ Church, offers 128 air-conditioned, beachfront rooms. Diving with Bubbles Galore Dive Shop. Rates per person are from $125 to $220. ☎ 246-435-8000, fax 246-435-8053.

Sam Lord's Castle, a luxurious, waterfront Marriott resort in Long Bay, on the Atlantic east coast, St. Phillip, features 234 air-conditioned rooms with all amenities. Tennis courts. Rates per day are from $210 to $248. ☎ 800-228-9290 or 246-423-7350, fax 246-423-5918. Diving with Underwater Barbados.

Welcome Inn Beach Hotel, Maxwell Coast Road, Christ Church, offers 110 rooms, diving with Underwater Barbados. Rates run from $185 to $330 in winter. ☎ 246-428-9900, fax 246-428-8905.

For villas and home rentals contact **Island Hideaways**. ☎ 800-784-2690 or 202-232-6137, fax 202-667-3392.

Crewed luxury yacht charters are offered by **Alleyne, Aguilar and Altman Ltd.**, St. James (none have compressors on board). ☎ 246-432-0840, fax 246-432-2147.

Other Activities

Horseback riding is offered by **Brighton Riding Stables**, ☎ 425-9381; **Caribbean International Riding Centre**, ☎ 433-1453; **Riding Beau Geste Farm**, ☎ 429-0139; or **Ye Olde Congo Road Stables**, ☎ 423-6180. Stables are near Bridgetown.

The **Sandy Lane Golf Course** at the Sandy Lane Hotel is a well-maintained 18-hole course. **Royal Westmoreland Golf & Country Club** offers contrasting challenges, stunning scenery and a succession of "feature holes." **Almond Beach Resort** features a par-three, nine-hole layout. It requires only a nine iron, wedge, sand wedge and putter. ☎ 422-4900. **Club Rockley** r offers an 18-hole layout, with a second nine holes playable from varying tee positions. ☎ 435-7873.

Deep-sea fishing for dorado, wahoo, sailfish, tuna and marlin is easily arranged by the hotel desks. Call **Blue Jay Charters**, ☎ 422-2098 or 230-3832, fax 425-2819, or **Deep Sea Adventure**, ☎ 428-5344.

Skyrider Parasail features a 32-ft boat with an integrated, self-contained launching and landing platform. ☎ 435-0570.

Windsurfing off the south coast can be arranged at the **Barbados Windsurfing Club** at Maxwell and **Silver Rock Windsurfing Club** at Silver Sands. ☎ 428-2866.

Submarine tours of the reefs are offered aboard the 28-passenger *Atlantis*. ☎ 436-8929.

Sightseeing

Ride on an electric tram into **Harrison's Cave** (☎ 438-6640) to explore beautiful underground water falls, Mirror Lake and The Rotunda Room, where the walls of the 250-ft chamber glitter like diamonds. Or view exotic tropical birds and native monkeys at the **Oughterson House Barbados Zoo Park**. History buffs will delight in finding 17th-century military relics like antique cannons and signal towers around the island.

The Barbados National Trust provides an open house program where **Historical Great Houses** are open for public viewing between 2:30 and 5:30 pm. Entrance is $6. A bus tour that includes entrance and transportation from hotels is $18. ☎ 809-426-2421.

A **Heritage Passport Program** offers visitors special admission to many of the island's historic attractions. Short-stay visitors can opt for the $12 minipassport. Children under 12 accompany adults for free.

Shopping

Barbados abounds with boutiques, galleries and shops, with department stores such as **Harrison's** and **Cave Shepherd & Co**. offering goods from around the world, particularly diamonds and Italian gold. Island specialties include handmade puppets and clay and wood figures, along with colorful silk-screened prints and fabrics. Pepper sauce and Barbados rum are also high on the list of popular take-homes. Most shops are in or near Broad Street, Bridgetown.

Dining

West Indian specialties and native seafood dishes like grilled flying fish and lobster are featured throughout the island. Bajan delicacies include *cou-cou* (a cornmeal and okra dish), pepperpot, a spicy stew, and *jug-jug*, a mixture of Guinea corn and green peas. Whether you're looking for a romantic five-star restaurant, beach-front café or Bajan buffet, Barbados has an endless number of dining options for every palate and budget. Restaurants range from small, front-porch cafés to large, luxury hotel dining rooms. Many hotels – Sandy Lane for example – offer a barbecue served to the music of steel bands or open-air discos. Fast food afficionados will enjoy **Chefette Drive-Thru**, Barbados' answer to the golden arches, open weekends from 10 am on Friday to midday Sunday. Chefette restaurants are located in Rockley, on Harbour Road, in Oistins, Holetown, Six Cross Roads, Broad St. and on Marhill St.

Josef's, in St. Lawrence Gap, Christ Church, serves fabulous gourmet fish and continental cuisine in a grand native home with a garden overlooking the sea. Meals are under $25. ☎ 435-6541.

Pisces Restaurant, located in the St. Lawrence Gap on the waterfront, is noted for West Indian specialties and fabulous rum pie. ☎ 435-6564.

Waterfront Café, the Careenage, Bridgetown, serves Bajan specialties and Creole cuisine, including pepperpot and melts, plus tapas. Meals run between $25 and $40. Nice view of the docks. ☎ 427-0093.

"Nu-Bajan" cuisine is served at **Koko's** on Prospect, St James. Meals are under $25. ☎ 424-4557. Seating overlooks the ocean.

Creole cuisine lovers should be sure to try the **Brown Sugar Restaurant** at the Aquatic Gap in St. Michael. Popular buffet lunch served in an old Barbadian home. Under $25. ☎ 426-7684.

Facts

Helpful Phone Numbers: Police, ☎ 112; ambulance, ☎ 115.

Recompression Chamber: Located in St. Annes, Fort Garrison, St. Michael. Contact Dr. Brown or Major Gittens at ☎ 436-6185.

Getting There: British West Indies Airlines (BWIA), ☎ 800-327-7401, offers regular service from London, Frankfurt, Stockholm, Zurich, New York, Miami, and Toronto. American Airlines, ☎ 800-433-7300, from New York. Air Jamaica, ☎ 800-523-5585, from US. Air Canada, ☎ 800-776-3000, and American Airlines from Canada. Inter-island service: BWIA, LIAT, Carib Express and Air Martinique. Barbados' Grantley Adams International Airport is modern and well kept.

Island Transportation: Taxi service is available throughout the island. (Note: cab fares should be negotiated before accepting service.) Local auto-rental companies are at the airport. National, ☎ 246-426-0603, P&S,☎ 424-2907; Corbins, ☎ 427-9531; Drive-A-Matic, ☎ 422-3000; Courtesy Rent A Car, ☎ 431-4160.

Driving: Traffic keeps to the left in Barbados.

Documents: Canadian and US citizens require a birth certificate with a current photo ID or passport and return ticket in order to enter Barbados. Entry documentation is good for three months.

Customs: Personal effects of visitors, including cameras and sports equipment, enter duty free. Returning US citizens may take back free of duty articles costing a total of US $600 providing the stay has exceeded 48 hours and that the exemption has not been used within the preceding 30 days. One quart of liquor per person (over 21 years) may be carried out duty free. Not more than 100 cigars and 200 cigarettes may be included.

Note: Cameras and dive equipment should be registered with Customs **before** you leave the US.

Currency: Barbados dollar (BD)=US $1.98.

Climate: Temperatures vary between 75 and 85°F. Average rainfall is 59 inches.

Clothing: Lightweight casual clothing is recommended. A jacket for men may be desirable for visiting nightclubs or dressy resort restaurants. Swimsuits, bikinis and short shorts are not welcome in Bridgetown shops or banks.

Electricity: 110 volts AC, 50 cycles.

Time: Atlantic Standard (EST + 1 hr).

Language: English with a local dialect.

Taxes: A 10% service charge is added to the bill at most hotels. A sales tax of 5% is also added to hotel and restaurant bills.

Religious Services: Anglican, Baptist, Catholic, Methodist, Moravian, Seventh Day Adventist, Jehovah's Witnesses.

For Additional Information: Barbados Board Of Tourism, 800 Second Ave., NY, NY 10017, ☎ 800-221-9831. *In NY*, 212-986-6510. *In Florida*, 150 Alhambra Circle, Suite 1270, Coral Gables, FL 33134, ☎ 305-442-7471, fax 305-567-2844. *In Barbados*, Harbour Road, Bridgetown, WI, ☎ 246-427-2623/2624 or 800-744-6244, fax 246-426-4080. Website: http://www.barbados.org.

Barbados

Bonaire

If you love beach diving, head for Bonaire. Its surrounding reef starts at the shoreline, where a huge and varied marine population awaits. Vibrant ocean life and calm waters protected by the island's crescent shape, have earned Bonaire acclaim as a world-class dive and snorkeling vacation destination. Strict conservation laws preserve its bountiful coral reefs.

Topside, Bonaire is a colorful island with 15,000 resident flamingos at its southern tip, which is rimmed by miles of pink coral-rock beaches. Kralendijk, its capital, sparkles with bright, pastel buildings. To the north, narrow roads wind through green mountains and cactus-laden deserts, where more than 190 species of tropical birds reside. Rare species include bright green Amazon parrots, ruby-topaz hummingbirds, pearly-eyed thrashers, and Caribbean parakeets. At the island's southern tip, home of the Antilles International Salt Company, mountains of glistening white salt offer a striking contrast to the blue Caribbean. At day's end a green flash follows the setting sun.

The second largest of the Netherlands Antilles islands, Bonaire sits well out of the hurricane belt – 1,720 miles south of New York, 50 miles north of Venezuela – and therefore protected from reef damage. Bonaire offers dependably dry weather and calm seas most of the year, though changing global weather patterns bring an occasional storm and water temperature drop in midwinter.

With only 22 inches of rain annually, there is no freshwater run-off, so water visibility is typically 100 ft or more. And because sites are close to shore, visitors can pick up a tank and dive anytime day or night. Bright yellow painted rocks along the beach road mark the dive and snorkeling sites. Excellent snorkeling exists off all the south coast beaches.

Less than a mile from the west coast is Klein Bonaire (Little Bonaire), an islet surrounded by beautiful coral reefs. The sheltered waters between Bonaire's western shores and Klein Bonaire are always smooth – perfect for diving and snorkeling anytime. Bonaire's north coast, by contrast, is battered by strong waves that pound against rocky, coral cliffs.

History

Arawak Indians inhabited Bonaire for centuries before Amerigo Vespucci claimed discovery in 1499. The word Bonaire comes from the Arawak "bonah," which means "low country."

Spain attempted to colonize the island between 1527 and 1633, but in 1634 the Dutch claimed the island and established a military base to defend against Spain. In 1639 the Dutch West India company developed Bonaire for salt production, corn planting and livestock breeding. The company imported 100 African slaves and ran the island for the next 160 years.

The British occupied Bonaire briefly during the early 1800s, but the Dutch regained control in 1816 and established a government plantation system based on commercial crops. With the abolition of slavery in 1863, the operations became unprofitable and the island was divided and sold.

Over the next 90 years a severe economic recession forced many Bonaireans to migrate to Curacao and Aruba seeking work in the oil industry. By the 1950s, however, Bonaire's economy recovered. The salt pans were modified to use solar energy and became the most successful such plants in the world. Tourism was introduced and divers have since come from around the globe.

Bonaire Marine Park

In 1979, the Netherlands Antilles National Parks Foundation (STINAPA) received a grant from the World Wildlife Fund for the creation of the Bonaire Marine Park. The park was created to maintain the coral reef ecosystem and ensure continuing returns from scuba diving, fishing and other recreational activities.

The park incorporates the entire coastline of Bonaire and neighboring Klein Bonaire. It is defined as the "sea bottom and the overlying waters from the high-water tidemark down to 200 ft (60 m)."

All visitors are asked to respect the marine park rules – no sitting on corals; no fishing or collecting of fish while scuba diving; no collecting of shells or corals, dead or alive. Spearfishing is forbidden. Anchoring is not permitted except in the harbor area off town (from the yacht club to the new pier). All craft must use permanent moorings, except for emergency anchoring. Boats of less than 12 ft may use a stone anchor.

Popular dive sites are periodically shut down to rejuvenate the corals. Moorings are removed and placed on different sites.

Dive & Snorkeling Sites

Hotels and dive shops offer daily trips to nearby offshore sites. Most are less than a 10-minute boat ride, but you don't need a boat or even a mask to see Bonaire's reefs. They grow to the surface in many areas and are visible from the shore. Excellent beach dives exist along the shores of the leeward side, where channels have been cut allowing access to deeper water. These reefs slope down to a narrow ledge at 30 ft, then drop off to between 100 and 200 ft. Expect to pay a $10 "annual" fee for using the marine park. Most of the resorts

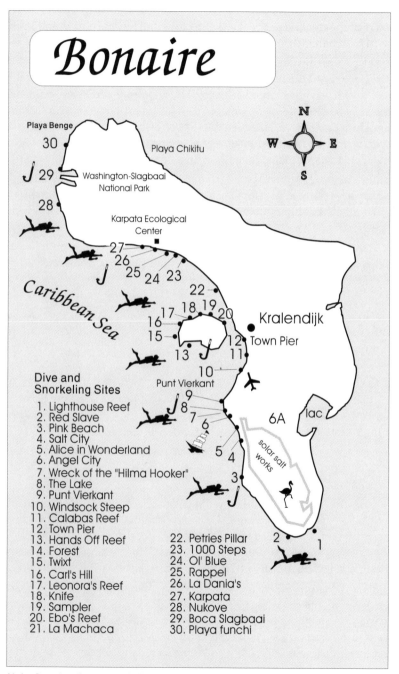

Bonaire

Playa Benge

30

Playa Chikitu

♪ 29

Washington-Slagbaai
National Park

28

Karpata Ecological
Center

27
26 25 24 23

Caribbean Sea

22

17 18 19
16   20
15

Kralendijk
●

12 Town Pier

13   11

10
Punt Vierkant

9
8
7 6

6A   lac

solar salt
works

**Dive and
Snorkeling Sites**

1. Lighthouse Reef
2. Red Slave
3. Pink Beach
4. Salt City
5. Alice in Wonderland
6. Angel City
7. Wreck of the "Hilma Hooker"
8. The Lake
9. Punt Vierkant
10. Windsock Steep
11. Calabas Reef
12. Town Pier
13. Hands Off Reef
14. Forest
15. Twixt
16. Carl's Hill
17. Leonora's Reef
18. Knife
19. Sampler
20. Ebo's Reef
21. La Machaca

22. Petries Pillar
23. 1000 Steps
24. Ol' Blue
25. Rappel
26. La Dania's
27. Karpata
28. Nukove
29. Boca Slagbaai
30. Playa funchi

5 4

3

2   1

Note: Bonaire sites are periodically closed down for rejuvenation.
Check with local dive shops for availability before diving on your own.

and dive shops offer guided snorkeling trips that include a map and instructional text materials.

☆☆☆ **Lighthouse Reef** takes its name from the nearby Willemstoren Lighthouse and is located at the southernmost point of the island. It is a shore dive, which can be entered at the lighthouse or from nearly any point west. Due to the surf, this dive is only recommended for experienced open-water divers. During calm seas, however, this site can also be dived by the novice if accompanied by a qualified dive master or instructor.

Lighthouse sparkles with sea plumes, sea fans, star, yellow-pencil, and brain corals. Marine life tends to be larger than at most other sites and includes parrot fish, schoolmasters, snappers, and sea turtles. Old anchors and chains rest in this area, the remains of ships wrecked prior to the lighthouse's 1838 opening.

☆☆☆☆ To reach **Red Slave**, drive south from Kralendijk, past the Solar Salt Works beyond the second set of slave huts. Strong currents and surf limit this site to experienced open-water divers.

The size and number of fish at Red Slave is spectacular. It is not unusual to spot four-foot tiger, yellowfin, or Nassau groupers. Gorgonians, orange crinoids, and black corals are found on the southern slope. Artifacts from pre-lighthouse wrecks rest on the slope, such as anchors and ballast stones from the 1829 shipwreck *H.M.S. Barham.*

☆☆☆☆ **Pink Beach**, named for the unusual pinkish tint of the sand, is either a boat or shore dive. Drive south from Kralendijk, past the Solar Salt Works, to the rock marked "Pink Beach." Park along the road and walk north to the beach. The mooring offshore marks the start of the dive.

Seaward of the mooring are clumps of staghorn coral and gorgonians. Schools of goatfish, porgies and horse-eye jacks feed in this area, with many large barracudas.

☆☆☆☆ One of the favorite boat dive areas is **Alice in Wonderland,** a double-reef complex, separated by a sand channel and extending from Pt. Vierkant south toward Salt Pier. A number of good dive sites exist within this reef system, all marked by dive buoys. **Angel City**, the most popular, starts at about 30 ft, then drops off to a deep channel. Swim down the first reef slope to a narrow sand channel, keeping right. One of the largest purple tube sponges you will ever see is at the channel's northern end.

Scattered throughout the shallow terrace are stands of staghorn, star, giant brain, and flower corals – home to goatfish, jacks, groupers and trunkfish. Farther down is a garden-eel colony, queen conchs, and swarms of fish. Initially,

Sea lion, Galapagos.
Photo © Marc Bernardi, Aquatic Encounters

Sally Lightfoot crab, Galapagos.
Photo © Marc Bernardi, Aquatic Encounters

Facing Page: West Wall, Grand Cayman
Photo courtesy Cayman Islands Department of Tourism

Dolphin Swim, Theatre of the Sea, Islamorada, Florida Keys.
Photo © Jon Huber

Grouper off Grand Turk Wall.
Photo © Connie Rus, Sea Eye Diving, Grand Turk

Facing Page: Wall dive, Andros, Bahamas.
Photo Courtesy Small Hope Bay Lodge

Christ of the Abyss, John Pennekamp Park, Key Largo, Florida Keys.
Photo © Monroe County Department of Tourism

Avalon Harbor, Santa Catalina.
Photo © Catalina Island Visitors Bureau

Facing Page: Shark Arena, Bahamas.
Photo Courtesy Stuart Cove's Dive South Ocean, New Providence Island

Orange barrel sponge, Jan Thiel Marine Park, Curaçao.
Courtesy Curaçao Tourist Board

Snorkeling, South Shore, Bermuda.
Courtesy Bermuda Department of Tourism

Facing Page: Snorkeling over brain coral, Half Moon Caye, Belize.
Photo by Tony Rath, Belize Tourism

Whaleshark, Galapagos.
Photo © Marc Bernardi, Aquatic Encounters

Snorkeling, Kauai.
Courtesy Sea Fun Kauai

Facing: Tube Sponge.
© Jean Michel Cousteau's Out Islands Snorkeling Adventure

Red-lipped batfish, Galapagos.
Photo © Marc Bernardi, Aquatic Encounters

Seahorses, Galapagos.
Photo © Marc Bernardi, Aquatic Encounters

Facing: Sunset, Florida Key
Photo © Jon Hube

Marble grouper, Bonaire.
Photo © Jon Huber

Shrimp on anemone, Bonaire.
Courtesy Bonaire Tourism

Facing: Cruise ship pier, Bonaire
Photo © Jon Huber

the garden eels look like a bed of grass, but will retract into the sand if you wave your arm over them.

☆☆☆ Boat dives in Bonaire are inexpensive ($16 and up) and very convenient but, if you miss the boat, **Angel City** can be reached by swimming from shore. Drive to the Trans World Radio transmitting station, south of Kralendijk – its huge tower is easy to spot. Follow a track before the station entrance, which leads to the shore. From there, enter opposite the Angel City buoy.

☆☆☆☆**Salt City** is a boat or shore dive located at the southern end of "Alice in Wonderland." To reach Salt City, drive south from Kralendijk past the salt loading pier (very visible). You'll spot a large buoy south of the pier. Enter along the left "bank" formed by the large "sand river," a wide sand stretch that eventually drops off the shallow terrace into a short, reef slope "island."

The terrace is landscaped with star, fire, elkhorn and staghorn corals. Sea life is superb, featuring scad, palometa, big groupers, snappers, garden eels, tilefish and French angelfish.

☆☆☆ **The _Hilma Hooker_**, a 250-ft freighter, lies right offshore just north of Angel City Reef. Reached from the beach or by boat, this is Bonaire's most spectacular and notorious shipwreck. The ship was seized during a drug raid when a member of the Antillean Coast Guard discovered a false bulkhead. The crew abandoned the freighter and fled the island. Because of an unmanageable leak, Bonaire law enforcement agents were afraid that the ship would sink and damage the reefs, so they towed the ship out to where she now lies, creating an intriguing dive site. The wreck rests on a sandy bottom at 91 ft. Divers should stay outside the wreck and monitor bottom time.

☆☆☆☆ **The Lake** is yet another part of the "Alice in Wonderland" complex. Sea plumes, purple tube sponges and a profusion of groupers, coneys, rock hinds and moray eels are in residence.

☆☆☆ **Punt Vierkant** is marked by the first buoy past the small lighthouse north of the "Alice in Wonderland" complex. To reach the site, drive south from Kralendijk past the Belnam residential area and toward the lighthouse. On the swim out you'll be joined by trunkfish, groupers and snappers. As you descend, the fish are larger and the rays more numerous. Pastel gorgonians and sponges decorate the wall.

☆☆☆ **Windsock Steep** is known for great snorkeling. This dive is off the small sand beach opposite the airport runway. Watch out for fire coral as you explore the shallow terrace. The bottom is sandy, but stacked up with sergeant majors, angelfish, snappers, trumpetfish and barracudas.

Facing: Woman kissing dolphin.
Courtesy UNEXSO, Grand Bahama

☆☆☆☆ **Calabas Reef**, just off the beach in front of the Divi Flamingo Resort, is reached by swimming over a sand shelf. Giant brain and star corals grow from the slope. Old anchors are scattered about. To the north is a small sailboat wreck. The hotel pier is well lit after dusk, making it an easily accessible and attractive night-dive spot.

Reef inhabitants are parrot fish, French angels, damsels, Spanish hogfish and yellow snappers. Spotted, goldentail and chain morays peek out from the crevices.

☆☆☆☆**Town Pier** refers to the "old pier" in the center of town, between the customs office and the fish market. Both the Town Pier and the neighboring new cruise-ship pier are popular for night dives. Bright sponge crabs and several species of decorator crabs materialize with darkness, disappear with daylight. Because water entry and finding one's way around the maze of pilings gets tricky, we find this site more interesting, and much more fun as a guided tour with Bonaire's "Touch-the-Sea" guru, Dee Scarr. She knows where to find all the good stuff. For details, contact Dee from the US, ☎ 011-599-7-8529.

For safety reasons, diving under the piers is subject to permission from the Harbormaster. All divers must check into the Harbormaster's office, located at the old fort with the cannon, next to the main government building, ☎ 8151. Double-check with the tugboat captain on duty before entering the water.

☆☆☆ Off the main road, in front of the Habitat dive shop is *La Machaca*. Ideal for night and warm-up dives, this site is named after a small, wrecked fishing boat. Every variety of fish found in Bonaire's waters can be seen here by divers and snorkelers. Mr. Roger, a huge green moray, along with an old tiger grouper, friendly rock beauties, and two black margates inhabit the wreck.

☆☆☆ **Petries Pillar** derives its name from the colony of pillar coral that grows on the reef face. To reach this site travel north toward Gotomeer, turn left about 4/10 of a mile after the last house onto an unpaved road. Follow that road down to the sea. Fine for boat or shore entry.

☆☆☆☆☆ **1,000 Steps (Piedra Haltu)** may be either a boat or a shore dive, though a boat dive may be easier and will definitely save you carrying your gear down the (actual count, 67) steps. To reach 1,000 Steps, drive north from town along the scenic road towards Gotomeer until you reach the entrance of the Radio Nederland transmitting station. On your left are steep concrete steps leading down the mountainside to a sandy beach and the site.

Swim through the marked channel to a sandy shallow terrace. Gorgonians and flower corals are abundant. Lavender shrimp, barracuda, black durgons, yellowtail snappers, horse-eye jacks and schoolmasters populate the reef.

☆☆☆☆ **Ol' Blue**, a favorite with snorkelers for its walls of reef fish, cleaning stations and calm waters, may get choppy when the wind kicks up. Get there by driving north along the scenic road to Gotomeer past the transmitting station to the white coral-rubble beach. The dive site is where the road descends to the ocean and the cliff bends away from the road.

☆☆☆☆☆ **Rappel**, one of the best dives on the island, was named for its sheer cliff face. Divers have been known to "rappel" down the wall. Usually a boat dive, it may also be reached by swimming out from Karpata.

Rappel's exceptional marine life includes orange seahorses, green moray eels, spiny lobster, squid, marbled grouper, orange tube coral, shrimp, encrusting sponges, black coral and dense pink-tipped anemones.

☆☆☆☆☆**Nukove** lies off a little road between Boca Dreifi and Playa Frans. It is a particularly nice shore dive with a channel cut through the jungle of elkhorn coral that grows to the surface.

Numerous juveniles, shrimp and anemones may be seen in the cut. To the south are huge sponges, black coral, crinoids and sheet and scroll corals. Scrawled filefish, black durgons, grouper, wrasses and barracuda are in residence.

☆☆☆☆ **Boca Slagbaai** provides opportunity to see the best examples of buttress formations in Bonaire water. In addition, green morays, white spotted filefish, tarpon and barracudas are in abundance. Slagbaai boasts six concrete cannon replicas, halved and buried for the 1974 film, *Shark Treasure*.

To reach this dive, drive through the village of Rincon into Washington/Slagbaai National Park, where you will follow the green arrows to Slagbaai. The center of the bay is sand, but a swim to the north brings you across ridges and valleys of coral. Excellent snorkeling is to the south, where two real cannons may be viewed at the southernmost point of the bay.

☆☆☆☆ **Playa Funchi**, in Washington/Slagbaai National Park, is another popular snorkeling area. From Rincon, follow the green or yellow signs. Enter next to the man-made pier and swim north for the best snorkeling. Rays, parrot fish, rock hinds, jacks, groupers and angels swim through fields of staghorn coral. On shore, picnickers are greeted by hoards of fearless lizards in search of scraps.

Klein Bonaire

The dive sites surrounding Klein Bonaire are great for both diving and snorkeling. Some may be closed down for rejuvenation.

☆☆☆☆☆ **Leonora's Reef**, on the north side, is a snorkeler's paradise heavily covered with yellow pencil coral, fire coral, star coral and elkhorn stands on a narrow shallow terrace. West of the mooring are pillar coral formations. Expect to be greeted by masses of fish. "Attack" yellowtail snappers and tiny royal blue fish are joined at cleaning stations by tiger, yellowmount and rare yellowfin groupers.

☆☆☆☆ **Hands Off Reef** was named in 1981 when an experiment was conducted to determine whether inexperienced and camera-carrying divers do more damage to the corals than others. "Hands Off," as the name implies, was not to be dived by photographers or resort course classes, designated solely as a control for later comparison to unlimited-access dives.

The reef slope is alive with black margate, grouper, rockhinds, parrots. Some of the narrow valleys of the drop-off zone contain the remains of coral-head "avalanches" worth exploring.

☆☆☆☆ Nearby is **Forest**, another fabulous snorkeling and diving spot. The reef starts at 15 ft, dropping off to undiveable depths. This site is named for the abundant black coral "trees" growing from the wall at 60 ft. Two-ft queen triggerfish, morays, filefish, black durgons, puffers and an abundance of small critters roam the "forest."

☆☆☆☆☆ **Twixt** is just north of Forest, around the southwest bend of Klein Bonaire. It provides excellent opportunities for wide-angle photography, with huge basket sponges, sea whips, black coral, enormous pastel fans, tube sponges and star corals. Depths range from 15 to 100 ft. The coral wall slopes down to a sandy bottom. Seas are almost always calm and flat here.

☆☆☆☆ Large groupers frequent the pillar coral cleaning station at the upper edge of **Carl's Hill**. Named after photographer Carl Roessler, this spot is great for snorkeling and diving. The drop-off begins at 15 ft and drops sharply to 80 ft, creating a narrow precipice called Venus Mound. An occasional strong current cleanses the huge purple finger sponges on the slope. West of the mooring, divers will find a buttress and sand valley, lined with coral rocks and cleaning stations – areas where fish line up to have barber or "cleaner" shrimp pick parasites from their mouths.

☆☆☆☆ **Ebo's Reef** (aka Jerry's Jam) is superb for video and still photography. Shallow enough for snorkeling, the drop-off starts at 20 ft and slopes off to a sandy bottom at 150 ft. Dramatic overhangs of black coral grow in less than 30 ft of water. Masses of grunts, Spanish hogfish, groupers, sergeant majors, parrot fish and yellowtail swarm the shelf. Small tunnels along the shelf are good hiding places for juvenile fish and small critters.

☆☆☆☆ **Knife Reef** is excellent for snorkeling and diving. A shallow, half-circle of elkhorn coral creates a mini "lagoon" protecting star coral heads, gorgonians, and a multitude of fish. Bermuda chubs, peacock flounders, lizardfish and yellowhead jawfish rove the shallow terrace. The drop-off zone is fairly barren (the result of reef slides), but gorgonians, stinging coral, and yellow pencils thrive.

☆☆☆☆ Another snorkeler's delight is **Sampler**. Resident spotted eels and hordes of tamed, friendly fish will charm you as you investigate the lovely pillar- and staghorn-coral formations.

Touch the Sea

Learn to pet moray eels, tickle sea anemones, get a manicure from a cleaner shrimp, massage the tummy of a "deadly" scorpionfish and befriend marine animals from which one normally keeps a safe distance. Diving with Touch-the-Sea creator Dee Scarr is an experience divers won't soon forget.

Ms. Scarr recommends that divers not try these antics without first participating in her program, which includes classroom and underwater time. Bring or rent a camera; you'll enjoy shooting these normally hard-to-approach creatures.

Arrangements to dive with Dee Scarr must be made prior to your trip to Bonaire by writing to her c/o Touch the Sea, PO Box 369, Bonaire, Netherlands Antilles, or calling 8529 on the island. From the US, ☎ 011-599-7-8529. A maximum of four divers may participate in one dive. Touch the Sea programs close during summer months.

In the US, specialized land programs are offered for universities and groups.

"Touch the Sea" is a PADI Specialty Certification available to all certified divers. Environmentalist Dee Scarr is author of *Touch the Sea, Coral's Reef,* a children's book, and *The Gentle Sea.*

Dive Operators

 For local calls, dial just the last four digits of the phone numbers listed.

Black Durgon Scuba Center, at the Black Durgeon Inn, offers reef and wreck diving trips by reservation. Resort and certification courses. ☎ 011-599-7-5736, fax 011-5-997-8846. E-mail: bkdurgon@bonairelive.com. Write to: PO Box 200, Bonaire, NA.

Buddy Dive at the Buddy Beach & Dive Resort offers trips and courses from beginner through instructor, including Nitrox. All courses can be conducted in four different languages. This PADI five-star, Gold Palm IDC center features the only drive-through airfill station in the Caribbean, possibly the world. The center also has a photo/retail shop, repair shop, rental shop, lockers and rinse basins. They offer guided dives from their boat or from the shore. The shop is

Courtesy Buddy Dive Center

The Caribbean's first drive-through air-fill station at Buddy Dive Center.

beachfront and reef front – just one giant stride in. A la carte rates: shore dive $12, one-tank boat dive $32, two-tank boat dive $60, snorkel boat trip $12. Unlimited airfills for six days $99. ☎ 599-7-5080, fax 599-7-8647. E-mail: buddydive@ibm.net.

Carib Inn Dive Shop is a full-service dive shop at the Carib Inn that features reef trips, beach diving, instruction, equipment sales, rental and repair. Use of a tank costs $12 per day, $5 for an additional fill. Boat trips, $15. Regulator with combo and octopus rig rents for $7 per day. Use of BCD, $7 per day. Snorkeling gear, $7. Computer, $10 per day. Their beach-diving package costs $99 for unlimited airfills and use of tank for six days includes weights and belt; $279 buys 12 boat dives over six days with unlimited airfills and use of tank with weights and belt. PADI referrals. PADI courses from resort to dive master. ☎ 011-599-7-8819, fax 011-599-7-5295, or write PO Box 68, Bonaire, NA. E-mail: bruce@caribinn.com.

Dee Scarr's "Touch the Sea" meets at the town pier and features personalized dives with an opportunity to interact with reef fish, moray eels. Super photo opportunities. Diving with Dee is a real treat. Closes during summer. ☎ 011-599-7-8529.

Dive Inn, next door to the Sunset Inn, offers scuba packages, PADI courses, reef trips, picnic trips. Six days of unlimited shore diving costs $99; add six boat dives for a total of $175. ☎ 011-599-7-8761, fax 011-599-7-8513. Or write PO Box 362, Bonaire, NA. E-mail: diveinn@bonairenet.com.

Slave huts.

Photo © Jon Huber

Bonaire

Peter Hughes Dive Bonaire, at the Divi Beach Resort & Casino, specializes in reef trips; resort certification and advanced courses; underwater photo and video courses. Daily E-6 and color print processing. Equipment sales, rental, and repair. Dive packages. ☎ 011-599-7-8285, fax 011-7-8252 in Bonaire. E-mail: george@bonairenet.com.

Sand Dollar Dive and Photo, within the Sand Dollar Condominium Resort complex, offers PADI certification, advanced, rescue, and divemaster courses. Reef trips, park trips, underwater photo and video courses. Same-day E-6 and print processing. Equipment sales, rental and repair. Fishing, sailing, snorkeling, water skiing. ☎ 800-288-4773, or 011-599-7-5252, fax 011-599-7-8760.   E-mail: sand$dive@bonairenet.com.   Website: www.interknowledge.com/bonaire/sanddollar.

Sunset Beach Dive Center offers full PADI certification, six days of shore diving for $99; add six boat dives for a total of $175. ☎ 011-599-7-8330. E-mail: sunsetdive@bonairenet.com.

Toucan Diving at the Plaza Resort Bonaire offers a variety of shore and boat-dive packages, courses including Nitrox ($193), advanced open water certification ($363), referrals ($223), rescue diver ($383), rusty diver ($96) and resort course ($77). ☎ 011-599-7-2500, fax 011-599-7-7133.

Jerry Schnabel & Dos Winkel's Underwater Photo Tours, adjacent to Toucan Diving, offers still and video equipment and tours. ☎ 011-599-7-2500.

Great Adventures Bonaire, at the Harbour Village Beach Resort, offers certification and underwater photography programs, boat and shore dives, night dives and equipment rental. ☎ 800-424-0004, 011-599-7-7500, fax 7505. E-mail: harbourvillage@bonairelive.com.

Habitat Dive Center at Captain Don's Habitat is a PADI facility offering resort, certification and advanced courses, reef trips and 24-hour shore diving. ☎ 800-327-6709, 011-599-7-8290, fax 011-599-7-8240, or write PO Box 88, Bonaire, NA. E-mail: jack@habitatdiveresorts.com.

Accommodations

Rates subject to change.

 For local calls, dial only the last four digits of the phone numbers listed.

Bonaire's entire tourist trade revolves around its beautiful reefs. All but three of the island's hotels were built in the last 20 years and are designed especially to accommodate divers. All have dive shops attached or nearby. Money saving dive/accommodation packages can be arranged through any hotel listed below. Rates listed are winter prices.

Buddy Beach & Dive Resort sits just north of Kralendijk, offering 68 luxury oceanfront apartments with cable TV, air-conditioning, fully equipped kitchens, nicely furnished living rooms. Restaurant and PADI five-star training facility on premises. Pool. Rooms range from $97 to $254 per night. Drive and dive packages, from $989 per person for seven nights, include six boat dives, unlimited airfills for six days, vehicle rental (often a pick-up truck). ☎ 800-359-0747 for Rothschild Dive/Travel packages, 800-786-3483 for Caribbean Dive Tours; direct 011-599-7-5080, fax 011-599-7-8647. E-mail: marketing@buddydive.com.

Bruce Bowker's Carib Inn has 13 guest rooms. Oceanfront accommodations are air-conditioned and have cable TV. Maid service, pool. Full-service scuba facilities. Studio/one-bedroom, $99-$119, two bedrooms $139. ☎ 011-599-7-8819 or write PO Box 68, Bonaire, NA. E-mail: caribinn@bonairenet.com.

Divi Flamingo Resort & Casino is a beachfront resort on the beach overlooking Calabas Reef. A few rooms have balconies directly over the water where you can view the reef and see fish swimming by. All rooms are air-conditioned with private bath. Two pools, tennis, jacuzzi. Two open-air restaurants, casino, dive shop. Room rates for winter are: standard, $150; deluxe, $240. Credit cards accepted. ☎ 800-367-3484, direct 011-599-7-8285, or write Divi Hotels, 6340 Quadrangle Drive, Suite 300, Chapel, NC 27514.

Lions Dive Hotel Bonaire features 42 ocean-view, one- and two-bedroom apartments with patio or balcony, each with a fully equipped kitchen. Amenities are freshwater pool with sundeck, waterfront restaurant and dive shop, diving and fitness school. Winter rates for a suite are from $160-$395 per day, a two-bedroom suite from $315. ☎ 888-546-6734 or 800-786-3483; direct 011-599-7-5580, fax 01-599-7-5680.

Plaza Resort Bonaire, a 198-unit luxury hotel, offers divers full service through the on-premises Toucan Diving shop and school, with IDD, PADI, and NAUI instruction, custom dive boats, rental equipment and classroom facilities. The Sports and Entertainment Department provides snorkeling, water-skiing, banana boating, knee boarding, tube rides, windsurfing, kayaking, tennis, beach volleyball, aqua jogging, water-polo, body-fit training and has Boston Whalers and catamarans for rent. The casino features 80 slot machines, roulette, and card games. Recent additions to this plush resort include a Mexican restaurant, racquetball and squash court, basketball court, minimarket, first-aid center, jogging track, playground, still and video camera rental. Jr. suite rates per day in winter (December 18-April 15) are $180-$400. Dive packages available. ☎ 800 766-6016 or 800-786-DIVE; direct 011-599-7-2500, fax 011-599-7-7133.

Harbour Village Beach Resort sits opposite Klein Bonaire on a powdery sand beach close to town. Sixty-four spacious air-conditioned rooms, one- and two-bedroom suites with French doors leading to patios or terraces, cable TV, telephones, hair dryers. Pool, three restaurants, bar, marina, dive shop. Meeting and banquet facilities. Rooms are $275-$405; suites, $445-$705. Packages available. ☎ 800-424-0004; in Bonaire, 011-599-7-7500, fax 011-599-7-7507. E-mail: harbourvillage@bonarielive.com.

Captain Don's Habitat offers deluxe, oceanfront cottages, cabanas, villas, studios. Rates are from $195 to $485 daily. Entire villas from $420-$485 daily. Dive shop, open-air restaurant, bar, pool, gift shop. Credit cards accepted. ☎ 800-327-6709 or 011-599-7-8290; fax 305-438-4220 or 011-599- 7-8240, or write PO Box 115, Bonaire NA. Guests who are certified divers can take out tanks and dive the reef off the beach 24 hours a day. E-mail: maduro@netpoint.net.   Website: www.habitatdiveresorts.com   or www.maduro.com.

The Sunset Inn, overlooking Kralendijk Bay, comprises five double rooms and two suites within walking distance of town. Accommodations are air-conditioned, have refrigerators, electronic safes and remote cable TV. Rates from $80 to $100. ☎ 800-328-2288, 407-774-9000 or 011-599-7-8291, fax 011-599-7-8118.

Sand Dollar Condominium Resort features luxurious, air-conditioned ocean front condominiums with kitchens, private baths, cable TV, balcony or terrace. Dive shop on premises with excellent diving and snorkeling off the beach. Tennis, pool bar, grocery store, sailing, babysitting. Studios, $155 summer, $165 winter; one-bedrooms, $180 summer, $215 winter; two-

Bonaire landscape.

bedrooms, $200 summer, $220 winter. Packages. For meals add $45 per day, per person. ☎ 800-288-4773, 407-774-9322 or 011-599-7-8738, fax 011-599-7-8760.   E-mail: sanddollar@bonairenet.com.   Website: www.interknowledge.com/bonaire/sanddollar.

Happy Holiday Homes rents one-, two- or three-bedroom homes with air-conditioning, living room, US cable TV and radio, dining room, fully equipped kitchen, patio and barbecue area. All are close to southern beaches. Rates start at $75 per day. Call for brochure: ☎ 610-459-8100, ext. 204, or 011-599-7-8405,   fax   011-5997-8605.   E-mail: 103665.1405@ compuserve.com. Website: www.interknowledge.com/bonaire /happy- holiday.

Other Activities

Exploring **Washington-Slagbaai Park** is a nice day's alternative to diving. One of the first national parks in the Caribbean, it is home to over 190 species of birds, thousands of towering candle cacti, herds of goats, stray donkeys, lizards and more lizards. The park covers the entire northern portion of the island. Its terrain is varied and those who are ambitious enough to climb some of the steep hills are rewarded with sweeping views.

Cars can be taken through the park. Two driving trails offer visitors a thorough tour of the park or a shorter excursion. A map, available at the entrance gate, indicates points of interest. The park is open from 8 am to 5 pm, though no one is permitted to enter after 3:30 pm. Small entrance fee. Be sure to pack a picnic lunch, binoculars, a camera, sunscreen and plenty of drinking water. Opportunities for exotic bird photography are outstanding.

Driving south you'll pass roadside cliffs with 500-year-old Arawak Indian inscriptions. Just beyond is **Rincon**, the island's oldest village. A drive to the southern tip of the island will bring you past primitive stone huts that were once homes to slaves working the salt flats. It is hard to imagine how six slaves shared one hut when you see the small size of them. Nearby, 30-foot obelisks were built in 1838 to help mariners locate their anchorages. Farther down is the island's oldest lighthouse, **Willemstoren**, built in 1837.

*A few **flamingos** can always be seen at the Gotomeer salt ponds, but much larger flamingo congregations take shelter at the solar salt flats on the southern end of the island. You must watch from the road as the area is a sanctuary, but the huge gathering of birds (10,000 to 15,000) makes a spectacular display. Every day at sunset, the entire flock flies the short trip to Venezuela. During spring, a highlight is seeing the fluffy gray young. It is only after months of consuming brine shrimp that they attain their characteristic pink color. Since the birds are extremely shy, bring binoculars.*

Guided bus tours of the national park or entire island are available through **Bonaire Sightseeing Tours, ☎** 8778, or **Baranka Tours, ☎** 2200.

Ernest van Vliet's **Windsurfing Bonaire** features top-of-the-line equipment and classes for beginners to advanced board sailors. Production or custom boards can be rented by the hour, day or week. He even provides transportation to and from island resorts twice a day.

Tours through the tiny capital city of **Kralendijk** ("coral dike" in Dutch) are highlighted by the colorful, well-preserved buildings such as Fort Oranje, Queen Wilhelmina Park, Government House and the miniature Greek temple-style fish market. The town pier makes for an interesting stop, as do any one of Kralendijk's open-air bars and restaurants. Sunset watching is best from Pink Beach at the southeastern end of the island.

Dining

Restaurants in Bonaire offer a unique selection of local, Creole and seafood dishes. Enjoy a delicious Cantonese dinner at the **China Garden Restau-**

rant (☎ 8480) – an old restored mansion at 47 Kaya Grandi; or Caribbean seafood and steak dishes at **Banana Tree Restaurant** (☎ 2500) at the Plaza Resort. Driving a few miles north of Kralendijk on the coast road brings you to the **Bonaire Caribbean Club** (☎ 7901) for a cozy seaside and caveside lunch or dinner (bring bug repellent). Chefs at the **Beefeater Restaurant** (☎ 7776), Playa Grande # 3, will prepare a banquet of fish or steak dishes at your table. Vegetarian favorites are found at **Je Mar Terrace** (☎ 5012), Kaya Grandi 5.

Carry-out and sit-down casual meals are offered by the **Green Parrot Restaurant** at the Sand Dollar Condominium Resort (☎ 5454).

Local foods include juwana, a stew or soup made from local iguana; piska hasa, a fried fish dish served with funchi and fried plantains; tutu, funchi with frills – cornmeal mush with black-eyed peas; and goat stew made with onions, peppers, tomato, soy sauce and spices.

In Kralendijk, local dishes are served at the **Supercorner** on Kaya Simon Bolivar (☎ 8115); **Seumar's** on Kaya Simon Bolivar; and **Kunuku Warahama** on Kaminda Lac. Fast food lovers will delight in finding **Kentucky Fried Chicken** and **Cozzoli's Pizza** in the Harborside Mall.

Facts

Helpful Phone Numbers: Police, ☎ 8000; taxi, ☎ 8100; airport, ☎ 8500; San Francisco Hospital, ☎ 8000 or 8900.

Nearest Recompression Chamber: San Francisco Hospital on the island.

Getting There: ALM offers regularly scheduled service to Bonaire's Flamingo International Airport from Miami and Atlanta. Air Aruba offers direct service out of Newark, Baltimore, Miami, Philadelphia and Tampa. American Airlines offers regularly scheduled service to Curacao with connections via ALM to Bonaire. Guyana Airways from La Guardia connects with ALM in Curacao.

Driving: Foreign and international licenses accepted. Traffic to the right.

Language: The official language for Bonaire is Dutch, but residents speak Papiamento – a blend of Dutch, African and English. English and Spanish are widely spoken.

Documents: US and Canadian citizens may stay up to three months providing they prove citizenship with a valid passport, birth certificate or a voter's registration card accompanied by a photo identification.

All visitors should have a confirmed room reservation before arriving and a return ticket. A visa is required for visits over 90 days.

Customs: US citizens may bring home $400 worth of articles including one quart of liquor and 200 cigarettes. Canadian citizens may bring in C $300 of goods once each calendar year.

Currency: Netherlands Antilles florin or guilder, but US dollars are widely accepted. US $1=NA fl 1.77.

Credit Cards: Widely accepted.

Climate: Mean temperature 82°F year-round; 22 inches rainfall annually.

Clothing: Casual lightweight. A wetsuit is not necessary most of the year, but water temperatures occasionally drop down in mid-winter, especially in late January and February.

Electricity: 127 volts, 50 cycles. Adapters are necessary.

Time: Atlantic (EST + 1 hr).

Tax: Airport departure tax, $10.

Religious Services: Roman Catholic, Seventh Day Adventist, Jehovah's Witnesses.

Additional Information: Tourism Corporation Bonaire, 10 Rockefeller Plaza, Suite 900, NY, NY 10020. ☎ 800-BONAIRE (266-2473). E-mail: 102372.3337@ compuserve.com. Website: www.bonaire.org.

Bonaire

British Virgin Islands

Windswept and wildly beautiful, the British Virgins encompass more than 60 sparsely inhabited islands and rocks that lie 60 miles east of Puerto Rico. Most tourist activity centers around the four larger islands Tortola, Anegada, Virgin Gorda and Jost Van Dyke. Except for Anegada, which is a flat coral slab surrounded by shallow reefs, the islands are mountainous and of volcanic origin. The highest point is 1,781-ft Mt. Sage on Tortola.

The capital and chief port is Road Town on Tortola, the largest island and home to 80% of the BVI residents, with a population of 17,000. A toll bridge connects Tortola to Beef Island and the international airport. An efficient ferry service, in some cases a short hop by light aircraft, takes visitors to the other main islands of Virgin Gorda, Jost Van Dyke and Anegada. Other BVI islands include Cooper Island, Ginger Island, The Dogs, Great Camanoe, Necker Island, Guana Island, Mosquito Island, Peter Island and Eustatia Island.

Save for a few clubs and discos, nightlife consists of stargazing and moonlit dives. Overall, BVI life is relaxed, yet retains some British formality in terms of dignity and manners. Crime is rare and nudity is not encouraged. Visitors are asked to respect the residents' wishes by covering up in town and dressing "appropriately" in restaurants and bars.

The BVI's prime attractions are its sheltered coves, isolated beaches and protected marine parks. Superb snorkeling and diving exists around the out islands with towering coral pinnacles, underwater caves, canyons, massive boulders, lava tunnels and almost 200 different wrecks. Most areas have little surge and only gentle currents. Visibility runs from from 50 to over 100 ft.

Clustered around the Sir Francis Drake Channel and protected from high wind and waves, the islands are enormously popular with sailors. In fact, half the BVI tourist "beds" are aboard the hundreds of yachts in Tortola's marinas.

The best time to visit the BVI is between October and June, with warmest water temperatures between mid-March and early December. Reduced rates at hotels and on charter boats are available from May through November. Hurricane season is from July through October. Air temperature ranges between 80 and 90°F year-round with an occasional drop in February.

History

In 1493 Christoper Columbus discovered the islands and named them St. Ursula y las Once Mil Virgenes (St. Ursula and the Eleven Thousand Virgins.)

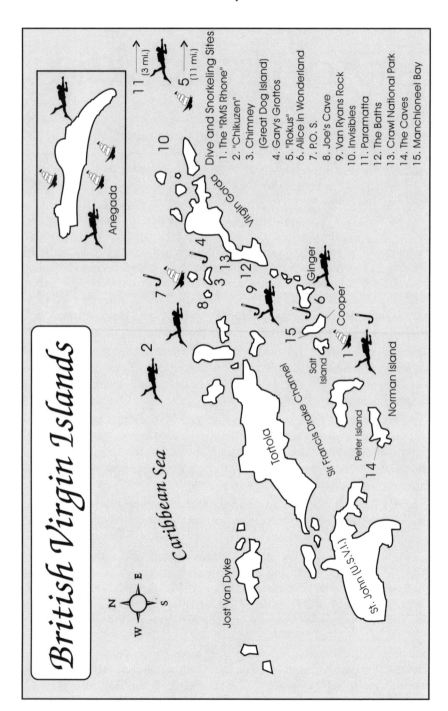

British Virgin Islands

Caribbean Sea

Jost Van Dyke

Tortola

Sir Francis Drake Channel

Salt Island

Peter Island

Norman Island

St. John (U.S.V.I.)

Cooper

Ginger

Virgin Gorda

Anegada

Dive and Snorkeling Sites

1. The "RMS Rhone"
2. "Chikuzen"
3. Chimney
   (Great Dog Island)
4. Gary's Grottos
5. "Rokus"
6. Alice in Wonderland
7. P.O.S.
8. Joe's Cave
9. Van Ryans Rock
10. Invisibles
11. Paramatta
12. The Baths
13. Crawl National Park
14. The Caves
15. Manchioneel Bay

11 (3 mi.)
5 (11 mi.)

At that time peaceful tribes of Indians roamed the BVI and remained its principal residents until the turn of the 17th century.

During the 1500s, pirates set up base on Tortola, an ideal spot to attack ships trying to navigate the treacherous reefs of Sir Francis Drake Channel. Buccaneers such as Blackbeard Teach, Bluebeard, and Sir Francis Drake became legendary.

By 1672, the pirates were forced out by English planters who, with slave labor, developed the land for farming. They thrived on the export of bananas, sugarcane, citrus fruits, coconuts, mangoes and root crops until slavery was abolished in the early 1800s. Today, tourism has replaced agriculture as the islands' largest employer. Politically, the islands are a British colony administered by an executive council with a governor.

Best Dive & Snorkeling Sites

☆☆☆☆☆ **Wreck of the *R.M.S. Rhone***, featured in the movie *The Deep*, is by far the most popular dive in the BVI. Struck by a ferocious hurricane in October, 1867, the Royal Mail Steamer *Rhone* was hurled onto the rocks at Salt Island as its captain, Robert F. Wooley, struggled desperately to reach open sea.

The force with which the 310-ft vessel crashed upon the rocks broke the hull in two, leaving two superb dive spots – a great snorkeling area at the stern, which lies in 30 ft of water amid rocks and boulders, and a good area for diving at the bow, 80 ft down on a sandy bottom. The top of the rudder sits just 15 ft below the surface. Its superstructure, encrusted with corals, sponges, and sea fans, provides a dramatic setting for underwater photography.

Fish greet divers and snorkelers as they enter the water. Living among the wreckage is a 300-pound jewfish, a very curious four-ft barracuda named Fang, schools of snappers, grunts, jacks, arrow crabs, squirrel fish, and yellowtail. The *Rhone* is a boat-access dive. Sea conditions are usually calm; recommended for novices. Visibility is usually excellent, from 50 to over 100 ft. Also, The *Rhone* is a national park and off-limits for coral collecting and spearfishing. The wreck is located off Black Rock Point on the southwest tip of Salt Island.

☆☆☆☆ **The *Chikuzen***, a 268-ft steel-hulled refrigerator ship that went down off Tortola's east end in 1981, lies in 75 ft of water. Currently in use as a fish condominium, the wreck is blessed with visibility so good that you can stand on the bow and see the stern.

Tenants of the *Chikuzen* include several large sting rays, occasional black tip sharks, schools of yellowtail, filefish, barracudas, octopus, drum fish, and jewfish. The ship rests on her port side, allowing easy entry. Coral covers the hull. A fine choice for novice divers. By boat access only. The outstanding visibility and large number of marine animals make for excellent photography.

☆☆☆ **The Chimney**, located at Great Dog Island off the west end of Virgin Gorda, is a spectacular coral archway and canyon covered with a wide variety of soft corals, sponges and rare white coral. Hundreds of fish follow divers and snorkelers along the archway to a coral-wrapped, tube-like formation resembling a huge chimney. Inside the Chimney are circling groupers, crabs, brittle starfish, spiny lobsters, banded coral shrimp, queen angels, tube sponges and schooling fish. This is a favorite spot for close-up photography. Maximum depth of the Chimney is 45 ft. The many shallow areas and protected-cove location make this a "best snorkel dive," as well as a good selection for the scuba diver. Boat access only. Some surge and currents when wind is out of the north.

☆☆☆ **The *M/V Inganess*** , a wreck sunk by BVI dive operators as an artificial reef after a storm snapped its anchor chain, lies off the southern tip of Cooper Island. The 136-ft freighter sits in 95 ft of water, its masts at 45 ft. Two national park moorings mark the sight. A good show of invertebrates and fish inhabit the wreck. Boat access.

☆☆☆ **Mountain Point** lies near the shoreline, four miles north of Spanish Town on Virgin Gorda. It is a shallow reef characterized by three huge arches which give the feel of swimming through a tunnel. At the end of the "tunnel" divers find a cave guarded by a friendly moray. This rocky area is teeming with shrimp, squid and sponges. The site is susceptible to north swells, but when calm the cove is a choice spot for a night dive. The average depth is 30 ft.

☆☆ **Great Dog Island's** south side drops off to a shallow reef with 10-to-60-ft depths. Nice elkhorn stands hide spotted and golden moray eels, spiny lobster and barber shrimp. Good for novice divers when seas are calm.

☆☆☆☆☆ **Alice in Wonderland**, a coral wall at South Bay off Ginger Island, slopes from 45 ft to a sandy bottom at 75 ft, with most interest at 60 ft. Named for its huge mushroom corals, villainous overhangs, and gallant brain corals, this ornate reef shelters long nose butterfly fish, rays, conch and garden eels. Visibility is good and seas are usually calm. Alice in Wonderland is a boat dive, good for photography, free diving, and novice through expert scuba diving.

☆☆☆ **Blonde Rock**, a pinnacle between Dead Chest and Salt Island, starts at 15 ft below the surface. Coral-encrusted tunnels, caves and overhangs support a wealth of crabs, lobsters and reef fish. Good for novice divers when seas are calm. Boat access.

☆☆☆ **Santa Monica Rock**, a sea mount, sits about a mile south of Norman Island. Depths range from 10 to 90 ft. Currents attract spotted eagle rays, sharks and other pelagics.

☆☆☆ **Joe's Cave**, an underwater cavern on the west side of West Dog Island, can be explored by swimming from the entrance at 20 ft down to 75 ft, where you'll find a magnificent opening to the sky. Corals and boulders form the cave's outer walls. Eels abound. Rough bottom terrain accents the masses of gleaming copper sweepers inside. During periods of north swell, this area can get rough, but more often calm seas prevail. Skill level required varies with weather.

☆☆☆ **Van Ryan's Rock**, in Drake's Channel, sits off collision Point on Virgin Gorda. The top is at 16 ft and the bottom at 55 ft, with boulders and coral leading down to a sandy plain. Nurse sharks, eels, huge turtles, lobster, jacks, spade fish, and barracuda circle it. Divers should take care to avoid the huge clumps of fire coral. A strong current is occasionally encountered. Experienced divers. No national park moorings.

☆☆☆ **Invisibles**, a sea mount off Tortola's northeast tip, is a haven for nurse sharks, eels, turtles and all types of reef fish from the smallest to the largest. Diver Gayla Kilbride describes this area as a "Symphony of Fish." Depths go from three ft to 65 ft, a nice range for both snorkeling and diving.

Snorkeling

Snorkeling gear may be rented or borrowed from most hotels and charter boats, although it is best to have your own to insure a comfortable fit. Be sure to bring your camera. Snorkeling trips are offered by the dive shops.

☆☆☆☆ **The Baths**, at the southern tip of Virgin Gorda, encompasses the islands' most famous beaches. The area, a natural landscape of partially submerged grottoes and caves formed by a jumble of enormous granite boulders, is a favorite beach-access snorkeling area and one of the biggest tourist attractions in the BVI. The caves shelter a variety of tropical fish. Find this area by taking the trail that starts at the end of the Baths Road. A small bar just off the beach rents snorkel equipment. Beware of the dinghies while you are snorkeling! There are a lot of them in the area. The Baths is a favorite of cruise ship visitors.

☆☆ **Spring Bay**, neighboring the Baths, has a gorgeous sandy beach and good snorkeling.

☆☆ **Crawl National Park**, a great spot for beginning snorkelers, also on Virgin Gorda, is reached via a palm-lined trail from Tower Road, just north of the Baths. A natural pond created by a boulder formation is ideal for children.

☆☆☆ **Smugglers Cove**, off the beaten path on the northwest end of Tortola, may be tough to find but is well worth the effort. The last mile leading

British Virgin Islands

to this spot is rough driving. There are two lovely reefs, about 100 ft out, with crowds of grunts, squirrel fish, parrot fish and some good-sized trunk fish to keep you company. Depths are shallow and seas usually calm. Good for children. The beach is shaded by palms and sea grape trees. No restrooms or changing facilities, but there is an honor bar with sodas, beer and some snacks and a phone with a couple of taxi numbers.

Guests of the neighboring Long Bay Beach Resort are shuttled to Smugglers Cove twice a day.

☆☆ **Brewers Bay**, on Tortola's north coast road, has two good snorkeling sites, one to the left along the cliffs with depths from eight to 10 ft , the other in the center of the beach opposite the rock wall edging the road. The reef starts close to shore and stretches out in shallow depths for a long way. Schools of trumpet fish, barracuda, octopus, stingrays and sergeant majors inhabit the area.

☆☆☆☆ **The Caves** at Norman Island are accessible by boat. It is a favorite snorkeling-photo site, bright with sponges, corals and schools of small fish. The reef slopes down to 40 ft. Moorings are maintained by the National Park Trust.

 Norman Island is rumored to have inspired Robert Louis Stevenson's Treasure Island and the Caves are reputed to be old hiding places for pirate treasure.

☆☆ **Manchioneel Bay**, Cooper Island, has a beautiful shallow reef with packs of fish around the moorings.

☆☆☆☆☆ **Loblolly Beach**, on Anegada's northern shore, is one of the best shore-entry snorkeling spots in the Caribbean when winds are calm. Coral heads teeming with fish and invertebrates are close to shore. Visibility can exceed 100 ft. There is usually some surf, but it breaks on the front of the reef, which is quite a distance from shore. The Big Bamboo bar and restaurant on the beach is worth the trip. Owner Aubrey Levons welcomes everyone with island stories and hospitality. Loblolly Beach is reached by taxi, bike or jeep from the Anegada Reef Resort docks.

Avoid this area during strong winds. The sea gets stirred up and visibility drops from super to silty, while the beach becomes a sand blast area. Spring and summer are usually the best times to snorkel Anegada.

Anchoring on Anegada Reef is prohibited. Diving Anegada is currently banned, but snorkeling day trips can be arranged through the dive operators. Dive BVI offers a particularly nice snorkeling trip aboard their fast 45-ft Sea

Lion to Anegada, which also includes beachcombing and a local lobster lunch at the Big Bamboo Bar and Restaurant.

Additional excellent snorkeling sites are found on the northeast corner of **Benures Bay**, Norman Island, or the **Bight and Little Bigh**t, also off Norman Island. At **Peter Island**, try the south shore at **Little Harbor** and the western shore at **Great Harbor**. **Diamond Reef** on the southeast side of **Great Camanoe** can be reached by dinghy fom Marina Cay. The shallow reef sits straight out from the utility pole on the shore.

Long Bay, near Smugglers Cove, Tortola, has pretty corals and the biggest fish, but water entry is difficult as the coral grows to the surface.

 A wetsuit top, shortie, or wetskin is recommended for night dives and winter diving. Snorkelers should have some protection from sunburn. The BVI reefs are protected by law, and no living thing may be taken. "Take only pictures, leave only bubbles."

Dive Operators

Dive BVI Ltd., a PADI five-star shop, operates out of Leverick Bay, Virgin Gorda Yacht Harbour and Marina Cay. Owner Joe Giacinto has been diving and snorkeling the BVI for 33 years and knows all the best spots. Rates, which include the park fee are $86 for a two-tank dive, $228 for three two-tank dives. Will rendezvous with boats. Snorkeling trips are offered to Anegada and other spots aboard the *Sealion*, a fast 45-ft wave-piercing catamaran. Courses from resort up through assistant instructor are available. Write: PO Box 1040, Virgin Gorda, BVI. ☎ 284-495-5513 or 800-848-7078, fax 284-495-5347. E-mail: dbvi@caribsurf.com.

Underwater Safaris, at the Moorings Mariner Inn on Tortola and Cooper Island, offers fast 42- and 30-ft dive boats, full service, rendezvous with yachts, PADI certification. The Tortola shop is the largest retail dive shop in the BVI. Rates: $55 for a one-tank dive, $80 for a two-tank tour. Hotel/dive and sail packages. Write: PO Box 139, Road Town, Tortola, BVI. ☎ 800-537-7032 or 284-494-3235, fax 284-494-5322.

Baskin' in the Sun at the Prospect Reef Resort Marina has two custom dive boats. Rates: $65 for a one-tank tour; $85 for a two-tank; $25, snorkel trip. Super service; you never carry a tank or gear. PADI five-star dive center. Package tours can be booked through Tropical Reservations, 8890 Coral Way, Suite 220, Miami FL 33165. ☎ 305-554-4020; direct 284-494-2858/9, fax 284-494-4303. E-mail:reservations@baskininthesun.com.

Blue Water Divers, at Nanny Cay on the south side of Tortola, serves divers staying at the Windjammer. Blue Water Divers operates a 47-ft catamaran and a 27-ft dive boat. Dive tours are to the eastern sites in the BVI, such as Jost Van Dyke, as well as all the sites in the channel. ☎ 284-494-2847.Write: PO Box 846, Road Town, Tortola, BVI. E-mail: bwdbvi@caribsurf.com.

Island Diver Ltd. at Village Cay Marina, Road Town, offers reef and wreck tours, resort courses and snorkeling. ☎ 284-494-3878/5236-7.

Kilbride's Sunchaser Scuba, at the famous Bitter End Yacht Club on Virgin Gorda, features a variety of dive packages, courses and services. Their boats take you to 50 different dive locations. Despite a change in ownership, you will still be escorted by any one of 16 diving Kilbrides. As personal friends of the "better mannered fish," the Kilbrides provide a diving tour that is educational as well as entertaining. Tours can be booked by writing to Sunchaser Scuba, Box 46, Virgin Gorda, BVI. ☎ 800-932-4286 or 284-495-9638; fax 284-495-7549. Mail may take as long as six weeks, so write early. Sunchaser serves the North Sound resorts; their tours cover all the islands. Resort courses through PADI certification and open water checkouts are available. Rates: $60 for a one-tank dive; $85 for a two-tank tour. Rates include all equipment except wetsuits. Non-divers can come along for a small fee. E-mail: sunscuba@caribsurf.com.

Rainbow Visions Photography at Prospect Reef offers underwater, still and video camera rentals. Processing. Custom videos and portraits. ☎ 284-494-2749. Write: PO Box 139, Road Town, Tortola, BVI.

Sailing & Scuba Live-Aboards

Sail-dive vacations are an easy way for divers to enjoy a variety of sites and destinations. Live-aboard yachts are chartered with captain, captain and crew or "bare" to qualified sailors. Navigation is uncomplicated; you can tour most of the area without ever leaving sight of land. Most boats carry snorkeling gear as standard equipment; some of the large craft have compressors. And every dive shop offers some type of arrangement to accommodate seafarers.

With sailing almost a religion in the BVI, it is easy to customize a live-aboard dive or snorkeling vacation. If you are an experienced sailor and diver you can charter a bareboat and see the sights on your own. If you've never sailed before or have limited experience, you can "captain" a crewed yacht to find the best dive spots. If you've never sailed or dived, but want to learn both, you can charter a yacht with a crew that includes a divemaster (often the captains are qualified dive instructors) or arrange to rendezvous with a dive boat. Or you can book a week-long cruise on a commercial live-aboard where you'll meet other divers. Prices on private charters vary with the number of people in your

Sandy Cay, BVI.

party. With four to six people, a crewed yacht will average about the same cost as a stay at a resort.

One of the world's largest trimarans (105 ft), **Cuan Law** was specifically designed with the scuba diver in mind. As with most live-aboards, you are offered "all the diving you can stand." *Cuan Law* accommodates 20 passengers in 10 large, airy double cabins, each with private head and shower. Rates from April through December start at $1,650 per person for seven days and six nights. Transfers, tips, alcohol and scuba instruction are NOT included.

Cruises are sometimes booked up to a year in advance. ☎ 800-648- 3393 or write Trimarine Boat Company, PO 4065, St. Thomas, USVI 00803. E-mail: cuanlaw@caribsurf.com. Website:www.diveguideint.com/cuanlaw.

The Moorings Ltd. offers "Cabin N Cruise" tours for those wishing to enjoy a fully crewed sailing vacation without having to charter an entire yacht. ☎ 800-535-7289. Dive arrangements must be made separately. See detailed listing below.

Bareboating

Private sailing yachts with diving guides and instructors are available from most of the charter operators listed below. You can arrange for your own personal live-aboard diving or snorkeling vacation. Be sure to specify your needs before going.

Bareboating can be surprisingly affordable for groups of four or more. Boats must be reserved six to nine months in advance for winter vacations and at least three months in advance for summer vacations.

Experience cruising on a similar yacht is required and you will be asked to fill out a questionnaire or produce a sailing resume. Instructor-skippers are available for refresher sailing. A cruising permit, available from the Customs Department, is required. For a complete list of charter companies contact the BVI Tourist Board at ☎ 800-835-8530 or write 370 Lexington Ave., Suite 1605, New York, NY 10017.

The Moorings Ltd., Tortola, has been operating for 30 years. Their charter boats include 32- to 55-ft monohulls and catamarans.

A three-day sailing vacation can be combined with a four day resort/diving vacation at the Moorings Mariner Inn. Write to The Moorings, Ltd., 19345 US Hwy 19 N, Clearwater, FL 33764. ☎ 800-535-7289 or 813-535-1446. Website: www.moorings.com.

Offshore Sailing School uses the Moorings boats and offers a Sail 'N Dive vacation with the Prospect Reef Resort. The package includes the complete Learn to Sail course and PADI Dive certification, eight nights accommodations and all course materials. Classroom and on-water instruction is held Monday through Thursday alternating between midday and afternoon with one full day of sailing on Friday or Saturday. On-water instruction is held Monday through Thursday in half-day sessions. They also offer a Learn to Sail vacation (from $1,195 per week), which can be mixed with dive expeditions through the Prospect Reef Resort. Rates for the Sail 'N Dive course and accommodations are $1,643 based on a double in summer, April 20th to December 20th; $1,743 from December 12 to April 19; $1,594 from October 13 to November 16. ☎ 800-221-4326.

A Fast Track to Cruising course, offered by Offshore Sailing School, includes the complete Learn to Sail course and Moorings/Offshore Live Aboard Cruising course on consecutive weeks. Available starting Sundays year-round (two-person minimum for Live Aboard cruising), the package includes 10 days/nine nights accommodations ashore, six days/five nights aboard a Moorings yacht, Learn to Sail and Live Aboard Cruising courses, textbooks, certificates, wallet cards, logbook, full-day practice sail, split yacht provisioning during onboard portion of Live Aboard Cruising course (five breakfasts, five lunches, three dinners), graduation dinners ashore, airport or ferry transfers in Tortola. Per-person rates for a double between April and May 1, $3,120; May 2 to mid-July, $2,775; mid-July to October 30, $2,675. ☎ 800-221-4326 or 941-454-1700, fax 941-454-1191. Write to: Offshore Sailing School, 16731 McGregor Blvd., Ft. Myers, FL 33908.

Yacht Promenade, a sleek, 65-ft tri-hull sailing yacht for couples or groups of six to 12, features on-board scuba facilities, spacious air-conditioned cabins, full breakfasts, lunches, cocktails, hors d'oeuvres and three-course gourmet dinners. There are five guest staterooms, one in each outer hull and three at the rear of the center hull, three queen-sized berths and two that are larger than king and can be converted into four single berths. A 20-ft Wellcraft launch whisks divers off to all the best spots. Cost of $1,450 per week per diver includes use of 11-ft kayaks, a sailing dinghy, and a windsurfer. Non-divers' discount $100. For 12 divers the price drops to $1,195 per person. Gear rental, $90 per week. Pick up at Village Cay Marina, Road Town, Tortola. ☎ (US) 800-526-5503 or 284-494-6020 or 284-494-0999, fax 284-494-5577. E-mail: promcruz@caribsurf.com.

Mooring Buoys

In order to protect the BVI's fragile coral reefs, boats are required to use National Parks Trust (NPT) mooring buoys when visiting the following areas: The Baths, The Caves, The Indians, Pelican Island, Carrot Shoal; also dive or snorkeling sites at Peter, Norman, Ginger and Cooper Islands, the Wreck of the *Fearless*, Dead Chest, Blonde Rock, the Dogs, Guana Island, the wreck of the *Rhone* and the *Rhone's* anchor. All users of the moorings must have a valid NPT moorings permit, which can be obtained at their office in Road Town, or at BVI Customs Offices, local charter boat companies and brokerages.

Mooring buoy colors indicate the use for that mooring. White is for scuba diving only; orange or red are for snorkeling or any day use; yellow moorings are for commercial dive operations only; blue are for dinghies.

 Note: Mooring on the reefs surrounding Anegada is prohibited.

Accommodations & Anchorages

Website: www.britishvirginislands.com/divebvi.

Tortola

Every type of accommodation is available in the BVI from tents to cottages, guesthouses, condos, luxury resorts to live-aboard sailboats and motor yachts. Reservations can be made through your travel agent or the BVI Tourist Board at ☎ 800-835-8530, or in New York, 212-696-0400. Locally owned properties start at $40 per night for a room. For a copy of the Intimate Inns brochure, ☎ (US) 800-835-8530. Website: www.bviwelcome.com.

Island Hideaways rents upscale private homes and villas. ☎ 800-784-2690 or 410-884-3636, fax 410-884-3636.

Long Bay Beach Resort on Tortola's north shore has 82 deluxe hillside and beachfront accommodations. Transfers, three two-tank dives, beach, restaurant, tennis, pitch & put golf. Rates start at $899 per person per week for a seven-night dive vacation with hillside accommodations, breakfasts, four dinners, one-day car rental, airport transfers and shuttle to diving. Dive packages with Baskin in the Sun. ☎ 800-729-9599. Write: PO Box 433, Road Town, Tortola, BVI.

The Moorings-Mariner Inn, Tortola, is home port to The Moorings charter boat operation. It has no beach. The poolside bar and restaurant are just a few steps from Underwater Safaris, the largest retail shop in the BVI.

The resort offers a new Shore 'N Sail vacation with three nights aboard a luxurious sailing yacht (snorkeling only) with your own skipper and provisions, plus four nights at the resort diving with Underwater Safaris. ☎ 800-535-7289, 284-494-2332, fax 727-530-9747, or write The Moorings-Mariner Inn, 1305 US 19 S., Suite 402, Clearwater, FL 34624. E-mail: yacht@moorings.com. Website: www.moorings.com.

Nanny Cay Resort & Marina, two miles southwest of Road Town, has 41 air-conditioned rooms from $180 per day in winter; $110 in summer. TV, phones, pool, restaurant, bar, tennis, windsurf school and on-site dive operation, Blue Water Divers. Winter dive packages start at $635 per person for four nights accommodations and three two-tank boat dives, $1,101 for seven nights with six two-tank dives. ☎ 800-74CHARMS or 800-742-4276 or 284-494-4895, fax 914-424-3283. Write: PO Box 281, Road Town, Tortola, BVI. E-mail: nanresv@caribsurf.com.

Prospect Reef Resort is a sprawling 10-acre resort on the west end of Road Town, Tortola, facing Sir Francis Drake Channel. The resort has over 130 rooms ranging from studios to standard rooms, full apartments, and luxury villas. This resort is the largest on Tortola and offers six tennis courts, miniature golf, two restaurants for casual food and drinks, and three pools. Rooms are cooled by ceiling fans and a breeze from the sea. An excellent buffet is served at the resort's Harbour Restaurant on Saturday nights. Scuba packages with Baskin' in the Sun. Winter rates are $990 for seven nights, including accommodations and three boat dives; summer, $773. Winter room rates range from $147 per day. (17% tax/service charge included in rates.) ☎ 800-356-8937, 284-494-3311. Write: Box 104, Road Town, Tortola, BVI.

Sugar Mill, on the northwest shore of Tortola, is a village of hillside cottages built around the remains of a 360-year-old sugar mill. Its proprietors, Jeff and Jinx Morgan, are famous for their gourmet meals (they write for *Bon Appétit*). The old sugar mill houses the restaurant, where you may dine by candlelight. The menu changes nightly. Small beach. Their "Adventure Package" includes seven nights deluxe accommodation, six-day vehicle rental, four gourmet dinners at the Sugar Mill's restaurant, six one-tank dives with Baskin' in the Sun, a resort course, two shallow dives for beginners, gourmet picnic for two, full-day sail to neighbouring islands with lunch and drinks, an autographed copy of *The Sugar Mill Caribbean Cookbook* by Jiff & Jinx Morgan, and a bottle of Sugar Mill rum. Winter rates (December 2-April 14) for the package are $1,713 with dives, $1,483 without dives; spring rates (April 15-May 31 and November 1-December 20) are $1,396 with dives, $1,166 without. Summer rates (June 1-October 31) are $1,324 with dives, $1,094 without. Rates are per person based on double occupancy (single rate not available). ☎ 800-462-8834 or 284-495-4355, fax 284-495-4696. Write PO Box 425, Tortola, BVI. Website: www.sugarmillhotel.com.

Treasure Isle Hotel, Roadtown, has 40 air-conditioned rooms, three suites, pool, restaurant, bar. Dive packages with Underwater Safaris. Room rates are from $253 in winter, $143 mid-season, from $104 in summer. ☎ 800-437-7880.

Marina Cay

Marina Cay, a six-acre island off the northeast tip of Tortola, features Dive BVI's newest dive and water sports center, offering daily dive and snorkeling trips, ocean kayaks, two new Hobie catamarans, Pusser's Fine Dining and a large Company Store.

Marina Cay Resort has four one-bedroom units and two two-bedroom villas that accommodate up to 16 guests. All have been recently refurbished. Room per-day rates are $175 in winter, $120 in summer for double occupancy room and $450 in winter, $295 in summer for a lagoon villa. Continental breakfast included. Taxes extra. ☎ 284-494-2174 or fax 284-494-4775. Dive/accommodation packages may be reserved through Dive BVI. ☎ 800-848-7078.

Virgin Gorda

The Bitter End Yacht Club on Virgin Gorda's North Sound offers guest rooms in luxury villas along the shore and hillside or on a Freedom 30 liveaboard yacht. The club bar is the favorite story-swapping place for sailing and diving folk. Daily scuba trips, arranged through Kilbride's Underwater Tours, leave from the Bitter End Docks every morning. Rates are for couples. Deduct $100 per day for a single. Add $100 for an extra person. A suite in winter with all meals for two costs $700 per day or $4,550 for seven nights. Diving is extra. If you prefer to stay aboard a yacht, the same package costs $480 per day or $3,360 per seven nights. ☎ 800-872-2392, 284-494-2746, or write PO Box 46, Virgin Gorda, BVI.

Biras Creek Estate, located on a 140-acre peninsula, can be reached by scheduled ferry from Tortola. The resort has 34 luxury villas with garden and

British Virgin Islands

ocean views overlooking North Sound. Recently refurbished, the resort provides complimentary use of Boston Whalers, windsurfers and 25-ft sailboats. Diving, extra, is arranged at the desk. Rates for a room (double occupancy) and three meals daily are from $570 in winter, $425 in summer. Call for special family packages. ☎ 800-608-9661 or 284-494-3555, fax 284-494-3557. E-mail: biras@caribsurf.com. Write: PO Box 54, Virgin Gorda, BVI. Add 17% to cover tax and service.

Leverick Bay Hotel, on Leverick Bay, offers a variety of unique, affordable accommodations. Winter rates start at $135 per day for a room; summer, $120. Small beach. Diving, water-skiing, kayaking and small boat sailing are through Dive BVI. ☎ 800-848-7078 or 284-495-7328. E-mail: dbvi@caribsurf.com.

Little Dix Bay features 96 luxury suites and guest rooms starting at $250 per day in summer (May-November), $550 per day during the high season (January 3 to March 31). The resort rests on a half-mile of pristine beach surrounded by tropical gardens. Paradise Watersports on-premises offers scuba and snorkeling tours. ☎ 800-928-3000 or book through your travel agent.

Peter Island Resort & Yacht Harbour offers luxurious beachfront rooms overlooking Sprat Bay and the Sir Francis Drake Channel. Excellent snorkeling off the beach. Dive BVI facility on site. Winter room rates are from $4,725 per week for a couple, summer from $3,815 per couple for a week (seven nights). ☎ 800-346-4451 or 800-323-7500; direct 284-495-2000, fax 284-495-2500. Add a 17% surcharge.

Anegada

Tiny Anegada, 12 miles northwest of Virgin Gorda, covers just 15 square miles. This off-the-beaten-track coral atoll, surrounded by uninterrupted beaches and gorgeous reefs, is home to 250 residents and a huge community of exotic Caribbean birds including a flamingo colony, herons, terns and ospreys. Shipwrecks and coral heads abound, a delight for divers and snorkelers, but sailors beware – approaching the island by boat can be treacherous without local knowledge and eyeball navigation. Snorkeling, diving and fly fishing, done from shore, is outstanding.

Much of the island's interior is a preserve for 2,000 wild goats, donkeys and cattle. Not for the average tourist, but a great spot if you want to get away from it all. Expect encounters with a ferocious mosquito population; carry as much repellent as you can. Fly in from Beef Island, Tortola or go by boat from any of the marinas.

Anegada Reef Hotel, on Setting Point, offers great beaches, snorkeling and fly fishing, 20 air-conditioned rooms, tackle shop. Winter rates are from $180 per day, summer from $150. Rates include breakfast, lunch and dinner (sur-

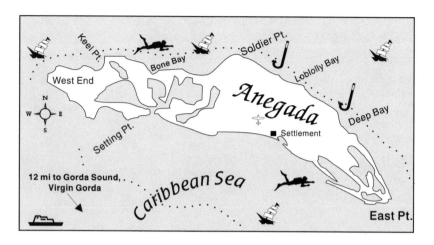

charge for lobster). Informal restaurant. Jeep and bicycle rentals. A 15% service charge and 7% tax are added to the bill. Three-night deposit required. ☎ 284-495-8002, fax 284-495-9362.

Anegada Beach Campground offers 8x10-ft tents, a restaurant and snorkeling tours. Winter rates are $36. Bare site is under $10. ☎ 284-495-9466 or write to Box 2710, Anegada, BVI.

Pristine Anchorages

Deadman's Bay, on the eastern tip of **Peter Island**, is a short sail out of Road Harbour that takes no more than an hour or two. Once there, you will find a long white sand beach at Peter Island Yacht Club. Yachtsmen are requested to anchor in the Bay's extreme southeastern corner and should be aware that the area is prone to a swell, especially in the winter months.

Salt Island. Heading upwind from Deadman's Bay is Salt Island, once a regular stopping-off point for ships requiring salt for food preservation on the trade routes. This is also the location of the BVI's famed wreck of the *Rhone*, which sank off the island in 1867. At Lee Bay, just north of the *Rhone*, moorings are provided for those diving the wreck in order to minimize anchor damage. Both Lee Bay and Salt Pond Bay off the settlement can be rough anchorages and are recommended for day use only.

Cooper Island's Machioneel Bay, located on the island's northwest shore, is a good lunch stop for those sailing upwind to Virgin Gorda. There is a dock for dinghies and a beach for swimming. The Cooper Island Beach Bar serves lunch, dinner and drinks.

The Virgin Gorda Baths, one of the BVI's most famous landmarks, lies on the southwestern shore of Virgin Gorda. Randomly placed large granite boulders form small grottoes and pools on the beach's edge, great for exploring

British Virgin Islands

and snorkeling. As with all these north shore anchorages, a swell can prevent overnight anchoring.

North Sound, Virgin Gorda, offers the yachtsman a wide array of overnight anchorages, and a variety of good dining spots. The harbor sits along the eastern tip of the island and is well protected by surrounding islands Mosquito, Prickly Pear and Eustatia. Boats over five ft in draft should use the Sound's northern entrance at Calquhoun Reef; shallow drafts can use the Anguilla Point entrance in calm weather only.

The Dogs make a good stopping-off point for sailors on their way from North Sound to Jost Van Dyke; they are also a popular diving and snorkeling venue. On calm days the best anchorages are the bay to the west of Kitchen Point on George Dog, as well as on the south side of Great Dog.

Trellis Bay, Beef Island, is a well-protected anchorage fringed by a semicircular beach. It serves as the location for Boardsailing BVI, the Conch Shell Point Restaurant and The Loose Mongoose Beach Bar. At the Bay's center is The Last Resort, an English-style restaurant whose owner, Tony Snell, puts on a one-man cabaret act.

Marina Cay lies north of Trellis Bay and offers a restaurant, bar, small beach and moorings. It is fringed by coral and one should enter from the north.

Sandy Cay, east of Little Jost Van Dyke, is uninhabited and offers a long stretch of white sandy beach. The water is deep almost until the shore; the area is prone to swells and not a good anchorage year-round.

The Baths.

Courtesy BVI Tourism

Little Harbour, Jost Van Dyke, a quiet, easy-to-enter lagoon touts three restaurants, all with local food and atmosphere at the shore's edge.

Great Harbour, Jost Van Dyke (south coast), is the locale of Foxy's Tamarind Bar and several other good West Indian restaurants. A small settlement bordering a white sand beach fringes this picturesque harbor. The anchorage is fairly well protected and the holding good.

White Bay, Jost Van Dyke, lies west of Great Harbour and features a white sand beach, small hotel and a restaurant. A channel through the center of the reef allows entrance to the anchorage, which is subject to winter swells.

Norman Island's main anchorage is **The Bight**.

Pelican Island and the **Indians** are near The Bight and offer good snorkeling and excellent scuba diving.

Soper's Hole, one of Tortola's three main ports of entry, lies at the very west end of the island and is both deep and sheltered. Ferries to St. Thomas and St. John leave from here daily. There are several nearby restaurants and marinas.

Road Harbour, Tortola's largest harbor, skirts Road Town, capital of the BVI. Here one finds customs and immigration facilities, good supermarkets and shops, marinas, restaurants and a boatyard all within walking distance of the harbor. Brandywine Bay and Maya Cove, which also offer restaurants, are two more anchorages just beyond Road Harbour.

Other Activities & Sightseeing

Hiking and exploring are popular in the BVI. You will find deserted dungeons, sugar mills, pirate caves, rain forests and wooded trails. Tennis courts as well as horseback riding are provided by some of the hotels. Boardsailing and windsurfing equipment is available at many of the resorts.

Tortola

The 2.8-acre **J.R. O'Neal Botanic Gardens** in the center of Road Town feature a beautiful waterfall, lily pond and exotic tropical plants and birds. Nearby, on Main Street, is the **Virgin Island Folk Museum**, which displays many artifacts from the *Rhone* and from early plantations. Hikers and botanists will find huge elephant-ear plants, and lush ferns under a canopy of mahogany and manilkara trees at **Sage Mountain National Park**. Mt. Sage peaks at 1,780 ft.

If you are cruising the BVI, be sure to visit **Stanley's** in Cane Garden Bay on the weekend, where the steel band is reputed to be the best in the islands.

British Virgin Islands

Virgin Gorda

Visitors will find the ruins of an 18th-century sugar mill at Nail Bay on Virgin Gorda's west coast. And just south of the Yacht Harbor at Little Fort National Park is some masonry from an old Spanish fortress. Monster granite boulders are at the Spring Bay beach between Little Fort National Park and the Baths.

Gorda Peak is a 265-acre national park with a wealth of mahogany trees and exotic plants.

There are small shops (not duty-free) around Road Town, Tortola and Spanish Town, Virgin Gorda, specializing in local crafts and gifts.

Dining

Tortola

Rhymer's Beach Bar and Restaurant at Cane Garden Bay, Tortola, is a favorite among the locals. Serving fresh fish and lobster, it has Buffet Night on Tuesday and Saturday. Open for breakfast, lunch and dinner. ☎ 54520.

Scatliffe's Tavern, another local favorite in Road Town, Tortola, specializes in local food such as fish soup made with coconut milk, conch fritters, ribs, and lobster dishes, followed by fresh lime pie. Near the high school. ☎ 42797.

Carib Casseroles, on Tortola, has a "Meals on Keels" service for bareboaters experienced with boil-a-bags as well as sit-down service. Food is a combination of Caribbean, French, Greek and Creole. Peanut Creole soup, curry and casseroles are featured here. Moderate.

Virgin Gorda

The Bath & Turtle is a patio tavern in the Yacht Harbour serving breakfast, lunch, and dinner. Burgers, sandwiches, and homemade soups. ☎ 55239.

Mad Dog near the Baths specializes in sandwiches all day. Spectacular view! ☎ 55830.

The Olde Yard Inn features a library and classical music. Homemade soups, local seafood, gourmet specialties. ☎ 55544. Reservations.

Anegada

The Anegada Reefs Hotel, Anegada, serves lunch at their beach bar and specializes in barbecued lobster for dinner. Local fish or steak, chicken and ribs are also available. Moderate to expensive. ☎ 58002. VHF Ch 16.

Mosquito Island

Drake's Anchorage, on Mosquito Island, has been written up in *Gourmet* magazine for its fabulous Caribbean lobster and local fish dinners. Meals include fresh baked bread, soup, appetizer, salad, dessert and coffee. Moorings are available for a low overnight charge. ☎ 42254. VHF Ch 16.

Jost Van Dyke

Sandcastle at White Bay on Jost Van Dyke serves gourmet fish dishes, lobster, orange-glazed duck, fresh breads and desserts for lunch and dinner in the open-air restaurant on the beach. **The Soggy Dollar Bar** offers the original "Painkiller." No credit cards. Reservations on VHF Ch 16. Prices are moderate to high.

Foxy's in Great Harbor (south coast) serves roti and sumptuous burgers for lunch, local lobster and steak for dinner. A favorite with the yachting crowd. ☎ 59258.

Peter Island

Peter Island Hotel and Yacht Harbour offers lunch at the Beach Restaurant from 12:30 to 2 pm. Dinners are formal; men must wear a jacket and women, "cocktail" attire. ☎ 52000. Expensive.

Facts

Nearest Recompression Chamber: The nearest chamber is on St. Thomas in the neighboring USVI.

Getting There: San Juan, Puerto Rico is the airline hub for the Caribbean, with frequent service to all parts of the US, Canada and Europe. Beef Island is the major airport of Tortola and the BVI. Flights to San Juan with connections to the BVI from the United States on American (☎ 800-433-7300), Delta and Continental Airlines. Atlantic Air BVI, Sunaire Express or American Eagle fly from San Juan to Beef Island. Gorda Aero Services (☎ 52271) flies to Anegada from Tortola on Mon, Wed, and Fri. Inter-island ferry service is also available from St. Thomas to St. John and Tortola. Ferries run from Tortola to Virgin Gorda, Peter Island, Jost Van Dyke. Baggage can sometimes be delayed by a day on the small airlines. Divers carrying a lot of equipment should fly direct to St. Thomas and take a water ferry, to avoid having to change planes.

Car rentals: *(Tortola)* Hertz, ☎ 54405; Avis,☎ 43322; ITGO, ☎ 42639; International, ☎ 42516. *(Virgin Gorda)* Speedy's, ☎ 5-5240.

Taxi Service: Available from Beef Island Airport, Road Town Jetty, West End Jetty and from the dock on Virgin Gorda. *(Tortola)* BVI Taxi, ☎ 52378 or 42875; Andy's Taxi, ☎ 55252; Style's Taxi, ☎ 42260. *(Virgin Gorda)* Mahogany Taxi, ☎ 55542.

Driving: Valid BVI driving license required. A temporary license may be obtained from the car rental agencies for $10. Driving is on the left-hand side of the road. Maximum speed is 30 mph. Bicycles must be registered at the Traffic Licensing Office in Road Town. Cost of registration is $5. License plate must be fixed to the bicycle.

Fishing: The removal of any marine organism from BVI waters is illegal for non-residents without a recreational fishing permit. ☎ 43429.

British Virgin Islands

Documents: A valid passport is required to enter the BVI. For US and Canadian citizens, an authenticated birth certificate or voter registration card with photo identification will suffice. Visitors may stay up to six months, provided they possess ongoing tickets, evidence of adequate means of support and pre-arranged accommodations. Visitors from some countries may need a visa. ☎ 284-494-3701.

Currency: US Dollar. Personal checks not accepted.

Clothing: Casual, light clothing; some of the resorts require a jacket for dinner. Avoid exposed midriffs and bare chests in residential and commercial areas. Nudity is punishable by law. A wetsuit top, shortie, or wetskin is recommended for night dives and winter diving. Snorkelers should have some protection from sunburn.

Time: Atlantic Standard (EST + 1 hr).

Language: English.

Climate: The BVI are in the tradewind belt and have a subtropical climate. Average temperatures are 75 to 85°F in winter and 80 to 90°F in summer. Nights are cooler. The hurricane season extends from July through September.

Taxes: There is a departure tax of $10 by air and $5 by sea. The hotel accommodation tax is 7%.

Religious Services: Methodist, Anglican, Roman Catholic, Seventh Day Adventist, Baptist, Jehovah's Witness, Pentecostal and Church of Christ.

For Additional Information and a list of all guesthouses, apartments, hotels, campgrounds, charter operators, and restaurants, contact the BVI Tourist Board. *(Tortola)* PO Box 134, Road Town, Tortola, British Virgin Islands, ☎ 284-494-3134. *(New York)* BVI Tourist Board, 370 Lexington Avenue, Suite 1605, New York, NY 10017, ☎ 800-835-8530 or 212-696-0400. *(United Kingdom)* BVI Tourist Board, Banks Hoggins O'Shea FCB Travel Marketing, 54 Baker St, London W1M1DJ, ☎ 171-240-4259. Website: www.bviwelcome.com.

Cayman Islands

Grand Cayman, Cayman Brac & Little Cayman

Dubbed "The Islands that Time Forgot" by the *Saturday Evening Post* in the early 1950s, the Caymans today have become one of the world's top dive-travel destinations. Some 480 miles, and an hour's flying time south of Miami, this Caribbean trio entertains more than 200,000 visitors each year.

Physically beautiful, each island is blessed with an extraordinary fringing reef, superb marine life and sparkling, palm-lined beaches.

Underwater Cayman is a submerged mountain range, complete with cliffs, drop-offs, gullies, caverns, sink holes and forests of coral. The islands are the visible above-the-sea portions of the mountains. At depth, the Cayman Trench drops off to more than 23,000 ft.

Grand Cayman, the largest and the most developed of the three, boasts world-class dive operations, restaurants and scores of luxury hotels and condominiums. The islands' no-tax status, granted by Britain in the 1700s because of the heroic action of Caymanians in saving the lives of passengers and crews of 10 sailing ships, has attracted numerous corporations and banks. Its capital, Georgetown, ranks as the fifth largest financial center in the world, with nearly 600 international banks.

Cayman Brac and Little Cayman lie 89 miles northeast of the big island and are separated by a seven-mile-wide channel. Both wildly beautiful, each has its own special personality.

Little Cayman is *very quiet*, virtually untouched by developers. The smallest of the three islands – only 10 square miles – it has about 35 permanent residents. There are no shops, restaurants, movie theaters or traffic. Phones are few and far between. Small resorts cater almost exclusively to divers and fishermen.

With daily direct flights from North America and easy access from many other parts of the globe, most divers head first for Grand Cayman. Its famed Seven Mile Beach is headquarters for dive activity. More adventurous divers seeking a unique wilderness experience flock to the Brac and Little Cayman for superlative wall dives. Little Cayman is also noted for unsurpassed flats fishing.

When to Go

Late summer and fall bring the chance of a hurricane, but diving is possible year-round. Conditions are generally mild, although steady winds can kick up some chop. When this happens, dive boats simply move to the leeward side of the island and calmer waters. Air temperature averages 77°F. Water temperature averages 80°.

History

As with many other Caribbean islands, the discovery of the Caymans is attributed to Christopher Columbus, who first saw them on his second voyage while en route from Panama to Cuba in 1503. Amazingly, his primitive ships were able to negotiate the coral reefs with little trouble. He named these islands "Las Tortugas" for the countless marine turtles who came to Cayman beaches to breed. The turtles, which lived in captivity for long periods, became a source of fresh meat for the sailors, and the Cayman Islands became a regular stop for exploring ships.

Marine Regulations

With a dramatic growth in tourism and an increase in cruiseship arrivals, the islands have enacted comprehensive legislation to protect the fragile marine environment. It is an offense for any vessel to cause reef damage with anchors or chains anywhere in Cayman waters. Marine areas are divided into three types: Marine Park Zones, Replenishment Zones and Environmental Zones.

The **Marine Park Zones** outlaw the taking of any marine life, living or dead, and only line fishing from shore and beyond the dropoff is permitted. Anchoring is allowed only at fixed moorings. (There are more than 200 permanent moorings around the islands.)

In a **Replenishment Zone**, the taking of conch or lobster is prohibited, and spear guns, pole spears, fish traps and nets are prohibited. Line fishing and anchoring (at fixed moorings) are permitted. Spearguns and Hawaiian slings may not be brought into the country.

Environmental Zones are the most strictly regulated. There is an absolute ban on the taking of any kind of marine life, alive or dead; anchoring is prohibited and no in-water activities of any kind are tolerated. These are used as a breeding ground and nursery for the fish and other creatures that will later populate the reef and other waters.

The Marine Conservation Board employs full-time officers who may search any vessel or vehicle thought to contain marine life taken illegally. Penalties may include a maximum fine of CI $5,000 or imprisonment, or both.

Stingray City appeals to novice and experienced divers.

Courtesy Cayman Islands
Department of Tourism

Grand Cayman

Best Dive & Snorkeling Sites of Grand Cayman

Grand Cayman, noted for its fabulous wall-diving, has steep drop-offs on all sides. The **West Wall**, a drop-off that runs parallel to Seven Mile Beach, offers the most convenient diving on the island. Most dive operators are located in this area, and many hotels offer dive and snorkeling trips to the sites – all five- to 10-minute boat rides. Flat-bottom dive boats attest to the calm seas. Several beach dives are possible. More sites along the **South Wall** have recently opened, particularly for experienced divers and photographers. This area is defined by a barrier reef that breaks the surface and serves as a coral fence. Conditions here are more demanding.

The **North Wall** also lays claim to some of the most spectacular dive sites because of its unusual coral formations and frequent pelagic sightings.

Cayman Islands

Least explored is the **East End Wall**, often referred to as the last frontier.

Water temperature holds steady at 82°F, while visibility ranges from 100 to 150 ft. The coral reefs are exceptionally healthy, largely due to the conservancy measures enforced by the dive shops.

✰✰✰✰✰ **Stingray City** is the most photographed dive site in the Caymans, if not the entire Caribbean. Pictured in all the tourist board ads, the subject of endless travel articles and an Emmy-award-winning film by Stan Waterman, this gathering of Southern stingrays in the shallow area of North Sound is a marine phenomenon that has thrilled scuba divers and snorkelers since their discovery by two dive instructors, Pat Kinney and Jay Ireland in 1986.

After observing the normally solitary and shy rays gathering regularly at a shallow site where boats cleaned their conch and fish, Kinney and Ireland began hand-taming exercises, carefully avoiding the razor-sharp, venomous spine in their whip-like tails. When safe hand-feeding became a predictable event, they invited small groups of divers and snorkelers out to watch.

Today, the 20-member cast of rays are big celebrities, luring curious visitors – as many as 150-200 per day – from across the globe. The location is shallow, 12-20 ft, ideal for snorkelers as well as divers. Feeding time occurs whenever a dive or snorkeling boat shows up.

✰✰✰✰✰ **Trinity Caves**, off the north end of Seven Mile Beach, winds into a maze of canyon trails between 60 and 100 ft. Reef features consist of gigantic barrel sponges, black coral, towering sea whips, sea fans, and a host of critters. Huge groupers and turtles, lobsters, squirrel fish, and schooling reef fish inhabit three cathedral-like caves for which the site is named. Their walls grasp clusters of pink anemones, vase sponges, and star corals. Sea conditions are generally calm, with an occasional light current. Exceptional visibility. Suggested for experienced divers.

✰✰✰✰ **Orange Canyon**, north of Trinity Caves, glows with vibrant orange elephant-ear sponges. The reef starts at 45 ft, the edge of a deep wall adorned with sea plumes, lavender sea fans and bushy corals – cover for shrimp, sea cucumbers, brittle stars, arrow crabs, file fish, turtles and small octopi. Calm seas.

✰✰✰✰ **Big Tunnels**, north of the Seven Mile Beach area, feature a 50-ft coral archway linked to several tunnels and ledges bursting with rainbow gorgonians, sea fans, basket sponges, tube sponges, and branching corals. Eagle rays drift by walls of sea urchins, anemones, grunts, puffer fish, bigeyes, and shrimp. Big morays peek from the ledges. An occasional nurse shark appears. Depths average 110 ft, with excellent visibility. Experience recommended.

☆☆☆☆ **The Wreck of the *Balboa***, a 375-ft freighter, rests at 30 ft in George Town Harbor, 200 yards off the town pier. A favorite night dive, its twisted wreckage creates interesting video and still opportunities. Seas are calm, with good visibility, though several divers visiting the wreck at one time may kick up silt. Schools of sergeant majors, grouper, queen and French angels mingle about the hull.

☆☆☆ **Aquarium** sits close to shore off the center of Seven Mile Beach. As the name implies, this spot serves as a grand meeting center for most every species of fish in the Caribbean. Count-and-name-the-fish is the favorite sport at this 35-ft-deep coral grotto. Be sure to tote a waterproof fish ID card or book.

Spotted trunkfish, parrot fish, snappers, file fish, spotted morays, butterflyfish, queen angels, queen triggerfish, puffers and schooling barracudas inhabit Aquarium. Though hard to see through the crowds of fish, the reef is very pretty, with nice stands of staghorn coral, sponges and soft corals. Visibility is superb. Calm seas make this a good choice for new divers.

☆☆☆ **The Wreck of the *Oro Verde*** lies 30 to 50 ft beneath the surface, straight out from the Holiday Inn on Seven Mile Beach. After this 180-ft freighter ran aground in 1976, local dive operators scuttled the wreck to create an artificial reef. The hull, intact, is very photogenic. Divers are warmly greeted by its inhabitants – Spanish hogfish, French angels, snappers, butterflyfish, blue tangs, and rock beauties. Seas are calm.

☆☆☆ **Tarpon Alley**, a coral canyon, mirrors schools of giant silvery tarpon, mammoth grouper and sting rays. Large pelagics flash by too. The "alley," south of Orange Canyon, lies partially in the Seven Mile Beach replenishment zone. Top of the canyon walls are at 60 ft. Outside drop-offs plunge to several thousand ft. Surface conditions are occasionally choppy.

☆☆☆☆ **Grand Canyon**, an enormous channel enclosed by jagged, perpendicular mountains off Rum Point, is the favored north shore dive. The walls display a cornucopia of sponges, sea whips, sea fans, hard corals and critters. Depths start at 60 ft and drop off. Experience a must. Excellent visibility.

☆☆☆ **Japanese Gardens**, a series of long coral ridges off the island's south tip, blossom with elkhorn and antler corals, vase sponges and schooling fish. Depths start at 50 ft.

Snorkeling

Patch reefs and coral heads teeming with reef fish lie just a few yards off several of the island's swimming beaches. The best shore spots are found off **West Bay Cemetery, Seven Mile Beach, Eden Rock Dive Center** in **Georgetown, Smith Cove, Treasure Island Resort beach, Rum Point**

Club, Parrots Landing, Seaview Hotel, Coconut Harbour, Sunset House, Pirates Inn, Frank Sound Half Moon Bay, East End Diving Lodge and **Morritt's Tortuga Club**. Depths range from three to 20 ft. Clearer water and more dramatic coral formations are found farther offshore and may be reached by boat. Snorkeling cruises, some with dinner or lunch, are offered by the hotels and dive shops. Snorkelers are urged to inquire about currents and local conditions in unfamiliar areas before attempting to explore on their own.

Swimmers off the Rum Point Club beach should stay clear of the channels, which have rip tides. Grand Cayman's **Southwest Point** shows a good variety of juvenile reef fish and invertebrates on a rocky bottom close to shore. Currents beyond 100 yds are dangerous.

A trail marked by a round blue and white sign with a swimmer outline denotes access through private property to the beach. All Cayman beaches are free for public use.

☆☆ **Smiths Cove**, south of George Town, shelters a shallow reef whiskered with pastel sea fans and plumes. Trumpet fish, squirrel fish, schools of grunts, sergeant majors, butterfly fish, parrot fish and angels offer constant entertainment. The reef sits 150 ft from the beach at Southwest Point. Depths are from 15 to 45 ft.

☆☆ **Eden Rocks**, favored by cruise ship groups, lies less than 200 yds offshore from the Eden Rock Diving Center. Depths range from five to 40 ft. The reef features beautiful coral grottoes, walls, caves and tunnels – and tame fish. If you've yet to befriend a fish, this area offers the proper social climate. Good visibility and light currents are the norm here.

☆☆ **Sand Bar** at Stingray City in North Sound is home to several tame stingrays. Depths are shallow to 12 ft. Boat access. Trips departing from Georgetown or Seven Mile Beach are either a half- or full-day tour.

East End Diving

Grand Cayman's rural East End, 20 miles across the island from Seven Mile Beach, offers an entirely different dive-vacation setting. Devoid of shopping centers, traffic jams and commercial establishments, this wilderness region lures divers who relish a slower, laid-back pace, uncrowded beaches and uncharted dive sites. Underwater terrain is similar to West Wall sites, with fabulous walls, overhangs, caves, tunnels, grottos and remnants of shipwrecks. There are no moorings.

Large turtle entertains divers off Seven Mile Beach.

Courtesy Cayman Islands Department of Tourism

Strong currents sometimes rule out a number of the sites in this area, but they greatly benefit the marine life by carrying nutrients that encourage the growth of gigantic, brilliant colored sponges and soft corals. Fish life is outstanding, with passing palegics, walls of tarpon, gigantic jewfish, eagle rays, green and hawksbill turtles. Whale sharks have been spotted here during winter.

Dive Operators

Costs for a two-tank dive average $60 to $70; one-tank dives, $45. Snorkeling trips range from $25 to $35. All the dive shops that offer boat tours have Stingray City tours. These average $50 from the west coast. Most shops rent photo, video, dive and snorkeling gear. Trips include tanks and weights. Resort and certification courses are offered everywhere. Unless otherwise noted, shops accept American Express, MasterCard or Visa credit cards.

Abanks' Watersports on South Church Street is a short walk from downtown Georgetown and paradise Beach Club. This PADI shop offers dive and snorkel trips, resort and certification courses. A two-tank dive trip costs $60 to $70. Snorkelers pay $30. Boats carry 14 divers. ☎ 345-945-1444, fax 345-949-6290, E-mail: abanksx@aol.com.

Ambassador Divers, a PADI shop located at Ambassadors Inn in George Town, specializes in computer diving. They offer one- and two-tank dives, certification and resort courses, snorkeling trips, gear rental, video rental, trips to 345-Stingray City. Dive/accommodation packages. ☎ 800-648-7748 or 345-949-8839, fax 345-949-8839. Write to PO Box 2396 GT, Grand Cayman, BWI.

Aquanauts Diving at Morgan's Harbour is a short run to the North and West Walls. Complimentary shuttle for Seven Mile Beach area guests. Boats carry 16 divers. Two-tank dive costs $65, snorkelers pay $25. ☎ 345-945-1990, fax 345-945-1991. E-mail: aquanaut@candw.ky.

Bob Soto's Diving Ltd. is a PADI five-star facility with Seven Mile Beach locations at the Treasure Island Hotel and the Scuba Centre, near Soto's Reef. The operation offers dive and snorkeling trips, underwater photo and video services, camera and gear rentals, open water PADI certifications, completion dives, and comfortable custom dive boats. Complete dive/accommodation packages with Grand Cayman hotels and condominiums available. Two-tank dive $65, snorkelers pay $25. Boats carry 20 divers. ☎ 800-262-7686, 345-949-2022, fax 345-949-8731. E-mail: bobsotos@candw.ky. Write to PO Box 1801, Grand Cayman, BWI.

Capitol's Surfside has been serving the Seven Mile Beach area for 28 years. Dive boats carry 20 divers. Courses and trips for scuba and snorkeling. All rentals. Two-tank dive $60, snorkelers pay $25. ☎ 800-543-6828 or 345-949-7330, fax 345-949-8639.

Capt. Marvin's Aquatics' large boats carry 40 divers. Located in West Bay, this experienced dive operation offers scuba and snorkeling trips, Stingray City tours, courses and gear rental. ☎ 345-945-4590, fax 345-945-5673. E-mail: captmvn@candw.ky. Write to PO Box 413, West Bay, Grand Cayman, BWI.

Cayman Diving School offers courses ranging from Resort to Dive Master. ☎ 345-949-4729, fax 345-949-4729. E-mail: rivsport@candw.ky. Write to PO Box 1308, George Town, Grand Cayman, BWI.

Celebrity Divers in George Town features small, personalized tours with 10 or fewer divers on board. Snorkeling and Stingray City tours. ☎ 345-3410. No credit cards.

Clint Ebanks Scuba Cayman Ltd. on West Bay Road offers certification and resort courses, one- and two-tank dive trips, Stingray City tours, and snorkeling trips. Gear rental. ☎ 345-949-3873, fax 345-949-6244.

Crosby Ebanks C & G Watersports at Coconut Place Tropic Center specializes in dive and snorkeling trips to Stingray City. ☎ 345-945-4049, fax 345-945-5994. E-mail: crosby@cayman.org. Website: www.cayman.org/crosby/.

Dive N Stuff's 12-passenger boats tour all the spots off Seven Mile Beach and offer special tours of Stingray City. PADI certification courses, gear rentals. ☎ 345-949-6033, fax 345-949-6033. E-mail: divenstuff@cayman.org. Website: www.cayman.org/divenstuff/.

Dive Time Ltd. in Georgetown also has PADI and NAUI certification, one- and two-tank six-passenger boat dives, photo, video, snorkel and dive gear rental. ☎ 345-947-2339, fax 345-947-3308.

Divers Down, Georgetown, specializes in PADI Nitrox certification courses. Their custom, eight-passenger boat takes off for two one- or two-tank dive trips daily. Gear rentals. ☎ 345-945-1611, fax 945-1611.

Don Foster's Dive Cayman, a full-service facility based on Seven Mile Beach, offers certification and resort courses, daily dives, rental and a photo center. Plus, snorkeling excursions, waverunners and sailboats. ☎ 800-83-DIVER, or 972-722-2535, fax 972-722-6511 E-mail: dfd@candw.ky. Website: www.donfosters.com.

Eden Rock Diving Center touts unlimited shore diving on GeorgeTown's waterfront, with guided tours of Eden Rocks Reef and Devil's Grotto. Certification with PADI, NAUI and SSI. Photo, video, dive and snorkel gear rentals. They sell underwater cameras, tropical T-shirts and gifts. ☎ 345-949-7243, fax 345-949-0842. E-mail: edenrock@candw.ky.

Fisheye of Cayman offers scuba tours aboard three custom dive boats to the north, west and south sides of the island, including Stingray City. Snorkelers may join dive trips to Stingray City and North Wall based on space availability. Trips include free use of underwater cameras. Accommodation packages. E-mail: fisheye@candw.ky. Website: www.fisheye.com. ☎ 800-887-8569, 345-945-4209, fax 345-945-4208.

Indies Divers at Indies Suites visits both North and West wall sites. Boats carry 12 divers. PADI certification and resort courses. Nitrox training. Snorkelers welcome. Niceties include illustrated briefings, fresh fruit and towels. ☎ 800-654-3130 or 345-945-5025, fax 345-945-5024. E-mail: indiessuites@worldnet.att.net.

Ocean Frontiers, Cayman's newest operation, offers East End diving. Snorkelers welcome on the 12-passenger boats. PADI courses. Gear and photo rentals. ☎ 345-947-7500, fax 345-947-7500. E-mail: oceanf@candw.ky. Website: www.oceanfrontiers.com.

Off the Wall Divers offer personalized dive/snorkeling tours. ☎ 345-947-7790, fax 345-947-7790. E-mail: otwtim@candw.ky. No credit cards.

Ollen Miller's Sun Divers on Seven Mile Beach features small groups, personalized service for divers and snorkelers. ☎ 345-947-6606, fax 345-947-6706. No credit cards.

Cayman Islands

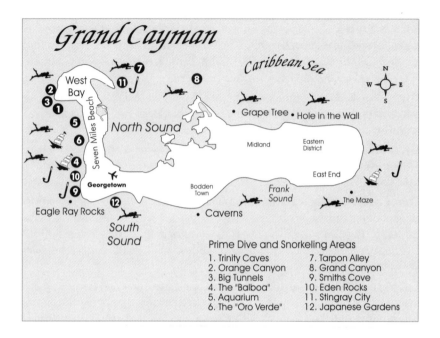

Prime Dive and Snorkeling Areas

1. Trinity Caves
2. Orange Canyon
3. Big Tunnels
4. The "Balboa"
5. Aquarium
6. The "Oro Verde"
7. Tarpon Alley
8. Grand Canyon
9. Smiths Cove
10. Eden Rocks
11. Stingray City
12. Japanese Gardens

Parrots Landing Watersports Park, a half-mile south of downtown Georgetown, has excellent shore diving on four beautiful, shallow reefs 30 yds from their dock and a wall dive 115 yds out. Seven 20-passenger dive boats visit the South Wall, West Wall and Northwest Point. A 60-ft sailing catamaran, the *Cockatoo*, sails from North Sound to Stingray City. Squid is provided for snorkelers to hand feed the rays. PADI and NAUI certifications. On shore, the park features picnic tables, sun deck and a half-dozen friendly Cayman parrots. Park shuttle boats and buses will pick you up anywhere along Seven Mile Beach. SSI and YMCA check-out dives. The park offers complete air/accommodation/dive packages with your choice of any hotel or condo on the island. ☎ 800-448-0428 or 345-949-7884. E-mail: parrots@ candw.ky. Write to 218 S. Church Street, George Town, Grand Cayman, BWI.

Peter Milburn's Dive Cayman Ltd. has been on the island for 18 years. Their 14-passenger boats make three dive/snorkel trips daily. Dive gear rental. ☎ 345-945-5770, fax 345-945-5786. E-mail: pmilburn@candw.ky. No credit cards.

Red Sail Sports, at the Marriott Resort, across from the Hyatt Regency and at the Westin Casuarina on Seven Mile Beach, offers dive and snorkeling trips, PADI certification courses and daily resort courses. Snorkel and dive trips, dinner and cocktail cruises. Waterskiing and parasailing. ☎ 800-255-

6425 or 345-947-5965, fax 345-947-5808. E-mail: redsail@candw.ky. Website: www.redsail.com.

Resort Sports Limited, at Beach Club Colony and Spanish Bay Reef hotels, offers resort courses and PADI, NAUI or SSI certification. Camera and gear rentals for scuba and snorkeling. Night dives, Stingray City trips and snorkeling tours. ☎ 345-949-8100, fax 345-949-5167.

River Sport Divers Ltd. at the Coconut Place Shopping Center in West Bay, offers instruction and caters to all levels of divers. ☎ 345-949-1181, fax 345-949-1296.

Seasports picks up divers by boat at hotels and condos along Seven Mile Beach. Small groups. PADI, NAUI courses. Snorkelers welcome. ☎ 345-949-3965, fax 345-945-6383.

Seven Mile Watersports on Seven Mile Beach, offers dive and snorkeling tours. ☎ 345-949-0332, fax 345-949-0331. E-mail: smbort@candw.ky.

Sunset Divers at Sunset House provides scuba instruction and dive packages, but is best known for its Underwater Photo Centre, operated by Cathy Church. The Centre offers 35mm and video camera rental, processing and photo instruction for all levels. Very informal and friendly, with personalized service. ☎ 800-854-4767 or 345-949-7111, fax 345-854-7101. E-mail: sunseths@candw.ky. Website: www.sunsethouse.com. Write to PO Box 479, Grand Cayman, BWI.

Soto's Cruises, for advanced and certified divers, visits all the popular West Wall sites. ☎ 345-945-4576, fax 945-1527. Write to PO Box 30192, Seven Mile Beach, Grand Cayman, BWI.

Tortuga Divers Ltd., at the Morritt's Tortuga Club on the East End, operates two 34-foot custom dive boats that accommodate up to 14 passengers. The shop has a nice range of services and courses for beginning divers and snorkelers. ☎ 345-947-2097, fax 345-947-9486. E-mail: tortugad@ candw.ky.

Treasure Island Divers at the Treasure Island Resort, offers instruction, shore dives, snorkeling trips, sail cruises to all four sides of Grand Cayman. Their 45-foot boats have freshwater showers, marine heads and a sundeck that shades the bottom deck. Their first trip leaves at 8 am. ☎ 800-872-7552 or 345-949-4456, fax 345-949-7125, E-mail: tidivers@netrunner.net. Website: www.tidivers.com. Write PO Box 30975 SMB, Grand Cayman, BWI.

Dive Resorts & Accommodations

Grand Cayman has accommodations and packages for every budget and every need. All dive shops listed above offer a money-saving, dive accommodation package, some with air. For a complete list of guest houses, cottages and condos, contact the Cayman Islands Department of Tourism, 6100 Blue Lagoon Drive, Suite 150, Miami, FL 33126, ☎ 800-346-3313 or 305-266-2300, fax 305-267-2932. New York, ☎ 212-682-5582, fax 212-986-5123. United Kingdom, ☎ 071-491-7771, fax 071-017-1409. Canada, ☎ 800-263-5805 or 416-485-1550, fax 416-485-7578. Grand Cayman, ☎ 345-949-0623, fax 345-949-4053. Website: www.caymanislands.ky.

Seven Mile Beach Resorts

Caribbean Club features beautiful beachfront villas that start at $285 per day in winter, from $175 in summer. Dive trips arranged. ☎ 345-945-4099, fax 345-945-4443. E-mail: reservations@caribclub.com. Website: www. caribclub.com.

Treasure Island Resort, a 25-acre beachfront luxury hotel, features 280 spacious air-conditioned rooms. All have ceiling fans, satellite TV, in-room safes and mini-bars. Resort facilities include a well-equipped dive shop, gourmet restaurant, two freshwater pools, tennis and entertainment. Winter rates for a standard double room start at $220 per day. Summer, $155. ☎ 800-203-0775 or 345-949-7777, fax 345-949-8672. Call for current dive package rates.

Hyatt Regency Grand Cayman, on Seven Mile Beach and the centerpiece of the Britannia Golf and Beach Resort, has a complete watersports center and full-service spa. Standard rooms run from $305 in winter, from $190 in summer. Deluxe from $385. ☎ 800-233-1234 or 345-949-1234, fax 345-949-5526.

Westin Casuarina Resort offers 343 luxurious guest suites, all water sports – diving, snorkeling, fishing, windsurfing – restaurant, jacuzzi, pool, handicap access, tennis, photo center, lush tropical grounds, and a lovely stretch of Seven Mile Beach. ☎ 800-228-3000 or 345-945-3800, fax 345-949-3804. Write to PO Box 30620, Seven Mile Beach, Grand Cayman, BWI.

George Town Area

Beach Club Colony, George Town, offers all-inclusive packages starting at $230 per day in winter, from $180 in summer. Lovely palm-lined beach. Restaurant. Resorts Sports Limited on premises offering dive and snorkeling trips. Tennis, photo shop. ☎ 800-482-DIVE or 345-949-8100, fax 345-945-5167. Write to PO Box 903, George Town, Grand Cayman, BWI.

Coconut Harbour, south of Seven Mile Beach, has suites with mini-kitchens, cabana bar and open air restaurant, shore diving on Waldo's Reef out front. Parrot's Landing Dive Shop on premises. Children under 12 stay free with parents. Rates include continental breakfast daily. Winter room rates, $152. Summer, $145. ☎ 800-552-6281 or 345-949-7468, fax 345-949-7117. Write to PO Box 2086 GT, Grand Cayman, BWI.

Indies Suites, a beachfront 41-suite hotel, features a pool, jacuzzi, bar, and handicap access. Apartments rent from $180 per day in summer, $285 in winter. Indies Divers on premises runs dive and snorkeling trips to Stingray City, the North and West Walls, gear rental. ☎ 800-654-3130 or 345-947-5025, fax 345-947-5024.

Spanish Bay Reef Resort, an all-inclusive resort, includes room, meals, beverages, bicycles, scuba/snorkel lesson, snorkeling equipment, airport transfers, taxes and gratuities. Winter rates, per day, per person are from $210, summer from $170. ☎ 800-482-DIVE or 345-949-3765, fax 345-949-1842. Write to PO Box 903, George Town, Grand Cayman, BWI.

Sleep Inn Hotel features standard and deluxe guest suites from $120 in summer, $185 in winter. Watersports can be arranged. ☎ 800-SLEEP-INN or 345-949-9111, fax 345-949-6699. E-mail: sleepinn@candw.ky.

Sunset House, a 59-room resort owned and operated by divers for divers, sits south of Seven Mile Beach. Good diving and snorkeling from the beach! Room rates for a standard start at $110 in summer, $135 in winter. Packages for five nights, four days of two-tank diving and unlimited shore diving start at $662.50. ☎ 800-854-4767 or 345-949-7111, fax 345-949-7101. E-mail: sunseths@candw.ky. Website: www.sunsethouse.com. Write to PO Box 479, George Town, Grand Cayman, BWI.

East End

Cayman Diving Lodge has 14 guest rooms, a club-like atmosphere, and all-inclusive dive or snorkeling packages. Call for current rates. Snorkelers join the dive trips, or may choose to explore the shallow reef in a protected lagoon off the resort's beach. Dive trips are more adventurous than in the Seven Mile Beach area. Expect some current, but with it comes a host of marine life and robust corals and sponges. Super for divers who prefer to be off-the-beaten-track. ☎ 800-TLC-DIVE or 345-947-7555, fax 806-798-7568. E-mail: divelodge@aol.com. Website: www.divelodge.com.

Morritt's Tortuga Club caters to those seeking luxurious oceanfront accommodations in a very private setting. The 121 air-conditioned suites feature kitchenettes, TV and phones. Pool, jacuzzi, restaurant, bar, laundry facilities and Tortugas Divers shop on premises. Room rates start at $145 in summer, $175 in winter. ☎ 800-447-0309 or 345-947-7449, fax 345-947-7299. E-mail: reservations@morritts.com. Write to PO Box 496-GT, East End, Grand Cayman, BWI.

Other Activities

Fishing, windsurfing, parasailing, and tennis are offered at most condos and resorts. An 18-hole, a nine-hole and a special Cayman course are located

Cayman Islands

next to the Hyatt Regency Grand Cayman. On the latter, you use special light-weight balls that travel about half the distance of a normal ball. Grand Cayman's night clubs and larger hotels offer live entertainment and dancing. The Cayman National Theater presents live performances of drama, comedy and musicals.

Sightseeing

The capital city, George Town, has a well-scrubbed look not always found in the Caribbean. Visitors can tour the area by foot, taxi, moped or rental car. Courtesy phones at the airport connect to the car rental dealers. Driving is on the left. Along George Town's waterfront several historic clapboard buildings have been lovingly restored and converted into souvenir shops, galleries and boutiques. Native crafts such as black coral and tortoise shell jewelry along with imported goods may be purchased here.

Heading north along the famed Seven Mile Beach you come to the largest congregation of hotels, condos, shopping malls and restaurants. Each morning dive boats line up here and offer door-to-reef service to resort and condo guests.

A side trip to the Cayman Turtle Farm is always fun, as is a visit to Hell, the town where visitors delight in having mail postmarked to send back home.

Dining

Grand Cayman offers visitors an enormous variety of choices in dining. Shopping centers along West Bay Road house several fast food eateries such as Burger King, Pizza Hut, Kentucky Fried Chicken and TCBY Yogurt. For su-perb local specialties such as conch stew, curried chicken and native fish try the **Cracked Conch** by the sea on West Bay Road, **Myrtles** on N. Church St. or the **Almond Tree** on N. Church St. near George Town.

For more formal dining – all seafood – try the **Wharf**, waterfront on West Bay Road, ☎ 949-2231, **Seaharvest Restaurant** in front of Sunset House, ☎ 945-1383, **The Lobster Pot**, above Bob Soto's Dive shop, or **Ristorante Pappagallo** on West Bay Road, set in an exotic, modern thatched-hut-style building.

Cayman Brac

Often called the loveliest of the islands, this 12-mile strip of land is rumored to be the resting place of pirates' treasure. Lying some 87 miles east of Grand Cayman, Cayman Brac's (brac is Gaelic for bluff) most striking feature is a 140-foot-high limestone formation covered by unusual foliage, including flowering cactus, orchids and tropical fruits such as mango and papaya. Rare species of birds, including the endangered green, blue and red Caymanian parrot, inhabit the island, which is a major flyway for migratory birds. Resident brown booby birds soar the cliffs. Cayman Brac is also known for its many caves where pirates, in earlier centuries, took refuge and, according to legend, buried their treasures. In fact, a peg-legged turtle pirate is the country's national symbol. Native fir, palm and papaya trees shade the narrow streets. Fragrant thickets of bougainvillea, hibiscus, periwinkle, and oleander surround the islanders' houses, many of which were built with wood salvaged from the wreckage of ships that crashed on the reefs. A visit to the **Cayman Brac Museum** in Stake Bay offers a look at the history of shipbuilding on the island.

Activities other than diving and snorkeling are limited. There are a few restaurants scattered along the main road that also feature elevated caves with ladders for the tourists; **NIM Things** gift shop which sells fabulous handmade woven bags, local crafts and post cards; and the main town area which has a convenience store, post office, gift shops and the island museum.

Best Dive & Snorkeling Sites of Cayman Brac

☆☆☆ **Wreck of the *Tibbetts***, a 330-ft Russian destroyer built for the Cuban Navy, was renamed the *Captain Keith Tibbets* and deliberately sunk off the northwest coast of Cayman Brac on September 17, 1996. The vessel, the most exciting new dive attraction in the Cayman Islands, is easily accessible from shore if you don't mind a 200-yd swim, but is favored as a boat dive. All levels of divers may explore several swim-throughs, including the bridge and upper deck. Fore and aft cannons, missile launcher and machine gun turrets remain on the ship. Snorkelers may easily view the top of the radar tower at 20 to 25 feet and the bridge at 80 feet below the surface.

☆☆☆☆ **The Hobbit**, off the Brac's southeast tip, presents divers with a fairy-tale setting of giant barrel sponges and dazzling corals inhabited by chubs, turtles, queen angels, octopi, grunts and queen triggerfish. Average depth runs 70 ft. Suggested for intermediate to advanced divers. Excellent visibility. Boat access.

☆☆☆☆ **Radar Reef** encompasses a series of coral pinnacles and canyons, each home to a splendid variety of elkhorn, star, and brain corals, lavender sea fans, tube and barrel sponges, feather dusters, and sea whips. Inhabitants of this lively community include turtles, sting rays, octopi, and swirls of tropicals. A normally calm surface and shallow depths – from 30 to 60 ft – make this a good choice for new divers. Boat access or swim out from the beach adjacent to Island Dock.

Cayman Islands

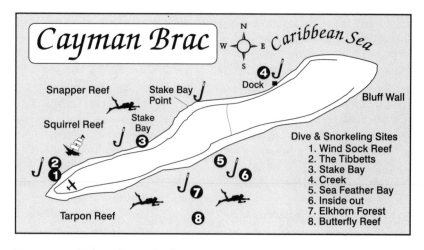

Cayman Brac Snorkeling

Several excellent shore-entry points exist off the north and south shores. Wind conditions determine which area is calm. Usually, if the north shore spots are choppy, the south shore is calm. Check with area dive shops for daily conditions.

North Shore

☆☆☆☆ **WindSock Reef** and the **Wreck of the _Tibbetts_**, in White Bay off the northwest coast is the Brac's most popular snorkeling spot. The reef, which lies close to the shoreline, shelters elkhorn and brain coral patches while providing haven for a good variety of juveniles and tropicals. This spur and groove reef encircles gardens of elkhorn, pillar corals, sea fans, orange sponges and gorgonians. Angels, barracudas, butterfly fish, file fish, trumpet fish and critters hide in the ledges and crevices. Expect good visibility and usually calm seas. Typical inhabitants are stoplight parrot fish, blue tangs, midnight parrot fish, sergeant majors, turtles, grey angels, grunts, trumpet fish and triggerfish. Shore area depths range from four to 20 ft.

The mast of the _Tibbetts'_ wreck breaks the surface and is easily spotted from the beach. Some prefer snorkeling the wreck, which lies 200 yds offshore, from a boat; but if you're in good shape, you can swim out. The top of the wreck lies 20 to 25 ft below the surface. See scuba section for details. Check with area dive shops before venturing out. Visibility is usually 100 ft or better.

To reach White Bay, travel the North Shore Rd (A6) west from the airport to Promise Lane. Turn left. The beach entry point is behind the closed Buccaneer Inn Hotel.

☆☆ **Stake Bay**. Find this spot by turning off the North Shore Rd at the Cayman Brac Museum. Reef terrain, depths and fish life are similar to White

Bay. Sea conditions usually calm, but will kick up when the wind is out of the North.

☆☆ **Creek** lies off the north shore. A turn towards the shore from Cliff's Store on the North Shore Rd (A6) will lead to the Island Dock. Enter from the beach area left of the dock, facing seaward. Dense patches of elkhorn predominate. Depths are shallow to 30 ft. Angels, small turtles, and sergeant majors swarm the reef. Wind speed and direction determines the conditions, though seas are usually calm with a light current.

Additional entry points are found at the boat launching areas, where cuts have been blasted through the dense coral. Parking is available along the north road.

South Shore

☆☆ **Sea Feather Bay**, off the South Shore Rd at the Bluff Rd crossing, provides haven for pretty wrasses, turtles, blue parrot fish, grouper, indigo hamlets, squirrelfish, porkfish, blue tangs, and rockfish. Reef terrain is comprised of long stretches of dense elkhorn interspersed with tube sponges, fire coral, rose coral and gorgonians. After a big storm, this area becomes a wash-up zone for some strange cargo, such as rubber doll parts and unusual bottles, which may come from Cuba. Expect some surge and shallow breakers. Visibility is good, though silt may churn up the shallows following a storm.

Experienced snorkelers may want to dive the barrier reef at the southwestern tip of the island. Water entry is best by boat, but if you enjoy a long swim you can get out to the reef from either the public beach or one of the hotel beaches.

Cayman Brac Dive Operators & Accommodations

Almond Beach Hideaways, the Brac's newest accommodations, offer roomy two- and three-bedroom villas on a white sand beach. Dive and snorkel from the beach. Villas that sleep six are priced from $185 per day. ☎ 800-972-9795 or 541-426-4863, fax 541-426-4863. E-mail: brac@almondbeach.com. Website: www.almondbeach.com.

Brac Aquatics Ltd. offers certification courses, reef tours and gear rentals. ☎ 800-544-2722 or 345-948-1429, fax 345-948-1527.

Brac Reef Beach Resort and **Reef Divers** has comfortable air-conditioned rooms with satellite TV, a great beach, fresh water pool, whirlpool, beach bar and restaurant. Complete dive/accommodation packages start at $889 in summer, $1,046 in winter, for five nights, three meals daily, three one-tank dives per day, ground transfers and bicycles. For seven nights, $1,269 in summer, $1,492 in winter. Unlimited beach dives. ☎ 800-327-3835 or 813-323-8727, fax 345-948-1207. Dive shop 345-948-1323, fax

Cayman Islands

Photo ©Jon Huber 1999

"Soon Come" sits on its own private beach. (See listing below)

948-1207. E-mail: bestdiving@aol.com. Website: www.braclittle.com. Write to PO Box 56, Cayman Brac, BWI.

Brac Caribbean Beach Village offers 16 condo units from $185 per day for a standard, from $245 for deluxe. Each unit has two bedrooms, air-conditioning, ceiling fan and telephone. Beachfront. ☎ 800-791-7911 or 345-948-2265, fax 345-948-1111.

Divi Tiara Beach Hotel and **Peter Hughes Dive Tiara** cater almost exclusively to divers and snorkelers. This first-class resort features a freshwater pool, jacuzzi, tennis, 71 spacious, air-conditioned rooms, auto rentals, sailboards, bicycles and paddleboats. Snorkeling and diving are found right off the resort's palm-lined beach. Dive Tiara spares no effort to make every dive trip relaxing, safe and fun aboard any one of six custom-designed dive boats. The shop offers tours to the best dives of Cayman Brac as well as Little Cayman daily. A seasoned boat crew readily assists divers with gear set-ups and getting in and out of the water. There's no need to lug your gear back and forth to your room; it stays overnight in a gear storage room on Tiara's dive pier. Room rates based on a double are $125 for a standard, $145 for deluxe. One-tank dives are $30, two-tank, $55. Snorkelers pay $40 for a boat trip. Package rates available. ☎ 800-367-3484, 800-661-DIVE or 345-948-1553, fax 345-948-1563. E-mail: divtiara@candw.ky. Write to Divi Tiara Beach Hotel, PO Box 238, Stake Bay, Cayman Brac, B.W.I.

La Esperanza offers two-bedroom and three-bedroom condos from $70 in summer, $110 in winter.

There are other facilities, such as **Soon Come,** a charming, modern two-bedroom oceanfront house for rent on the isolated South Shore. Very nice! Rents for $150 per day from December 18 to April 18; $100 per day the rest of the year. ☎ 212-447-0337, fax 212-447-0335. E-mail: clofting@aol.com.

Little Cayman

Populated by fewer than 100 people, Little Cayman retains a rural and unhurried ambiance. Its grass runway, unpaved roads and limited phone service attest to its long-standing reputation as a great get-away vacation spot. Activities include diving, snorkeling, fly fishing and counting iguanas. When you visit Little Cayman, keep in mind that there are no stores. Items such as aspirin, mosquito repellent, decongestants, and sun lotion should be packed from home. Few accommodations offer air-conditioning.

Best Dives of Little Cayman

☆☆☆☆☆ **Bloody Bay Wall** is one of the top dives in all the Caymans. The "Wall" peaks as a shallow reef at 15 ft and drops off to an unfathomed bottom. Bright orange and lavender tube sponges, pastel gorgonians and soft corals flourish in the shallows.

An extremely friendly six-foot barracuda named Snort may join your dive at Bloody Bay Wall, flashing his pearly whites while cheerfully posing for videos and still photos.

Eagle rays blast by the wall along with slow-moving turtles and huge parrot fish. Spotted morays peek from the walls. Sea conditions are usually calm, although a stiff wind will churn the surface. Divers of all levels will enjoy diving Bloody Bay Wall. Super snorkeling in the shallows. Boat access.

☆☆☆☆ **Little Cayman Wall,** off the island's west end, starts shallow with a blaze of yellow, orange and blue sponges at 15 ft, then drops off to unknown depths. Soft corals, big barrel sponges decorate the wall. Great for snorkeling and diving. Boat access.

The Western half of the wall is called the "Bloody Bay Wall" and the eastern half "Jackson Wall."

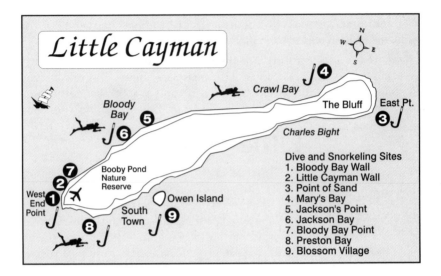

Snorkeling

Little Cayman has several superb snorkeling spots with visibility often exceeding 100 ft. Ground transportation to beach-access sites is easily arranged through the dive operators. For the ultimate in free diving head out to **Bloody Bay** and **Spot Bay** off the north shore, where the seas are calm and the marine life spectacular. The boat ride takes about 25 minutes. Average depth on top of the North Wall is 25 ft.

☆☆☆ **Point of Sand**, off the southeast end of Little Cayman, is excellent for experienced and beginning snorkelers. A gentle current flowing from west to east maintains very good visibility. The bottom is sandy with many coral heads scattered about. Marine life is fine and the site is accessible from the shore. Ground transportation can be arranged from the resorts.

☆☆☆ Good snorkeling at Mary's Bay starts 50 yds from the beach inside the barrier reef. There is no current and visibility runs about 30 to 50 ft. A host of fish and invertebrates inhabit the shallows. Depths run three to eight ft. The bottom is turtle grass, requiring booties or other submersible footwear. An old shack on an otherwise deserted shore marks the spot. Perfect for beginners.

☆☆ **Jackson Point**, aka School Bus, is for experienced snorkelers only. Swim out about 75 yds from the beach, where you'll see a small wall towering from a sandy bottom at 40 ft to 15 ft. Hundreds of fish, rays and turtles congregate in the shallows. Corals and sponges carpet the area. Swimming another 50 to 60 ft brings you to a much larger wall that drops off to extraordinary depths.

☆☆ **Jackson Bay** resembles Jackson Point except for the bottom of the mini-wall, which drops off to a depth of 50 to 60 ft. Beach access.

☆☆☆ **Bloody Bay Point**, recommended for seasoned snorkelers, requires a 100-yd swim out to the reef. The bottom eases down to about 30 ft before the drop-off to the Great Wall begins. Well worth a visit for the spectacular coral and marine life.

☆ **Preston Bay**, just east of the lighthouse, provides another good shore-entry choice for beginning snorkelers. Maximum shoreline depth is six ft and visibility 30 to 50 ft. Swarming fish and a white sandy bottom offer endless photo opportunities.

☆☆ **Blossom Village**, a lovely, shallow reef, displays crowds of reef fish and critters amidst staghorn and brain corals at depths from four to eight ft. Boat access. A light current maintains 50-100 ft visibility.

Little Cayman Dive Operators & Accommodations

Little Cayman dive operations are smaller than those on Cayman Brac and Grand Cayman.

Conch Club Condominiums feature luxurious two- and three- bedroom town homes on a private beach. All amenities. Pool, jacuzzi, dive boat. Room rates start at $300 in summer for a two-bedroom, $350 for three-bedroom; in winter, $350 for two-bedroom, $400 for three-bedroom. Three dives aboard their new dive boat cost $95 per person, per day. ☎ 800- 327-3835 or 813-323-8727, fax 813-323-8827. E-mail: conchclub@aol.com. Website: www.conchclub.com.

Little Cayman Beach Resort features air-conditioned rooms, fresh water pool, jacuzzi, cabana bar, tennis, restaurant, and a full-service dive/photo operation. Bicycles. Rates per person for a double, including three meals and three one-tank dives daily, five nights $1,204 in summer, seven nights $1,714. Five nights $1,370 in winter, seven nights $1,949. Lower rates for non-divers. ☎ 800-327-3835 or 813-323-8727, fax 813-323-8827.

Southern Cross Club, a fishing and diving resort comprised of five double cottages, warmly welcomes divers. Divemasters will take you to all the top dive and snorkel sites on Bloody Bay Wall or South Shore. Snorkelers mix with scuba groups. IANTD Nitrox facility. Resort courses are available. Rooms run from $134 in summer to $162 in winter. ☎ 800-899-2582 or 345-948-1099, fax 345-948-1098. E-mail: relax@southerncrossclub.com.

Website: southerncrossclub.com. Write to Southern Cross Club, PO Box 44, Little Cayman, Cayman Islands, BWI.

Sam McCoy's Diving and Fishing Lodge, on the North Shore, offers rustic accommodations for up to 14 divers (seven rooms). Rooms in the main lodge are air-conditioned with private bath. Twenty-ft fiberglass runabouts are used for reef trips. Shore diving from Jackson's Point. Rates per day start at $191 per person. Dive packages available. ☎ 800-626-0496 or 345-948-0026, fax 345-948-0057. E-mail: mccoy@candw.ky. Website: www.cayman.com.ky/com/sam. Or write to Carl McCoy, PO Box 711, George Town, Grand Cayman, BWI.

Pirates Point Resort features rustic guest cottages and a guest house on seven acres of secluded white beach. Owner Gladys Howard offers friendly service, all-inclusive dive packages from $210 per person summer, $230 winter, per day. ☎ 800-327-8777 or 345-948-1010, fax 345-948-101

Cayman Live-Aboards

The *Cayman Aggressor III*. Based in George Town, this luxury yacht features double staterooms and one quad which holds 18 passengers, along with a salon, carpeting, E-6 film processing, air-conditioning, TV, video equipment and hot showers. Nitrox, rebreather rentals and courses. Enjoyable meals, including soups and salads, chicken, turkey, native fish and snacks, are prepared on board. Packages cover transfers, meals, diving, tanks, backpacks and weights. Prices are commensurate with those of Cayman land resorts. Write to Aggressor Fleet, PO Drawer 1470, Morgan City, LA 70381. Week-long tours range from $1,695 to $1,895. ☎ 800-348-2628, fax 504-384-0817. E-mail: divboat@aol.com or divboat@compuserve.com. Website: www.aggressor.com.

Little Cayman Diver II offers week-long tours to the reefs and walls surrounding Little Cayman. All-inclusive rates range from $1,595 to $1,695, with occasional specials as low as $1,095. The yacht is 90 ft long and accommodates 10 to 12 passengers in five cabins. Each cabin is the width of the boat, has air-conditioning and sits above the water line. Offers unlimited, unstructured 24-hour diving. ☎ 800-458-2722 or 813-269-4542. Write to PO Box 273781, Tampa, FL 33688.

Facts

Nearest Recompression Chamber: George Town. This chamber is operated and staffed 24 hours a day by the British Sub-Aqua Club. ☎ 555 or 911 for help.

Getting There: Cayman Airways (☎ 800-G-CAYMAN) provides scheduled flights from Miami, Houston, Atlanta, Tampa and Orlando to Grand Cayman with connecting flights to Cayman Brac and Little Cayman. Northwest, United, American and Air Jamaica fly nonstop from gateway cities into Grand Cayman. During peak season (December 15-April 15) charter flights direct from many major snowbelt cities to Grand Cayman are available from Cayman Airways. Flight time from Miami is one hour. Grand Cayman is a regular stop on many cruise lines as well.

Island Transportation: Rental cars, motorbikes, and bicycles are available on Grand Cayman and Cayman Brac. Friendly and informative taxi drivers are stationed at hotels and other convenient locations.

Driving: As in England, driving in the Cayman Islands is on the left. A temporary license is issued for a few dollars to persons holding US, Canadian or international licenses.

Documents: Proof of citizenship and an outbound ticket (birth certificate, voter's registration certificate) are required from US, British, or Canadian citizens. No vaccinations are required unless you are coming from an epidemic area.

Customs: The penalties for trying to bring drugs into the Cayman Islands are stiff fines and, frequently, prison terms. No spearguns or Hawaiian slings permitted into the country.

Currency: The Cayman Island Dollar, equal to US $1.20.

Climate: Temperatures average about 80°F year-round. The islands are subject to some rainy periods, but generally sunny and diveable.

Clothing: Casual, lightweight clothing. Wetskins or shorty wetsuits are useful to avoid abrasions, as are light gloves for protection against the stinging corals. Snorkelers should wear protective clothing against sunburn.

Electricity: 110 volts AC, 60 cycles. Same as US.

Time: Eastern Standard Time year-round.

Tax: There is a 6% government tax on accommodations. A service charge of 10-15% is added to hotel and restaurant bills. Departure tax is US $12.50.

Religious Services: Catholic, Protestant, Baptist, Mormon and non-denominational churches are found on Grand Cayman.

Additional Information: (*United States*) The Cayman Islands Department of Tourism, 6100 Blue Lagoon Drive, Suite 150, Miami, FL 33126-2085. ☎ 800-G-CAYMAN, 800-327-8777 or 305-266-2300, fax 305-267-2932. (*New York*) 420 Lexington Ave, Suite 2733, New York, NY. ☎ 212-682-5582, fax 212-986-5123. (*United Kingdom*) 6 Arlington Street, London, SW1A 1RE England. ☎ 0171-491-7771, fax 0171-409-7773. (*The Cayman Islands*) Grand Cayman, Box 67, Grand Cayman, Cayman Islands, BWI. ☎ 345-949-0623, fax 345-949-4053. Website: www.caymanislands.ky.

Cayman Islands

Cozumel & Akumal

Cozumel

Cozumel, Mexico's largest island and top Caribbean dive destination, lies 12 miles off the Yucat n Peninsula, separated by a 3,000-ft-deep channel. Dense jungle foliage covers most of this islands interior, but its surrounding coast welcomes visitors with miles of luxuriant, white sand beaches.

Topside tourist activity centers around San Miguel, the island's cultural and commercial center, which boasts an impressive seaside maze of shops, cantinas and restaurants. An ultra-modern cruise-ship terminal accommodates ocean liners and ferries arriving daily from the mainland. Most dive resorts are scattered along the west coast, where calm waters prevail.

A 1961 visit by Jacques Cousteau first brought attention to Cozumel's spectacular diving and its incredible water clarity. Its fringing reef system is fed by warm, fast-moving Yucat n currents (a part of the Gulf Stream) as they sweep through the deep channel on the west side of the island. These currents bring a constant wash of plankton and other nutrients that support thousands of exotic fish. Immense rays and jewfish populate the spectacular drop-offs and wrecks on the outer reefs; sea turtles nest along the beaches from May to September. Visibility remains a constant 100 to 150 ft year-round, except during and after major storms.

Despite an onslaught of divers, Cozumel's reefs and marine life are better than ever. Once a mecca for spearfishermen, all of the reefs surrounding the island are now protected as a marine park. Those of you who may remember the dive operators' requests for qualifications being "You dive before?" will now be asked for C cards. A functional, free-to-divers recompression chamber is in operation.

When to Go

The best time to visit Cozumel is from December to June. Water and air temperatures average 80°F year-round, with hotter conditions in summer. Summer and fall often bring heavy rains or hurricanes.

History

Cozumel was first inhabited by the Maya Indians, who settled as early as 300 AD. They named it Ah-Cuzamil-Peten, place of the swallows. Remains of their temples and shrines still can be found.

During the 1800s Cozumel was a busy seaport stopover for ships carrying chicle (used to make gum) from Central America to North America.

Best Dives of Cozumel

Most tours include a shallow dive on the inner reef and a drift dive along the outer wall. Currents on the drift dives vary with the weather from very mild to too-strong-to-stop-for-a-photograph. The dive boat drops you off at one end of the reef, then follows your bubbles as you drift with the current to a predetermined point where you surface to rendezvous with the boat.

A maximum depth of 120 ft is enforced by the dive operators. Novice divers may wish to avoid the strong currents associated with drift diving and stick to the inner reefs.

☆☆☆☆☆ The **Palancar National Park** reef complex, off the southwestern tip of the island, encompasses more than three miles of winding tunnels and coral canyons. Its most prominent feature is a 12-ft bronze statue of Christ, created by sculptor Enrique Miralda to commemorate the first Catholic Mass said on the island. The statue stands in 40 ft of water at the north end of the reef known as Big Horseshoe. Depths on the inner reef range from 30 to 60 ft. Visibility exceeds 100 ft. The drop-off on the reef's outer wall is laced with immense coral arches and tunnels – shelter to huge crabs, lobsters and all types of morays. Vibrant growths of tree-sized sea fans, yellow and lavender tube sponges, barrel sponges, giant sea whips and pink-tipped anemones adorn the walls.

Huge towering coral pinnacles on the south end of Palancar provide excellent photo and video opportunities. Fish are abundant, with gigantic parrot fish and groupers, schools of pork fish and grunts everywhere. Many of the groupers are tame and may be hand fed. At depth you'll find a profusion of black coral.

☆☆☆☆ **San Francisco Reef** offers underwater photographers a kaleidoscope of seascapes with an array of pastel gorgonians and sea fans, vase and barrel sponges, coral arches, caves and tunnels. Usually a drift dive, with huge angels, rays, groupers, and sea turtles greeting you along the way.

Depths along the reef ledge are from 20 ft to 70 ft. The wall then drops off to channel depths. Visibility is excellent – usually 150 ft.

☆☆☆ **Paraiso Reef North** is a popular shallow dive just north of the cruise ship pier in San Miguel. The reef is accessible by swimming straight out 200 yds from the beach at the Hotel Sol Caribe or by dive boat. The remains of a twin engine airplane, sunk intentionally as part of a movie set, rest at 30 ft, creating a home for a vast array of fish life. Huge green morays, eagle rays, turtles, yellowtail, French angels, schools of pork fish, butterfly fish, and queen trigger fish may be found. The reef is a good choice for novice divers.

Snorkeling

Good snorkeling may be found all along Cozumel's east coast beaches. The reefs off the beaches at both the Scuba Club Galapago Resort and Playa San Francisco have some nice stands of elkhorn and brain coral with a constant show of juvenile tropicals and inverte- brates.

☆☆☆**The Chancanab Lagoon**, south of the cruise ship pier at Laguna Beach, is protected from wind and waves. Ideal for snorkeling, depths range from very shallow to about 30 ft. Schools of grunts, angel fish, damsel fish, trumpet fish, turtles, and snapper dart between the clumps of coral. Seafans and soft corals adorn the reef. Visibility runs about 75 ft, sometimes better. Snorkeling gear may be rented from shops on the beach. Changing rooms, freshwater showers and lockers are available. Small admission fee. A botanical garden and restaurant are on the premises.

A pretty snorkeling-depth reef aprons the south end of neighboring Isla Mujeres. Enter from the shore at Playa Garrafon, four miles from town. This spot – El Garrafon (the carafe) – is one of the most populated (by fish and swimmers) in the Caribbean. Just wade out from the beach with some cracker crumbs and you'll immediately be surrounded by crowds of friendly fish. Ideal for first-time snorkelers. The beach has a dive shop, showers, refreshment stands and shops.

Cozumel Dive Operators

To telephone or fax any of the Mexican listings from the US, dial 011 52 + 987 + the five digit number. In Mexico just dial the last five digits.

Most of the dive shops offer three- to seven-day reduced-rate dive packages. Before forking over your money, ask if refunds are given for missed dives and whether you can get that in writing. Some divers prefer to pay each day rather than risk missing the boat and losing the price of a trip.

Aqua Safari, on the ocean at 5th St. South, offers drift dives on Palancar Reef, night dives, rentals and repairs. Custom dive boats can accommodate up to 20 divers. Multilingual dive guides. Expect to dive with a crowd during high season and to carry your own gear. ☎ 011-52-987-20101, fax 011-52-987-20661. Write to: PO Box 41, Cozumel, Quintana Roo, Mexico 77600. E-mail: dive@aquasafari.com. Website: www.aquasafari.com.

Blue Bubble Divers has sunset dives, wreck and reef dives. Dive/accommodation packages from $400. Guides are friendly and helpful. Good briefings. Punctual. ☎ 800-878-8853, 011-52-987-21865, fax 011-52-987-21865. Write to 5th Ave. South, Cozumel Quintana Roo, Mexico 77600. E-mail: bubbles@cozunet.finred.com.mx. Website:www.gssolutions.com/bluebubble.

Caribbean Divers International visits Palancar, Santa Rosa and Maracaibo reefs. Dive as a group. No computers. NAUI, PADI and PDIC courses. Bilingual staff. ☎ 011-52-987-21080, fax 011-52-987-21426. Write to Box 191, Cozumel, Quintana Roo, Mexico 77600.

Del Mar Aquatics offers courses, trips, services. Dive/accommodation packages offered. Two boats carry 30 divers each. Expect crowds. ☎ 011-52-987-21833, fax 011-52-987-21833. Write to PO Box 129, Cozumel, Quintana Roo, Mexico 77600.

DIMI Educational Dive Center features all the best reef dives plus cave and cavern diving. Nitrox. Boats carry eight divers. Four night hotel/dive packages from $175 per person. ☎ 011-52-987-22915, fax 011-52-987-23964. E-mail: dimidive@cozumel.czm.com.mx. Write to Av. Rafael Melgar #45-B, Cozumel, Quintana Roo, Mexico.

Coral Head off Isla Mujeres.

Dive Palancar at the Diamond Resort has trips aboard a 44-ft custom dive boat to Palancar and Santa Rosa plus inland cenote (cave and cavern) dives. Beach diving tours. Dive and snorkeling courses. Seven-night hotel/dive packages from $1,000. English-speaking guides. Boats on time. Fine service. ☎ 800-247-3483, 011-52-987-23443, ext. 895.

Dive Paradise offers personalized tours for divers and snorkelers. Boats carry a maximum of seven divers. Nitrox available. Computers are required if you want to join their experienced diver program. Snorkelers may join trips for $35. Shaded boats. ☎ 011-52-987-21007, fax 011-52-987-21061. E-mail: applep@cozumel.czm.com.mx. Website: www.dparadise.com. Write to 601 Melgar, Cozumel, Quintana Roo, Mexico 77600. Hotel/dive packages are offered by Landfall Productions. ☎ 800-525-3833. E-mail: lndfall@aol.com.

Dive With Martin offers punctual, personalized tours to sites around the entire island perimeter. Small groups on fast boats plus excellent service make this operation very popular. Write to 601 Melgar, Cozumel, Quintana Roo, Mexico 77600. ☎ 281- 859-0700, 011-52-987-22610, fax 281-859-7720, 011-52-987-21340. E-mail: dwm@flash.net. Website: www.flash.net/~dwm.

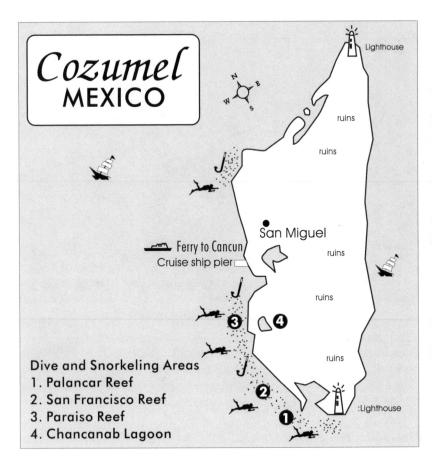

Cozumel
MEXICO

Lighthouse

ruins

ruins

San Miguel

ruins

Ferry to Cancun
Cruise ship pier

ruins

ruins

Dive and Snorkeling Areas
1. Palancar Reef
2. San Francisco Reef
3. Paraiso Reef
4. Chancanab Lagoon

ruins

Lighthouse

Diving Adventures tours the best reefs from San Miguel down to Santa Rosa. ☎ 888-338-0388, 011-52-987-23009. E-mail: diventur@cozumel. czm. com.mx. Write to Calle 5 #2 Cozumel, Quintana Roo, Mexico 77600.

Marine Sports offers hotel/dive packages with the Fiesta Inn. Boats tour Palancar Underwater Park. ☎ 800-FIESTA-1, 011-52-98722899, fax 011-52-987-22154.

Nitrox Solutions offers IANTD and PADI Nitrox certifications to all levels. Their spacious training facility and Nitrox fill station is equipped with the latest in training materials and the DNAx Membrane System from Undersea Breathing Systems in Florida. (DNAx is considered by many to be the most advanced system to date.) In-town, Calle 3 and the Waterfront, two doors from the Bahia Hotel. ☎ 800-967-1333 or 011-52-967-5666. E-mail: nitrox@cozumel.czm.com.mx. Website: www.islacozumel.net/diving/nitrox.

Papa Hogs Scuba Emporium, San Miguel, visits the southern sites, Barracuda Reef. ☎ 800-780-3949, 011-52-987-21651, fax 011-52-987- 21651. E-mail: diving@papahogs.com. Website: www.papahogs.com.

Scuba Cozumel, a five-star PADI Dive Center and first-class operation, visits Palancar National Park aboard comfortable custom boats carrying four to 12 divers. Catamarans of 43 ft carry bigger groups. No crowds. Dive/hotel packages with Scuba Club Dive Resort (formerly the Galapagos Inn) ☎ 800-847-5708.

Scuba Du at the Hotel Stouffer Presidente offers personalized dive tours, small groups, Nitrox and fast custom boats. Dive-hotel packages. ☎ 011-52-987-21379, fax 011-52-987-24130. Write to PO Box 137, Cozumel, Quintana Roo, Mexico 77600.

Cozumel Accommodations

To telephone or fax any of the Mexican listings from the US, dial 01152 + 987 + the five digit number.

Hotel Presidente Inter-Continental, two miles south of town at the Chancanab Lagoon, features a large pool, tennis, restaurants, entertainment and dive packages with Scuba Du. Rates for hotel and diving for two start at $222 per person, per day, for hotel, breakfast buffet, daily two-tank dive. Good snorkeling off the beach. ☎ 800-346-6116 or 800-298-9009.

Casa Del Mar, an affordable dive resort across the street from the beach, has 196 air-conditioned rooms, telephones, on-site dive shop, snorkeling reef in front of hotel, sand beach, shopping arcade, gardens, pool, and restaurant. The bar is built from salvaged shipwrecks. Accommodation rates start at $120 per night for single or double. ☎ 800-435-3240 or 011-52-987-21900. E-mail: www.delmar@cozumel.com.mx.   Website: www.mexicoweb.com/travel/coz201.html.

Allegro Resort, located 10 minutes from the best reefs, is a first-class, all-inclusive dive resort. On site, Dive Palancar provides PADI five-star services and a choice of five daily dive-trip departure times. Resort features 350 deluxe rooms, children's program, good restaurants, pool and a variety of water sports and activities for adults and kids. ☎ 800-433-0885, E-mail: info@dsi-divetours.com. Website: www.dsi-divetours.com.

Fiesta Inn Cozumel offers 180 clean, air-conditioned deluxe rooms, all with satellite TV, telephones, balconies, purified drinking water, large swimming pool, jacuzzi, tennis court, karaoke bar and Café La Fiesta, which serves delicious Mexican and international dishes. Snorkeling is available off the resort beach. Direct ☎ 800-FIESTA-1 or 011-52-987-22899, fax 011-52-987-22154.

Fiesta Americana Cozumel Reef features 172 deluxe ocean- and reef-view rooms and four parlor suites with satellite TV, private terraces, room service. On-site scuba shop, Dive House Cozumel, visits all the best southwest sites. Amenities include two lighted tennis courts, fax service, equipment storage lockers, custom charters, gym and jogging trail, two restaurants, gift shop, poolside snack bar car, bike and moped rentals and purified water. Night dives and snorkeling trips. Hotel direct, ☎ 800-FIESTA-1 or 011-52-987-22622, fax 011-52-987-22666. Website: www.fiestamexico.com.

Paradisus Cozumel sits on Cozumel's longest stretch of natural beach. Located two miles from town on the northeast side of the island, this all-inclusive hotel offers air-conditioned deluxe ocean-view and garden-view rooms with terraces, remote control satellite TV, telephone with international dialing. King-size or two double beds. For diving and snorkeling trips, guests must travel to the Paradisus Beach & Dive Club on the southern side of the island. Beach Club features restaurants, dive shop, training pool, changing rooms, lockers, showers and a variety of non-motorized and motorized water sports, plus horseback riding. Hotel guests have complimentary use of non-motorized sports equipment – kayaks, Sailfish, wind surfers and spyaks. Lunch for guests is no charge. ☎ 888-341-5993, 011-52-987-20411, fax 011-52-987-21599. E-mail: paradisu@cancun.rce.com.mx.

Plaza Las Glorias, within walking distance of San Miguel, is a charming four-story, pueblo-style 170-room resort. Air-conditioned rooms have balconies or patios. Features include a dive shop, boutique, two restaurants, pool and ocean views. Room rates range from $133 to $189. ☎ 800-342-AMIGO or 011-52-987-22000, fax 800-562-1989 or 011-52-987-21937.

Scuba Club Galapago (formerly the Galapago Inn) is both casual and elegant, with thatch-roofed huts lining the beach, a pool with three mosaic sea turtles, air-conditioned rooms (each with a refrigerator and spacious closet), gourmet dining and an on-site dive shop. Just offshore is a nice snorkeling reef. The inn operates five roomy dive boats, and offers photography and scuba courses, E-6 film processing and professional service. Write to Aqua-Sub Tours, PO Box 630608, Houston, TX 77263. ☎ 800-847-5708; or 713-783-3305. Website: www.scubaclubcozumel.com.

Villablanca Garden Beach Hotel, in front of Paradise Reef, features 50 air-conditioned rooms and suites with phones, sunken tubs, ceiling fans and refrigerators. Pool, white sand beach. Divers picked up at hotel's private pier. Dive/hotel packages from $490 include seven nights accommodations, five two-tank dives with Dive Paradise, complimentary snacks and beverages on dive trips. ☎ 916-563-0164, fax 916-924-1059. E-mail: landfall@ pattravel.com.

Sightseeing & Other Activities

Diving and sport fishing are the main activities on Cozumel, followed by wind surfing, jetskiing, and water-skiing, which are offered by the resorts. The widest range of watersports rentals is at Playa San Francisco.

San Miguel's main tourist areas are **Plaza del Sol**, where you'll find cafés, craft shops, jewelry stores, restaurants and fast food joints, and the **Malecon**, Cozumel's seaside boardwalk. While touring the town stop in at the **Museum of the Island of Cozumel**, a two-story, former turn-of-the-century hotel that features displays of island wildlife and anthropological and cultural history. Between May and September the museum runs marine biologist-led tours to witness the sea turtles lay eggs on the eastern shore.

The Chankanab Lagoon Botanical Gardens, two miles south of town, has 300 species of tropical plants and trees and an interesting Mayan museum.

Farther south, you'll come to the **Celarain Lighthouse**, which you may climb for a spectacular view of the area. Be sure to clear your visit first with the resident caretaker.

Rent a jeep to explore the windward east coast of Cozumel. You'll find pounding surf and marvelous stretches of uninhabited beaches lined with mangroves and coconut palms. It may be wise to avoid swimming here because of the dangerous currents and strong undertow, except at **Playa Chiquero**, a protected crescent-shaped cove, and **Playa Chen Rio**, which is protected by a rock breakwater.

Remains of Mayan temples and pyramids can be found at the northern end of the island. Guided tours to explore **San Gervasio** (once the Mayan capital), also on the north end, may be booked through most large hotels. Ferry trips to the larger, more impressive Mayan ruins on the mainland can be booked in town at the International Pier. Most dive packages include a side-trip to **Tulum**, a Mayan walled city built in the late 13th century, or to **Isla Mujeres**, a fabulous nearby snorkeling island.

Sightseeing flights around Cozumel, to neighboring islands, or the mainland can be arranged at the airport.

Dining

Local lobster, native grilled fish and a variety of Mexican dishes such as tacos, enchiladas or caracol (a giant conch) predominate at Cozumel's restaurants and roadside stands. Several superb native eateries within a few blocks of the pier offer island specialties such as grilled turtle, grilled fish in banana leaves, conch cocktail and spicy steak strips. All in all, dining is quite good in Cozumel whether you choose romantic garden dining with strolling serenaders or a fast snack at one of the many stands.

Music is featured at most restaurants and hotel bars on Cozumel, and the island has a number of discos, including Scaramouche and Neptuno.

Pepes Grill, on Ave. Rafael Melgar, features savory steaks, lobster and seafood. ☎ 2-02-13.

Café Del Puerto, at the plaza, is one of Cozumel's best spots for lobster and crab. Youll be entertained with live guitar music. ☎ 2-03-16.

El Portal offers fabulous Mexican-style spicy breakfasts. ☎ 2-03-16.

Carlos 'N Charlies and Jimmy's Kitchen, on Ave. Rafael Melgar 11, is a divers' favorite for Mexican steaks and seafood. ☎ 2-01-91.

La Palmeras, at the pier (27 Rafael Melgar), is a good spot for breakfast and lunch. ☎ 2-05-32.

La Laguna, on the beach at Chankanab National Park, serves up tasty shrimp, crabs and fish. ☎ 2-05-84.

Pizza Rolandi, on Ave. Melgar 22, specializes in Italian favorites.

Akumal

Akumal (place of the turtle) lies 60 miles south of Canc n on Mexico's Yucat n Peninsula in an area known as the Tulum Corridor. Laid-back and off the beaten track, this tiny resort community originated as a section of a large coconut plantation. It wasn't until 1958 that Mexican treasure divers salvaging a sunken Spanish galleon discovered great sport diving opportunities along the off-shore barrier reef. Pristine corals and sponges, frequent turtle sightings, silky white sand beaches and terrific beach snorkeling have popularized Akumal with local divers and a discriminating group of visitors. Three dive operators serve the area.

Drawbacks exist for those who like pampered diving. Akumal dive guides are friendly and helpful, but they do not carry, store or wash your gear. The diving is not easy in terms of services. Divers schlep their own tanks, weights and equipment to and from the boats. The boats are open, with ladders – no platforms, no sun canopies. On the other hand, most sites lie close to shore, a five- to 10-minute boat ride. Spearfishing is prohibited.

Akumal dive operators also offer divers and snorkelers freshwater tours to jungle pools or cenotes, which are sunken limestone caverns with dazzling stalagmites and stalactites. These inland adventures include a jungle trek through nature's most exotic gardens.

When to Go

The best time to dive Akumal is October through April. Weather is very hot in May and June and rain is heavy during July, August and September.

Best Dives of Akumal

Akumal's ocean scuba sites are gentle drift dives with easy pickups along a barrier reef that parallels the shoreline of Akumal Bay, neighboring Half Moon Bay and nearby Yalku Lagoon. Snorkeling opportunities exist all along the coast.

The reef structure comprises three distinct systems running parallel to one another at progressively greater depths. The inner reef, a network of patch reefs, ranges from three to 35 ft, with huge stands of elkhorn and formations of boulder, brain and plate corals. An expanse of white sand separates the inner reef from the middle reef which is three miles long at depths from 40 to 55 ft. Several reef areas are shot through with coral caves and tunnels. Farther out, a well-developed outer reef from 60 to 125 ft features more outstanding caverns and canyons. Abundant tropicals inhabit the patch reefs and the middle reef. Larger fish and turtles roam the outer reef.

Frequent sightings of loggerhead, green and hawksbill turtles that nest along Yucat n beaches highlight many dives. Currents normally run less than one knot.

Snorkelers exploring from the beach can swim up to the breakers on the reef. Conditions inside are normally calm, with depths from three to 20 ft.

☆☆☆ **Akumal Shark Caves**, at 40 ft, shelter six or more nurse sharks and walls of porkfish, grunts, and snapper. Cavern walls blossom with rose gorgonians, lettuce corals, yellow seafans, flower and brush corals. Orange vase sponges and soft corals proliferate in the gently moving current. Drift dive. Expect some surge. Experience suggested.

☆☆☆☆ **La Tortuga**, named for the big turtles that paddle by, slopes from 70 to 80 ft. Located outside the reef, this site offers a slightly more challenging current. Surface can get rough at times. Good to excellent visibility.

☆☆☆ **The Nets**, at 45 ft depth, and **El Mero**, at 75 ft, both adjacent to Shark Caves, normally have excellent visibility, vibrant red sponges, star corals, sea feathers, and soft corals. Terrain slopes into a labyrinth of canyons, tunnels and overhangs. Both spots provide habitat to arrow crabs, sea cucumbers, lobsters and shrimp. Lots of tunnels and small caves. French and queen angels, sergeant majors, trigger and parrot fish bob with the current. Gentle drift dive.

Photo Courtesy Myra Bush

Club Akumal Beach.

The Cenotes

Cenotes are freshwater pools with submerged limestone caverns. "Gin clear" best describes the visibility, though you may pass through a thermal layer of soup as you drop down to more crystal clear water. Scuba depths average 40 to 60 ft. You'll see fish, but the magnificence of these limestone caverns lies in the fantastic stalagmites and stalactites. Lights make the colors stand out and your dive more exciting.

Akumal, Cozumel and Canc n dive shops offer guided cenote (cavern) tours to certified divers. Unlike cave diving, you stay within close sight of the entrance. No special certification required. Before signing up for a cenote trip make sure your guide is cave-certified by one of the national associations: National Association for Cave Diving (NACD), National Speleological Society Cave Diving Section (NSS CDS) or International Assocation of Nitrox and Technical Divers (IANTD). The guide should also be wearing doubles with octopus rigs and using a continuous guideline (a rope to lead you back to the surface should one of you kick up the silt and decrease the visibility to zero). Groups should be very small. A thorough briefing on emergency procedures should precede the dive.

Be sure to maintain neutral buoyancy to avoid kicking up the silty bottoms and smashing the flowstones. Keep a close watch on your air supply. Don't explore passageways on your own. You'll need a wet suit; water temperatures in the cenotes average 70°F. Cenote dives cost about $45 per tank.

☆☆☆ **The Car Wash, Gran Cenote, Temple of Doom** and **Dos Ojos** are favorite cavern dives in Akumal. All average 50 to 60 ft depths. Temple of Doom requires jumping from a ledge 15 ft above the pool.

Some of these caverns are partially above water and shallow enough for snorkelers, who are offered specialty tours.

☆☆☆☆ **Nohoch Nah Chich**, listed in the *Guinness Book of World Records* as the world's longest underwater cave system, was also featured in the PBS TV series, *The New Explorers*, as one of Yucat n's most exciting caverns. Visitors snorkel in the shallow fresh water amidst brilliant white stalactites and stalagmites. Unlimited visibility and the open, expansive quality of the caverns offer breathtaking views.

Joining a jungle walk and snorkeling expedition to Nohoch Nah Chich involves a mile-and-a-half trek through impressive flora. Horses or donkeys carry your gear. Be sure to apply sun protective lotions and bug repellent and wear a hat that will shade your face. Not suitable for young children or people with severe disabilities or medical problems.

Akumal Snorkeling Sites

Uncrowded beaches, secluded bays and a healthy marine population make Akumal delightful for family snorkeling vacations.

☆☆☆ **Akumal Bay's** best snorkeling is off the beach in front of the Club Akumal Caribe. Depths range from three ft to 20 ft with coral heads leading out to the breakers at the barrier reef. A variety of corals, sea fans, sponges, reef fish, occasional moray eels, barracudas, jacks, grouper, sting rays, parrot fish and turtles inhabit the bay. Bottom terrain is sandy, with coral heads scattered about. Bay conditions inside the barrier reef are almost always tranquil.

☆☆☆ **Half Moon Bay**, about three minutes down the interior road from Akumal Bay, resembles Akumal Bay in terrain and marine life. This is a residential area, but anyone can use the beach.

☆☆☆☆ **Yalku Lagoon**, at the end of the interior road, a short drive from Half Moon Bay, features partially submerged caves, throngs of fish and crystal clear, tranquil water. Fresh water mixing with seawater provides nutrients and aquatic plants that attract rich marine life. Big parrot fish, angels, Spanish hogfish, rays, juvenile turtles and spotted eels nibble on the plants around the rocks. A natural entrance from the sea ensures a constant mix of nutrients. The outlying barrier reef protects this magnificent natural aquarium from wind-driven waves and rough seas. Enter the lagoon from the head of the bay or climb down the big rocks anywhere along the shore. Guided boat and beach-entry snorkeling tours are offered by the dive shop at Club Akumal Caribe.

Snorkeling Up & Down the Coast

☆☆ **Chemuyil.** Several sheltered bays and secluded beaches with good shore-entry snorkeling exist along the coast. About six miles south of Akumal, the dirt road turn-off at KM 249 leads to Chemuyil, a quiet, horseshoe-shaped cove of tranquil water edged by a lovely, powder-white beach. A shallow snorkeling reef crosses the mouth of the bay. A small beach bar (the Marco Polo) serves fresh seafood, cold beer and soft drinks. Full camping facilities and a few tented palapas for overnight rental are available.

☆☆ **Xel-Ha** (pronounced Shell ha). About 20 miles south of Akumal lies, this is the worlds largest natural aquarium, covering 10 acres of lagoons, coves and inlets teeming with exotic fish. Platforms above the rocky limestone shore provide sea life viewing for non-swimmers. Unlike Akumal, this spot is packed with tourists. Busloads of avid snorkelers arrive regularly in season.

A small admission fee is charged. On-site showers, shops, a maritime museum, seafood restaurant and Subway sandwich shop serve visitors. Snorkeling gear is available for rent. Despite the crowds, most snorkelers, especially those touring with children, immensely enjoy this spot. Venture across highway 307 to visit some small ruins.

☆☆ **Xcaret** (Scaret), Mayan for little inlet, about 40 miles north of Akumal, is a private ranch turned aquatic theme park. Once a Mayan port, this novel playground now features dolphin swims and snorkeling through the underground river, which flows through a series of open-ended caves. A mix of fresh and saltwater nourishes sea plants, which in turn feed armies of fish that entertain between 400 and 500 snorkelers per day. The effect is like drifting through a very big, very pretty, shaded pool stocked with fish. Holes in the roof of the river caves filter light into a spectrum of colors.

Topside features include a wild-bird aviary, butterfly pavilion, saltwater aquarium, botanical garden, a couple of Mayan temple ruins, and the Museum of Mayan Archaeological Sites, with scale models of 26 Mayan ceremonial sites found on the Yucat n peninsula. There are three restaurants, two snack bars, one cafeteria, showers, lockers, photo center, horse shows, gift shops and a sundeck with spectacular ocean views. Crowded, but very user-friendly.

The open-air restaurant, **La Peninsula**, offers a good selection of entrées and remains open at night. **La Caleta**, another alfresco restaurant near the inlet, specializes in spicy seafood.

The Maya prized Xcaret, believing that its waters could purify bodies and souls. Thus it became important as a place to take a sacred bath before crossing the sea to Cozumel to worship Ixchel, Goddess of Fertility.

We can't guarantee the soul-purifying properties, but most snorkelers find Xcaret a fun day or half-day diversion. Mike Cherup, one of our snorkeling researchers returning from Xcaret, claims he found relief from back pain there!

Akumal Accommodations

Hotel Club Akumal Caribe features a variety of air-conditioned accommodations and an on-site dive shop. On the main beach choose from spacious Maya bungalows with garden views or first class hotel rooms facing the pool and ocean. All are clean and modern with full baths, air conditioning, ceiling fans and compact refrigerators. Also on the main beach is the Cannon House Suite, with two bedrooms, two baths, living room and kitchen.

Two-bedroom condos on Half Moon Bay have one king-size bed, two twins, kitchens and living rooms. Winter rates range from $99 per night for a bungalow, $120 for a hotel room, and from $370 for a three-bedroom villa.

Contact the reservation office for additional accommodation rates and information. In the US, ☎ 800-351-1622; in Canada, ☎ 800-343-1440; in Texas, ☎ 915-584-3552; in Mexico, ☎ 800-351-1622. E-mail: clubakumal@ aol.com.

Akumal Dive Operators

Akumal Dive Center at Club Akumal offers cenote, jungle, cave and open-water diving with top-notch dive masters. Groups are small and tours are personalized. Guides are environmentally aware and enforce local marine sanctuary regulations. C-cards are a must. Cave dives only to certified cave divers. ☎ 800-351-1622, 011-52-987-59025, fax 915-581-6709. E-mail: clubakumal@aol.com.

Aquatech Villas DeRosa in Aventuras Akumal features technical training, Nitrox, rebreathers, cave and cavern diving. ☎ 011-52-987-59020, fax 011-52-987-59020. E-mail: 105107.2445@compuserve.com.

Mike Madden's Cedam Dive Centers are at four locations – Club Oasis Puerto Aventuras, Beach Club Hotel Puerto Aventuras, Robinson Club Tulum and Club Oasis Aventuras Akumal. Tours include reef diving, cavern diving, day trips to Cozumel and cave diving for certified cave divers. Snorkeling trips offered to Nohoch, the world's longest underwater cave (the Indiana Jones Jungle Adventure). All levels of certification are offered from Open Water Diver through Scuba Instructor, with special courses in night diving, deep diving and photography. Cavern and Cave certifications are available with NACD, NSS-CDS and IANTD instructors. Technical certifications such as Nitrox, Deep Air and Trimix are also offered. ☎ 011-52-987-35147, fax 011-52-987-35129. E-mail: mmaden@cancun.rce.com.mx. Website: www.cedamdive.com.

The trip from Cancún to Cozumel by boat takes 40-60 minutes.

Facts

Helpful Phone Numbers: Police (Cozumel), ☎ 20092; hospital (Cozumel), ☎ 20140.

Nearest Recompression Chamber: On the mainland there is a recompression chamber run by doctors trained in hyperbaric medicine in Playa del Carmen. On Cozumel, there is a chamber in San Miguel, ☎ 22387.

Getting There: Direct flights to Cozumel and Canc n from the US are offered by American Airlines, ☎ 800-733-4300, Continental, United, Northwest, Mexicana and Aero Mexico. There are additional domestic flights from Acapulco, Canc n, Guadalajara, Mexico City, Merida, Monterey, and Veracruz. Cruise ships from Miami: Norwegian Caribbean Lines, Holland America, Carnival. Cozumel island also can be reached by bus ferry, car ferry and hydrofoil from Canc n. Isla Mujeres is reached by bus ferry, car ferry and air taxi from Canc n. AeroCozumel and Aerocaribe fly between the islands. Cozumel is a 40- to 60-minute boat trip from Canc n.

Island Transportation: Taxi service is inexpensive and readily available. Mopeds, cars and Jeeps may be rented in town or at the airport. Book rental cars in advance of your trip.

Departure tax: $18.

Driving: On the right.

Documents: US and Canadian citizens need a tourist card. To obtain one, you must show a valid passport or birth certificate with raised seal. Citizens of other countries should contact their nearest Mexican consulate for regulations. The tourist card is necessary to leave the country as well and may be obtained from the Mexican consulate or your airline prior to departure.

Customs: Plants, flowers and fruits may not be brought into Cozumel. Persons carrying illegal drugs will be jailed. You may bring three bottles of liquor and one carton of cigarettes. Dogs and cats should have a current vaccination certificate. Divers carrying a lot of electronic or camera gear, especially video equipment, should register it with US Customs in advance of the trip.

Water: Drink only bottled or filtered water to avoid diarrheal intestinal ailments. Also avoid raw vegetables, the skin of fruit, and foods that sit out for any length of time.

Cozumel & Akumal

Currency: The exchange rate of the Mexican peso fluctuates a great deal. At this writing US $1=5.5 nuevos pesos. Banks are open weekday mornings. Major credit cards and travelers checks are widely accepted in Akumal, Canc n and Cozumel.

Climate: Temperatures range from the low 70s in winter to the high 90s in summer, with an average of about 80°F. Winter months bring cooler weather; summer and fall, chance of heavy rain.

Clothing: Lightweight, casual. Wetsuits are not needed, but lightweight (1/8) short suits or wetskins are comfortable on deep wall dives.

Electricity: 110 volts; 60 cycles (same as US).

Time: Central Standard Time.

Language: Spanish; English widely spoken.

For Additional Information: *In New York*, Mexican Government Tourist Office, 405 Park Avenue, Suite 1400, NY, NY 10022. ☎ 800-446-3942 or 212-421-6655, fax 212-753-2874. *In California*, 10100 Santa Monica Blvd., Los Angeles, CA 90067. ☎ 310-203-0821. *In Florida*, 128 Aragon Avenue, Coral Gables, FL 33134 ☎ 305-443-9160. *In Canada*, Mexican Government Tourist Office, Suite 1526, One Place Ville Marie, Montreal, Quebec, Canada H3B 2B5. ☎ 514-871-1052, fax 514-871-1052. *In the UK*, Mexican Government Tourism Office, 60/61 Trafalgar Square, 3rd Floor, London, England WC2N 5DS. ☎ 44-171-734-1058, fax 44-171-930-9202. Website: www.mexico-travel.com/.

Curaçao

Curaçao, the largest of five islands that make up the Netherlands Antilles, which include Bonaire, Saba, Sint Maarten and St. Eustatius, is a dry and hilly island completely surrounded with rich coral reefs – many within a stone's throw of shore. Its coastline sparkles with beautiful sand beaches, secluded lagoons and snorkeling coves.

Willemstad, its capital, is delightfully Dutch, with open-air markets, narrow streets and rows of shops offering imports from all over the world. It is best known for its colorful Dutch-colonial architecture. According to legend, the first governor of Curaçao suffered from migraine headaches due to glare from the white houses and ordered all residents to paint their homes pastel. The rows of pastel-colored town houses with gabled roofs, red tile and rococo-style facades in downtown Willemstad are probably the most photographed sights on the island.

St. Anna Bay, like an Amsterdam canal, divides the capital city in two parts – the Punda and the Otrabanda. A pontoon walking bridge, which opens several times a day to allow cruise ships to dock in town, connects the two sides of the city.

Christoffel Park in the northwestern sector of Curaçao is marked by the island's highest peak. The volcanic crest of Mt. Christoffel dominates the landscape, rising 1,250 ft above the sea. Undulating hills are punctuated with the evergreen wayaca and cacti, reaching as much as 10 ft from the parched land like outstretched fingers.

History

Curaçao's heritage and history is long and multi-faceted. The original inhabitants of Curaçao were the Caiquetio Indians (one of their tribes were called the "Indios Curaçao"). In 1499, when Alonso de Ojeda, a Spanish navigator who sailed with Columbus, discovered the island and the Indians, he named it for them.

Later, in 1634, the Dutch captured Curaçao, forcing evacuation by the Spaniards and the Indian natives. By 1635, only 50 of the 462 inhabitants were native Indians and approximately 350 were Dutch soldiers. The island became one of the leading slave and salt trade centers for the Dutch West Indies Company.

Elkhorn stand in Jan Theil Marine park dwarfs diver.

For many years, England and France tried to conquer the island. The English were successful in 1800, but were defeated two years later by the Dutch. England eventually recaptured the island, only to give it back as a result of the Treaty of Paris in 1815.

By the mid-1800s, Curaçao's population was as varied as any in the world. One-time soldiers married Curaçaoan women and established a livelihood on the island. Merchants from Europe stayed. Others were freed slaves who chose to remain on the island. All carried a part of their culture and tradition to this tropical paradise.

Curaçao's harbor became the site of one of the world's largest oil refineries in 1914, following the discovery of oil in Venezuela.

Best Dive & Snorkeling Sites

Like its sister islands, Aruba and Bonaire, Curaçao lies far south of the hurricane belt and offers clear skies and good diving year-round. Most dives require a boat. The reefs and wrecks are "a stone's throw from shore," but the "shore" adjacent to the best reefs is often formed of jagged, razor-like, ironshore cliffs. Seas along the south coast – locale of the underwater park – are usually dead calm in the morning, but may kick up a three- or four-ft surge in mid-afternoon.

The **Curaçao Underwater Park**, established in 1983 by the Netherlands Antilles National Park Foundation (STINAPA), stretches 12 miles from the Princess Beach Hotel to East Point . It features 20 dive sites marked by numbered mooring buoys and another 10 unmarked sites. Within the park, divers and snorkelers find crystal-clear water and spectacular subsea landscapes. The reefs are in pristine condition, with many yet to be explored. Diving did not become popular in Curaçao until the 1980s, when officials realized the potential for additional tourist growth. Before then, the island was promoted solely for honeymoons, sport fishing and sailing.

Although the park's terrain features dramatic coral walls with deep drop-offs, there is excellent diving in the shallow waters, with 50-foot brain coral, gigantic sponges, huge, perfectly formed trees of elkhorn and enormous, lush seafan gardens. Visibility is a dependable 100 ft.

To the west is the (not yet official) **Banda Abao Underwater Park**, with more than 21 outstanding dive and snorkeling sites.

☆☆☆☆ For the very adventurous, the westernmost dive site, **Wata Mula**, features a sloping reef and cave frequented by huge moray eels, groupers, nurse sharks and rays. This area is diveable only on very calm days and only with an experienced dive guide. Seas at this end of the island are often very rough, with strong currents. Yet, visibility and marine life is outstanding. Suggested for experienced divers in top physical condition.

☆☆☆☆ In the Santa Cruz/San Nicolas area lies **Mushroom Forest**, the most beautiful site of the Banda Abao Underwater Park. This gently sloping reef is highlighted by giant mushroom-shaped star corals at 50 ft. The mushroom shapes were created by boring clams and sponges eroding the coral bases. A large cave lies along the cliffs where you can occasionally find sleeping nurse sharks. High cliffs make beach access difficult; best bet is to contact a local dive shop making boat trips to the site.

☆ At the end of Mushroom Forest is **Playa Lagoen**, a snorkeling beach nestled between two massive rock formations. Snorkelers will find some juvenile fish and small coral heads along the rocks. Be sure to tote a floating dive flag as small fishing boats weave in and out of the area. Energetic divers can swim out about 150 yds to the drop-off.

☆☆☆ South of Playa Lagoen, sea turtles and occasional mantas are sighted at the **Black Coral Gardens** off Boca St. Martha. Steep drop-offs, 60 to 130 ft, support a colossal black coral forest. Nearby is Mike's Place, known for a giant sponge locally called the "double bed."

☆☆☆☆ **Sandy's Plateau**, at Jan Thiel Park, is a 12-minute swim toward the right (northwest) side of the lagoon, Jan Thiel Bay. This brings you to a large shallow plateau leading to a coral covered wall. It is an excellent spot for

Curaçao

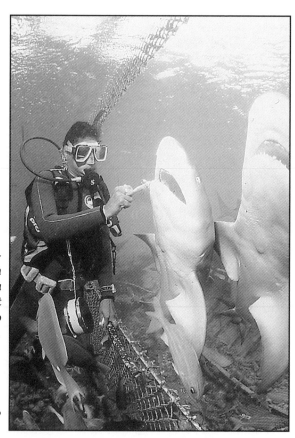

Divers safely hand-feed sharks through tiny holes in a Plexiglas partition at the Curaçao Seaquarium.

Courtesy Curaçao
Tourist Board

novice divers and snorkelers. The terrain is a combination of walls and steep slopes colored with lavender and pink star corals, yellow pencil corals and orange tube sponges. Lush stands of elkhorn coral grow to within 10 ft of the surface. Dense coral flows around an undercut ledge from 10 to 30 ft. Soldierfish, trumpetfish and schools of sergeant majors hover at the ledge. Normally some wave action and current, but expect 100 ft+ visibility. An eight-minute swim northwest of Jan Thiel lagoon will put you over **Boka Di Sorsaka**, a deeply undercut ledge at 30 ft. Many sponges, corals and small reef fish.

☆☆☆☆ Unique shark dives for the less intrepid are available at the **Curaçao Seaquarium**. Here, stingrays, lemon and nurse sharks inhabit a tidal pool built near the edge of the Seaquarium reef. Wire fencing fitted with Plexiglas windows separates the sharks and rays from the divers. Small holes in the Plexiglas allow divers to photograph or pass fish through to feed the sharks.

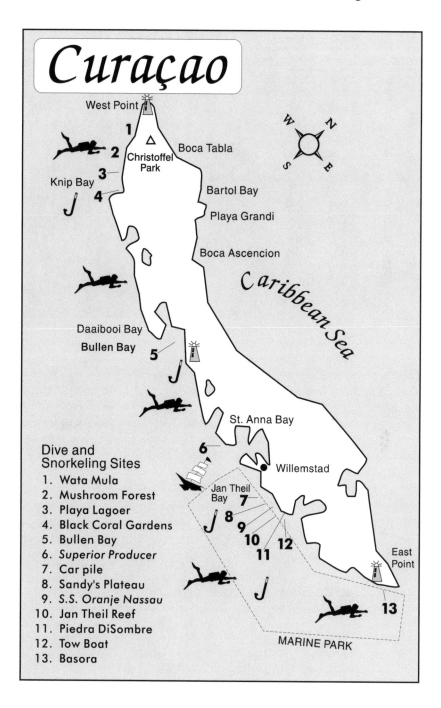

Curaçao

West Point

1

2

Christoffel
Park

Boca Tabla

3

Knip Bay

4

Bartol Bay

Playa Grandi

Boca Ascencion

Caribbean Sea

Daaibooi Bay

Bullen Bay

5

St. Anna Bay

6

Willemstad

Dive and Snorkeling Sites

Jan Theil
Bay

7

1. Wata Mula

8

2. Mushroom Forest

9

3. Playa Lagoer

10

4. Black Coral Gardens

11   12

5. Bullen Bay

East
Point

6. *Superior Producer*

7. Car pile

8. Sandy's Plateau

9. *S.S. Oranje Nassau*

10. Jan Theil Reef

13

11. Piedra DiSombre

12. Tow Boat

MARINE PARK

13. Basora

Photo © Curacao Tourism

Tugboat.

Offshore from the Curaçao Seaquarium in Jan Thiel Bay lies the wreck of the ☆☆☆☆ **S.S. Oranje Nassau**, a Dutch steamer that ran aground here on the Koraal Specht over 80 years ago. Also known as *Bopor Kibra*, Papiamento for broken ship, this is a shallow dive and a favorite spot for free diving. The seas are always choppy over the wreck. Entry is best from the diveshop docks adjacent to the Seaquarium. Check with the divemaster for the day's conditions.

This area is known for outstanding corals. Depth starts shallow, with large pillar and star corals, seafans, huge brain coral, and gorgeous stands of elkhorn. It then terraces off to a wall starting at 50 ft. Fish life includes swarms of blue chromis and creole wrasses, French angels, barracuda and jacks. Sea conditions are choppy – recommended for divers and snorkelers with some ocean experience.

☆☆☆☆ **Jan Thiel Reef**, just outside of Jan Thiel Bay, is a fabulous snorkeling site. Lush, shallow gardens at 15 ft are alive with a mass of gorgonians, two-foot lavender sea anemones, seafans, long, purple tube sponges, pastel star, leaf, fire, pencil and brain corals. Fishlife is superb, with walls of grunts, trumpetfish, parrot fish, angels and small rays. Added buoyancy from a snorkeling vest or shorty wetsuit will help you stay clear of the fire coral. You can swim from Playa Jan Thiel, just east of the Princess Beach Hotel. The beach has changing facilities and is a favorite for picnics. Admission fee.

☆☆☆ **Piedra Di Sombre** sits between Caracas Bay and Jan Thiel Bay. Ideal for snorkeling and diving, the site is a steep wall covered with abundant seafans, seawhips, wire coral, star coral, club finger coral and rows of gorgonians. Depths are from 30 ft to 125 ft. Numerous black corals grow on the wall. Reef residents are lizardfish, black durgons, angelfish and barracuda.

☆☆☆☆☆ **The *Superior Producer*** is Curaçao's favorite wreck dive. The 100-ft freighter sank in 1977 when her heavy cargo of clothing shifted. The ship is intact and stands upright on a sandy plain at the foot of a steep, coral-covered slope. The wreck is encrusted with orange, red, purple, green and yellow corals and sponges. Clouds of silversides command the wheelhouse; rays and porpoises are frequently sighted. The site has a mooring buoy and is most conveniently reached from a boat, but can also be reached by a rugged 10-minute swim from shore. The closest water-entry point is from the Curaçao public swimming pool at the Rif recreation area. Top of the wreck is at 90 ft, with sections of the mainmast reaching up to within 40 ft of the surface. This is an early morning dive; the seas have not had a chance to build and visibility is best then. Divers should watch the tables or dive computer as several bounty hunters have ended up in the island's recompression chamber.

☆☆☆ The mooring for **PBH** is in front of the Princess Beach Hotel. This reef starts shallow enough for snorkeling and drops off at 40 ft. Arrow crabs, octopi, and hordes of juvenile fish swim the shallow terrace. Black corals and large grouper are found at depth.

☆☆☆ **Car Pile**, by the Princess Beach Hotel, is an artificial reef constructed from piles of old car and truck wrecks. Depth is 60 to 125 ft. Watch out for jagged pieces of metal and avoid getting under the heaps as the mass is not dependably stable. The wrecks are completely covered over with corals, algae and sponges, with resident lobsters, crabs and fish. You can reach it by swimming out from the hotel beach. Expect a light to moderate current.

☆☆☆ **Tug Boat**, the favorite shallow dive in the Curaçao Underwater Park, is intact, sitting upright on a sandy shelf, and can be explored at 15 ft. Tube corals, Christmas trees worms, sponges and sheet corals cover the wheelhouse. Schools of reef fish frolic around the bow. Great for wide-angle photography. Divers can continue down a steep drop-off to explore black corals, vase and basket sponges. The wreck is accessible only by boat, a short ride from Caracas Bay.

☆☆☆☆ Choppy seas are usually encountered enroute to **Black Rock/ Piedra Pretu**, near the easternmost corner of the coast, but the effort is paid back with exposure to one of the most spectacular wall dives in the Caribbean.

Curaçao

You will see dense black-coral bushes and soft corals. Staghorn, elkhorn, soft corals, and sea fans cover the shallow terrace, which drops off to a vertical wall. Depths are from 20 to 150 ft. This is a 12-mile boat ride from the nearest dive operator and can take an hour if the seas are rough (and they usually are).

☆☆☆☆ **Basora** is the easternmost dive site on Curaçao. Changing conditions prevent Basora from being a regular trip by dive operators. On a good day it is a rough one-hour boat ride. However, when conditions allow, this is a memorable dive. Rich with huge brain and star corals and towering pillar formations. Black coral and strangely shaped star corals grow along the drop-off. Sheets of star corals drape the wall. Fish include monster grouper, sting rays and morays. Pay attention to your location and depth; the current often runs two knots.

☆☆☆ **Bullen Bay**, just north of the park, has an outstanding protected, shallow area for snorkeling and a nice drop-off for diving. Yellow pencil corals and pretty white sea plumes highlight the reef. Average depth is 40 ft.

☆☆☆☆☆ **Klein Curaçao** (little Curaçao) is an uninhabited island about a two-hour boat ride east of Curaçao. It is a rugged strip of desolate volcanic rock which plunges into a most spectacular reef. A constant parade of scorpion fish, red-legged hermit crabs, yellow stingrays, spotted morays, yellow frogfish, eagle rays and huge turtles whistle by the wall.

The shelf drops 100 ft into a blaze of orange elephant-ear sponges, purple tube and rope sponges, black corals, huge seafans and massive boulder corals.

Beaches

Curaçao is surrounded by beautiful beaches, from popular hotel beaches to intimate secluded coves. Along the southern coast, there are free public beaches at **West Point Bay, Knip Bay, Klein Knip, Santa Cruz, Jeremi Bay** and **Daaibooi Bay. Knip Bay** is the largest and loveliest swimming beach on the island. Snorkeling is good along the adjacent cliffs.

The main private beaches, which charge a small fee per car, are **Blauw Bay, Jan Thiel, Cas Abao, Barbara Beach** and **Port Marie**.

Beware the manzanilla tree, with its small green apples, that borders some beaches. Its sap will cause burns and blisters on wet exposed skin. Its fruit is poisonous.

Dive Operators

Reef and wreck diving and snorkeling trips may be booked through the following operators. Most offer certification courses.

All West Diving & Adventures Curaçao at West Point Beach. Contact Hans & Bernardien v/d Eeden. ☎ 5999-8640102, fax 8640107.

Aqua Diving, Grote Berg. Contact Arjan Meule. ☎ 011-5999-8649700, fax 8649288.

Atlantis Diving, Drielstraat 6. Roland de Kneg, Manager. ☎ 011-5999-4658288, fax 4658288.

Big Blue Diving, Club Seru Coral, Koral Partier 10. Manager, Tom Zeck. ☎ 011-5999-5605454, fax 4624188.

Coral Cliff Divers, Coral Cliff Hotel at Santa Martha Bay. Owner/Manager Marlies Feijts. ☎ 011-5999-8642822, fax 8642237.

Curaçao Seascape, on the beach at the Curaçao Caribbean Hotel, has fast, comfortable, custom dive boats and friendly service. Snorkelers welcome. Manager, Eva Van Dalen. ☎ 011-5999-4625000, fax 4625846.

Diving School Wederfoort/Sami Scuba Center, at Marine Beach Club St. Michiel Bay. Eric & Yolander Wederfoort owners. ☎ 011-5999-8684414, fax 8692062.

Eden Roc Diving Center, Holiday Beach Hotel, Pater Euwensweg 31, Willemstad. ☎ 011-5999-8648400, fax 8648400. Website: http://tradereps.com/dive/edenroc.html.

Habitat Curaçao Dive Resort, Rif St. Marie. Albert Romijn, Manager. ☎ 5999-8648800, fax 8648464.

Holland Diving Curaçao, Hotel Holland, F.D. Rooseveltweg #534. ☎ 5999-8697060, fax 8697060.

Ocean Divers Curaçao, Socratesstraar 15b. Shirley Pikeur, Manager. ☎ 011-5999-4657254, fax 4657254.

Peter Hughes/Princess Dive Facility, at the Princess Beach Resort & Casino, Holiday Inn Crowne Plaza Hotel, offers reef trips and certification courses. Lex Kleine, Manager. US, ☎ 800-932-6237; Curaçao, 011-5999-4658991, fax 4655756. E-Mail: dancer@winnet.net.

Red Sail Sports, at Curaçao Marriott Hotel, Piscadera Bay. Staff carries gear and tanks. Towels provided. US, ☎ 800-255-6425; Curaçao, 011-5999-7368800, fax 4627502.

Scuba Do Dive Center, at Jan Thiel Beach & Sports Resorts. Contact H. Ferwerda. ☎ 5999-7679300, fax 7679300.

Toucan Diving, Valk Plaza Hotel, Plaza Piar. Bibi Rutten, Manager. ☎ 011-5999-4612500, fax 4616543.

The Ultimate Dive Store, at Orionweg 23. Robby v/d Heuvel, Manager. ☎ 011-5999-5608713, fax 4654431.

Curaçao

Coral-encrusted anchor amidst seafans.

Courtesy Curaçao
Tourist Board

Underwater Curaçao, adjacent to the Seaquarium, at the Lion's Dive Hotel, is a PADI five-star facility. Their double-decker dive boats can easily accommodate large groups. Underwater Curaçao's services include round-trip mini-van service from your hotel or cruise ship. ☎ 011-5999-4618100, fax 4618200.

Travel Packages

Diving is taking off in Curaçao, with new watersports facilities and dive resorts opening their doors. A wide range of accommodations are available. Some hotels offer villa-style arrangements and apartments, and there are a variety of smaller, more intimate guest houses and inns. Dive/vacation packages, including mid-week air fare from the US, start at $538. Packages can be booked through the resorts, travel agents, or these dive tour operators:

- **Landfall Productions**, ☎ 916-563-0164, fax 916-924-1059, E-mail: landfall@pattravel.com.

- **Ocean Connections**, Houston, TX, ☎ 800-331-2458 or 800-364-6232, fax 713-486-8362.

- **Dive Tours**, Spring, TX 77379, ☎ 800-328-5285, fax 281-257-1783. Website: www.dsi-divetours.com. E-mail: info@divetours.com.

- **Caribbean Dive Tours**, Marietta, GA, ☎ 800-786-3483, fax 404-565-0129.

Accommodations

Prices subject to change. All are in US dollars.

Coral Cliff Resort & Beach Club is nestled in the Santa Marta cliffs on its own private beach. Each unit has a fully equipped kitchenette and panoramic vistas. Casino, restaurant, meeting room, satellite TV, tennis court and watersports. Reserve through your travel agent. Summer, $145-$210; winter, $180-$240. ☎ 011-5999-641-610, fax 641-781.

Curaçao Caribbean Hotel & Casino is a huge beachfront hotel with watersports, casino, shopping gallery, tennis, five restaurants, beach bar. Dive packages with Seascape Diving. Five minutes from town. Winter rates for four days/three nights, with four dives for a double, start at $468 per person. For eight days/seven nights, $938 per person. Includes room, airport transfers, discount booklet, free shuttle bus to and from town, tax and service charge, diving, tanks, backpack, weights, belts, unlimited air for shore diving, lockers, T-shirt, service charge on diving. Reserve through your travel agent or ☎ 800-545-9376 or 203-831-0682, fax 203-831-0817. Write to PO Box 2133, Curaçao, NA.

Habitat Curaçao, on the southwest coast in St. Marie, offers restaurant, pool, satellite TV, tennis courts and a variety of watersports. Unlimited diving 24 hours a day with all-inclusive packages for eight days/seven nights starting at $649. US, ☎ 800-327-6709, fax 305-438-4220. Curaçao, 011-599-9-864-8800, fax 864-8464. E-mail: maduro@netpoint.net.

Holiday Beach Hotel & Casino is located on Coconut Beach facing the Curaçao Underwater Park. The 200-room hotel has a complete dive shop, beach, casino, two restaurants, open-air bar, pool, satellite TV, tennis courts and meeting rooms. Handicapped facilities. Rooms are spacious and modern. AC, visitor information hot-line in rooms and children's rates available. Summer $110-$120; winter, $150-$165. PO Box 2178, Curaçao, NA. US and Canada, ☎ 800-444-5244. Curaçao, 011-5999-462-5400, fax 462-5409. Website: www.hol-beach.com.

Kadushi Cliffs Resort, remote, beachfront location with 12 rooms. Restaurant kitchens, meeting facilities, pool, satellite TV. Rates for summer and winter, $195-$295. US, ☎ 800-523-8744. Curaçao, 011-599-9-864-0200, fax 864-0282. E-mail: kadushi@cura.net.

Lions Dive Hotel & Marina is a luxurious 72-room oceanfront dive complex adjacent to the Curaçao Seaquarium. Rooms overlook the Curaçao Marine Park and the *Orange Nassau*. Rooms are air-conditioned and have an ocean-view balcony or terrace. The resort features three restaurants, fitness center and dive shop, Underwater Curaçao. Resort and certification courses are available. Summer, $105-$125; winter, $120-$145. US, ☎ 800-451-9376; Canada, 800-468-0023. Curaçao, 011-5999-461-8100, fax 461-8200. Write to International Travel and Resort Dive Desk, 25 West 39th Street, NY, NY 10018.

Plaza Hotel & Casino, oceanfront with 235 rooms, has a casino, restaurants, dining, meeting facilities, pool, watersports and satellite TV. IDD diving school on premises. Summer, $100-$140; winter, $100-$140. Write to PO Box 813, Willemstad, Curaçao, N.A. US, ☎ 800-766-6016. Curaçao, 011-5999-4612500, fax 4618347.

The Princess Beach Resort & Casino, overlooks the ocean on a long white-sand beach. Luxury accommodations, swim-up bar, shopping arcade, restaurant and casino. Dive and snorkeling sites off the beach. Summer, $145-$585; winter, $210-$735. Diving with Peter Hughes. ☎ 800-992-2015. In Curaçao, 011-5999-736-7888, fax 461-4131.

Curaçao Marriott has a beachfront location with 248 rooms. Casino, three restaurants, fitness center, facilities for handicapped, pool, satellite TV, tennis courts and watersports. Summer, $180-$725; winter, $255-$975. ☎ 800-223-6388, 011-5999-7368800 or fax 011-5999-4627502.

Other Activities

Wherever there is wind and water you are sure to find **windsurfing** – a cross between sailing and surfing. The area of the Spanish Water Bay at the southeast end of the island is the spot for testing your board skills. If you haven't tried it before, take a lesson from a pro. The basics can be learned within a few hours from a certified instructor. Experienced boardsailors should head for the **Marie Pompoen Area** near the Seaquarium. The winds average 12-18 knots, and blow from left to right when facing the water. Check with your hotel's front desk for more information. Sailboards, Sunfish sailboats, and jetskis are rented at most of the hotels' watersports centers.

The Curaçao Golf & Squash Club, near the office for the refinery, offers a nine-hole, oiled-sand course. Stiff tradewinds add to the challenge. There are two squash courts that are open all week. ☎ 873590 for reservations.

Horseback riding the beach trails or through the Kunucu (countryside) can be arranged with the Ashari Ranch (☎ 8690315) or Rancho Alegre (☎ 8681181).

In addition to horseback riding, active travelers can jog along the special paved path at the **Rif Recreation Area Koredor,** a two-mile stretch of palm-lined beachfront about a mile from Willemstad's pontoon bridge.

Deep-sea fishing charters complete with bait and tackle can be arranged for about $50 an hour for a party of four through the marinas at Spanish Water Bay or through the hotel watersports centers. Sportfishing is for marlin, tuna, wahoo and sailfish. Hook and line fishing is allowed in the underwater parks.

Curaçao

Sightseeing

Architecture is the big topside attraction in Curaçao. Walking tours of Willemstad and the surrounding countryside are offered by **Old City Tours**. Scheduled departures are on Tuesdays and Saturday at 9 am, with pickup by jeep at your hotel. A variety of escorted tours for groups of four or more are offered by **Casper Tours, Blenchi Tours** and **Taber Tours**. Arrangements may be booked through most hotels. Taxi tours are about $15 per hour and take up to four passengers.

Many of the hotels offer a free shuttle van to and from Willemstad every half-hour until evening. Traffic in town is busy and walking is the best way to see the town. The main town area (Punda) is safe for tourists, but there are occasional robberies. Avoid the long, narrow streets on the outskirts of town. One area is a government-sanctioned red-light district established to serve transient seamen and is best left unexplored.

In the 1700s, lavish homes and plantations, known as *landhuisen* or landhouses, were built in the countryside. Government and private funds have assisted in the restoration of many of these homes, which now serve as museums, shops, restaurants and even the famous **Seniour Curaçao Liqueur Factory.**

Landhuis Jan Kock, built in 1650, on the road to Westpunt (near Daaibooi Bay), is one of the oldest buildings on the island. Said to be haunted, the *landhuis* was restored as a museum in 1960. On Sundays from 11 am to 6 pm, Dutch-style pancakes and local specialties are served. Nice gift shop.

Landhuis Brievengat, a Dutch version of the 18th-century West Indian plantation, was torn down and rebuilt. It now operates as a museum and cultural center, open daily from 9:30 am to 12:30 pm. It is just north of Willemstad.

The beautifully restored 1700 **Landhuis Ascension**, originally a plantation house, is a recreation center for Dutch marines stationed on the island. An open house featuring local music, handicrafts and refreshments is held on the first Sunday of the month.

Landhuis Habaai is the only remaining "Jewish Quarter" home built by early Sephardic settlers. Located in Otrobanda (St. Helena), the plantation home has an authentic cobbled courtyard.

Landhuis Chobolobo is home to the Senior Curaçao Liqueur Factory, which distills and distributes the world-famous Curaçao liqueur using the original recipe and distilling equipment from the early 1900s.

 Curaçao liqueur was the result of an agricultural mistake. When Spaniards landed on the island in the early 1500s, they planted hundreds of orange trees. The arid climate and sparse rainfall did not provide appropriate growing conditions for the citrus crop, and inedible, bitter fruit was produced. The settlers were not dismayed. They discovered that the orange peel, when dried in the sun, produced an aromatic oil which could be used to prepare a variety of drinks and foods. Today, the fruit is used to produce Curaçao liqueur. Visitors can tour the factory weekdays from 8 am to noon and 1 to 5 pm to view the process and sample the liqueur.

The island's **Amstel Brewery** manufactures Amstel Beer – the only beer in the world brewed from distilled sea water. Tours available on Tuesday and Thursday at 10 am.

In downtown **Willemstad**, just a few minutes walk from the pontoon bridge, is a colorful floating market. Scores of schooners tie up alongside the canal offering fresh fish, tropical fruits, produce, and spices. Vessels arrive daily from Venezuela, Colombia and other West Indian islands. Park where you can and walk, as traffic is heavy and stopping on the narrow street is tough.

At the western end of the island is **Christoffel National Park** and **Mt. Christoffel**. A protected wildlife preserve and garden covering 4,500 acres of land, the park has been open to the public since 1978 and features 20 miles of one-way trails through fields of cactus, divi divi trees and exotic flowers. Wild iguanas, rabbits, donkeys, deer and more than 100 species of birds inhabit the preserve. If you love roller coasters, you will love the big rolling hills of this park. Drive slowly. Hiking trails are very rugged and should be traveled in the cool morning hours. The park is open Monday through Saturday. Admission is US $9; a guide can be hired for about US $14.

Walking tours are popular and may be arranged, in advance, through most hotels. Jeeps and four-wheel-drive vehicles are available for rent.

Boca Tabla is the site of a wonderful cave that opens to the sea. You walk the sand path to the cave entrance (signs lead the way) and climb down a path of huge boulders for a spectacular view of crashing waves into the cave entrance. Very photogenic!

Because Curaçaons believe women make the ocean angry or more active, a woman may be asked to stay in the cave to liven up the attraction. So strong is this belief that, during a rescue operation off the north shore in 1992, a woman reporter was asked to leave the area so that male divers might do their job more easily.

An even more spectacular natural wonder is **Wata Mula**, a 30-ft-wide crater that tunnels to the open sea. Huge waves crash and recede rhythmically while spewing fountains of froth and rainbows high into the air. Both dramatic and mesmerizing, it is a photo buff's delight. Take care if you are driving. The ground is sharp ironshore. The land meets the sea quite abruptly and, without warning, shoots straight down jagged cliffs into crashing waves. Plus, the area is badly littered with broken beer bottles.

You'll see 20-ft sharks, turtles as big as manhole covers, giant moray eels and more than 400 species of fish, crabs, turtles, anemones, sponges, corals and marine life at the **Curaçao Seaquarium**. A "Touch Tank" allows children to pick up starfish, sea urchins and other small sea animals. All species in the 75 hexagonal aquariums are native to the surrounding waters.

The Seaquarium complex also has two restaurants, a magnificent beach and gift shop. It's open daily from 10 am to 10 pm. Admission fee.

Other attractions include the **Arawak Clay Factory**, the **Curaçao Museum**, the **Hato Caves** near the Hotel Holland, the **Botanical Garden and Zoo**, and numerous old fortresses such as **Rif Fort, Fort Amsterdam** and **Fort Nassau**.

Dining

With culinary influences from more than 40 countries, Curaçao offers a wide and wonderful variety of restaurant choices, including Dutch, Indonesian,

Creole, Swiss, Chinese, French, South American, Indian, Italian and American cuisine. They range from casual eateries to gourmet restaurants, many with spectacular views. Popular fast-food eateries are scattered about the island. Local food is usually chicken, fish or meat in a thin sauce made of onions, peppers and tomatoes, with French fries or a biscuit-like pancake.

The **Golden Star Bar and Restaurant**, in town at Socratesstraat 2, is the place for goat stew and fungi or other local cuisine at low prices. Hamburgers, sate (skewered meat or fish), bacon and egg sandwiches, sailfish cakes, and fried chicken are on the menu too. Open for lunch and dinner. ☎ 54795 or 54865.

La Pergola, at Waterfort Arches in the Punda section of Willemstad, is a fine Italian restaurant with lovely views and excellent food. Local seafood, pasta, and steaks. Expensive, but a definite memorable treat. Reservations a must. ☎ 4613482.

Rumours, at the Lion's Dive Hotel, is open daily for breakfast, lunch and dinner and features meat dishes and fresh catches of the day. ☎ 4617555.

For the charm of a typical Dutch coffee house with Creole and international dishes, try the **Bon Appetit** lunchroom in the heart of Willemstad's shopping center, at Hanchi Snoa. ☎ 4616916.

The Landuis Groot Davelaar houses the 18th-century **De Taveerne Restaurant & Wine Cellar**. An international lunch and dinner menu also features fine wine and cheeses. Closed Sunday. Reservations. ☎ 7370669.

History buffs and romantics will love candlelight dining at the **Fort Nassau Restaurant**. The fort sits high over Willemstad with a 360° panoramic view of St. Anna Bay. Both the food and view are spectacular! Open daily from 7 to 11 pm and for lunch Monday to Friday from noon to 2 pm. Prices for lunch average $15 per person. Dinner entrées (à la carte) are from $22. ☎ 4613086 or 4613450.

Fine seafood, from Creole red snapper to Spanish specialties, such as paella mariner, are offered by **El Marinero Seafood** in Biesheuvel, at Schottergatweg Noord 87B. Reservations, ☎ 79833.

Fort Waakzaamheid Bistro is known for its BBQ, salad bar and fresh seafood. In Otrobanda, at Berg Domi. ☎ 4623633. For downhome Antillean dishes, there is **March,** an open-air restaurant where you can choose your lunch from dozens of Curaçaoan delicacies cooked up in giant pots. Low, low prices.

In West Punt, stop in at **Jaanchie's Restaurant** for conch stew, goat stew and fried or broiled fish. Located at Westpunt 15. ☎ 8640126. This is a beautiful, open-air restaurant with a garden atmosphere. Local folk artists' work decorates the columns. Very casual, very charming, very special. Excellent local dishes. Average prices.

Fincamar at Lagoen K-27 at West Point is marked by a huge horse sculpture outside. This seafood restaurant is one of Curaçao's finest. The back wall is open to scenic views of West Point's towering cliffs. European atmosphere. Prices for dinner entrées start at $18 sans service charges. ☎ 8641377.

Fast food fans will find their fill at Breedestraate in Willemstad.

Facts

Helpful Phone Numbers: Police: ☎ 114. Taxi Service, ☎ 616711. Island Bus Service, ☎ 684733.

Nearest Recompression Chamber: St. Elisabeth Hospital, ☎ 624900 or 625100.

Getting There: ALM Airlines flies from Atlanta four times a week.

Getting Around: Car Rental, ☎ 689410 or 617568. Curaçao also has an excellent bus system to transport visitors around the island.

Language: The official language is Dutch, but English and Spanish are spoken as well. Most residents speak Papiamento, a blend of Portuguese, Dutch, African, English, French and some Arawak Indian.

Documents: Passports are not required for US and Canadian citizens. Travelers will need proof of citizenship and a return or continuing ticket. A passport or birth certificate is necessary for reentering the US.

Customs: Arriving passengers may bring in 400 cigarettes, 50 cigars, 100 cigarillos, two liters of liquor. There is a duty-free shop at the airport.

US residents may bring home, free of duty, $400 worth of articles, including 200 cigarettes, and one quart liquor per person over 21 years of age plus $25 worth of Edam or Gouda cheese for personal use.

Airport Tax: For international flights, $10; for inter-island flights, $5.65.

Currency: The guilder, or florin, is the Netherlands Antilles' currency. The official rate of exchange is US $1=1.77 NA florins. However, US dollars and major credit cards are accepted throughout the island.

Climate: Curaçao's tropical climate remains fairly constant year-round. The average temperature Is 80°F and less than 23 inches of rain fall annually. The island is outside of the hurricane belt and its cooling trade winds average 15 mph.

Clothing: Snorkelers should bring wetskins or long-sleeve shirts to protect from the sun. Wetsuits are comfortable when making several deep dives, but warm ocean temperatures make them unnecessary baggage for the average sport diver. Topside dress is casual, lightweight. Topless sunbathing is practiced on some beaches. Jackets are required for a few restaurants.

Electricity: 110-128 volts, AC (50 HZ), which is compatible with American electric razors and blow dryers. Adaptors are not needed. The Lions Dive Hotel has 220 volts.

Religious Services: Protestant, Catholic, Jewish, Episcopal, Seventh Day Adventist.

Curaçao

Additional Information: Curaçao Tourist Board, 475 Park Avenue South, Suite 2000, NY, NY 10016,☎ 800-287-2226 for brochures, 800-270-3350 for information or 212-683-7660, fax 212-683-9337. E-mail: ctdbny@ctdb.com.

In Miami: 330 Biscayne Boulevard, Suite 808, Miami, FL 33132, ☎ 305-374-5811, fax 305-374-6741. E-mail: ctdbmiami@ctdb.com.

In Curaçao: The Curaçao Tourism Development Bureau, Pietermaai 19, PO Box 3266, Curaçao, Netherlands Antilles; ☎ 011-599-9-461-6000, fax 011-599-9-461-2305. E-mail: ctdbcur@ctdb.com. Website: www.Curaçao-tourism.com.

US Virgin Islands

Discovered by Columbus in 1493, the US Virgin Islands (USVI) comprise three main islands: St. Croix, St. John and St. Thomas. Each has a distinct personality and flavor, and since they are close together you can choose one island as your base and still catch the fun of the other two. They offer an enormous variety of reefs, wrecks and drop-offs, all in crystal clear water protected from strong currents and heavy seas.

Before becoming an American territory, the USVI lived under six different flags. It still preserves a rich and varied culture. Wander through old Danish arcades covered with tropical flowers in the historic town of Christiansted on St. Croix; visit Bluebeard's Castle on St. Thomas; or stroll around the partially restored ruins of the Annaberg Plantation on St. John.

St. Croix

The largest of the USVI, St. Croix plays host to over 50,000 visiting snorkelers and divers per year, the main attraction being Buck Island National Park – the most famous snorkeling spot in the world. Scuba divers will find their share of reefs, walls and wrecks to dive.

Picturesque St. Croix, once a Danish territory, is known for its easy lifestyle and warm hospitality. The streets of Christiansted, its tiny capital, are lined with 18th-century buildings in pastel pinks, blues and yellow. Tropical flowers greet the visitor everywhere. At night, shops, restaurants and nightclubs come alive with reggae music and island hospitality.

The small town of Frederiksted is laced with wide tree-shaded streets that lead to a lovely waterfront with arcaded sidewalks. After a devastating fire in 1878, Frederiksted was rebuilt in the Victorian style. Flowering vines now cling to the balustrades of the gingerbread frames the Cruzans built over the Danish masonry. Much of the best diving and snorkeling around St. Croix is accessible by beach entry.

Best Dives of St. Croix

☆☆☆ **Long Reef**, a six-mile-wide shallow reef on the outskirts of Christiansted Harbor, offers a variety of dives. The bottom gently terraces from the shallows to an average depth of 50 ft, reaching 80 ft at some spots. Hundreds of small coral caves and crevices along the reef shelter French an-

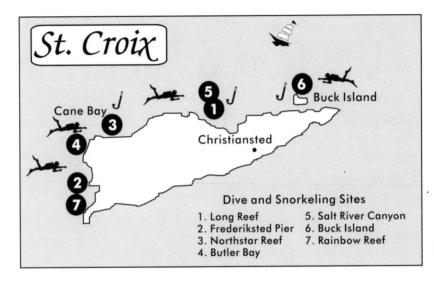

St. Croix

Cane Bay

Buck Island

Christiansted

Dive and Snorkeling Sites

1. Long Reef   5. Salt River Canyon
2. Frederiksted Pier 6. Buck Island
3. Northstar Reef   7. Rainbow Reef
4. Butler Bay

gels, parrot fish, rays, turtles, morays, octopi, lobsters and goatfish. A docile nurse shark makes frequent appearances. Huge brain and elkhorn coral formations prevail. An old barge intentionally sunk at 60 ft near the harbor channel attracts a healthy fish population. Visibility varies. Recommended for snorkelers and novice divers.

☆☆☆☆ **The Frederiksted Pier** offers the ultimate night dive at St. Croix. Underwater pilings, carpeted with red, yellow and orange sponges, provide cover for seahorses, iridescent tube sponges, octopi, baby morays, juvenile fish, brittle stars, puffers, featherdusters, parrot fish and tube anemones. Take your dive light. Beware the stinging corals and red do-not-touch-me sponge. Entrance to the dive site is by climbing down a steel ladder or taking a giant stride off the end of the pier. Before entering the water, be sure to see the Harbor Master at the pier, C-card in hand. ☎ 772-0174. Diving is prohibited when a ship is in.

☆☆☆☆ **Northstar Reef**, a spectacular wall dive at the east end of Davis Bay, is recommended for intermediate or experienced divers. Beach entry is possible here but most divers opt for boat access because of the rocky terrain.

Beautiful staghorn thickets and brain corals decorate the wall. A sandy shelf at 50 ft leads to a spooky cave and a hefty green moray eel. Huge anchors from 18th-century sailing ships lie scattered about. Marine life includes a superb collection of schooling tropicals, pelagics, turtles, morays and eagle rays. Expect an occasional moderate current.

☆☆☆ **Butler Bay**, on the island's west shore, harbors four shipwrecks: the 170-ft *Rosaomaira*, which sits in 100 ft of water; the 140-ft *Suffolk Maid*, an old fishing trawler at 90 ft; the *Northwind*, a retired tugboat at about 60 ft; and the *Virgin Island*, a 300-ft barge sunk in 1991, resting at 70 ft. The wrecks are part of an artificial reef system that also includes old cars and trucks, music boxes, typewriters, and a vast array of other items. Wreck residents include goat fish, groupers, snappers, hogfish, parrot fish, turtles, rays, and angelfish. Recommended for intermediate to experienced divers.

☆☆☆ **Salt River Canyon**, a deep, submerged canyon formed by the out-flow to the Salt River, features two distinct dives off its east and west walls. Salt River East, with interest between 40- and 100-ft depths, is famed for the massive orange elephant ear sponges and black corals that decorate its precipice. The area's usual good visibility allows a long look at resident bigeyes, grunts, barracuda, blue chromis and sting rays. Suggested for intermediate divers.

Salt River West plunges from 40 to more than 130 ft. Plate corals cascade down the reef slope and large purple tube sponges make a wonderful fore-ground for wide-angle photography.

When seas are calm, it is an excellent spot for novices. Visibility, normally good, may decrease during stormy weather.

☆☆☆ **Cane Bay Drop-off** is the favorite beach dive. The drop-off lies about 140 yds off the beach and is suitable for scuba and snorkeling, with depths ranging from the surface to 120 ft. Inside the reef, calm waters and a decent fish population make this spot a favorite of snorkelers. Light surf along the shore. Light current at the drop-off. Park along the road at Cane Bay Beach.

Additional shore-entry dives are best at Davis Bay and Butler Bay. Visibility close to shore is weather-dependent and decreases when a lot of rain and wind churn the bottom. Equipment may be rented at any of the dive shops.

Best Snorkeling of St. Croix

☆☆ **Buck Island Reef** continues to capture the hearts of Caribbean tour-ists despite noticeable wear from hurricanes and a daily blitz of snorkelers. Es-tablished by President John F. Kennedy as a national monument, this 850-acre sanctuary houses an underwater national park.

As in most national parks, Buck Island has its own rangers, only here they sport swim trunks and patrol in powerboats. There are also the standard park guide markers, but at Buck Island they stand at a depth of 12 ft, embedded in the sands along the ocean floor. Each day, catamarans, trimarans, sloops, and yawls unload what the islanders call the wet set. The Buck Island welcom-ing committee includes green parrot fish, snappy sergeant majors, grouper, rainbow-striped angelfish and the silvery Bermuda chub. Beginners and ex-perienced snorkelers alike can experience this underwater fantasy in an un-usually safe atmosphere. The reefs of Buck Island lie only 100 yds off the coast

US Virgin Islands

and no trail is more than 15 ft deep. As snorkelers enter the park, they are welcomed by a blue and white plaque shimmering below the surface. One marker (number 8) next to an unusual round coral full of veins inquires, "What would you name this coral?" The next marker says, "You are right. Brain Coral." Arrows and signs guide the swimmer along the underwater trail and give the precise names of coral and other growths below the surface.

More than 300 species of fish are identified. One species that audibly demands attention is the small striped grunt, which can be clearly heard underwater. The National Park Service maintains a careful watch, but one familiar park rule – Don't Feed the Animals – does not apply here. Swimmers can feed the fish as often as they like. Grouper, a favorite fish to hand-feed, come readily at the slightest beckoning.

Since the reef park is strictly non-commercial, you are advised to rent gear before heading out. Whether you're coming from St. Thomas, St. Croix or St. John, you can obtain equipment readily on all three islands. And getting there is half the fun. Most hotels on St. Croix offer a shuttle service to Christiansted, where you can select almost any kind of boat imaginable. Charter boats of every description line the docks of the Christiansted harbor. Boats to Buck Island are widely available at low cost.

 Make sure you stop over on Buck Island Beach, a pristine stretch of powdery, white sand created in part by parrot fish gnawing on the coral reef and excreting sand.

From Buck Island Beach, a wildlife trail leads 200 ft to an observation tower, which gives a grand view of the lagoon and reef. A trip to Buck will be one of the most memorable experiences of your visit to the Virgin Islands. Areas of Buck Island reef away from the snorkeling trail are suitable for scuba.

Dive Operators of St. Croix

All of the dive operators on St. Croix require a C-card.

Cane Bay Dive Shop, on the beach at Cane Bay, offers walk-in dives to the Cane Bay Drop-Off, which sits about 140 yds off the beach. Snorkeling tours. Hotel and dive packages available. Boat dives $60, beach dives from $35, beach night dives from $40. PADI courses. ☎ 800-338-3843 or 340-773-9913. Write to PO Box 4510, Kings Hill, St. Croix, USVI 00851.

Dive Experience is at the Club St. Croix in Christiansted. Owner, Michelle Pugh is a diver-medic instructor as well as a PADI instructor. This PADI five-star facility offers all certifications, including a four-day certification, a resort course, rentals, photography equipment . Dive Experience offers boat dives around the island and will shoot personalized videos. Hotel and dive packages are available. ☎ 800-235-9047, 340-773-3307 or write Box 4254, Christiansted, St. Croix, USVI 00822.

Mile Mark Watersport/Dive St. Croix in Christiansted offers wall and wreck diving trips, night dives, Buck Island trips, camera rentals, resort through certification courses, and accommodation package tours with several different resorts. ☎ 800-523-3483 or 340-773-3434, fax 340-773-9411. Mile Mark Watersports also offers sportfishing, water skiing, parasailing, board sailing and island tours. ☎ 800-524-2021, local 773-2628. Write to 59 Kings Wharf, Christiansted, St. Croix, USVI 00820.

Virgin Island Divers is located at the Pan Am Pavilion in Christiansted. All certification ratings and rentals. Beach dives, boat, night and wreck dives, custom dive boats. ☎ 800-544-5911 or 340-773-6045 or write Pan Am Pavilion, Christiansted, St. Croix, USVI 00820.

Anchor Dive Center is a PADI five-star, IDC training facility. Resort to instructor courses. Located at the Salt River Marina, they are three minutes from Salt River Canyon. ☎ 340-778-1522 or 800-532-3483. Write to PO Box 5588, Sunny Isle, St. Croix, USVI 00823. E-mail: anchordivecenter@juno.com

Cap'n Dicks Scubawest offers boat, beach and pier dives plus wall and reef dives. Resort, rescue, dive master and advanced courses. ☎ 800-352-0107 or 340-772-3701. Write to 330 Strand St., Frederiksted, St. Croix USVI 00840. E-mail: scubawest@msn.com.

Sea Shadows is in Cane Bay and at Kings Wharf. Owners Libby Wessel and Steve Fordyce are beach diving specialists. The shop also operates two dive boats that tour all the sites around St. Croix.

St. Croix Ultimate Bluewater Adventures (SCUBA) in the Caravele Arcade, offers personalized service for divers of all experience levels . The shop also books Busk Island snorkeling tours, deep sea fishing charters and jet ski and kayak rentals. Dive-hotel packages available. ☎ 877-STX-SCUBA or 340-773-5994. Website: www.stcroixscuba.com.

Accommodations

For current rates via the Web: http://st-croix.com/rates.

St. Croix offers a wide range of luxury resorts, villas, condominiums, inns and guest houses. Like the neighboring British Virgin Islands, the waters around the USVI are excellent for sailing. Many visiting divers combine a week of bare boating or live-aboard sailing with sub-sea exploring. The following are resorts that cater to divers and offer package deals. (Add 8% tax to room rates.)

US Virgin Islands

The Buccaneer Hotel in Christiansted also offers packages with Caribbean Sea Adventures. The resort features three beautiful beaches, three restaurants, a spa, shopping arcade, eight tennis courts, an 18-hole golf course and all water sports. Dive and snorkeling trips leave from the resort dock for Buck Island. Rates are from $185 (summer), $250 (winter) per night for a double in a standard room. Cottages range from $245 to $1,370 per week (summer), $385 (winter) per night. ☎ 800-223-1108 or 340-773-2100; write PO Box 492477, Los Angeles, CA 90049.

Chenay Bay Beach Resort offers beachfront cottages with kitchens from $215 per day. ☎ 800-548-4457, fax 340-773-2918.

Hibiscus Beach Hotel, a small, friendly Caribbean-style hotel, rents oceanfront rooms with patios or balconies from $190 per night. TV, phone, restaurant. White sand beach. ☎ 800-442-0121, fax 340-773-7668.

The Waves At Cane Bay offer spacious seaside studios with balconies, pool, beach, restaurant. Scuba and snorkeling off the beach. Rooms are from $170 per night. Nice! TV, no phones. ☎ 800-545-0603 or 340-778-1805, fax 340-778-4945. PO Box 1749, Kingshill, St. Croix, USVI 00850.

Cane Bay Reef Club features six two-room suites with full kitchens, balcony overlooking the sea. Saltwater pool. Rates are from $175 per day. PO Box 1407, Kingshill, St. Croix, USVI 00851. ☎ 340-778-2966. Website: www.canebay.com.

For additional rentals try **Island Villas**, ☎ 800-626-4512, fax 340-773-8823. From $1,200 per week. E-mail: carphil@viaccess.net www.ecani.com/island.villas.

Dining

The US Virgin Islands are considered the mecca of haute cuisine in the Caribbean. From the islands' rich mixture of cultures – Spanish, French, English, Danish, Maltese, Dutch and American – its pungent local spices and fresh tropical fruits, local chefs create dishes to dream about. So many fine restaurants have opened up within the last five years, we can only give a hint of the many options.

Bacchus. In a historic townhouse in the heart of Christiansted on Queen Cross Street, this sophisticated dining spot has a menu boasting prime cuts of beef carved according to each diner's preference, as well as fresh local fish, lobster and vegetarian selections. Extensive wine list. ☎ 692-9922.

Cheeseburgers in Paradise on Rt. 66. Diners will encounter a congenial crowd any time of day or night at this relaxed, open-air spot on St. Croix's east end. If not ordering what many consider to be the largest and best burgers on the island, diners may opt for the grilled chicken, hummus burrito or chili dog.

Nachos with homemade salsa and a "Paradise Margarita" are the perfect accompaniments. ☎ 773-1119.

A St. Croix landmark, located upstairs on Strand Street in the heart of downtown Christiansted, **Comanche** is famed for its Casablanca ambiance and native island character. The lunch menu includes an array of interesting soups, appetizers and sandwiches, and dinner time features numerous innovative entrées flavored with local island ingredients. A favorite choice is the susu chicken curry served in a fresh pineapple shell. ☎ 773-2665.

Dino's. Amidst colorful European artwork and surrounded by dramatic floor-to-ceiling windows, diners can savor Northern Italian and Mediterranean cuisine made famous by chef Dino DiNatale. Located on the grounds of the Buccaneer Hotel, Dino's bistro offers elegant dining with panoramic views of the sparkling lights of Christiansted. ☎ 773-2100, ext. 723.

Duggan's Reef (on the east end, Rt. 66). A favorite among locals and visitors alike who come for the lunch menu which features eggs Benedict, flying fish, quiches, soups, salads and more. Dinner is equally delicious, with menu options such as rack of lamb, filet mignon or lobster pasta. Relax in the open-air, informal atmosphere overlooking the Caribbean Sea and Buck Island. ☎ 773-9800.

The Galleon (on the east end). Traditional French and northern Italian favorites top the dinner menu at this elegant, relaxed restaurant on Green Cay Marina. The Caesar salad for two comes highly recommended, as does the "Galleon," a grilled filet mignon dish with lobster sauce Béarnaise. Other entrées of note are the ch teaubriand, rack of lamb for two and the aiguillette de canard. Local fresh fish and lobster are on the menu daily. ☎ 773-9949.

Diners have an ample menu from which to make lunch and dinner selections at **Gertrude's**, a long-time favorite on St. Croix. Hot and cold sandwiches, fresh salads and hearty homemade soups satisfy the lunch-time palate, while dinner selections include escargot, conch fritters and other fresh seafood, chicken and steak favorites. ☎ 778-8362.

Harvey's Restaurant. This friendly family establishment in Christiansted has a menu replete with West Indian favorites such as buttered conch, goat stew and local lobster prepared with onion and spice topping. Fresh local fish is served poached, stewed or fried with creole sauce and seasoned rice and beans. Entrées are accompanied by local sweet potatoes, fried plantain, fungi and West Indian-style stuffing. Homemade pies flavored with guava, pineapple and coconut are on the house! ☎ 773-3433.

A highly esteemed name among St. Croix's restaurants, **Kendrick's** (King Cross Street) resides in Christiansted's historic Quin House complex, offering dinners in the courtyard or within the charming West Indian cottage. Whether

US Virgin Islands

an appetizer, pasta dish, delicately seasoned entrée of fresh local fish or other house specialty, each selection is prepared to suit each diner's fancy. ☎ 773-9199.

No Name Café (on King Street). A beautiful fountain and circular stairway lend to the romantic atmosphere of this popular restaurant located in a historic downtown Christiansted courtyard. No Name is famous for its variety of fresh grilled fish, stuffed pork tenderloin, vodka pasta and an array of delicious soups, appetizers and desserts. ☎ 773-8228.

Located in the Buccaneer Hotel's main building, **The Terrace** offers covered, open-air dining with views overlooking the resort's manicured fairways, Caribbean Sea and Christiansted harbor. In addition to daily breakfast, the restaurant offers dinner nightly, boasting a menu rich with the fusion of European and classic Caribbean accents. ☎ 773-2100.

Nestled in a breezy tropical garden in the heart of downtown Christiansted, **Tivoli Gardens** (on Strand Street, Pan Am Pavilion) serves salads, sandwiches and hot entrées such as shrimp curry and coquilles St. Jacques for lunch-time diners. The dinner hour features sumptuous favorites such as lobster-stuffed mushroom caps, steak Diane, broiled lobster and other fresh fish and pasta selections. Homemade ice creams and the ever-popular chocolate velvet dessert are the perfect conclusions. ☎ 773-6782.

A lively Caribbean café with an Italian accent, **Tutto Bene** (in downtown Christiansted, on Company Street) boasts a well-rounded menu of appetizers, salads and pasta dishes. Homemade desserts, coffee and drinks provide the perfect nightcap to this café's highly acclaimed cuisine. Menu changes daily. ☎ 773-5229.

Nestled right along the Christiansted harbor at Hotel Caravelle, **Wahoo Willy's** has an extensive lunch and dinner menu from which to select such savory items as wood-fired pizzas, steaks, lobster and catch-of-the-day entrées. Breakfast buffet seven days a week, as well as a West Indian buffet every Monday night. ☎ 773-6585.

The Buccaneer Hotel's Brass Parrot on St. Croix promises a feast to remember. Situated just 20 minutes outside of historic Christiansted, the restaurant combines a taste of past glory with a stunning modern decor. The Haitian chef prepares fine continental cuisine with a touch of the islands. Specialties include conch with hot lime sauce; shrimp Bahia, giant shrimp sautéed in garlic butter and topped with brandy and pineapple liqueur; or a rack of lamb carved at your table. In a more informal setting, diners will enjoy the lively **Club Comanche Restaurant**, on the second floor of an old Danish townhouse in Christiansted. Favorites here are cucumber soup, prime rib, rack of lamb, and lobster. For dessert, try key lime pie.

Caneel Bay, St. John.

The Wreck Bar on Hospital Street is the place for West Indian atmosphere. Opens for dinner 4 pm, Monday through Saturday. Specials are fish and chips, fried shrimp and beer batter onion rings. Entertainment includes crab races and guitar music. Cash only.

The Stone Terrace Restaurant, overlooking Cruz Bay Harbor, offers international cuisine in a casually elegant atmosphere. ☎ 693-9370. E-mail: raintree@islands.vi.

Visitors to **Dowie's**, Frederiksted, can sample local specialties such as bullfoot soup, kallalloo, conch in butter sauce and fish pudding. Breakfast and lunch are served Tuesday through Friday from 7 am to 2 pm, and Saturday breakfasts consist of fritters, johnnycakes, salt fish, fry fish and bush tea. ☎ 772-0845.

The Garlic Press on St. Croix is a casual family-style restaurant known for its fried calamari, hot antipasto, "build-your-own" calzones and hot subs. Lunch and dinner. Opens 11:30. ☎ 773-1100.

St. John

The smallest and most verdant of the USVI, St. John is truly the most virgin. The island is an unspoiled sanctuary of natural beauty and wildlife. Two-thirds of the 28-square-mile island and most of its stunning shoreline comprise the Virgin Islands National Park, part of the US National Park system. Here nature flaunts her majestic mountains, emerald valleys and lush tropical vegetation. St. John is the best choice for beachfront camping.

Best Dives of St. John

The best dives of St. John are from the out islands, Congo Cay and Carvel Rock. Shallow dive sites are found around the south shores of Reef Bay and the west shores of Cruz Bay.

☆☆ **Congo Cay** is a favorite site for dive boats based at St. John and St. Thomas. It is a rocky islet located between them. Visibility is usually good. As with many of the small cays, the rocky submerged areas are home to large schools of fish. The coral mounds, some of which have been beaten up by the sea, are decorated with soft corals and brightly colored sponges. Currents are occasionally strong here.

☆☆☆ **Carval Rock** is a short boat ride from the north end of St. John. Try this dive only if weather and sea conditions permit, as strong currents may exist under less than perfect circumstances. Recommended for very experienced divers only. The attraction here is the schools of very large fish and eagle rays. The submerged part of the rock is covered with sponges, gorgonians, basket stars, and false corals.

☆☆ **Fishbowl Reef**, just south of Cruz Bay, is a nice shallow dive for novices and snorkelers. Divers swim along ledges sparkling with beautiful elkhorn and staghorn coral. Soft corals undulate in the shallows. Many kinds of small reef fish are found hiding in the crevices.

Best Snorkeling Sites of St. John

Half-day and full-day snorkeling excursions by boat are available, exploring outer reefs or shipwrecks. Lucy Portlock, **Pelagic Pleasures**, ☎ 340-776-6567, at the Caneel Bay Resort, offers boat snorkeling excursions to all the best sites around St. John. If you're not staying at Caneel Bay, sign up at Hurricane Alley in the Mongoose Junction Mini Mall.

☆☆☆ **Trunk Bay** on the north shore of the island has a clearly marked underwater trail, with abundant soft and hard corals, yellowtail, damsel fish, and occasional turtles. The reef is shallow and is just off beautiful Trunk Bay Beach. Top-side here is great for snapshots. Average depths: 10 to 15 ft.

☆☆☆ **Salt Pond Bay**, at the southeast end, is never crowded and is blessed with ample shade trees. Coral reefs stretch from both points of the Bay, offering snorkelers a full day's worth of adventure. Many fish and marine animals make their home here.

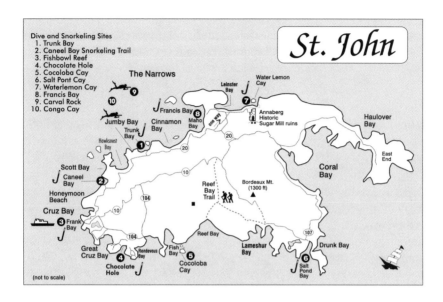

Dive and Snorkeling Sites
1. Trunk Bay
2. Caneel Bay Snorkeling Trail
3. Fishbowl Reef
4. Chocolate Hole
5. Cocoloba Cay
6. Salt Pont Cay
7. Waterlemon Cay
8. Francis Bay
9. Carval Rock
10. Congo Cay

St. John

The Narrows

Water Lemon Cay

Leinster Bay

Annaberg Historic Sugar Mill ruins

Haulover Bay

Francis Bay

Jumby Bay

Cinnamon Bay

Maho Bay

Trunk Bay

Hawksnest Bay

East End

Scott Bay

Caneel Bay

Honeymoon Beach

Cruz Bay

Frank Bay

Coral Bay

Bordeaux Mt. (1300 ft)

Reef Bay Trail

Great Cruz Bay

Rendevous Bay

Chocolate Hole

Fish Bay

Cocoloba Cay

Reef Bay

Lameshur Bay

Drunk Bay

Salt Pond Bay

(not to scale)

☆☆☆ **Chocolate Hole**, at the east side of the mouth of Chocolate Bay, is distinguised by several rocks sticking up out of the water. The reef is just to the west of these. Reef depths are from four to 15 ft. Hordes of fish, including grunts, squirrelfish, blue chromis, parrot fish, rays and turtles, wander about. Seas usually very calm unless the wind is from the south. Good for all levels.

☆☆ **Waterlemon Cay**, a national park, offers terrific fish watching for experienced swimmers. To get there, drive to Annaberg Sugarmill ruins, park and hike down the road to the beach (half a mile). Swim along the east side of the bay to Waterlemon Cay. There are loads of big Caribbean starfish in the sand and walls of fish all around the island, including big yellowtail snapper and jawfish. This spot is usually calm in summer, but choppy in winter when the wind is out of the northeast. Tidal currents may exist.

☆☆ **Caneel Bay Snorkeling Trail** is limited to guests of the Caneel Bay Resort or boaters who enter from the sea, but Caneel Bay's main beach is open to the public and offers some nice fish watching.

☆ **Francis Bay** is easiest by boat, but you can reach it by driving to the Annaberg Sugar Mill, then left to Francis Bay. The last stretch of road is gravel and dirt. Rocks, corals and plenty of fish.

☆☆ **Cocoloba Cay**, a bare rocky site attached to St. John by rock, coral and sand, requires boat access. The east side has huge coral formations, some 15-ft high, which died long ago, but now have new coral growing on top. Large coral patch reefs exist along the west side. Depths range from five to 30 ft. Highlights are angel fish, schools of blue tang, spadefish, jacks, pompano and an occasional shark. This area is usually rough, good only on days with the wind from the north or northeast. Experienced ocean swimmers only. Boaters should anchor about 100 yds east of the cay.

Dive Operators

Hurricane Alley, Mongoose Junction, offers rentals and dive trips. ☎ 340-776-6256. You can also sign up for a memorable snorkeling adventure with our favorite snorkologist, Lucy Portlock of Pelagic Pleasures ☎ 340-776-6567. Or write PO Box 1570, Cruz Bay, St. John, USVI 00830.

Cinnamon Bay Watersports Center, located at Caneel Bay Resort, operates a 42-ft custom dive boat complete with compressor. Dive trips are offered to the outer islands (cays) and reefs. Day trips to the *R.M.S. Rhone*, an outstanding wreck dive, located nearby in the British Virgin Islands, can be arranged for groups. Dive packages with Caneel Bay Resort are available. ☎ 340-693-8690. Write to PO Box 720, Cruz Bay, St. John, USVI 00831.

Snuba of St. John offers underwater tours at Trunk Bay. Snuba is a cross between snorkeling and scuba with surface-supplied air. No experience needed. Ages eight and up. ☎ 340-693-8063.

Accommodations

For current rates via the web: http://st-john.com/rates.

Caneel Bay Resort occupies a 170-acre peninsula that adjoins the Virgin Islands National Park. There are 171 guest units in low-profile buildings scattered about the grounds, three restaurants, seven white sand beaches and seven tennis courts. The resort is known for the gardens where over 500 tropical plant species grow. Divers may combine a week with Little Dix Bay Resort on Virgin Gorda (transfers handled by the resort) or sailing on Hinckley yachts ranging from 40 to 50 ft. Room rates are from $400 to $700 per day; $750 for a cottage. ☎ 800-928-8889 or see your travel agent.

Westin Regency St. John sprawls over 34 exotic acres with a gigantic freshwater pool covering a quarter-acre and offers 280 luxury guest rooms with all amenities. Under 18 stay free. Good snorkeling off the beach. Cruz Bay Watersports (☎ 693-8000), on premises, offers dive and snorkeling trips. ☎ 800-228-3000 or 340-693-8000, fax 340-779-4985.

Cottages by the Sea features full kitchens, white sand beach, patios. Snorkeling off the beach. Rates from $115 per day. ☎ 800-323-7252, fax 340-772-1753.

Condos & Apartments

Cruz Bay Villas, high on the mountainside near town, rent for $160 per night. ☎ 340-776-6416. Website: www.cruzbayvillas.com.

Dining

Serving Pacific Rim cuisine with an oriental influence, **Asolare** provides a gorgeous view of Cruz Bay. Open daily from 5:30 to 9:30 pm, except on Tuesdays. Reservations are recommended. ☎ 779-4747.

Coccoloba Grill & Bar. Fine dining is the order of the evening at this premier hilltop restaurant at The Westin Resort, St. John. With spectacular open-air views overlooking the resort's expansive gardens and Great Cruz Bay, Coccoloba features specialty cuisine celebrating native Caribbean spices and flavors. Open for dinner on Tuesdays, Thursdays and Saturdays only, 6:30-10 pm. ☎ 693-8000.

Casual dining by day and elegant dining by night is offered at **Dinner with Andre**, built to cozily accommodate only 24 diners at a time. Home to sandwich shop Chilly Billy's during the day, nightfall introduces an intimate dining spot where diners enjoy delectable French cuisine created by Chef Andre Rosin, for whom the restaurant is named. In downtown Cruz Bay. ☎ 693-8708.

Located in Caneel Bay Resort's former Sugar Mill Restaurant, **Equator** boasts imaginative cuisine inspired by the countries which border the equator. Menu selections combine the best local seafood and island produce with the robust flavors and spices native to South America and Thailand. Entrées include pepper-cured tandoori lamb with Egyptian cous cous, Brazilian T-bone steak with churrasco sauce and wok-fried catfish with Polynesian fried rice. ☎ 776-6111.

In Cruz Bay on the grounds of the Raintree Inn, **Fishtrap** has a tropical patio setting and offers fabulous seafood specials nightly. Conch fritters are a must for any diner, and the popular rum cake gets rave reviews from those who've saved room for dessert. ☎ 693-9994.

In the popular Mongoose Junction shopping complex, **Global Village on Latitude 18** offers Cruz Bay diners a quiet and intimate atmosphere in which to savor unique dishes combining both local and imported ingredients. In addition to offering a late afternoon "sandy feet menu" featuring snacks, salads and sandwiches, the restaurant delights evening diners with specialties including cashew-encrusted mahi mahi and grilled margarita-marinated shrimp. Global Village, in Cruz Bay, is open daily for breakfast, lunch and dinner. Brunch is served every Sunday. ☎ 693-8677.

US Virgin Islands

Diners at **Morgan's Mango** in Cruz Bay enjoy an eclectic blending of Caribbean and Gulf cuisines in a relaxed, open-air atmosphere. The menu includes a brie quesadilla with fresh island salsa, Cajun shrimp with bayou mayonnaise, voodoo snapper from Haiti, grilled mahi mahi with Cruzan rum and mango sauce, and more. The bar features more than 25 tropical drinks like the Mango Smash, Green Iguana and Mango Margherita. ☎ 693-8141

A recent addition to Cruz Bay's Wharfside Village, **Panini Beach** is right on the water and provides an elegant setting for both indoor and outdoor dining. Specializing in northern Italian cuisine. ☎ 693-9119.

Doubling as a restaurant and night club, **Paradiso** offers a versatile menu of lunch and dinner entrées. Located in Mongoose Junction, Cruz Bay, the restaurant caters to hungry lunch-time crowds with soups, salads, cheeseburgers and pizzas personalized with a variety of toppings. The dinner hour features such American favorites as steak, chicken and fish accompanied by double-stuffed potato or country mashed potatoes. ☎ 693-8899

Situated on tranquil Coral Bay on St. John's east end, **Sera Fina** is a quaint seaside bistro with European-based cuisine and other cultural specialties. Fresh seafood and pasta dishes are flavored with a delectable mix of international ingredients, and homemade desserts change daily. ☎ 693-5630.

Campgrounds

Camping/snorkeling trips are popular on St. John. Bring your own gear.

Cinnamon Bay Campground, PO Box 720, Cruz Bay, St. John, USVI 00830. Rates range from $30 to $145 plus 8% tax per day for cottages, campsites and tents on Cinnamon Bay Beach in the national park. ☎ 800- 539-9998 or 340-776-6330, fax 340-776-6458. Dive packages available, windsurfing and sailboat rentals.

Maho Bay Camps, PO Box 310, St. John, USVI 00830. Luxury camping, white sand beach, watersports and gourmet restaurant. From $105 per day. ☎ 800-392-9004.

St. Thomas

St. Thomas is the second largest of the USVI and site of the capital, Charlotte Amalie. Provincial yet cosmopolitan, modern yet rich in history, it can be seen in a day. Divers should save an afternoon for shopping. Duty-free prices and keen competition make it a bargain-hunter's dream. In the narrow cobblestone streets and arcades of Charlotte Amalie you'll find designer shops housed in 200-year-old restored warehouses that were once full of molasses and rum. For those content to idle away some topside time, St. Thomas boasts sugar-white beaches. It is in these calm sands that St. Thomas's history, rich and tumultuous, lies hidden. The sheltered coves once harbored some of the most bloodthirsty pirates in Caribbean history.

The architecture and people of St. Thomas reflect the island's many-cultured past. Dutch, French and Spanish historic sites sit side-by-side with contemporary resorts. For those mixing scuba diving and sailing, St. Thomas is the home port to a number of charter operators.

Though some beach-entry diving exists here, the prettiest reefs and clearest waters are found around the outer cays. Some dive shops offer trips to the wreck of the *R.M.S. Rhone* in the British Virgin Islands.

Best Dives of St. Thomas

☆☆☆ **French Cap Cay** is well south of St. Thomas, but worth the long boat trip for both divers and snorkelers. This reef complex displays an enormous array of corals, caves, tunnels, and a spectacular sea mount. Visibility is often unlimited. The reef is teeming with fish, rays and critters. Beautiful lavender, orange, and yellow vase and basket sponges grow on the walls, interspersed with orange and red corals and unblemished stands of elkhorn. A light current is usually encountered here.

☆☆ **Capella Island** is just east of Little Buck Island. The reef here begins at 25 ft. Divers swim down through coral-encrusted canyons to a beautiful rocky bottom where basket sponges, soft corals and pillar coral grow. The visibility, often excellent, is weather-dependent. Fish life is abundant.

☆☆ **Saba Island**, a short boat trip from the St. Thomas's harbor, is a favorite one-tank dive. Depths are 20 to 50 ft. The reef at Saba Island is very pretty; divers swim through staghorn thickets and pillar corals. Large boulders cover the bottom, which is at a depth of about 50 ft. You may encounter surge; a number of divers have been tossed into the fire coral on the reef.

Best Snorkeling Sites of St. Thomas

Coki Beach, on the north shore of St. Thomas, is a favorite beach dive and snorkeling site. The beach is adjacent to Coral World, an underwater viewing tower. The reef here ranges in depth from 20 to 50 ft. Divers swim down a sand slope amid schools of snappers, French and queen angels, and an occasional baby shark. The reef has small coral arches and recesses, a favorite hiding place for small fish, sea turtles and stingrays. Star coral, sponges, crinoids, and rock are characteristic of the reef at Coki Beach. This is a fine first dive site.

☆☆☆ *Cartanser Senior*, a 190-ft wreck, sits just off Little Buck Island in 35 ft of water. It is filled with schools of squirrel fish, morays, angels, butterfly fish, sergeant majors, angels and damsels, all of whom will approach you looking for a snack. Visibility is often good.

US Virgin Islands

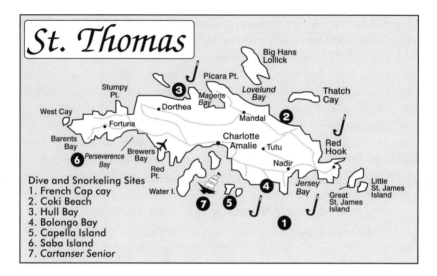

St. Thomas

Big Hans Lollick
Picara Pt.
Stumpy Pt.
Magens Bay
Lovelund Bay
Thatch Cay
West Cay
Dorthea
Mandal
Fortuna
Barents Bay
Charlotte Amalie
Tutu
Red Hook
Perseverance Bay
Brewers Bay
Nadir
Red Pt.
Dive and Snorkeling Sites
1. French Cap cay
2. Coki Beach
3. Hull Bay
4. Bolongo Bay
5. Capella Island
6. Saba Island
7. Cartanser Senior
Water I.
Jersey Bay
Little St. James Island
Great St. James Island

☆ **French Cap Cay** has the best visibility for snorkeling and free diving photography (see overall description above). The reef has many shallow areas full of large sea fans, antler coral, and elkhorn.

Additional good beach snorkeling exists at **Hull Bay** on the north coast and **Bolongo Bay**, plus the resort beaches at **Sugar Bay Resort, Renaissance Grand Beach, Secret Harbor Beach, Sapphire Beach, Point Pleasant Resort, Marriott's Morning Star Resort, Grand Palazzo**, and **Carib Beach**.

St. Thomas Dive Operators

Aqua Action, at Secret Harbour Beach Hotel, features custom dives to area sites. Accommodation packages. ☎ 340-775-6285 or write Red Hook, Box 15, St. Thomas, USVI 00802.

Chris Sawyer Diving Center has three locations, one at the Renaissance Grand Beach Resort at Coki Beach, American Yacht Harbor and the main operation at Compass Point Marina. The shops offer resort courses as well as PADI and NAUI scuba certifications. All gear, including underwater photo equipment, is available for rental. A fast 42-ft dive boat shuttles divers to all the best dives around St. Thomas and its outer islands. Escorted beach-snorkeling tours. ☎ 800-882-2965 or 340-775-7320. Write to 6300 Estate Frydenhoj, 29 St. Thomas, USVI 00802. E-mail: sawyerdive@worldnet.att.net. Website: www.sawyerdive.vi.

Caribbean Divers, at Red Hook, has boat dives and PADI certification classes. ☎ 340-775-6384.

Coki Beach Dive Club specializes in beginner courses and tours. Nikonis rentals. ☎ 800-474-COKI or 340-775-4220.

Dive In!, at the Sapphire Beach Resort, a full-service PADI facility, visits the sites around St. Thomas. Snorkelers may join the dive tours when sites are shallow. Equipment rentals and scuba courses. ☎ 800-524-2090 or 340-775-6100 ext 2144.

St. Thomas Diving Club, at the Bolongo Bay Beach Club, specializes in dive and snorkel excursions to local and BVI sites. Nitrox diving. ☎ 340-776-2381, 340-777-3232. E-mail: bill2381@viaccess.net. Website: www.st-thomasdivingclub.com.

Sea Horse Dive Shop at the Crown Bay Marina, offers cruise ship and hotel pick-up. The shop visits 58 different reef and wreck sites. ☎ 340-774-2001.

Accommodations

For current rates via the web: http://st-thomas.com/rates.

St. Thomas has a seemingly endless variety of accommodations. You'll find quaint guesthouses, cozy inns, resorts on secluded beaches, romantic mountain-top villas, condos, and hotels.

Bolongo Bay Beach & Sports Club offers diving packages in cooperation with the on-premises St. Thomas Diving Club. This all-inclusive resort offers 75 air-conditioned beachfront units with telephone, color TV, kitchenettes, and balconies. Nightly entertainment. Sports facilities include four tennis courts, a Sunfish sailboat fleet, resort yacht *Heavenly Days*, snorkeling, volleyball courts and board games. Informal atmosphere. Children under 15 free in room. Beach bar. Winter rates run from $550 per person, per day, including all meals, taxes, and service charge for a double. Room rates from $205. Good snorkeling off the beach. ☎ 800-524-4746 or 340-775 1800, fax 340-775-3208; or write 50 Estate Bolongo, St. Thomas, USVI 00802.

Renaissance Grand Beach Resort, a deluxe beachfront resort at Pineapple Beach on the east shores of St. Thomas, features 315 rooms, all air-conditioned, two pools, three restaurants, entertainment, and TV. There are dive packages with Chris Sawyer Diving Center, on the property. Room rates in winter are from $335 for garden view to $445 for ocean view. Summer rates start at $235 per night, double occupancy. Child under 18 free in room. Guided beach snorkeling excursions with dive shop. Write PO Box 8267, St. Thomas, USVI 00801. ☎ 800-421-8188 or 800-HOTELS1 or 340-775-1510, fax 340-775-2185.

Marriott's Frenchman's Reef Resort, a full-service 408-room luxury beachfront resort, provides diving and snorkeling tours, freshwater pool, tennis and seven restaurants. Recently renovated rooms have TV, phones and tropical decor. Day rates from $350. ☎ 800-524-2000, fax 340-776-3054.

Sapphire Beach Resort, on the northeast coast, offers 171 suites with full kitchens, TV, phone, handicap access, day-long children's program. Under 12 free in room. Dive In! dive shop on premises has PADI courses, equipment rentals, dive and snorkeling tours. Freshwater pool, tennis, three restaurants. ☎ 800-524-2090, fax 775-4024.

Best Western's Carib Beach Resort on south coast Lindbergh Bay, features affordable ocean-view rooms with private balconies. Two miles from town. Freshwater pool, phones, TV. Rooms from $159. ☎ 800-792-2742 or 340-774-2525, fax 340-777-4131.

Best Western's Emerald Beach Resort, a quarter-mile from the airport, two miles to downtown, features 90 deluxe, beachfront rooms overlooking beautiful Lindberg Bay. Rooms have balconies, cable TV, direct dial phone, hair dryers, coffee makers. There is a freshwater pool. Admiralty Dive Shop on premises offers boat dives. Nice white sand beach. Children under 12 stay free. Rates are from $199 to $249. ☎ 800-233-4936, fax 776-3426.

Secret Harbor Beach Resort on Nazareth Bay, the southeast Caribbean side, offers 171 luxury rooms in a tranquil beachfront setting. Per-day room rates run from $425 for one bedroom to $435 for a two-bedroom suite. Children under 13 stay free. Good snorkeling off the beach on a small reef with tropicals, turtles and rays. Aqua Action Dive Shop on premises provides rentals, courses, dive and snorkeling boat trips. Dive packages available. ☎ 800-524-2250 or 340-775-6550, fax 775-1501.

Small Hotels & Condos

Admiral's Inn has 16 ocean-view rooms from $99 to $149 per day with cable TV, AC, phone. Sea pool with sandy beach area. Diving and snorkeling must be arranged through local dive shops. ☎ 800-544-0493, fax 340-774-8010.

Blazing Villas, adjacent to Renaissance Grand Beach Resort, features boat diving and shore snorkeling excursions with Chris Sawyer Diving, on property. Guests use all of Rennaissance Resort's facilities. Suites feature full kitchens or kitchenettes, phones, TV, handicap access, tennis, beach. Winter rates start at $160 per night. Under 12 stay free with adults. Add 10% service charge. ☎ 800-382-2002 or 340-776-0760, fax 340-776-0760.

Jean's Villas features villas and rooms on the grounds of the Renaissance Grand Beach Resort. Guests use the resort facilities. From $150 to $650 per night. ☎ 800-874-5326 or 340-777-7612, fax 610-941-6742.

Dining

The USVI's rich history has influenced many of the area restaurants. Both plain and fancy dishes highlight most menus. Savor a Caribbean lobster bouillabaisse in one of the restored 19th-century inns or try a delicious fish-fry on the beach while listening to strains of reggae or calypso.

Perched on a cliff overlooking nearby St. John, **Agave Terrace** specializes in fresh seafood prepared to suit each diner's fancy. Enjoy local lobster or one of the day's fresh catches, along with a tropical drink or from the award-winning wine list. At Colony Point Pleasant Resort on the east end. ☎ 775-4142.

Famous for its stunning views of St. Thomas' Charlotte Amalie, **Banana Tree Grille** sits high above cruise ships and yachts in the harbor at its legendary lookout in Bluebeard's Castle Hotel. The restaurant offers tempting entrées such as Thai-glazed salmon, coconut tempura shrimp and raspberry cabernet chicken, plus many great steak and pasta dishes. Key lime pie headlines the dessert menu, along with ice cream crêpes and bananas Foster. ☎ 776-4050.

Blue Moon Café. Palm trees along the beach and boats at anchor in the bay set the scene at this beachside restaurant in Secret Harbour Beach Resort on St. Thomas' east end. Beach-goers wander in to enjoy a lunch time menu of salads and tortilla-style sandwiches, and visitors for dinner choose from an excellent selection of salmon, mahi mahi, steak and prime rib dishes. Open every day for breakfast, lunch and dinner. ☎ 779-2262.

On St. Thomas' East End adjacent to the Red Hook ferry dock, **Café Wahoo** serves an eclectic menu of seafood and local favorites, including entrées with a French, Italian and Spanish influence. ☎ 775-6350.

Caesar's. Rippling waves on Charlotte Amalie harbor provide a serene backdrop to this classic Italian ristorante at Marriott Frenchman's Reef Beach Resort. Breakfast, lunch or dinner, Monday through Saturday. ☎ 776-8500.

Poised over Charlotte Amalie town and harbor at historic Blackbeard's Castle, **Café Lulu** blends sophisticated ambiance and exotic flair. The menu follows the theme of cultural fusion, drawing from Caribbean, Asian and Mediterranean cuisines. With "first courses" of grilled vegetable salads and tempura sashimi and "main courses" of cornmeal-crusted salmon and Chinese five-spice duck, Café Lulu offers some of the Caribbean's most creative dishes. ☎ 714-1641.

Famous for its spectacular location on the water at historic Villa Olga in Frenchtown, **The Chart House** has an unlimited salad bar and specialty breads to accompany such mouth-watering selections as prime rib, steaks, local lobster and fresh fish. Diners are encouraged to top off their meals with the restaurant's justifiably famous mud pie. ☎ 774-4262.

Craig & Sally's. This intimate Frenchtown restaurant has received numerous rave reviews in its four-year history for its eclectic cuisine. Entrées change daily based on chef Sally's whims and inspirations, and are accompanied by a wine list offering more than 200 choices from around the world. Open Wednesday through Friday for lunch, and Wednesday through Sunday for dinner. ☎ 777-9949.

Once a livery stable and cook shop more than a century ago, the building housing **Cuzzin's Restaurant**, on Back Street in Charlotte Amalie, today has been transformed into a comfortable dining room serving fresh Virgin Island dishes and seafood. Conch, lobster and fish are caught daily by island fishermen and prepared by West Indian chefs into curries, stews and other native dishes. "Cuzzin Nemo" – a melange of shrimp, lobster, conch and scallops over pasta – is a favorite, especially when accompanied by a local beverage of sea moss, maubi or ginger beer. ☎ 777-4711.

The Dining Room at The Ritz-Carlton, St. Thomas. This elegant restaurant, with pink marble decor and vaulted ceilings, has been recently expanded to capture views of the Caribbean Sea. Under the supervision of Executive Chef Alain Peraux, chef de cuisine Arnaud Berthelier prepares a stunning array of European specialties. The adjacent lounge, with a hand-carved wooden bar, offers cocktails and a selection of fine cigars.

Eunice's Terrace. Just west of the entrance to the Renaissance Grand Beach Resort, on the island's east end, sits this pleasantly roomy restaurant famous for its local, West Indian fare. Tempting native dishes such as conch fritters, old wife fish, sweet potato, peas and rice, fungi and fried plantain top the menu, along with other daily specials of steak and local fish and lobster. President Clinton and the First Family dined at Eunice's during their January 1997 visit to St. Thomas. ☎ 775-3975.

Gladys' Café. This charming café in Royal Dane Mall, downtown Charlotte Amalie, serves breakfast and lunch, Monday through Saturday, for hungry St. Thomas shoppers looking for a true taste of native cuisine. The breakfast menu offers bacon and eggs, omelettes, thick French toast and freshly baked breads; lunch time tempts with conch and fungi, saltfish and dumplings and mutton stew. Gladys even bottles her own hot sauce, attractively packaged for diners to carry home as a tasty souvenir. ☎ 774-6604.

A panoramic view of Charlotte Amalie harbor by day and the sparkle of town by night awaits at **Herve Restaurant & Wine Bar**, located on historic Government Hill. Serving a mixed menu of contemporary American and classic French cuisines with a bit of Caribbean flair, Herve offers everything from salads and cheeseburgers to seafood crepes and spicy conch fritters. Extensive wine selection. ☎ 777-9703.

A lovely spot for dinner on St. Thomas, **Hotel 1829** resides in a former home set just above the street on Government Hill. Surrounded by landscaped garden terraces and overlooking town and harbor, the hotel's charming old-world bar and dining room beckon visitors for a drink or meal amidst old brick walls and ship's ballast. Hotel 1829 offers a light menu of soups and salads, plus daily specials and well-known house favorites like rack of lamb, mixed seafood grill and wilted spinach salad prepared tableside. Chocolate or Grand Marnier soufflées are popular dessert selections. ☎ 776-1829.

Lindy's. Locals and vacationers alike have eagerly awaited the reopening of this restaurant at St. Thomas' Mafolie Hotel. With alfresco dining six nights a week, you can enjoy spectacular Caribbean sunsets over Charlotte Amalie harbor. Choose from an extensive menu of specialty shrimp, crab and lobster dishes. A tempting dessert menu features owner Mary Russ' award-winning fruit tart, key lime pie and chocolate chip macadamia nut tart. ☎ 774-8643.

Smuggler's Steak & Seafood Grill. On the grounds of St. Thomas' Renaissance Grand Beach Resort, this handsome tropical pavilion restaurant offers outstanding beef and fresh seafood selections. Known island-wide for its award-winning Sunday brunch, Smuggler's offers an enticing 12-foot-long, make-your-own Bloody Mary bar. ☎ 775-1510.

Regional American cuisine with a Caribbean flair is served at **Tavern on the Beach**, overlooking the beautiful white sands of Marriott's Morning Star Beach. Open 6:30-10 pm, Tuesday through Saturday. ☎ 776-8500.

In a historic 1854 building on Government Hill in Charlotte Amalie, **Zorba's** serves authentic Greek and Mediterranean food, homemade bread and pasta. President Clinton and the first family dined here during their winter vacation two years in a row. ☎ 776-0444.

Live-Aboards

Virgin Islands Charter Yacht League will rent you a sailing yacht and teach you how to sail. On some yachts crew includes a divemaster; some also have compressors aboard. Others arrange rendezvous with dive boats. ☎ 800-524-2061 or 340-774-3944. E-mail: V.I.C.L@worldnet.att.net. Advance reservations suggested.

Regency Yacht Vacations offers dive vacations aboard fully-crewed, live-aboard yachts from 40 to 100 ft. Scuba instruction, if desired, must be arranged in advance. ☎ 800-524-7676, 340-776-5950 fax 340-776-7631. E-mail: regenbvi@caribsurf.com or regency@viaccess.com. Write to 5200 Long Bay Rd, St. Thomas, USVI 00802.

Sightseeing & Other Activities

Check with your hotel or the tourist newspapers (available everywhere) for historic tours, rum factory tours, golf, tennis, deep sea fishing, bird walks, day sails, visits to Hassel Island, parasailing, and board sailing. Check nightclub listings for broken bottle dancing, fire eating, limbo dancing, steel bands, and local entertainment. Be sure to see a performance of the Mocko Jumbies on their 17-foot stilts or the Mungo Niles Cultural Native Dancers and Musicians. The dancers, ranging in age from 20 to well over 70, swirl and twirl in their bright red and white floral-motif costumes to the sounds of Qelbe or scratch music. For schedules, call the Reichhold Center on St. Thomas at ☎ 340-693-1559 or Island Center on St. Croix at 340-778-5272.

Facts

Recompression Chamber: St. Thomas Hospital, St. Thomas – constantly monitored. ☎ 340-776-2686, on island call 776-2686 for assistance.

Getting There: There are daily direct flights from the US mainland, via American Airlines, ☎ 800-433-7300, United Airlines, USAir and Delta. Other airlines serving the newly expanded Cyril E. King Airport on St. Thomas from Puerto Rico are American Eagle and Cape Air. Inter-island connections can be made by ferry, seaplane shuttle or one of the island airlines. US citizens must carry a passport if also traveling to the BVI. Caledonian Airways offers charter flights between London and St. Thomas during summer months.

Cruise Ships: The USVI's cruise ship schedule can now be accessed on the Internet. Web surfers can obtain specific information about cruise ship capacity, port calls and arrival and departure times by visiting www.ships.vi. Or call the Cruise Ship Activities Office at ☎ 340-774-8784, extensions 2252 and 2253. For cruise ships booked to St. Croix ☎ 340-772-0357.

Island Transportation: Taxi service is readily available on all three islands. Taxi rates are determined by law and those rates are available from your driver. Bus service and tours are available on St. Thomas and St. Croix. Car rentals: Thrifty, Avis, Budget, Hertz.

Driving: Traffic keeps to the left on all three islands. A US driver's license is required.

Customs: US residents are entitled to take home $1,200 worth of duty-free imports. A 10% tax is levied on the next $1,000.

Currency: US $, travelers checks, major credit cards. No personal checks accepted.

Climate: Year-round temperatures range from 76 to 82°F.

Clothing: Casual, lightweight, with sweaters for winter; jackets and ties needed for some resorts and eating establishments.

Electricity: 110 volts AC, 60 cycles (same as US).

Time: Atlantic Standard, which is one hour earlier than Eastern Standard.

Language: English.

Taxes: No sales tax. 8% hotel tax. Service charge may apply at some hotels and restaurants.

Religious Services: All denominations.

For Additional Information: United States Virgin Islands Division of Tourism, PO Box 6400, Charlotte Amalie, USVI 00804. *In New York*: 1270 Avenue of the Americas, NY, NY 10020. ☎ 800-372-USVI, 212-332-2222, fax 212-332-2223. Website: http://www.usvi.net.

Part III

Central America

Belize

Fascinating and exotic, Belize offers a world of tropical adventure to divers and snorkelers. It is a preserve for the largest barrier reef in the western hemisphere, second only to the Great Barrier Reef in Australia, the magnificent Blue Hole, a 1,000-ft ocean sinkhole, and home to three beautiful atolls – Lighthouse Reef, the Turneffe Islands and Glovers Reef. Within the reef system are hundreds of uncharted islands.

Just 750 miles from Miami, Belize lies on the Caribbean coast of Central America between Guatemala and Mexico. Populated by a mere 200,000 people, it is a country of approximately 9,000 square miles. It has inland mountain ranges with peaks over 3,500 ft, dense tropical jungles, a coastline of mangrove swamps, and 266 square miles of offshore coral islands. The 185-mile-long barrier reef parallels the shore from 10 to 30 miles out, with prime diving locations around the out islands.

With the exception of Ambergris Caye, tours to Belize out islands fall more under the realm of "expedition" or "safari" rather than "vacation." Its offshore accommodations and facilities are primitive by Caribbean standards – few TVs, phones or automobiles on most of the islands. Yet Belize's jungles and unspoiled reefs lure intrepid divers back again and again.

Visitors arriving in Belize City will find a safer environment than in the past, thanks to a special Tourist Police Force that has reduced crimes against tourists by 72%. Despite the improvement, it's still wise to avoid flashing expensive cameras, jewelry, or money around.

On the mainland outside Belize City one finds fairly rugged and varied terrain, alive with yellowhead parrots, giant iguanas, monkeys and a curious creature called the gibnut – described by Belizean author Robert Nicolait as a cross between a fat rabbit and a small pig.

The heart of dive tourism is **Ambergris Caye**, a bustling resort and fishing community, the largest of the out islands or "cayes." Its main town, San Pedro, is a few hundred yards from the **Hol Chan Marine Preserve**, the northernmost point of the Barrier Reef, and is the jump-off point to Belize's smaller cayes and atolls. Ambergris is just 20 minutes by air from Belize City or an hour and 15 minutes by ferry (see end of chapter for transportation details). The northern portion of Ambergris is accessible by boat only, but plans for a road are under consideration. Transportation on Ambergris and the other islands is by golf cart or on foot.

A new area for divers is **Placencia**, a quaint fishing village located on a 16-mile coastal peninsula, 100 miles south of Belize City. There are some coral heads off the beaches, but a half-hour boat ride will bring you to **Laughing Bird Caye**, a small island surrounded by pristine reefs, and the remains of old wrecks. Several Spanish galleons went down in this area over the years and occasionally a gold piece washes up on the beach. Placencia is an intriguing new place to explore.

Visit Belize during the dry season, from February to May. Annual rainfall ranges from 170 inches in the south to 50 inches in the north. Heaviest rainfall is from September to January. August is frequently dry.

The climate is sub-tropical, with constant brisk winds from the Caribbean Sea. Summer highs are rarely above 95° F, winter lows seldom below 60°. Bug repellent is always needed as mosquitoes and sand flies are a constant annoyance.

Belize has a long history of stable government. It is a member of the British Commonwealth, with a democratically elected government. The people are Creoles (African-European), Garifuna (African-Indian), Mestizo (Spanish-Indian), Maya and European. English is the official language and is widely spoken, as is Spanish.

History

Early inhabitants of Belize were the Maya, whose territory also included Mexico, Guatemala, Honduras and El Salvador. They left behind great ceremonial centers, pyramids and evidence of a dynamic people with advancements in the arts, math and science. The Maya inhabited Belize as early as 9000 BC and flourished as a master civilization until most of them mysteriously disappeared about 1000 AD. Theories about their fate range from massive death by natural disaster to speculation about spaceship travel to other planets. Remnants of this ancient culture show that Belize was a major trading center for the entire Mayan area. Today, a small population of Mayan descendants inhabit the countryside.

At Altun Ha (30 miles north of Belize City), an excavated Maya center, spectacular jade and stone carvings have been unearthed, including an ornately carved head of Kinisch Ahau, the Mayan Sun God. This head, weighing 9 pounds and measuring nearly six inches from base to crown, is believed to be the largest Maya jade carving in existence. Also uncovered was the Temple of the Green Tomb, a burial chamber that contained human remains and a wealth of jade pieces, including pendants, beads, figures and jewelry. Side trips to this and other jungle archaeological sites are offered by most dive-tour operators.

During the 17th century, Belize was colonized by the British and the Spanish. In 1862, the settlement became an English colony known as British Honduras. It gained independence in 1981. Today, it is the only Central American nation where English is widely spoken.

Best Dive & Snorkeling Sites

The Barrier Reef

☆☆☆ **Hol Chan Marine Preserve**, a five-square-mile reef area off the southern tip of Ambergris Caye, is characterized by a natural channel or cut that attracts and shelters huge communities of marine animals. Maximum depth inside the reef is 30 ft, allowing unlimited bottom time. The outside wall starts at 50 ft, then drops to beyond 150 ft. Schools of tropicals line the walls, with occasional glimpses of big turtles, green and spotted morays, six-ft stingrays, eagle rays, spotted dolphins and nurse sharks.

A constant flow of sea water through the cut promotes the growth of large barrel and basket sponges, sea fans, and beautiful outcroppings of staghorn and brain corals. Check tide charts before diving on your own; currents can be very strong in the channel at outgoing tides.

Diving all along the barrier reef is extraordinary. There are caves, dramatic overhangs, and pinnacles, all with superb marine life, though commercial fishing has taken its toll on the really big grouper, shark and huge turtles that were commonplace 10 years ago. The subsea terrain is similar throughout the area, with long channels of sand running perpendicular to the overall reef system. These cuts run seaward, allowing a constant change of nutrient-rich sea water to cleanse and feed the coral.

The inner reef, that area facing land, is shallow, with coral slopes that bottom out between 20 and 40 ft. Amidst its forests of stag horn and elkhorn are throngs of juvenile fish, barracuda, invertebrates, spawning grouper, stingrays, conch, nurse shark and small critters.

Diving the outer reef brings a better chance to see mantas, permits, jacks, black durgons, tuna, dolphin, turtles and sharks. Visibility is exceptional too. The reef profile outside is typically a sloping shelf to between 25 or 40 ft, which then plunges to 2,000 ft or more.

Live-aboard yachts that explore the entire coast are extremely popular in Belize, though local guides and tourist officials are working to attract more divers to their shore facilities and après-dive attractions.

Belize

The Atolls

Atolls are ring-shaped coral islands or island groups surrounding a lagoon. Most are in the South Pacific and are often the visible portions of ancient, submerged volcanoes. But those in Belize are composed of coral and may have been formed by faults during the shifting of land masses.

All three, Lighthouse Reef, Glovers Reef and the Turneffe Islands, are surrounded by miles of shallow reefs and magnificent, deep dropoffs. The sheltered lagoons are dotted with pretty coral heads and are great for snorkeling and novice divers. Outside, visibility exceeds 150 ft and marine life is unrivaled. Generally, the islands are primitive, remote and largely uninhabited, with the bulk of the population made up of free-roaming chickens, though each location has at least one dive resort and a resident divemaster.

☆☆☆☆ **The Turneffe Islands**, 35 miles from Belize City and beyond the barrier reef, are a group of 32 low islands bordered with thick growths of mangroves. The lower portion of the chain forms a deep V shape with **Cay Bokel** at the southernmost point. Reef areas just above both sides of the point are the favorite southern dive spots. Cay Bokel is where you'll find the Turneffe Island Lodge, a quaint resort offering dive services. West of the southern point are sheltered, shallow reefs at 20 to 60 ft depths. Along the reef are some old anchors overgrown with coral, a small, wooden wreck, the *Sayonara*, and a healthy fish population. Seas are rougher, currents stronger and the dives deeper to the east, but more impressive coral formations and large pelagics are found. The ridges and canyons of the reefs are carpeted by a dense cover of sea feathers, lacy soft corals, branching gold and purple sponges, anemones, seafans and luxurious growths of gorgonians. Passing dolphins and rays are the big attraction as they upstage the reef's "blue collar workers" – cleaner shrimp, sea cucumbers, patrolling barracuda, defensive damsel fish, schooling yellowtail, grunts and coral crabs. Snorkeling and diving are excellent, with outstanding water clarity, protected areas, and diverse marine life.

Rendezvous Point at the northernmost point is equal in sub terrain and diver interest, but is more often visited by fishermen. Much of the northern area is shallow mangrove swamp where tarpon, bonefish, shrimp and lobster proliferate.

☆☆☆☆☆ The most popular atoll, and that most visited by dive boats, is **Lighthouse Reef**. It lies 40 miles from Belize City and is the outermost of the offshore islands within the Belize cruising area. Lighthouse is a circular reef system featuring several islands and small cayes. On its southeast boundaries is a beautiful old lighthouse and Half Moon Caye Natural Monument, the first marine conservation area in Belize and a bird sanctuary for colonies of the red-footed boobies (sula sula), frigate birds, ospreys, mangrove warblers and

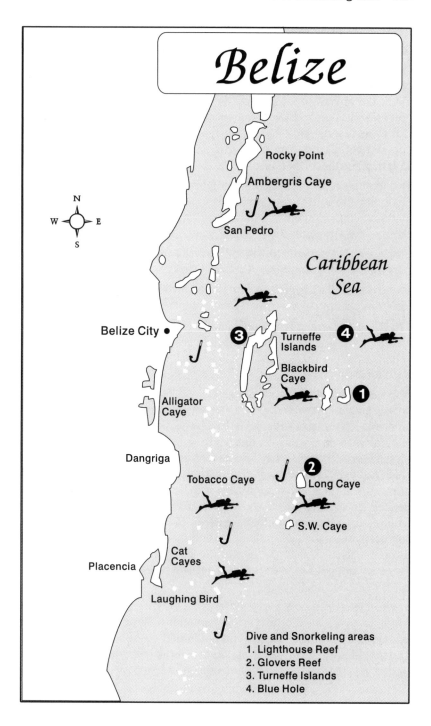

Belize

Rocky Point

Ambergris Caye

San Pedro

Caribbean Sea

Belize City

Turneffe Islands

Blackbird Caye

Alligator Caye

Dangriga

Tobacco Caye

Long Caye

S.W. Caye

Cat Cayes

Placencia

Laughing Bird

Dive and Snorkeling areas
1. Lighthouse Reef
2. Glovers Reef
3. Turneffe Islands
4. Blue Hole

white-crowned pigeons. Ninety-eight other species of birds have been re-corded on the caye.

Half Moon Caye Natural Monument has white sand beaches with a drop-off on the north side and a shallow lagoon on the south end. A dock with a pierhead depth of about six ft and an area for amphibious aircraft are on the north side of the island. Dive boats are required to anchor in designated areas to prevent reef damage. All boaters must register with the lighthouse keeper upon arrival. Coordinates of an approved anchorage for craft with a beam length of less than 120 ft are 17° 12'25' N 87° 33'11' W.

The lighthouse, situated on the tapering eastern side of Half Moon Caye, was first built in 1820. It was later replaced by another in 1848 and since reinforced by a steel-framed tower in 1931. Today the lighthouse is solar-powered. A climb to the top offers a spectacular view.

Endangered loggerhead turtles and hawksbill turtles come ashore to lay their eggs on the sandy southern beaches.

To the north is the Lighthouse Reef Resort, an air-conditioned colony of English villas catering to divers and fishermen.

☆☆☆☆☆ Near the center of Lighthouse Reef is the **Blue Hole**, Belize's most famous dive spot. From the air it looks like an apparition. The cobalt blue of the Caribbean abruptly changes to an azure blue circle. The heart of the circle is an indigo blue.

Approaching by water is not as breathtaking, but beautiful nonetheless. You know you are somewhere special. It is an almost perfect circle, 1,000 ft in diameter in the midst of a reef six to 18 ft below the surface. Inside the shallow reef, the walls drop suddenly to a depth of 412 ft, almost completely vertical for the first 125 ft. Here they turn inward and slightly upward. At 140 ft you reach an awesome underwater "cathedral" with alcoves, archways and columns. It is a huge submerged cave with 12- to 15-ft-wide stalactites suspended 20 to 60 ft from the cavern ceiling. Formed thousands of years ago, perhaps during the Ice Age, the cave was once above sea level. This is always a guided dive and should be attempted only by experienced divers, but novice divers are as entertained by the shallows surrounding the crater's rim as are those venturing down to the cave. Note: The nearest decompression chamber is in Ambergris Caye.

Travel time to and from the Blue Hole and the cost of your trip will vary according to the location of your accommodations. If you are staying on Ambergris Caye the trip will take an entire day and cost about $150. From the Turneffe Islands, travel time to and from is about half a day and the cost is included. If you are on a live-aboard, one of your stops will surely be the Blue Hole.

☆☆☆☆ South of the Turneffe Islands and Lighthouse Reef is the third and most remote atoll, **Glover's Reef**, the largest marine World Heritage Site. It is a reef system formed by coral growing around the edges of a steep limestone plateau. An almost continuous barrier reef encloses an 80-square-mile lagoon that reaches depths of 50 ft. The lagoon is an outstanding snorkeling spot, with over 700 shallow coral heads. Outside, the reef starts at 30 ft and drops to more than 2,000 ft. Visibility exceeds 150 ft. Grouper, queen trigger fish and parrot fish are in abundance. Mantas, pods of dolphins, spotted eagle rays and sea turtles are occasionally seen on the reefs. It is a spectacular diving and snorkeling spot, with more than 25 coral species to be explored and thousands of sheltered spots. The reefs remain largely unexplored and are seldom visited by live-aboards. Two dive/fishing resorts, Glovers Reef Resort and Manta Reef Resort, offer experienced guides and services.

Accommodations

Rates listed are for winter, in US dollars, and are subject to change with higher prices during the peak high season. Most resorts and restaurants accept US dollars, travelers checks, and major credit cards.

Direct dial service is available between Belize and the US and Canada. To call Belize, ☎ 011-501, drop the first zero from the local number, then dial the remaining numbers. E-mail, where available, may be used to book direct.

Ambergris Caye

There are flights between Belize City and San Pedro, the main town on Ambergris Cay, every 30 minutes from sunrise to sunset.

Tropica Beach Resort in San Pedro features 16 lovely rooms with air-conditioning, ceiling fans, private bath and porch. Diving with Reef Divers. Winter room rates are from $125 per day, summer from $95. Dive packages start at $385. Book through Dive Safaris, ☎ 800-359-0747 or 212-662-4858, fax 212-749-6172. E-mail: godive@divesafaris.com.

Ramon's Village in San Pedro offers 20 nice air-conditioned, thatched-roof bungalows with double beds and full baths. The resort has a poolside bar, saltwater pool, restaurant, and fully equipped dive shop offering reef trips and basic rentals. Relaxed atmosphere. Daily room rates start at $140 daily for a double, to $165 for a suite. ☎ 800-MAGIC 15 or 601-649-1990, fax 601-425-2411; or write PO Drawer 4407, Laurel MS 39441. Website: www.ramons.com.

Belize

Caracol Ruins, Cayo District.

Courtesy Belize
Tourist Board

Victoria House, on its own nine-acre beach, features 31 casually elegant rooms, suites, apartments and villas. An on-site PADI dive shop, restaurant and tour desk make this deluxe resort a popular spot with divers and snorkelers – coupled with the fact that the barrier reef lies three-quarters of a mile directly in front of the hotel. Day rates for standard air-conditioned rooms are from $180 for a double with air-conditioning; suites from $230, two-bedroom villas from $595, three-bedroom villas from $795. All rooms have private bathrooms with hot and cold running water, mini-refrigerators and ceiling fans. They include complimentary bicycles and round-trip transfers to and from the airstrip in San Pedro. Golf cart rentals available. Kayaks, board surfers, Sunfish and a small catamaran may be rented. The resort offers half- and full-day snorkeling trips, fishing trips, scuba diving, Blue Hole snorkel and dive trips, Turneffe Island tours, plus mainland sightseeing tours. ☎ 800-247-5159 or 404-373-0068, fax 404-373-3885. Local 011-501-26-2067, fax 011-501-26-2429. Or write to Victoria House, Ambergris Caye, Belize, Central America. E-mail: victoria@btl.com or info@victoria-house.com. Website: www.belize.com/victoriahouse.html.

Banyan Bay Villas, conveniently located 15 minutes on foot from San Pedro, features two-bedroom, two-bath villas with jacuzzi tub and shower in the master bedroom. Each unit sleeps four comfortably. Full kitchen with microwave, coffee maker, dishes, silverware. Dining room seats six. Each unit has a large veranda overlooking the sea. Three-level resort pool. Beach café serves breakfast, lunch, drinks and beverages. Golf cart rentals. Diving, fishing, mainland tours and snorkeling trips arranged at front desk. Winter rates for a single or double, $190 for ocean view, $215 for beachfront, $220-$245 triple, $250-$275 quad. Children under 12 sharing with parents stay free. Baby cribs at no charge. Taxi transfers from San Pedro Airstrip to and from hotel on arrival and departure. ☎ 011-501-26-3739, fax 011-501-26-2766. E-mail: banyanbay@btl.net. Website: www.banyanbay.com. Write to: PO Box 91, 100 Sea Grape Street, San Pedro, Ambergris Caye, Belize, Central America.

Belize Yacht Club, within easy walking distance of San Pedro Town and restaurants, features modern, Spanish-style, air-conditioned, one- and two-bedroom suites with fully equipped kitchens. Amenities include a freshwater pool, marina, bar, dive shop, fishing, snorkeling excursions. No restaurant. ☎ 800-396-1153 or 713-613-1920, fax 026-2768.

Caribbean Villas Hotel, three-quarters of a mile from San Pedro, features 10 air-conditioned beachfront luxury rooms and suites. Nice pier and beach. Hot tubs, elevated perch for bird watching. ☎ 800-633-4734 or direct 011-501-26-2715, fax 011-501-26-2885. E-mail: c-v-hotel@btl.net.

Paradise Resort Hotel, at the north end of San Pedro, features 24 charming tropical rooms, some with air-conditioning. Rates are $67.50 for an air-conditioned room in summer, $120 in winter. ☎ 800-451-8017.

Paradise Villas Beachfront Resort Condos offer one- and two-bedroom deluxe apartments with ceiling fans, air-conditioning, TV and kitchenettes. Restaurant. Rates are $90 to $150 per night plus 7% tax. No service charge. ☎ 501-792-2639, fax 510-791-5602. E-mail: susan@belize.com.

Journey's End, is an outstanding, beachfront hotel just 500 yds from the Barrier Reef. The 50-acre resort is accessible by water taxi – 10 minutes from the airstrip. Guests stay in luxurious beach cabanas, poolside villas, or waterfront rooms. All have been recently renovated. Amenities include a gourmet restaurant, tennis courts, beach bar, and freshwater Olympic pool with swim-up bar and grill. All watersports are offered. The 125-member staff caters to guests' every whim. Rates in summer (May-Dec 13th), seven nights, for a pool/garden room are $620, three nights $321; in winter (January 5-April 15) seven nights, from $872; three nights, from $432. Package includes round-trip air from Belize International Airport to San Pedro, land transfers to hotels, welcome cocktail, accommodations, continental breakfast and dinner daily, taxes, service charges. ☎ 800-460-5665 or 800-365-6232 or 713-780-1566, direct 501-26 2173, fax 501 26-2397. E-mail: Jornyend@neosoft.com.

Rocks Inn is on the beach within walking distance of San Pedro, restaurants, bars, and shops. The hotel offers attractive air-conditioned suites with modern appliances. No restaurant. Dive-travel packages available. ☎ 501-26-2326, 501-26-2358. E-mail: rocks@btl.net.

Belize

Sunbreeze Beach Hotel, a 39-room, air-conditioned beachfront hotel, teams up with Belize Undersea Adventures to offer a seven-night package for $683 including accommodations, five two-tank boat dives and transfers from Belize City. Rooms have private bath, ocean views, balconies, phone, cable TV. ☎ 800-327-8150 or 954-462-3400, fax 954-462-4100. E-mail: sunbreeze@btl.net. Website: www.belizenet.com/sunbreeze.html.

Sunset Beach Resort, one of San Pedro's newest inns, features air-conditioned junior and deluxe suites with cable TV, kitchens and a nice beach. Junior suites start at $160 per day, deluxe from $295. ☎ 940-627-2514, Direct 501-26-5020, fax 501-26-5023. E-mail: jowinmew@wf.net. Website: sunsetbeachbelize.com.

Caye Caulker

Tropical Paradise Resort features standard rooms with fans, traditionally constructed from local woods. suites with telephones, refrigerator, AC and TV. Amenities and services include restaurant and ice cream parlor, diving, snorkeling and fishing available. A good spot for getting away from the world. Day trips to San Pedro easily arranged. Book through International Expeditions, ☎ 800-633-4734.

St. George's Caye

St. George's Lodge is the only commercial establishment on Saint George's Caye. The lodge, which is beautifully handcrafted of exquisite local hardwoods, houses a dining room, rosewood bar, secluded sundeck and 12 private rooms cooled by tradewinds. In addition, there are four new thatched cottages, each with a private veranda overlooking the sea. All rooms and cottages feature private bath with shower, and windmill-powered electricity. (A 110-V AC converter is located in the lodge for recharging strobes, etc.) Gourmet meals featuring fresh lobster, broiled native fish, and outstanding conch chowder, followed by fabulous desserts created with local fruits, are the fare of the day at this lodge. Diving takes place on a shallow wall ranging from 40 to 100 ft, where there is a wide variety of corals and endless schools of fish. Visibility exceeds 100 ft. Rates per person, per day, include round-trip ground and boat transportation from Belize International Airport, private bath, three meals daily, tanks, weights, full diving privileges, two trips daily and maid service: $314 per day, $1,787 per week (cottages); $199 per day (lodge), $1,211 per week (double occupancy). Non-divers, $149 per person for a double, $172 single (lodge), $235 for a double, $1,439 for a week (cottage). Non-divers may swim from dive boats on a space-available basis. Nitrox diving available. Instruction extra. ☎ 800-678-6871 or 941-488-3788, fax 941-488-3953, local 011-501-212121. Write to St. George's Lodge, PO Box 625,

Belize City, Belize, C.A. E-mail: sgl.belize@btl.net. E-mail for reservations: aw2trav2bz@aol.com. Website: www.godiving.com.

Villas at Banyan Bay in San Pedro are deluxe, with two bedrooms and two baths, ocean views, air-conditioning, phone, cable TV, microwave, washer/dryer, security storage. Rates for two sharing a villa are $175 per villa per night; for four, $225 per night. Add 7% tax. ☎ 800-382-7776 or 011-501-26-3739, fax 011-501-26-2766. E-mail: banyanbay@btl.net.

South Water Caye

Escape the masses on this private 18-acre island off Dangriga, 35 miles south of Belize City. Transfers from the mainland are by the Blue Marlin Lodge launch or by charter flight. By boat, the trip takes about 90 minutes. Driving from Belize City to Dangriga takes about 2½ hours, or by air, 20 minutes.

The big plus for this pristine spot is easy beach diving and snorkeling on the barrier reef that sits 120 ft offshore. Sounds like a short swim, but actually the water is so shallow between the shore and the drop-off that it's really a short walk. Despite Belize's current trend toward marine conservation, spearfishing is allowed here.

The Blue Marlin Lodge, South Water Caye's sole resort, spreads over six acres. Catering primarily to divers and fishermen, the all-inclusive rustic lodge features nine clean, modern rooms (each with two double beds) cooled by ceiling fans and three air-conditioned cottages on the water's edge. All rooms have a private bath with hot and cold running water. The lodge produces its own 110 volt, 60 cycle power and has a desalinization plant to produce pure water. The restaurant and bar serve three sumptuous meals daily. Fresh fish, shrimp and lobster are nicely prepared. Snacks and beverages are served all day. The bar is always stocked with fine Caribbean rums and an assortment of other liquors and beers. No phones and no TV in the rooms or cottages, but there is a phone in the office that guests may use, and the bar has one satellite TV and a VCR. The lodge's dive office has an air compressor, tanks, weights and a small supply of gear. Bring your own personal equipment and snorkeling gear.

Dive/snorkel trips are aboard a fast Pro 42 dive boat or one of two 26-ft power boats. Fishing trips are aboard a 28-ft Mako.

All-inclusive dive packages for $1,443 per person, based on a double, from Saturday to Saturday, include pick-up in Dangriga, standard accommodations, three meals daily plus snacks, two boat dives daily (six days), unlimited shore dives. Add $360 for an air-conditioned cottage. ☎ 800-798-1558, 011-501-52-2243 or 011-501-52-2296. E-mail for reservations: bluemarlin@netrunner.net. E-mail for inquiries: marlin@btl.net. Website: www.bluemarlinlodge.com.

Belize

The Turneffe Islands

Turneffe Island Lodge accommodates guests either in 12 air-conditioned beachfront cottage rooms with private bath or at the main lodge. Cellular and fax service (no phones). American-owned and -operated, this delightful outpost lies approximately 30 miles from Belize City – a two-hour boat trip supplied by the lodge. Lodge rooms feature tropical decor and screened porches facing the Caribbean. Specialties from the gourmet dining room include local fish dishes, conch, and island-grown fruits and vegetables.

A sheer coral wall that starts at 40 ft and drops to more than 2,000 ft surrounds the entire island. Outstanding snorkeling reefs lie about 350 yards off the resort beach. Get there by either paddling one of the resort's four sea kayaks, sailing a Sunfish or taking the skiff. Rates per person of $1,350 plus tax for seven nights, seven days, include round-trip transfers from the Belize City airport, three meals daily, 17 single-tank dives, day trip to the Blue Hole, Half Moon Wall and Long Caye Wall, use of sea kayaks, windsurfer, sailboat, volleyball, horseshoes and lodging. Non-divers pay $1,095. Tanks and weights supplied. Bring your own personal gear. ☎ 800-874-0118, fax 770-534-8290. Write to PO Box 2974, Gainesville, GA 30503. E-mail: info@turneffelodge.com. Website: www.turneffelodge.com.

Dive/hotel/airfare packages from the US are offered through Landfall Productions, ☎ 916-563-0164, fax 916-924-1059. E-mail: landfall@pattravel.com

Blackbird Caye Resort, located 35 miles from Belize City within the Turneffe Reef Atoll on Blackbird Cay, is a real "ecotourist paradise." Unique and exciting, with miles of deserted beaches and jungle trails, the island sits close to 70 impressive dive sites with depths from 20 to 80 ft. Reefs are spectacular, with huge tube and barrel sponges, dramatic overhangs, large loggerhead turtles, dolphins, perfect coral formations. Lots of groupers and reef fish. Manatee sightings. Great snorkeling lies just 400 yds offshore, a five-minute swim. Calm waters inside the reef make it a safe spot for novices. Rate for an all-inclusive package is $1,350 for seven nights. Packages include airport reception, boat transfers, lodging, all meals (excellent, buffet-style), trails, three dives per day, air, tanks and weights. Dive shop on property. Morning and afternoon snorkeling excursions. Boat to the island departs from Ramada docks in Belize City promptly at 3:30, September-March; 4:30 pm, April-August. Travel time is four-five hours.

Accommodations are in thatch-roofed cabanas with ceiling fans and private baths. ☎ 888-271-DIVE (3483). E-mail: dive@blackbirdresort.com. Website: http://www.blackbirdresort.com.

Lighthouse Reef

Lighthouse Reef Resort on Northern Cay, a private island at the northern end of the Lighthouse Reef Reserve, boasts a protected lagoon perfect for snorkelers of all ages. For experienced divers, the resort's custom-built cruiser takes off for the best of Belizean adventure dives, including the fabulous Blue Hole and Lighthouse Reef where 15x10-ft basket sponges, kelp-like gorgonians and sea fans up to nine ft across thrive.

The resort offers luxury air-conditioned rooms and villas. Tropic Air meets incoming flights at Belize International Airport and transports guests to the resort's private airstrip. Flight time is 20 minutes. Diving packages: cabana $1,460 per diver, $1,040 per non-diver; mini-suite $1,615 p/p diver, $1,235 p/p non-diver. They run from Saturday to Saturday and include air-conditioned room with bath, three meals per day and snacks, three boat dives per day, night dives, tanks and weights. Rates are per person for a double; add approx $400 for a single. A fishing and diving package may be combined. ☎ 800-423-3114. Write: PO Box 26, Belize City, C.A.

Glovers Reef

Manta Reef Resort, a 2½-hour boat trip from Belize City, sits on 12 palm-studded acres at the southern tip of Glovers Reef Atoll, conveniently perched over a deep coral wall with easy beach entry. Guests unwind in modern, though simple, mahogany cabanas with private baths and showers. A spacious waterside restaurant and bar decorated with hand-rubbed native woods, fast dive boats, an E6 photo lab and gift shop fill most divers' vacation wishes. Rates are $1,350 per week (Saturday to Saturday), per person, double occupancy, including round-trip transfers from the mainland aboard their 48-ft boat, three meals daily, three boat dives per day, two night dives, unlimited beach dives. Fishing packages also available. ☎ 800-326-1724, local 011-501-232767, fax 011-501-234449. E-mail: info@mantaresort.com. Website: www.mantaresort.com.

Placencia

Placencia is a great spot for divers seeking off-the-beaten-track adventures and especially for those on a low budget. Forty cayes between the mainland and the barrier reef offer pristine diving and snorkeling. Placencia Village has guest rooms for as low as $20 per night. Affordable open-air bars serve pizza, chili and Creole fish dishes. Camping is available at the **Bonaventure Resort** in Seine Bight Village. For complete listings contact the Belize Tourist Board, ☎ 800-844-3688.

Rum Point Inn, a NAUI and PADI Dream Resort, three miles from Placencia Village, comprises 10 seaside cabanas, a main house and a small sandy swimming beach. E-6 processing. Pro-42 Auriga dive boat. Rates per person, per day, for a double are $191, $238 including meals. Add 7% hotel tax and 15% service charge on meals. Dive courses available. ☎ 800-747-1381 or 011-501-6-23239, fax 011-501-6-23240. You can also book through International Expeditions, ☎ 800-633-4734 or 205-428-1700. E-mail: 76735@ compuserve.com.

Turtle Inn, a mile north of Placencia Village, offers thatch-roofed, beach-front cabanas. Cabanas have private baths, solar-generated lighting and kerosene lanterns. There are a number of options for dive, snorkeling and jungle trips. Rooms start at $111 per night. Dive shop. Direct ☎ 501-623-244, fax 501-623245. Book through International Expeditions, ☎ 800-633-4734 or 205-428-1700. E-mail: turtleinn@btl.net.compuserve.com.

Nautical Inn, the newest resort on the Placencia peninsula in Seine Bight Village, features beachfront rooms with private baths, the Oar House Restaurant, transfers from Placencia airstrip, a gift shop, salon, scooter rentals, canoeing, scuba, snorkeling and jungle tours. Rooms that sleep two are $109 per day. Dives are $67 for two one-tank dives. ☎ 800-225-6732 or 011-501-6-22310. E-mail: seaexplore-belize@worldnet.att.net.

Singing Sands Inn features private individual thatch-roofed cabanas, modern on the inside, with private bathrooms. Excursions for diving, snorkeling and day-trip visits to Maya ruins and the Cockscomb Jaguar Preserve are offered. Book through International Expeditions, ☎ 800-633-4734 or 205-428-1700. E-mail: 76735@compuserve.com.

Soulshine Resort dive tours take off to Laughing Bird Caye, Ranguana Caye and Little Caye. This small dive resort offers clean accommodations, breakfast and dinner, five two-tank dives, transfers for rates starting at $1,060 per person, double occupancy. ☎ 800-890-6082. Website: www. soulshine.com.

The Placencia Dive Shop specializes in friendly service, with dive and snorkeling trips such as their Creole seafood feast and snorkel trip to nearby French Louis Cay. ☎ 501-62-3313 or 501-62-3227, fax 501-62-3226.

Sightseeing

Day trips to Belize's archaeological sites, the rain forest and Belize Zoo are offered by local tour companies in Belize City and Ambergris Caye or can be arranged as part of your trip in advance. Day rates are from $65 to about $200 from Ambergris Caye to inland sites, depending on where you are headed.

Altun Ha is the most popular Maya Ruin and least expensive from Ambergris Caye. Tour operators include a picnic lunch, ground and sea transportation.

Xunantunich (Maiden of the Rock) is on the west coast about 80 miles from Belize City. This is the largest ruin unearthed in Belize. Impressive views are had from the top of El Castillo, the main pyramid. Xunantunich is accessible only by ferry, which runs from San Jose Succotz daily between 8 am and 5 pm. Trips often include a tour of the Belize Zoo and a drive around Belmopan, Belize's capital.

Animals at the **Belize Zoo** are housed in naturalistic mesh and wood enclosures. The animals – jaguars, pumas, toucans, spider and howler monkeys, and the "mountain cow" – are all indigenous to Belize. They were originally gathered for a wildlife film. The zoo is 30 miles west of Belize City.

From Belize City, driving up the Western Highway to Mile Marker 21 will bring you to **Gracie Rock,** one of the sites used in the movie *Mosquito Coast,* where you'll find the remains of the huge icemaker blown up by Harrison Ford.

Guanacaste Park, about 50 miles southwest of Belize City, is a 50-acre parcel of tropical forest located in the Cayo District at the junction of Western Highway and Hummingbird Highway. It is named for the huge Guanacaste tree, which can reach a height of 130 ft with a diameter over six ft. More than a hundred species of birds have been spotted here.

The Blue Hole National Park & St. Hermans Cave are 12 miles southeast of Belmopan. This inland "Blue Hole" is a popular recreational spot where water, on its way to the Sibun River, emerges into the base of a collapsed sinkhole about 100 ft deep and 300 ft in diameter. St. Hermans Cave is 500 yards from the Hummingbird Highway and is accessible via a hiking trail from the Blue Hole. The nearest of the three known entrances is impressive – a large sinkhole funneling to a 65-ft entrance. Mayan pottery, spears and torches have been found here.

Dining

Divers staying on Ambergris Caye will find restaurants in the village of San Pedro offering fresh seafood and local dishes such as conch chowder, conch fritters, broiled snapper, shrimp, lobster, and rice dishes, often accompanied by home-baked breads or soups. Chinese food is also extremely popular. **Ramon's Village Restaurant**, ☎ 26-2071, offers a variety of fresh seafood in Chinese, Cajun and island dishes (breakfast, lunch and dinner). Try **Celi's**, ☎ 26-2014, next to the Holiday Hotel, for fabulous fish in beer batter and key lime pie (beach barbecue on Wednesdays), **Little Italy**, ☎ 26-2866, for great pizza, pasta and seafood (open for lunch and dinner), or **Elvi's Kitchen**, ☎ 26-2174, for lobster, conch and shrimp (open for lunch and dinner).

If you are staying at an out-island resort, meals are included in the price of the stay. Local fish, conch and chicken dishes are the usual.

Belize

Shopping

Small shops at the airport and resorts offer T-shirts, straw crafts and native carvings from mahogany, rosewood and ziricote, a two-toned wood indigenous to Belize.

Tours

The following tour companies run diving and/or combination diving/jungle expeditions of Belize. There are pre-planned packages for groups and individuals, or design your own and they will make all the arrangements. Most Belize tours from the US depart from Houston or Miami. Package rates for week-long trips are usually much lower than buying air, accommodations, diving, meals and transfers separately.

Dive Safaris provides deluxe vacations to Ambergris Caye and live-aboard vacations on the *Wave Dancer*. ☎ 800-359-0747 or 212-662-4858, fax 212 749-6172. Website: www.divesafaris.com.

Landfall Productions features well-planned, money-saving, all-inclusive dive vacations from the US, including transfers, diving and accommodations for seven nights to both resorts and live-aboards touring Belize. Call for group rates. ☎ 916-563-0164, fax 916-924-1059. E-mail: landfall@pattravel.com. Website: www.landfallproductions.com.

Tropical Adventures features a variety of Belize vacations to Ambergris Caye, Mainland Belize, Turneffe Island Lodge, Lighthouse Reef Resort, Manta Island Resort. Liveaboards on the *Belize Aggressor* and *Wave Dancer*. ☎ 800-247-3483 or 206-441-3483, fax 206-441-5431. Website: dive tropical.com.

International Expeditions Inc. offers custom-guided trips for the naturalist. Tours are well organized to consider both the skilled diver and novice snorkeler. ☎ 800-633-4734 or 205-428-1700. Write to Number One Environs Park, Helena, AL 35080.

Ocean Connection offers snorkeling, fishing and diving trips, with a choice of islands and hotels. Beach and jungle treks, Mayan ruins and Belize national park tours are their specialty. Budget rates. Combination tours with Mexico are possible. ☎ 800-934-6232, 713-996-7800, fax 713-996-1556. Or write 211 E. Parkwood #108, Friendswood, TX 77546.

American Canadian Caribbean Line Inc. features luxurious, small ship cruises from San Pedro to the Rio Dulce, Guatemala and cays between. No scuba, but they make several snorkeling stops at the best spots. Rates vary from $2,100 to $2,415 per person for 12 days. Airfare extra. ☎ 800-556-7450. Website: ACCL-smallship.com.

Live-Aboards

Belize live-aboards offer access to these pristine diving areas and are popular among those who thrive on 24-hour-a-day diving.

Nekton Diving Cruises caters to scuba divers and snorkelers. Their staff of 11 includes seven instructor who offer guided reef or wreck tours daily. A special 17-ft tender on board the 78-ft yacht is dedicated to carrying snorkeling guests to the best shallow spots. Tours depart Belize City.

The unique twin-hulled design of the yacht eliminates the rocking that causes most sea sickness. Cabins are roomy and nice. E-6 processing, complete audio/visual capabilities, spa, private baths and elevating dive platform.

Boat tours alternate Belize and the Bahamas. Rates for seven nights, six dive days range from $1,295 to $1,495 plus taxes. Call for schedules. ☎ 800-899-6753 or 954-463-9324, fax 954-463-8938. Website: www.nektoncruises. com. Write to: 520 SE 32nd Street, Fort Lauderdale, FL 33316.

Peter Hughes Diving operates the 120-ft *Wave Dancer*. ☎ 800-932-6237 or 305-669-9391. Or write 1390 S. Dixie Highway, Waterway II, Suite 2213, Coral Gables, FL 33146. Packages, ☎ 800-525-3833.

Belize Aggressor II is a 110-ft luxury yacht that carries 18 passengers. It offers all the amenities of a dive resort: air-conditioned private rooms, photo shop, film processing, mini-movie theater, plus fast cruising speeds. ☎ 800-348-2628 or write Aggressor Fleet Ltd., PO Drawer K, Morgan City, LA 70381. Packages through Landfall, ☎ 916-563-0164, fax 916-924-1059. E-mail: landfall@pattravel.com.

Facts

Belize

Helpful Phone Numbers: *(Police and ambulance)* Belize City, ☎ 90; San Pedro, ☎ 02-82095; Placencia, ☎ 06-23129. 911 works in some areas. *(Hospital)* Belize City, ☎ 02-77251 or 90. *(Tourist board)* ☎ 800-624-0686or 501-26-2012, fax 011-501-26-2338. *(Coast Guard)* ☎ 02-35312. *(Philip S.W. Goldson International Airport)* ☎ 02-52014. *(Maya Airways)* ☎ 2-44032/45968/44234 (service throughout Belize).

Nearest Recompression Chamber: San Pedro, Ambergris Caye. Emergency helicopter service from atolls. Dial 90 for assistance. **Note:** Readers Kay and George Shueppert report outstanding service from Antonia Guerrero, who is in charge of the chamber in San Pedro, with attending physician Dr. Otto Rodriquez and dive guides Patojo and Sabrina Paz.

Health: Anti-malaria tablets are recommended for stays in the jungle.

Airlines: Scheduled commercial service from the US and Canada is by American Airlines, ☎ 800-433-7300, ☎ Continental, 800-231-0856, and TACA. Tropic Air flies from Canc n, Mexico. ☎ 800-422-3435 or 501-26-2012, fax 011-501-26-2338. In Belize, Tropic Air, ☎ 2302, in San Pedro, 2012 or 2439, services major cities, Ambergris Caye and the out islands. Additional Belize cities are served by Island Air, ☎ 2219 or 2435, or Maya Airways, ☎ 2336, in San Pedro, 2515.

Private Aircraft may enter Belize only through the Phillip Goldson International Airport in Belize City. Belizean airspace is open during daylight hours. Pilots are required to file a flight plan and will be briefed on local conditions. Landing fee for all aircraft.

By Car: Belize can be reached from the US and Canada via Mexico, though reports of hold-ups on the roads deter most motorists. You must possess a valid driver's license and registration papers for the vehicle. A temporary permit will enable use of your vehicle without payment of customs. A temporary insurance policy must be purchased at the frontier to cover the length of stay in Belize. After three days, visitors must obtain a Belize driving permit, for which they need to complete a medical form, provide two recent photos and pay $20.

Private Boats must report to the police or immigration immediately. No permits are required. Boaters need documents for the vessel, clearance from last port of call, four copies of the crew and passenger manifest and a list of stores and cargo.

Documents: Visitors are permitted to stay up to one month, provided they have a valid passport and have a ticket to their onward destination. For stays longer than 30 days, an extension must be obtained from the Immigration Office, 115 Barrack Road, Belize City.

Transportation: Bus service around Belize City is readily available via Batty Brothers, ☎ 02-72025; or Z-Line, ☎ 02-73937/06-22211. Since few cars are available on the islands, transportation is usually arranged by the resorts. On the mainland, reservations can be made through National (☎ 800-CAR-RENT; in Belize, 2-31650) or Budget (☎ 800-927-0700; in Belize, ☎ 2-32435 or 33986). Reserve prior to trip. Jeeps and 4WD vehicles are mandatory on back roads. Avoid local car rental companies or carefully check vehicles for scratches or dents and have them documented by the rental company beforehand.

Ferries: Ambergris Caye can be reached by ferry boat from Belize City. *The Andrea I* and *Andrea II* operate from Belize City to San Pedro, leaving the docks of the Bellevue Hotel at 4 pm from Monday to Friday and 1 pm on Saturday, returning to Belize at 7 am. Also available to San Pedro is the *Miss Belize*, which runs daily. Tickets may be purchased from the Universal Travel Agency in Belize City. *Miss Belize* departs from the docks behind the Supreme Court building. Travel time to San Pedro is one hour and 15 minutes.

Departure Tax: US $15.

Customs: Personal effects can be brought in without difficulty, but it is best to register cameras, videos and electronic gear with customs before leaving home. American citizens can bring home $400 worth of duty-free goods after a 48-hour visit. Over that, purchases are dutied at 10%. Import allowances include 200 cigarettes or ½ lb tobacco; 20 fluid oz of alcoholic beverages and one bottle of perfume for personal use. **Note:** removing and exporting coral or archaeological artifacts is prohibited. Picking orchids in forest reserves is illegal.

Currency: Belize dollar=US 50¢.

Climate: Belize has a subtropical, humid climate. Average temperature 79°F. The rainy season is from April to December. Hurricanes form during late summer. Best time to visit is February through May, though summer diving when weather permits (mid-August) is often done in calm seas with excellent visibility.

Clothing: Lightweight clothing with long sleeves to protect against sunburn and a light sweater for evening wear. The dive resorts are extremely casual. Leave dress wear at home. Those who want to combine an expedition into the jungle with their diving vacation should check with the tour company. Bring mosquito repellent.

Gear: Divers' rental equipment is limited in Belize so be sure to bring all of your own personal equipment. The resorts do supply weights and tanks, but little else.

Electricity: 110/220V 60 cycles. Most island resorts run on generators, which are out of service for at least part of the day. Air-conditioning is limited on the out islands.

Time: Central Standard Time.

Language: English

Additional Information: Belize Tourist Board, ☎ 800-624-0686, 800-563-6011, fax 800-563-6033. In Belize, 011-501-2-31913, fax 011-501-2-31943. Write to: PO Box 325, Goal Lane, Belize City, Belize, C.A. E-mail: btbb@btl.net. Website: www.travelbelize.org.

Belize

Part IV

South America

Brazil

Brazil
SOUTH AMERICA
Rio de Janeiro
Atlantic Ocean
1. Fernando de Noronha

Brazil offers marvelous contrasts in geography, people and diving experiences. Brazil shares boundaries with every South American country except Chile and Ecuador. Its coastline extends over 11,919 miles, much of it as white sandy beaches.

Within its boundaries lie the beautiful Atlantic islands of Trindade and Fernando de Noronha, home to the Bay of Dolphins and the most interesting dive and snorkeling opportunities.

Fernando de Noronha & the Bay of Dolphins

Fernando de Noronha (Island of the Forbidden), a small chain of rocky islands and outcroppings, lie 200 miles from Recife, a resort community on Brazil's northern coast. These undeveloped islands are a natural sanctuary and breeding ground for spinner dolphins, green sea turtles, booby birds, and other wildlife. White, sandy beaches rim the largest islands.

The Bay of Dolphins on the northwest coast of the main island is habitat to a centuries-old community of spinner dolphins. This sheltered bay serves as both congregation and breeding ground for hundreds of the charming mammals. Eighteenth-century documents call this enchanted land the "Island of the Dolphins."

Calm and crystal clear waters prevail with unlimited visibility during dry seasons (October through December). Though occasionally frightened by scuba gear, the shy dolphins are extremely gentle and trusting, allowing some snorkelers to get very close. Rocky dropoffs provide refuge for walls of yellowtail, mammoth groupers, jewfish, snappers, squirrel fish, butterfly fish, surgeon fish, eagle rays, sea turtles, sting rays, octopus, and crustaceans. Bottom terrain varies with areas of coral patches, walls, caves and ledges.

Videographers will immediately recognize Fernando de Noronha as their own piece of heaven. The lively play of the dolphins as they leap, spinning several feet into the air, captivates everyone. Tank diving is allowed, although it is frowned upon by some conservationists who feel it unnerves the marine mammal community. Divers and snorkelers should exercise extreme consideration for this enchanting habitat. Take only pictures!

When to Go

The best time to plan a dive-vacation to Brazil is from October through December, the dry months. Rainfall is heavy from March through September, the heaviest during June, July and August.

Accommodations & Dive Operators

Vacationers from the United States and Canada will find a visit to the Bay of Dolphins easiest to arrange from home through a tour operator. Nordeste Linhas Airlines connects the islands to Recife.

Divers considering vacationing in Fernando de Noronha should note that it is essentially an unspoiled habitat and does not offer any resort amenities – no cities, no nightclubs, no tourist glitz. What it does offer, in addition to diving, is spectacular sunsets, a nightly festival of stars, a chance to unwind, and an opportunity to commune with nature.

The hotel, **Pousada Esmeralda**, offers guests clean, comfortable rooms overlooking the sea. Atlantis Divers shuttles divers and snorkelers aboard large, custom yachts. Dive-accommodation tours can be arranged through **Reef & Rainforest Worldwide Adventure Travel**, ☎ 800-794-9767, fax 415-289-1763, website reefrainfrst.com/brazildive.htm, or **Dive Tours**, ☎ 800-433-0885. E-mail: rnrtravel@aol.com.

Facts

Recompression Chamber: None. Stay shallow. Don't dive and fly the same day.

Getting There: American Airlines, Varig and United Airlines to Recife. Nordeste Linhas Airways fly from Recife to Fernando de Noronha.

Documents: Visitors to Brazil must carry a passport valid for at least six months and a tourist visa. Be sure to keep a separate record of your passport number, place of issue and date with you in case you lose it. Obtaining a replacement passport is no easy task.

Customs: Diving and camera gear should be registered with customs before you depart. Carry receipts with you if you are taking new products. While in Brazil you may purchase up to $300 worth of duty free products.

Currency: The Brazilian currency is the cruzado (Cz$) divided into 100 centavos. The official rate of exchange is published daily in the main Brazilian newspapers. Foreign currencies or travelers checks can be exchanged for cruzados at hotels, banks and tourist agencies. Travelers checks are recommended for currency here. Although international credit cards are accepted, they may billed at a higher rate than in the United States.

Climate: Most of Brazil lies immediately to the south of the Equator. As a result, there is very little seasonal variation. The climate is comfortably temperate in most of the country, and refreshing sea breezes often blow along the coast all year round, the temperatures usually ranging from 65 to 85°F. The hottest months of the year are January to March. The coldest months are July and August when the thermometer dips into the low 70s.

Clothing: Lightweight casual clothing is appropriate for the diving resorts. A sweater or light jacket is a good idea for cooler evenings. A full wetsuit is needed in Fernando de Noronha for scuba.

Time Zone: In most of the country and in the main cities, the time is three hours earlier than Greenwich (London) Mean Time. There is a maximum of two hours difference ahead of New York's time. When New York is on daylight savings time there is only a one-hour difference.

Electricity: 110 or 120 V, AC, 60 cycles in Rio. Some hotels have European- and American-type outlets. Adapters are readily available in most hotels, if needed.

Taxes and Service Charges: Tipping is expected by taxi drivers. In restaurants, because a service charge is added to the bill, only a small tip is left if the service is outstanding.

Vaccinations and Health Precautions: Vaccinations are not required to enter Brazil unless you are coming from an infected area. If traveling to the interior, check with your department of immigration and be sure to carry malaria prophylaxis pills. Drink only bottled water in Brazil and avoid unpasteurized milk, fruits and raw vegetables. Check the Government website for up-to-date health information: www.cdc.gov/travel/travel.html. Or www.travel.state.gov/travel_warnings.html.

Additional Information: The best information on diving Brazil comes from the tour specialists Reef & Rainforest, ☎ 800-794-9767, fax 415-289-1763, E-mail mrtravel@aol.com; Dive Tours, ☎ 800-433-0885; or Dive Safaris, ☎ 800-359-0747.

Brazil

Part V

The Pacific

Channel Islands

National Park & Marine Sanctuary

Located off the coast of Southern California, the Channel Islands National Park includes San Miguel, Santa Cruz, Anacapa, Santa Rosa and Santa Barbara Island. The National Marine Sanctuary, designated on September 22, 1980, extends six nautical miles from the shores of Channel Islands National Park. Diving is excellent off all of the islands.

Common to all the islands are colorful tide pools, wind-sculpted cliffs and sandy beaches, home to brown pelicans, sea lions and elephant seals. A relatively shallow shelf with an average maximum depth of 300 ft extends three to six miles around each island. Diving depths range from 15 to 100 ft. A few sheltered areas exist for snorkeling.

A huge community of marine life thrives in the reefs and kelp forests surrounding the islands, from microscopic plankton to huge blue whales and basking sharks. A mix of cold and warm currents that merge at the islands carry nutrients that support small fish and invertebrates, which, in turn, feed more than 800 species of marine life. In fact, San Miguel has the distinction of supporting six species of seals and sea lions. Seabirds such as the brown pelican and Xantus' murrelet thrive on the sanctuary's highly productive waters.

When to Go

Dive trips run year-round, but are weather-dependent. Storms and prolonged high winds, especially during winter months, may prevent dive and tour boats from crossing to the park.

Underwater visibility runs between 40 and 60 ft, except during a plankton bloom when areas become soupy. The best visibility exists between August and December. Since water temperatures range from 55 to 70°F, divers must wear a full 1/4-inch or thicker wetsuit, complete with hood, gloves, and boots, year-round.

Sections reprinted with permission of the National Oceanic and Atmospheric Administration and Channel Islands National Marine Sanctuary.

Kelp Forests

The dense kelp forests surrounding the islands are named for the large brown seaweed, *Macrocystis pyrifera*. Anchored to the rocky bottom by root-like holdfasts, the kelp plants extend to the surface from depths as much as 200 ft. The species has been known to grow two feet a day. Sheltered by the canopy formed at the surface, hundreds of animals and other species of seaweed flourish. On the rocky reefs where the kelp is attached, urchins, crabs and abalone graze among encrusting sponges and plumed worms. Small colonies of filter-feeding organisms and multi-colored snails are found on the leafy blades of the kelp. Many fish like the rubber-lipped surf perch and the large, colorful sheephead swim through the dense foliage. Fish and invertebrates also use the kelp for shelter and food.

Tide Pools

A great variety of ocean creatures may be found in the rocky intertidal area of the sanctuary. Tide pools form when pockets of water become trapped between the cracks and hollows of rocks as the tide recedes.

Marine Mammals

In the deeper water of the sanctuary dolphins, porpoises and whales can often be seen, while other predators such as sharks and seals hunt schools of fish. Of the more than 25 species of marine mammals known to inhabit the sanctuary, the seals and sea lions, known as pinnipeds, are among the most visible. At one time, pinnipeds roamed extensively along the southern California coast and hauled out on mainland beaches to breed. Hunting and development on the mainland have reduced their numbers and today the offshore islands and surrounding waters are among their last refuges. Together, the combination of isolation and a productive food source in the sanctuary provides favorable conditions for breeding. Six species of pinnipeds gather to breed, pup and nurse their young here. The seals and sea lions around San Miguel Island provide one of the world's outstanding wildlife displays.

Whales, dolphins and porpoises, known collectively as cetaceans, are the other group of marine mammals inhabiting sanctuary waters. The gray whale is a well-known seasonal migrant, and pilot whales as well as many others are frequently sighted in the sanctuary. During certain times of year, visitors may be fortunate enough to see pods of nearly a thousand common dolphins leaping clear of the water in unison. Bottlenose and Pacific white-sided dolphins often delight divers by "riding the bow" of their boats.

Diving

Divers should be experienced in ocean environments before visiting the northern Channel Islands.

Anacapa Island

Anacapa, actually three small islands, West Anacapa, Middle Anacapa and East Anacapa, connect by shallow sandbars. Their close proximity to the mainland – just 11 miles southwest of Oxnard and 14 miles from Ventura – makes them a popular dive spot. An ecological reserve has been established where no game can be taken. Within the reserve are large abalone, scallops and lobster caves teeming with life. Topside, the islands resemble a high-desert landscape countered by the seals and sea lions that haul out on their rocky shores. The brown pelican nests on the north side of West Anacapa.

When the fog horn is blowing, don't approach the lighthouse on foot beyond the warning sign. Severe hearing damage may result. Diving activities on the east end of East Island are not affected by the foghorn. January through March is whale-watch season.

Waters surrounding the island are open to the public for fishing and diving. Day visits ashore and camping are permitted. However, the disturbance, damage or removal of any rock, plant or animal is prohibited within the park. Fishing is permitted in accordance with State of California regulations, avail-

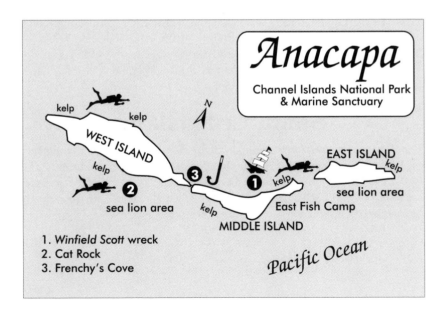

1. *Winfield Scott* wreck
2. Cat Rock
3. Frenchy's Cove

Channel Islands

able from the California Department of Fish & Game, Marine Resources Division 1416 Ninth St., Sacramento, CA 95814 (☎ 916-653-6281).

Best dives around Anacapa vary with the wind and sea conditions. Local charter dive boat captains are the best source of information. East Island has hiking trails, a campground, and a ranger station, as well as the lighthouse.

Best Dives of Anacapa Island

☆☆☆ The **Winfield Scott**, a 225-ft paddlewheel steamer, ran aground in dense fog and sank off Middle Anacapa in 1853. Remains of the wreck are scattered in 30 ft of water. Average visibility is 30 ft. The wreck is protected and nothing may be taken. Kelp beds are a short swim east of the wreck. Lobster, some abalone, sea urchins, starfish, and scallops may be found in this area. Check with local captains as to when you may take lobster and shellfish. Invertebrates may not be taken from waters less than 20 ft deep.

☆☆☆ **Cat Rock**, off the south shore of West Anacapa Island, has super diving when the southern swell is calm. The bottom is rocky, with depths from 40 to 60 ft. A variety of shellfish, including lobster, abalone, starfish and scallops, roam the seafloor. Sea conditions vary with wind. Check for currents before entering the water.

☆☆☆ **Goldfish Bowl**, off the western shores of West Anacapa Island, shelters masses of fish along a rocky reef.

Best Snorkeling Site of Anacapa

☆☆☆ **Frenchy's Cove**, at West Anacapa, has a beach and a good snorkeling area. Picnicking permitted. Depths range from 10 to 40 ft. Snorkelers will find colorful invertebrates, including red starfish, sea urchins, sponges, anemones and abalone. Some nice kelp stands. Seals sometimes visit the area, as well as bass, octopi and an occasional ray.

Santa Cruz Island

The largest of the northern Channel Island, Santa Cruz sits in the transition zone where warm currents from the south meet colder northern currents. The island's subsea terrain is riddled with abundant caves, rocky ledges and reef systems. Sea conditions change dramatically with the wind, but good diving can usually be found somewhere regardless of weather.

Best Dives of Santa Cruz

★★★★ **Gull Reef and Island** off Santa Cruz's southern tip is a photographer's favorite. A rocky bottom with kelp patches provides shelter for a wealth of fish, shellfish and lobster. Depths range from 10 to 70 ft. Good visibility.

★★★ **Wreck of the *Peacock*,** an old Navy minesweeper, offers some nice photo and fish-watching opportunities. Depths to 70 ft. Big bass inhabit the kelp strands.

San Miguel Island

This westernmost of the northern islands boasts outstanding natural and cultural features. Some of the best examples of caliche, a mineral sandcasting, are found here. Enormous numbers of seals and sea lions haul out and breed on its isolated shores. A type of island fox can also be seen. Over 500 undisturbed archaeological sites, some dating back thousands of years, are located here. Juan Rodriquez Cabrillo, discoverer of California, is believed to have wintered and died at Cuyler Harbor in 1543. Although his grave has never been found, a monument overlooking the harbor was erected in 1937.

During World War II and the Korean War, the US Navy used the island as a bombing range and later for missile testing. Staying on the trail is crucial since

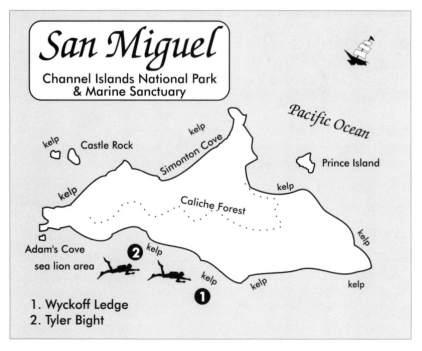

Channel Islands

live ordnance is still occasionally uncovered by shifting sands. Visitors who wish to travel beyond the beach at Cuyler Harbor must be accompanied by a Park Ranger. Contact park headquarters for information and permit applications.

If you travel by private boat, you must obtain a permit in advance to land on San Miguel. The island is open for day use. Camping is available during the summer. Both the US Navy and the National Park Service manage the island. Kelp forest diving around the island is excellent.

Underwater, San Miguel attracts large schools of rockfish that hover around towering pinnacles covered with invertebrates, sea stars, nudibranchs, anemones and cup corals.

Best Dives of San Miguel Island

☆☆ **Wyckoff Ledge**, off the south shore, offers divers a beautiful kelp forest and excellent visibility. Abalone, a variety of starfish, and sea anemones, as well as some corals and scallops, can be found on the bottom. This is a good area for photography. The wall starts at 20 ft, then drops off sharply to 90 ft. Sea conditions vary with wind and weather. A light current is always running.

☆☆☆ **Tyler Bight**, a protected cove on the south side of the island features a number of pretty rock formations and kelp gardens. Unusual starfish and flower-like anemones decorate the ledges and bottom. A number of scallops can be found around the rocks. This is a nice spot for underwater photography. Expect a light current.

Additional good diving exists around **Judith Rock** off the southwest shore. The wreck of the **S.S. Cuba**, a 307-ft Pacific Mail steamer that went down in 1923 lies off the western shore. The wreck of the **Comet**, a 145-ft, three-masted coastal lumber schooner that went aground on August 30, 1911, and **Nifty Rock**, are just east of Harris Point.

Santa Rosa

Santa Rosa, the second largest of the northern Channel Islands, is surrounded by rocky pinnacles and thick amber kelp forests. The best spots are off Carrington Point on the northern end, with depths from 20 to 60 ft and Talcott Shoal on the northwest tip, with depths from 10 to 100 ft. Talcott is often weathered out. Overall, subterrain is similar to Anacapa. Fish and invertebrates are abundant and diverse.

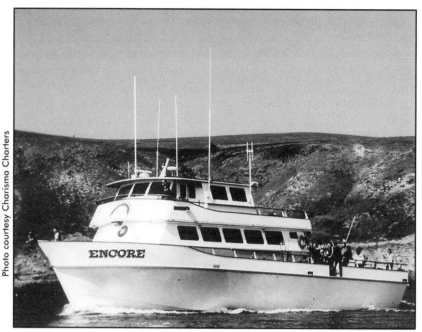

The Encore *visits the best sites off southern California.*

Best Dives of Santa Rosa

☆☆☆☆ The favored diving is around the pinnacles and kelp beds, but dive boats occasionally visit the wreck of the **S.S. Chickasaw**, a 439-ft freighter built in 1942 that ran into the south shore of Santa Rosa Island in heavy fog on February 7, 1962.

Santa Barbara Island

Famous for the large sea lion rookery along its western rocky shore, Santa Barbara Island also touts extensive kelp forest, caves and rocky reefs.

The island is quite a bit south of the main islands and is visited by dive boats from the Long Beach area. On shore, the island is fairly inhospitable.

Live Aboards

Dive trips from one to five days to San Miguel, Anacapa, Santa Cruz and Santa Rosa can be arranged with **Truth Aquatics, Inc.** at See Landing, Santa Barbara Harbor. Their three dive boats, the 65-ft *Truth*, the 75-ft *Con-*

Channel Islands

ception and 88-ft *Vision* were designed and custom-built specifically for divers. The Truth Aquatics fleet runs Channel Island excursions year-round. Their captains and crews are expert divers who know the islands well and can take you to the best spots. Each boat is outfitted with state-of-the-art navigational and safety equipment, hot showers, spacious galleys and large sundecks. The boats move to different locations throughout the day, providing as many dives as your bottom time will allow. Trips depart from Santa Barbara at 4 am, arriving at the dive location first thing in the morning. Hiking and kayaking available between dives. Non-divers welcome. Whale and dolphin sightings en route are common.

To receive a calendar of the trips, send a stamped, self-addressed envelope to Truth Aquatics, Inc., Sea Landing Breakwater, Santa Barbara, CA 93109. ☎ 805-962-1127, fax 805-564-6754. E-mail: taqua@ix.netcom.com. Website: www.truthaquatics.com.

Full-day and overnight trips to Santa Barbara Island and Santa Catalina can be arranged with **Sundiver** out of Long Beach. Sundiver skipper, Rich Wallace, a PADI instructor, employs a crew of dive professionals who have your safety and comfort in mind. The *Sundiver* is a 54x17-ft dive yacht that sleeps 22 persons. It has two hot showers, a full galley and a comfortable lounge. The boat is customized for scuba diving, but snorkelers and sightseers are welcome. ☎ 800-555-9446 or 562-493- 0951.Write to Captain Wallace at 160 Marina Drive, Long Beach, CA 90803.

Charisma Charters features the 80-ft *Encore* (see photo preceding page), a custom dive yacht with spacious bunk and state rooms.The vessel also has dual air compressors for rapid fills, circulating game tanks, four showers and a galley that seats everyone at once. Captain Kenny Hess knows Southern California waters well and is an avid diver. Charisma Charters publishes a monthly calendar of activities. To receive a copy, send a self-addressed, stamped envelope to: Charisma Charter Service, PO Box 590, Harbor City, CA 90710-0590. ☎ 310-541-1025.

Accommodations

There are no accommodations on these islands, but a wide selection of motels and hotels exist on the mainland in Santa Barbara, the jump-off point. Two are listed below. For a complete list and a vacation package on Santa Barbara ☎ 800-927-4688 or e-mail: webtech@sbjuide.com.

Santa Barbara Beach Travelodge, a 19-room motel, offers clean, modern, comfortable rooms. It is located at 22 Castillo St, Santa Barbara, CA 93101. ☎ 805-965-8527. E-mail: bchtrvl@west.net.

Harbor House, at 104 Bath St, Santa Barbara, CA 93101, is a small, friendly, family-run hotel. ☎ 805-962-9745. E-mail: info@beachmotel.com.

Camping

Primitive camping is available, but is not recommended unless you like extremely rugged living conditions. Transportation to any of the islands can be arranged through **Island Packers** (☎ 805-642-7688), authorized concessionaire to the Channel Islands National Park. Please note that weather can be a big problem for campers. Wind may blow for several days at a time and the only protection is what you have brought with you. Long periods of wet fog are not uncommon. Winter and spring rains turn the trails and campground into sticky mud. Sunscreen is a necessity. It is a harsh environment at best and a hostile and unforgiving one at its worst. Pets are not allowed on the islands at any time.

Sightseeing

Be sure to stop by the **Sea Center** on Stearns Wharf, Santa Barbara. The Center maintains an extensive educational program that features special tours and classes, tide pooling, whale watching, field trips to the Channel Islands and their surrounding waters. A wide variety of fabulous exhibits include life size models of whales and dolphins, undersea dioramas, aquariums and interactive computer/video displays. The remains of shipwrecks and Chumash Indian artifacts impart the region's cultural heritage. The Sea Center is open throughout the year. From June 1 through Labor Day weekend the hours are 11 am to 7 pm, seven days a week. The rest of the year it is open weekdays from noon to 5 pm and weekends and holidays from 11 am to 6 pm. Closed on Thanksgiving, Christmas and New Year's Day. ☎ 805-962-0885. Write to: 211 Stearns Wharf, Santa Barbara, CA 93101.

Facts

Getting There: All major airlines service Los Angeles International Airport. Train service aboard Amtrak is available to Santa Barbara, jump-off point for the Channel Islands. For details, ☎ 800-USA RAIL. Greyhound Bus travels from Los Angeles to Oxnard as well. Travel to the northern Channel Islands can be arranged through Island Packers, ☎ 805-642-7688.

Climate: Temperate; daytime temperatures vary from 80 down to 50°F. Frosts are very rare, but night and morning fog often blanket the islands. Average yearly rainfall is 10 to 12 inches, falling mostly during the winter months.

Clothing: Keep weather extremes in mind. Pack a jacket or extra sweater for evenings. The rainy season is from November to March. A full wetsuit is needed to dive the Northern Channel Islands, including gloves, boots and a hood.

Channel Islands

Time: Pacific Standard Time.

Using Your Own Boat: If you plan to take your own boat, refer to National Ocean Survey Charts 18720, 18727, 18728, 18729 and 18756. The Santa Barbara Channel is subject to sudden changes in sea and wind conditions, especially in the afternoons. Be familiar with local conditions. Cruising guides may be purchased at the park's Visitor Center. NOAA VHF-FM weather broadcasts – San Luis Obispo KIH-31, 162.55 MHz and Santa Barbara KIH-34, 162.40 MHz. For assistance, contact the US Coast Guard on Channel 16 of your marine band radio.

Landing Permits: To visit San Miguel Island and Santa Rosa Island you need a permit from park headquarters. Sea conditions around both islands are often rough; only experienced boaters with sturdy vessels should attempt the trip. Landing on privately owned Santa Cruz is by permit only. No landing is permitted on the eastern side. To land on the west side, contact The Nature Conservancy at 213 Stearns Wharf, Santa Barbara, CA 93101. ☎ 805-962-9111.

Additional Information: Contact Island Packers, 1867 Spinnaker Drive, Ventura CA 93001, ☎ 805-642-7688, or Channel Islands National Park at 1901 Spinnaker Drive, Ventura CA 93001, ☎ 805-658-5700.

The Visitor Center is located at the end of Spinnaker Drive in Ventura. Here you can view a 25-minute film, purchase publications, maps and nautical charts, and arrange for boat service to the islands.

For information on Santa Cruz Island, contact The Nature Conservancy, 213 Stearns Wharf, Santa Barbara, CA 93101 or The Sea Center 211 Stearns Wharf, Santa Barbara, CA 93101.

For information on boating or diving within sanctuary boundaries, write to Superintendent, Channel Islands Marine Sanctuary, 113 Harbor Way, Santa Barbara, CA 93109. ☎ 805-966-7107, fax 805-568-1582. E-mail: channel_islands@ ocean.nos.noaa.gov. Website: www.cinms.nos.noaa.gov.

Santa Catalina

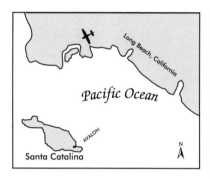

Of all the Southern Channel Islands (Santa Catalina, Santa Barbara, San Clemente, and San Nicolas), Santa Catalina, 22 miles off the coast of Los Angeles, is the undisputed jewel, with terrific diving and top-notch vacation facilities. Regular scheduled cross-channel boat and air service carry tourists to the island.

Avalon, the island's only city, sports a picturesque array of storybook cottages, cobblestone streets, flower gardens, boutiques, restaurants, and lovely hotels set in a beautiful background of canyons, mountains and Pacific blues.

Inland, wild boar, turkeys, bald eagles, island foxes, quail, deer and buffalo inhabit the countryside. Fourteen buffalo were brought to the island in 1924 for the filming of *The Vanishing American*, then were left here. In 1934, 11 additional buffalo were purchased to supplement the herd, which by then had increased to 19. Today there are approximately 200.

Sea lions and harbors seals take up residence at the east end of the island each summer.

Two Harbors, a small one-lodge village located at Catalina's isthmus, 23 miles by land or 14 miles by sea west of Avalon, offers rugged adventures, seaside camping, secluded coves and beaches. Diving and snorkeling is excellent. Regular bus service and a coastal shuttle connect this area to Avalon.

History

Catalina was first discovered in 1542 and named San Salvador by Don Juan Rodriguez Cabrillo, a Portuguese navigator searching for the Straits of Anian, a mythical passage connecting the Pacific and the Atlantic Oceans. Following Cabrillo's brief visit, the island was forgotten until 1602, when an expedition led by Don Sebastian Viscaino dropped anchor nearby. Viscaino renamed the island "Santa Catalina" for St. Catherine of Alexandria.

Viscaino found peace and friendliness among the resident American Indians, who had built a great temple they called Chiningchinich, dedicated to sun worship and a gathering place for all the Channel Island Indians. The temple, since buried by a landslide, was probably located at Empire Landing.

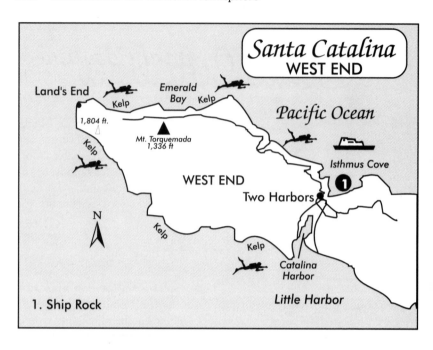

Santa Catalina
WEST END

Land's End

Kelp

Emerald Bay   Kelp

Pacific Ocean

1,804 ft.

Mt. Torquemada
1,336 ft

Kelp

Isthmus Cove

①

WEST END

Two Harbors

N

Kelp

Kelp

Catalina Harbor

1. Ship Rock

Little Harbor

By the mid-1800s Catalina's abundant wildlife attracted Russian hunters, who crewed their boats with fierce Aleuts and Kodiak Indians. Their prime target were the sea otters, valued for their fur.

The hunters killed everything in their path, including the entire Channel Island Indian population. The trusting sea otters were clubbed to death, their valuable furs sold to Chinese merchants in Canto and members of nobility in Russia. The greed and cruelty continued until the entire sea otter population was gone. The otters were thought extinct until the 1930s, when a small colony emerged off Monterey, California.

Much of the island's recent history comes from the people who lived and vacationed here – from the smugglers and missionaries of the 1800s to William Wrigley Jr. and some of Hollywood's biggest stars and literary giants. Stan Laurel and Oliver Hardy were among the many Hollywood favorites that frequented Avalon. American author Zane Grey's former home sits high above Avalon Bay and is now a popular hotel. On the other side of the bay, overlooking the entire city, is the former home of Mr. Wrigley – a grand, elegant estate that operates as the Inn on Mt. Ada, a four-star country hotel. Catalina's Tuna Club, the oldest fishing club in the US, attracted Cecil B. DeMille, John Wayne and Winston Churchill.

In 1892, the Santa Catalina Island Company was incorporated by the Banning brothers, who purchased the island. Today 86% of the island belongs to The Santa Catalina Island Conservancy, a nonprofit foundation incorporated in 1972. As part of an agreement with Los Angeles County, the

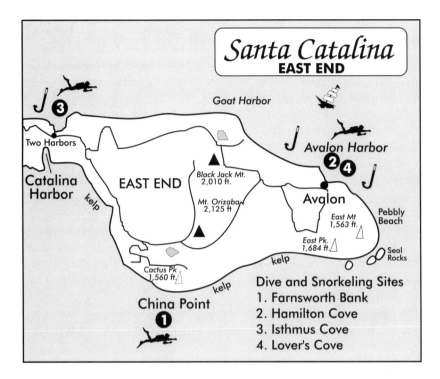

Santa Catalina
EAST END

Goat Harbor

Two Harbors

Avalon Harbor

Catalina
Harbor

kelp

EAST END

Black Jack Mt.
2,010 ft.

Mt. Orizaba
2,125 ft

Avalon

Pebbly
Beach

East Mt
1,563 ft.

East Pk.
1,684 ft.

Seal
Rocks

Cactus Pk
1,560 ft.

kelp

kelp

China Point

Dive and Snorkeling Sites
1. **Farnsworth Bank**
2. **Hamilton Cove**
3. **Isthmus Cove**
4. **Lover's Cove**

Conservancy's purpose is to preserve the island's resources while increasing access and improving recreational opportunities.

Best Dives of Santa Catalina Island

Huge rocks, deep caverns and towering kelp forests form Catalina's underwater landscape. Lobster and abalone abound.

Visibility is best during the winter months. Summer brings plankton blooms, which cloud the water. The average water temperature is 65°F (ranging from 57 to 71), necessitating a full wet suit for diving.

☆☆☆☆ **Farnswork Bank**, the island's most exciting dive, lies about three miles southwest of Ben Weston Point on Catalina's "Bach" or windward side. This rocky sea mount starts at 50 ft below the surface and drops off to over 150 ft. Some surge and a current which can be heavy at times is to be expected here. Visibility is usually outstanding. Sea urchins, anemones, pastel gorgonians, kelp, and rare lavender corals cover the mount. The coral is protected and should not be touched. Suitable only for experienced ocean divers.

☆☆☆ **Ship Rock**, an outcrop located offshore from the north side of Two Harbors, entices scuba-equipped wildlife photographers with friendly sea lions, seals, moray eels, lobster, colorful urchins, small horn sharks, octopus, keyhole limpets (mollusks similar to abalone), sea hares and perch. A 50-

minute boat ride from Avalon brings you here. Depths range from 100 to 110 ft. The bottom is sandy.

☆☆☆ **Isthmus Cover Harbor** marks the center point between Catalina's east and west portions. Diving along this drop-off is best on the rocky reef at depths between 20 and 40 ft. Sub- scenery features towering kelp patches inhabited by halibut and kelp bass, lavender and red sea urchins, pink anemones, starfish, and red gorgonians. Lobsters, moray eels and scallops peek from the crevices. Light currents make this spot good for snorkelers and novice divers.

☆☆ **Casino Point Underwater Park**, located at the edge of the Casino building in Avalon, is Southern California's first city- designated underwater park. Established in 1965 by the City of Avalon as a reserve, it is the only place within the city limits where diving is permitted and is a popular spot for snorkelers, first-time divers and experienced divers as well. Because it is protected, an abundance of marine life dwells there and several wrecks and artificial reefs have been established to provide additional habitats. Giant kelp forests flourish in the park.

The park area, on the ocean side of the point, is roped off to protect divers from the boats that pass through the harbor. Seas are generally calm. Depth is 10 to 90 ft.

Snorkeling

☆☆ **Lover's Cove**, east of Avalon Bay, is an easy entry from the small pebble beach next to the ferry landing. This marine reserve is protected from fishing, collecting and boats. The bottom is rocky, with patches of kelp. A number of friendly fish will follow you around in hopes of being fed. Frozen peas are the local fish- feeding favorite. Starfish, anemones, urchins, shrimp and some lobster can be found in the rocks and crevices. This area is calm, with little or no current running. Snorkel rental gear is available on site.

Snorkeling trips depart from **Joe's Rent-a-Boat** on the Pleasure Pier.

Dive Operators

Argo Diving Service has experienced guides who visit the best sites. The shop offers certification courses, introductory dives and boat trips. Owner Jon Hardy is a *Best Dives* contributor. ☎ 310-510-2208, fax 310-510-2337. Write to Jon Hardy, Box 2289, Avalon, CA 90704. E-mail: scubalab1@aol.com.

Catalina Diver's Supply, on the Pleasure Pier, offers scuba and snorkeling rental gear, repairs, air fills to 3500 psi, and dive charters. Dive packages with the Pavilion Lodge or Hotel Atwater. A two-tank morning dive costs $75. Includes lunch and soft drinks. Snorkelers can join for $40. ☎ 800-353-0330 or 310-510-0330, fax 310-510-0695. Website: www.catalina.com/cds or www.diveinfo.com/cds. Write to: Catalina Diver's Supply, PO Box 126, Avalon, CA 90704.

Catalina Scuba Luv, a PADI five-star facility, is also the largest shop on the island. They offer snorkeling and scuba tours, resort courses, retail sales, rentals, cameras, dry suits, rebreathers, Nitrox fills. Shark dives. ☎ 800-262-DIVE or 310-510-2350. E-mail: prneptune@aol.com. Website: www.padi.com.

West End Dive Center offers courses and boat trips to the best caves, reefs and kelp forests off the west end of the island. They have kayaking, scuba and snorkeling trips, beach dives, rentals, certification and refresher courses. Hotel-dive packages. ☎ 888-510-7979. Website: www.catalina.com.

Snorkeling Tours

Catalina Snorkeling Adventures, at Lover's Cove, provides gear rentals and tours. Open June through October. ☎ 877-SNORKEL.

Snorkeling Catalina features guided snorkeling trips to "hidden" Catalina coves. Trips depart daily from Joe's Rent-a-Boat on the Green Pleasure Pier in the middle of Avalon Harbor. $32 for adults, $22 for children. ☎ 310-510-0455. Website: www.flash.net/~snorkcat.

Wet Spot Rentals combines kayaking with a picnic lunch and snorkeling stops. Half-day costs $65, full day $95. Kayak rentals are available for $10 per hour for a single, $17 for a double or $30 and $50 per day. View-through boogie boards, wetsuits, fins and snorkeling gear are also offered. ☎ 310-510-2229. Website: www.catalina.com/wetspot.html. Write to: PO Box 231, Avalon, CA 90704.

Descanso Beach Ocean Sports, a short walk past the Catalina Casino building, rents kayaks, wetsuits and snorkel gear. The beach club restaurant and bar serves lunch. ☎ 310-510-1226. Website: www.catalina.com/CIX.html. Write to: Box 386, Avalon, CA 90704.

Accommodations

For a complete listing of hotels, campgrounds and inns, contact the **Catalina Island Visitors Bureau and Chamber of Commerce**. ☎ 310-510-1520, fax 310-510-7606. Website: www.catalina.com.

Rates vary dramatically with the season and availability. Check with individual hotels for current rates. Those listed are subject to change.

Catalina Express offers money-saving packages that may include round-trip boat passage from San Pedro.

Two- and three-night minimums are sometimes required for advance weekend reservations. Mid-week rates are lower than weekends. From November to February one night advance reservations are accepted by most hotels.

Some of the hotels frown heavily on scuba divers returning with dripping wetsuits, goodies bags and dive gear. If you are bringing your own gear and need to store it in your room, be sure to select an inn that specifies it is "diver-friendly."

Hotel Atwater sits in the heart of Avalon, just a stroll away from the beach. Walking distance to shops and restaurants. Twenty-four of their rooms have been remodeled. Suites have private baths, air-conditioning, color TV and cable; connecting rooms available. Bus tours are just across the street. Moderate. Major credit cards accepted. ☎ 800-446-0271.

Best Western Catalina Canyon Resort & Spa, Catalina's most complete resort and spa, features courtyard and mountain view rooms, many with private balconies. Rooms have tropical decor, cable TV, pool, sauna, jacuzzi. Packages. Open year-round. From $72.50. ☎ 800-253-9361.

Casa Mariquita Hotel sits one block from the beach, shops and restaurants. This lovely new Spanish-style hotel offers a friendly atmosphere. Air-conditioned rooms have cable TV, fridge, and phone. Packages offered year-round. Room rates from $75.50. ☎ 800-410-1192 or 310-510-1192, fax 310-510-2758.

Catalina Beach House Hotel, one block from the beach, features VCRs with free video library, kitchenettes, telephones, jacuzzi tubs and complimentary coffee. Free hotel shuttle. Packages available. Diver-friendly. Rooms from $50-$148. ☎ 800-97-HOTEL or 310-510-1078.

Catalina Island Inn, one-half block from the beach, is close to all the shops and restaurants. Newly redecorated in a tropical motif. King rooms feature a harbor view and balcony. Packages available. From $70. ☎ 800-246-8134.

Cloud "7" Hotel lies 400 feet from the beach, convenient to shops, restaurants and sightseeing. Air-conditioned rooms have TV, coffee brewer and refrigerator. From $75. ☎ 800-422-6836.

Hotel Villa Portofino, a charming hotel in the heart of Avalon, overlooks the bay. Amenities include a sundeck, restaurant, courtyards. Open year round. Rooms from $94. ☎ 800-346-2326 or 310-510-0555.

Hotel Vista Del Mar features oceanfront rooms, courtyard, fireplace, wet bar, refrigerator, full tile baths with skylighted dressing area, phone, A/C, TV, queen bed. From $85. ☎ 800-553-3481 or 310-510-1452.

LaPaloma Cottages have a New Orleans-style decor with iron balconies, vines, flowers. Rooms have private baths, queen beds. New units are non-smoking, with whirlpool tubs, VCR. Cleaning and storage facilities for divers. Low rates. ☎ 800-310-1505 or 310-5109-0737. E-mail: lapaloma@catalinas.net.

Seaport Village Inn, built in 1983, sits less than 400 steps from the beach, shops and restaurants. Choose from economy or luxury suites. All amenities.

New building for non-smokers. Diver-friendly services. Summer rates from $69 to $395. Packages. ☎ 800-2-CATALINA or 310-510-0344. E-mail: seaport@catalinas.net.

Snug Harbor Inn, Avalon's beachfront hotel ,features great views, jacuzzi tubs, fireplace, cable TV, telephone, king beds with down comforters. Rates higher weekends and in season. Rates from $104. ☎ 310- 510-8400. E-mail: snug@catalins/as.net.

West End

The historic **Banning House Lodge**, the sole inn at Two Harbors, features comfortable accommodations. Rates for two are from $119 to $191. ☎ 888-510-7979.

Intrepid divers wishing to explore the island's rugged West End will find tent cabins, tepees and tent sites at **Two Harbors Campground**, on the beach at Little Fisherman's Cove, a quarter-mile from the village of Two Harbors. Complete camping equipment rentals. ☎ 888-510-7979.

Other Activities

Hiking, fishing, tennis, golf, mountain biking and boating opportunities exist throughout Catalina. Rent paddle boards, pedal boats, small powerboats or row boats at **Joe's Rent-A-Boat** at the Avalon Pleasure Pier. Rent kayaks from **Descanso Beach Ocean Sports**, ☎ 510-1226. **Catalina Ocean Rafting** offers rafting trips, ☎ 800-990-RAFT or 310-510-0211. Website: www.catalina.com/OceanRaft.html. **Brown's Bikes** rents mountain bikes, beach cruisers, tandems, strollers and wheelchairs. ☎ 310-510-0986.

Hiking takes off from the Nature Center at Airport-In-the-Sky. Hiking into the interior requires a permit (no fee), which may be obtained at the Santa Catalina Island Conservancy's visitor office at 125 Claressa Avenue, Avalon. Permits are also required for biking ($50) and for camping the interior.

Take off with **Para-Sailing Catalina**, ☎ 510-1777, or tour the mountains on horseback. Guided trips leave from the **Catalina Stables**, ☎ 510-0478.

Catalina Island Golf Course caters to golfers of every skill level. Their unique nine-hole layout has been newly upgraded. Clubs and cart rentals. Pro shop sells clothing and equipment. ☎ 310-510-0530.

The Avalon Theatre in the Casino Building features nightly movies. ☎ 510-0179.

Yachting supplies and services are available in Avalon and at Two Harbors. Avalon is a no-discharge area and moorings are on a first-come, first-served basis. There are approximately 400 moorings at Avalon and 720 elsewhere in Catalina, including 249 at Isthmus Cove.

Sightseeing

The most famous sight has to be **The Casino Building**, Avalon's world-famous landmark and a stunning example of original Art Deco architecture. It houses a theater and ballroom. Located at the perimeter of the building is the **Catalina Island Museum**, the **Catalina Art Association Art Gallery** and a fitness center, as well as public restrooms. The Casino Ballroom, on the top floor, has been the site of major events since its grand opening in May of 1929.

Another favorite spot is **Airport-in-the-Sky** and the adjacent **Nature Center**. Owned and operated by the Santa Catalina Island Conservancy, the airport was built in the early 1940s at an elevation of 1,602 feet by leveling two mountain peaks. The airport's adobe-like architecture is enhanced by the native plant botanical gardens of the Nature Center. The airport sits 10 road miles from Avalon. Enter through the administration building, which features a native Indian artifacts display, the **Buffalo Springs Station Café**, a gift shop, and restrooms. Frequent bus service exists between the airport and Avalon. ☎ 310-510-2800 or 310-510-0143.

Discovery Tours, ☎ 310-510-TOUR, offers varied sightseeing opportunities. Their two-hour Skyline Drive Tour journeys 10 miles into Catalina's interior, where spectacular vistas, deep canyons, and buffalo await. Stops include the Catalina Nature Center at the Airport-in-the Sky. Adult $17, child (aged two-11)$8.50, senior (55+)$15.

Their 32-mile Motor Tour takes you to the Airport-in-the- Sky and Nature Center and along the island's Pacific side. A stop at El Rancho Escondido includes performances by Arabian horses, a chance to explore the trophy room of the prize-winning Wrigley Arabians and a browse through the Hidden Ranch Store. Adult $29.50, child $14.75, senior $26.

Discovery Tours also offers glass-bottom boat trips (adult $8.50, child $4.25, senior $7.50); Casino tours that visit the Avalon Theatre where Art Deco murals and a classic 1929 theater pipe organ, winding up in the world-famous Casino Ballroom (adult $8.50, child $4.25, senior $7.50). The most popular with divers and snorkelers is the Seal Rocks Cruise to the East End (no diving, just sightseeing; adult $8.50, child $4.25, senior $7.50).

Jeep Eco-Tours feature guided two-hour, half-day and full-day backroad nature tours to pristine beaches and awesome, near-vertical shoreline spots. Rates are $65 per person, two-passenger minimum, for the two-hour tour; $495 for the half-day, includes soft drinks and snacks for up to six passengers; $795 for the full-day, with lunch and soft drinks for up to six passengers. ☎ 310-510-2595, ext 0.

Dining

A variety of fine eateries, both plain and fancy, can be found on Catalina.

Sally's Waffle Shop features a variety of omelettes and waffles. It's on the beach next to Joe's Place at the foot of the Green Pleasure Pier. ☎510-0355.

Topless Taco's has a do-it-yourself buffet of toppings, homemade salsas, nachos, burgers, burritos, and more. Serve-yourself soda fountain. Eat in or take out.

Armstrong's Fish Market & Seafood Restaurant serves good mesquite-broiled seafood, steaks, chicken. Fresh sashimi, clams, oysters and mussels. Outdoor patio overlooks the bay. Full bar. Lunch from $6.95, dinner from $10.95. Located at 306 Crescent Ave. ☎ 510-0113.

The Blue Parrot Restaurant, overlooking Avalon Bay, serves American favorites. Lunch from $6.95, dinner from $11.95. Open seven days. It's located upstairs from the street entrance to Metropole Market Place. ☎ 510-2465.

The Busy Bee features ocean-view dining, breakfast, lunch and dinner. Drinks. Specialties include more than 100 items – large salads, fresh-ground burgers and fries. Stop by 306 Crescent.

Café Prego. Considered one of the best restaurants in Southern California by *LA Magazine*, this fine restaurant located on Crescent Avenue serves seafood, steak and Italian foods, including soup, hot bread and salad. Open 4:30 for dinner year-round. It's on the Bay at 603 Crescent. ☎ 510-1218, fax 310-510-2997.

Catalina Cantina, located on the boardwalk at 313 Crescent Ave, specializes in Mexican food and burgers. Full service bar. Great margaritas! Tops for people watching. Lunch from $5.95, dinner from $6.95. ☎ 510-0100.

Catalina Country Club, next to the golf course, is open to the public for dinner, lunch and cocktails. Outdoor patio. Lunch from $10.95, dinner from $15.95. ☎ 510-7404.

Coyote Joe's Restaurant & Bar offers Mexican and American food and drinks. Located one block up from the Green Pleasure Pier. Monday through Friday.

Descanso Beach Club features a delicious variety of appetizers, salads, sandwiches and charbroiled burgers, along with fresh fruit shakes. Open for lunch daily in summer. Weekends only during spring and fall. ☎ 310-510-1188.

Luau Larry's at 509 Crescent Ave, has ocean views, American food, tropical drinks, live music, and dancing. Lunch and dinner from $5. Sunday brunch from $11.95. ☎ 310-510-1919.

The Pancake Cottage serves breakfast and lunch. Favorites include omelettes, fresh fruit waffles, fresh squeezed orange juice, giant muffins. Open

6:30 am to 2 pm. Up the street from the Green Pier. 118 Catalina St. ☎ 310-510-0726.

Ristorante Villa Portofino offers award-winning regional Mediterranean cuisine – seafoods, pastas and fine wines. Casual oceanfront location. Rated "Avalon's Finest" by the *LA Times*. Dinner entrées from $8. ☎ 310-510-0508.

The Landing Bar & Grill/Kona Ken's in El Encanto Center on Avalon Harbor serves steaks, seafood, pasta, gourmet pizza; oyster bar, 14 micro beers on tap and super ocean view. ☎ 310-510-0486.

Facts

Recompression Chamber: A 24-hour chamber is located on Santa Catalina Island at the USC Wrigley Marine Science Center. For emergencies, ☎ 310-510-1053. For information, ☎ 310-510-0811.

Getting There: All major airlines service Los Angeles airport. From Los Angeles by car, take I-5 Freeway south and exit at the Pacific Coast Highway. Catalina Express provides boat transportation from both Long Beach and San Pedro Harbors. Travel time to Avalon is about one hour. Call for reservations, ☎ 310-519-1212.

Catalina Cruises offers year-round service from Long Beach Harbor. Travel time is one hour and 50 minutes. Reservations ☎ 800-228-2546. *Catalina Flyer* departs daily from Newport Beach's historic Balboa Pavilion. Travel time to Avalon is about 75 minutes. ☎ 714-673-5245.

Island Express Helicopter Service has daily flights from Long Beach Harbor (by the *Queen Mary*) and San Pedro, at the Catalina Terminal, ☎ 310-510-2525.

On-Island Transportation: Taxicabs, tram and bus services operate in Avalon. Most common modes of transportation are golf carts, bicycles and walking. Use of private automobiles is subject to city permit.

Catalina Safari Bus offers daily scheduled service in summer and weekends to the interior, ☎ 310-510-0303. Catalina Adventure Tours provides boat and bus trips, ☎ 310-510-0409. Tram, boat and taxi service to all points and places on Catalina is available through Catalina Transportation Co., ☎ 310-510-0025. Brown's Bikes rents bicycles, ☎310-510-0986.

Climate: Temperatures range between 50° and 68°F November through May.

Clothing: Lightweight during summer months with an extra sweater or jacket for cool evenings. Warmer fall clothing during winter months. A full quarter-inch wetsuit, with hood and booties, is needed for diving year-round.

For Additional Information: Catalina Island Chamber of Commerce and Visitors Bureau, PO Box 217, Avalon CA 90704. ☎ 310-510-1520, fax 510-7606. E-mail: info@catalinas.net. Website: www.catalina.com.

The Galapagos Islands

The Galapagos, a chain of mountainous volcanic islands, straddle the equator 650 miles west of mainland Ecuador. Thirteen major islands, six smaller ones and countless rocks rise from the Pacific Ocean to sprawl over 30,000 square miles. Only five islands are inhabited.

The United Nations Educational, Scientific and Cultural Organization (UNESCO) lists the Galapagos as a World Heritage Site. Equador declared the area a national park in 1959.

A Living Laboratory of Evolution

© Marc Bernardi, Aquatic Adventures

Over millions of years the winds and ocean currents carried animals and plants to the Galapagos. These species adapted to the Galapagos' rugged conditions and came to differ more and more from their continental ancestors. Today, many of the animals and plants that have evolved in the Galapagos never existed elsewhere. Different forms of the same species have evolved on different islands. More than 25% of the animals in the Galapagos live nowhere else on earth. Charles Darwin, observing the unique plant and animal life when he visited the archipelago in 1835 aboard the research ship *Beagle*, began to develop his theory of evolution. Darwin's visit to the Galapagos is regarded as a landmark in the history of science. He describes the Galapagos as a "living laboratory of evolution" in his book, *On the Origin of the Species.*

Marine Life

Intrepid divers and snorkelers who journey here experience an amazing panoply of sea life and birds. Fur seals, sea lions, penguins, bottle-nosed dolphins, colonies of huge moray eels, marine iguanas, red-lipped batfish, Sally Lightfoot crabs, octopi, Moorish idols and king angelfish are abundant. Five convening ocean currents, dominated by the icy Humboldt, bring in huge schools of hammerheads, whale sharks, giant sea turtles, groupers and pelagic fish, such as amber jack and barracuda. Plankton blooms attract manta and eagle rays. Orcas are occasionally spotted offshore.

Photo ©Marc Bernadi, Aquatic Encounters

Sealions on Rabida, a small islet off James Island.

Land Dwellers

Thousands of seabird nests crowd the islands' rocky cliffs and shores. Albatross, frigate birds, blue-footed boobies and the infamous Galapagos tortoise provide endless film and video subjects. Because the islands were uninhabited by humans when they were discovered in 1535, many of the animals had no instinctive fear of man. Many are still extraordinarily fearless.

Today, environmentalists concerns center on rapidly multiplying goat herds that compete with native wildlife for food. Some environmentalists have taken to shooting the goats. Fishermen poaching rare sea cucumbers, considered an aphrodisiac by some, are another ecological fear. One government attempt to restrict local fishermen from taking sea cucumbers resulted in an armed takeover of the Darwin Research Station on Santa Cruz.

When to Go

The best time to dive the Galapagos, especially if you want to visit the northern islands (Darwin & Wolf), is during December and January or May through June. These four months bring the doldrums, calmer seas, less wind, weaker currents.

Overall, the islands have two seasons. A hot, rainy season from January through May that brings the calmest seas, with water temperatures hovering around 70°F. Marine life is excellent, with manta rays, shark and schooling

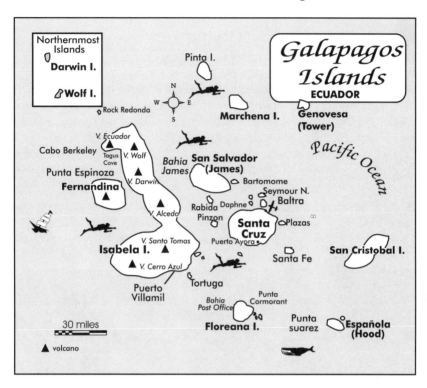

pelagic fish sightings. The days are hot and sunny; air temperatures average in the high 80s. Island tours are limited to 30 minutes, sometimes less. Sunburn is a major problem. The skies are often clear, but occasional heavy downpours are common. Many animals leave the trail areas. Some leave the islands until cooler weather returns.

June through December brings cooling winds and a light drizzle called "garua." The thermometer hangs around the mid-70s during the day, lower at night. Island topside tours are extended.

Between October and December seal pups are abundant, booby, frigate and albatross chicks can be seen. Underwater, shark sightings are good, but ray sightings are less frequent.

Getting to the Islands

Visitors arrive by plane on Baltra Island, where they are met by their guide and ship or yacht. Some of the islands have docks or dry landing areas while others have "wet landings" that require wading through the shallows to land. Bring two pairs of sneakers and three times as much film as you originally planned.

Diving

Divers should be in excellent physical condition and have recent experience in open-ocean diving. Unpredictable sea conditions bring swells, surges and currents strong enough to pull a diver's mask off. Visibility can drop from 60 ft to 20 ft in seconds. Changing currents, surges of fast-moving water and varying sea conditions make this a bad choice for new divers. Don't go if you're not an experienced open-ocean diver who likes adventurous vacations. This is not the best place for your first ocean dive, but it is a wonderful, special place for experienced divers. If you lack open-ocean experience, consider one of the less de- manding snorkeling and top- side expeditions.

Water temperatures vary from 65°F to 75° during August and September – the cooler months – and seldom rise above 80° at other times of the year. Thermoclines may lower the temperatures further. A three-sixteenths-inch

Photo ©Marc Bernadi, Aquatic Encounters

Giant tortoise on Santa Cruz.

Photo ©Marc Bernadi; Aquatic Encounters

full wet suit with an optional hooded vest is good most of the year. A quarter-inch wet suit works. Gloves are recommended at all times.

Divers should carry a loud surface signaling device on *every* dive. Circular currents and down currents are not uncommon and it is easy to get separated quite far from your group and boat. Visibility averages 50 ft.

Most week-long dive trips are either to Wolf and Darwin, the two northernmost islands, where high-voltage shark diving is assured. These are located about 100 miles or 20 hours by boat from the central islands, or the central southernmost islands – Santa Cruz, San Salvador and Isla Santa Maria.

Much of the diving is done from inflatables. Some have no ladders and require muscle and a big fin kick to get back in.

Best Dives of the Galapagos

Unique marine animals inhabit the Galapagos. Throngs of red lipped batfish color the waters off Marchena Island. Hammerhead sharks frequent Isabela, Marchena and are always seen at Darwin and Wolf. Penguins inhabit Bartholome Island. Mammoth, 50-ft whale sharks dwarf divers off Darwin and Wolf Islands.

 Wolf and Darwin Islands are for scuba diving only, visitors are not permitted on land. They are not protected from waves and trips are weather-dependent.

☆☆☆☆☆ **Darwin Island**, the most remote of the Galapagos, requires a 12- to 20-hour boat trip from Baltra. This area offers "high voltage" diving, with schools of hammerhead sharks, fur seals, dolphins, turtles, eagle rays, moray eels and an occasional whale shark. Lots of birds on the island. Currents may be stiff.

☆☆☆☆☆ **Wolf Island**, also in the northern sector, features more hammerheads at Shark Bay. Sting rays, dolphins, moray eels, hawksbill turtles and large schools of barracudas are often encountered. At least one operator runs a night dive to an underwater cave. Sea conditions vary. Currents may be stiff.

☆☆☆☆☆ **Cousins Dive Site**, off Isla Santiago, east of James Island, features a series of lava shelves that start at 15 ft, then shelve off in 10-15-ft increments down to about 150 ft. Masses of grunt-like salemas (native to the Galapagos) inhabit the area. Sea lions feeding off the schooling fish are common. King angelfish are often spotted, as are Galapagos sharks and jacks. Big black coral bushes adorn the ledges. This area is usually calmer, with less current than other spots.

Sea lions are very mischievous and they make the rules. Expect them to charge straight at you, take a nip at your arm or leg, tug on your wetsuit, pull off your mask if you let them – sometimes you can't stop them. If you don't want their full attention, keep your distance. During mating season the males may be aggressive. Give them space.

☆☆☆☆☆ The wildlife and conditions at **North Seymour Channel**, off Santa Cruz, depend on the currents. If a surge of nutrient-rich water blasts by, you will be in diver's Eden, awestruck by an influx of thousands of jacks, rainbow wrasses and reef shark. Visibility may drop from 70 ft to 20 ft and back again. Wedge into a crevice and watch the action shoot by. The bottom at 50-ft harbors a huge colony of garden eels.

☆☆☆☆☆ **Gordon Rocks** seem tame enough when you view them from the boat, but lookout below. The currents spin with hammerheads, reef sharks, turtles, and endless schooling fish. This is not a dive for the timid. Locals call it the "dishwasher." Expect strong currents.

☆☆☆☆ **Devil's Crown**, a few hundred yards offshore from Floreana, features a spectacular array of tropical fish, Galapagos sharks, sea lions, green sea turtles, eagle rays, marbled groupers and Moorish idols. The site encompasses two main pinnacle rocks separated by a sand channel. Depths average 40 ft. Expect fast currents.

Sightseeing

Both Spanish and English names are used interchangeably for the islands.

Santa Cruz (Indefatigable), the hub of the Galapagos, offers the most creature comforts and tourist amenities. It is home to the Charles Darwin Research Station at Puerto Ayora, where visitors can tour the Galapagos tortoise rearing pens. There is also the Tortoise Reserve, where mammoth 200-year-old tortoises roam free.

Small restaurants and shops offering post cards and T-shirts are at Puerto Ayora, a short walk from the research station.

Observe colonies of land iguanas and several different shallow-water birds at Dragon Hill on the northwest end of the island.

Isla Santiago (James), a four- to five-hour cruise north of Santa Cruz, is home to fur seals and flamingos at Puerto Egas. The flamingos feed at a salt extraction pit in a crater that lies a few miles from the coast. Espumilla Beach on Santiago also shelters flocks of flamingos. Wet landings at Sullivan Bay. Good snorkeling among the lava formations. The fur seals will jump in to swim with you.

Land iguanas and flamingos reside on Dragon Hill. Darwin's finches, mocking birds and yellow warblers live in the highlands.

Isla Bartolome (Bartholomew) is blessed with a dry landing site. Climb up a big staircase to the summit for a nice view of the area. Penguins and sea lions hang out around Pinnacle Rock. Sandy beach with good swimming and snorkeling.

Isla Floreana (Charles), one of the larger islands south of Santa Cruz and Isabela, features "The Barrel," a do-it-yourself postal service set up by 18th-century whalers that still works! Be sure to bring a stamped postcard along to try it out. The island also has a sandy beach at Point Cormorant, where sea turtles come ashore to lay eggs. An inland tidal pool shelters flamingos and other wading birds. Sea lion colonies haul out at nearby Loberla islet.

Isla Espanola (Hood), one of the southernmost islands, features a coral sand beach, sea lions, Sally Lightfoot crabs and several species of birds, including waved albatrosses, blue-footed boobies, masked boobies, swallow-tailed gulls, mockingbirds and cactus finches. Nice snorkeling at the beach and nearby islets.

At Punta Suarez, you walk on lava rocks along a trail edged with blue-footed and masked booby nests, colonies of marine iguanas and waved albatrosses. Sea lions, Darwin's finches and Galapagos doves are also on the island.

Isabela (Albemarle) is the largest of the Galapagos Islands. It boasts a dry landing. Inland, a steep, uphill climb takes you to Darwins' Saltwater Crater Lake. Penguins, flightless cormorants, boobies, pelicans and Sally Lightfoot Crabs patrol the beaches.

Galapagos Islands

Photo ©Marc Bernadi, Aquatic Encounters

Mosquera, a tiny islet, is home to a huge colony of sea lions that haul out in the sun. Give them a good deal of space during mating season and when pups are born.

North Seymour, a little island north of Sant Cruz and Baltra, is a good place to observe blue-footed boobies and frigate birds. Sea lions haul out on the windward side of the island.

San Cristobal, capital of the archipelago, is rarely visited by tour boats.

Genovesa (Tower) is noted for an incredible number of birds – frigate birds, red-footed boobies, lava gulls, doves, stormy petrels, noddy terns and Darwin's finches. There is a wet landing at Darwin Bay, which was formed by a collapsed volcano and a dry landing at Prince Phillip's Steps, where you'll find great snorkeling.

Live-Aboards

All prices subject to change. Call each operator for current rates. In addition to the cost of the live-aboard stay, expect to pay airfare from Ecuador to the islands (about $400 round-trip), a $100 entrance fee to the National Park, which encompasses all the islands and a crew tip of about $100 (cash or travelers checks) per diver. A departure tax of $25 must be paid in cash.

Getting all your luggage and gear to Equador, then to the Galapagos, can be laden with hazards. Visitors should buy cancellation insurance, DAN insurance, and baggage insurance – available through most tour operators.

Photo ©Marc Bernadi, Aquatic Encounters

Dive yacht Reina Silvia.

Land-based accommodations on the islands are limited. Most divers opt for tours aboard one of the live-aboard motor or sailing yachts. Snorkelers can join tours on the dive yachts, but will find snorkeling excursions offered by the government-sponsored cruise ships too. Airline and boat schedules always require an overnight stay on the mainland. Flights from the US arrive in either Guayaquil or Quito, Ecuador's capital city.

The 90-ft motor yacht **Reina Silvia** carries up to 16 divers in eight air-conditioned cabins with roomy, comfortable upper and lower bunks. The owner's cabin located on the upper deck, with a king-size bed, is available upon request. Each stateroom has its own private shower and bath. The yacht has a swimming/diving platform aft and an extended bow pulpit for whale and dolphin watching. It also features a stereo system with semi-individual controls, cassette and compact disc players, TV and VCR. A desalinator provides all the fresh water needed. The nine-person crew includes three dive masters, a multilingual naturalist-guide and a gourmet chef, who bakes brownies, pizza, cookies and other treats after every dive. Meals are excellent, varying from steak to fresh fish or lobster, with plenty of fruits and snacks in a spacious dining room. This boat tours only when the doldrums occur – December, January, May and June – to assure divers a look at both the northern and southern islands. Diving is off either an inflatable or wooden "panga" (Spanish for dinghy), guided or non-guided as you prefer. Tours include a good deal of topside sightseeing.

Galapagos Islands

Book through **Aquatic Encounters**, owned by dive master and underwater photographer Marc Bernardi, who is an expert on Galapagos diving, having made 34 trips to the islands. The base price of $3,125 per person includes four nights in a deluxe hotel in Quito, seven nights aboard the *Reina Silvia*, all meals aboard the boat, use of tanks and weights (no belts), transfers to hotels and back in Quito. NOT included are airfare to Equador or the islands. ☎ 800-757-1365, pin code 1815 or 303-494-8384, fax 303-494-1202. E-mail: aquatenctr@aol.com. Website: www.Aquatic Encounters.com. Write to: Aquatic Encounters Inc., 1966 Hardscrabble Place, Boulder, CO 80303. Free video available.

Lammer Law is a luxurious 95-ft trimaran sailing yacht that accommodates up to 18 guests in nine lovely, air-conditioned staterooms. Each cabin features a queen-sized bed that converts to twins, a private bath with flush toilet and shower. Fresh water is desalinized on board. A crew of nine caters to guests' needs. Tours are around the Central Islands. Trips to Wolf and Darwin are only made on specially designated itineraries. One land visit is made each day to a different island. An audiovisual entertainment center includes a VCR and television to relive the day's adventures. Credit cards are not accepted on the boat. Cruises cost $2,530 for seven nights, $3,614 for 10 nights. Whole-boat charters cost $40,450 for 18 people, seven nights. Book through Landfall Dive and Travel, ☎ 916-929-5555, fax 916-925-0958. E-mail: lwhillock@pattersontravel.com. Website: www. landfallproductions. com. Write to: 39675 Cedar Blvd., Ste 295B, Newark, CA 94560.

Galapagos Aggressors I & II, each 80 ft in length, are designed to pamper 14 guests in seven air-conditioned cabins. Staterooms feature a bath and radio/cassette player. Eight crew members provide services. Large TV in the salon. Divers each get their own locker to store gear. Film processing and camera rentals available on board. Offers more land tours for non divers. Seven nights costs $2,600. Make sure you specify "scuba charter" when you book. Hassle-free arrangements are offered by Landfall Dive and Adventure Travel, ☎ 916-929-5555, fax 916-925-0958. E-mail: lwhillock@patterson travel.com. Website: www. landfallproductions.com. Write to: 39675 Cedar Blvd., Ste 295B, Newark, CA 94560.

The Mistral II is a 74-ft luxury yacht that carries up to 12 passengers in six air-conditioned staterooms, each with private facilities. Specify "scuba charter." A seven-night stay with meals and two to three dives daily costs $2,100 (may change). The boat tours the central southern islands. Book through Landfall Dive and Adventure Travel, ☎ 916-929-5555, fax 916-925-0958. E-mail: lwhillock@pattersontravel.com. Website: www.landfallproductions.com. Write to: 39675 Cedar Blvd., Ste 295B, Newark, CA 94560.

Photo ©Marc Bernadi, Aquatic Encounters

Snorkeling Only

The Oceanic Society offers naturalist-led expeditions aboard *Tip Top II*, a comfortable yacht that accommodates 12 in six cabins. No scuba diving, but ample opportunity for snorkeling. For dates and costs contact Oceanic Society Expeditions, Fort Mason Center, Building E, San Francisco, CA 94123. Trips depart Miami or Los Angeles airport; rates from $3,390, including air from gateway cities. ☎800-326-7491 or 415-441-1106, fax 415-474-3395.

Metropolitan Touring operates three ships that carry up to 90 passengers, the recently renovated *Santa Cruz*, the *Isabela II* and the *Delfin II*, which combine tours with the Delfin Hotel on Isla Santa Cruz. No scuba diving , but snorkelers combining an-island-to-island tour will find plenty of snorkeling opportunities at the islands where it is allowed. Week-long trips from Sunday to Sunday cost from $1,616 per person for a double on the *Delfin*, from $2,955 per person on the *Isabela II*, from $3,010 on the *Santa Cruz*. Low season – March 16-June 14 and September 1-October 31 – cost less. Children under 12 sharing room with parents get 50% off. Book through Adventure Associates, ☎ 800-527-2500 or 972-907-0414, fax 972-783-1286. E-mail: info@ecuadorable.com. Website: www.ecuadorable.com.

Galapagos National Park Rules

1. No plant, animal, or remains of them (shells, bones, pieces of wood) or other natural objects should be removed or disturbed.

2. Do not transport any live material to the islands, or from island to island. Check your clothing before landing on any of the islands for seeds or insects and destroy them or keep them on your vessel for disposal later. Check your boot or shoe soles for dried mud before you leave your boat; this material will frequently contain seed and spores of plants and animals.

3. Do not take any food to the uninhabited islands. It is easy to introduce, together with the food, insects or other organisms that might be dangerous to the island ecosystems. The orange seed that you drop may become a tree.

4. Animals may not be touched or handled.

5. Animals may not be fed.

6. Do not startle or chase any animal from its resting or nesting spot. Exercise extreme care among the breeding colonies of sea birds. Be especially careful not to drive boobies, cormorants, gulls, or frigate birds from their nests. These birds will fly up if startled, often knocking the egg or chick to the ground or leaving it exposed to the sun. (A newly hatched booby chick will die in 20-30 minutes if exposed to the sun; frigate birds will also eat any unguarded chick).

7. Do not leave the areas designated as visiting sites. Stay on marked trails.

8. Litter must be kept off the islands. Disposal at sea must be limited to certain types of garbage only and in selected areas only. Keep rubbish (film wrappers, cigarette butts, chewing gum, tin cans, bottles) in a bag or pocket, to be disposed of on your boat.

Never throw anything overboard – sea lions will pick a tin can off the bottom and play with it, cutting their sensitive muzzles. Sea turtles, whales and mammals will eat plastic thrown overboard and die, for it blocks their digestive tract.

9. Do not buy souvenirs or objects made from plants or animals of the islands, with the exception of articles made from wood.

10. Do not paint names or graffiti on rocks.

13. All groups must be accompanied by a qualified guide approved by the national park.

15. Do not hesitate to show your conservationist attitude. Notify the National Park Service if you see any serious damage being done.

Facts

Nearest Recompression Chamber: None in the Galapagos, but the Ecuadorian navy operates one in Guayaquil and will send a small plane to Baltra for air evacuation. Getting to Baltra may be a problem as the northern islands are a 20-hour boat trip away. The southern islands are a few hours from each other too. At this writing, divers must pay some of the cost with cash up front or may be refused treatment. Prevention is best. The dive boats avoid repetitive dives and insist on the use of computers.

Getting There: Continental Airlines, ☎ 800-525-0280, American Airlines, ☎ 800-525-0280, Aerolinas Argentinas, Ecuatoriana and Salta.

Documents: Travelers must be in possession of a current passport. Some tour companies ask that it be valid for six months beyond the date of arrival.

Customs: US citizens are allowed to take back $400 worth of goods per person, duty-free. The next $1,000 worth is charged at a rate of 10%. Avoid products derived from any animal classified as endangered, black coral, tortoise shells, whalebone or sea lion teeth, certain skins or furs.

Cameras, computers and dive equipment should be registered with customs before you leave the US.

Currency: Ecuador's monetary unit is the sucre, which fluctuates frequently. Paper bills are available in 5, 10, 20, 100, 500, 1,000, 5,000 and 10,000 sucre notes. There is a one sucre coin. Smaller coins are called centavos. One US $ is equal to approximately 4,100 sucres at press time. All banks and exchange houses accept and exchange US dollars at similar rates.

Language: Ecuador has two official languages, Spanish and Quechua, the *lingua franca* of the Inca Empire. English is spoken in major visitor centers.

Departure Tax: $25 (must be paid in cash) US $ or sucres.

Climate: The average temperature in the Galapagos from December through May is 85°F. February is the hottest month. Between June and November, air temperatures hover in the 70s.

Clothing: Two bathing suits and casual lightweight sportswear cover most occasions on live-aboards. For hiking bring long-sleeved shirts, lightweight long pants, a rain jacket or plastic poncho, shoes suitable for wading, and sturdy hiking shoes.

Toiletries: Be sure to bring all toiletries you might need and a small first-aid kit. Don't forget the band-aids, antibiotic ointment, aspirin, sunburn cream, sunblock, sunglasses, shampoo and a seasickness preventative medicine.

Time: Ecuadorian time is one hour earlier than New York. The Galapagos are on the same as New York time.

Drinking Water: Unsafe on mainland Ecuador. Drink only bottled water. Live-aboards have their own desalinization equipment so there's always plenty of fresh water.

Electricity: 11 volts, 60 cycles in mainland Ecuador.

Additional Information: Contact the tour operators listed under "Live-Aboards"– Aquatic Encounters, ☎ 303-494-8384, fax 303-494-1202; Landfall Dive and Adventure Travel, ☎ 800-525-3833 or 510-794-1599; Adventure Associates, ☎ 800-527-2500 or 214-907-0414, fax 214-783-1286. Special Expeditions also offers cruises with snorkeling, ☎ 800-425-2724. Also try Oceanic Society Expeditions, ☎ 800-326-7491 or 415-441-1106, fax 415-474-3395. If you want to plan a stay on land, contact your local travel agent.

Galapagos Islands

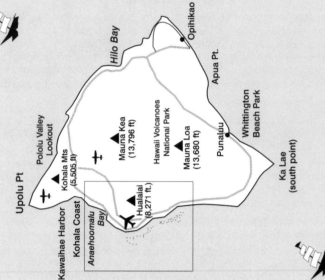

Hawaii
KONA COAST
HAWAII

Kona Coast
Dive & Snorkeling Sites
1. Anaehoomalu Bay
2. Kaiwi
3. Casa Cave
4. Manta Rays
5. Red Hill
6. Aquarium
7. Palimono Point

Kealakekua Bay
State Underwater
Park

Kailua Kona
Kahaluu
Keauhou

INSET

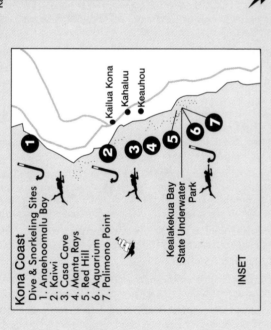

Upolu Pt

Kawaihae Harbor

Kohala Coast

Anaehoomalu Bay

Pololiu Valley Lookout

Kohala Mts (5,505 ft)

Hualalai (8,271 ft.)

Mauna Kea (13,796 ft)

Hawaii Volcanoes National Park

Mauna Loa (13,680 ft)

Hilo Bay

Opihikao

Apua Pt.

Punaluu

Whittington Beach Park

Ka Lae (south point)

Hawaii

Hawaii's six main islands – Kauai, Oahu, Maui, Molokai, Lanai and Hawaii – are unparalleled in beauty, with volcanic mountains, swaying palms, wild orchids, exotic plants and spectacular black and white sand beaches. Inland, sugarcane plantations and pineapple fields stretch for miles.

Underwater Hawaii offers a magical world of lava tubes, tunnels, archways, cathedrals, caves, and reefs. Thirty percent of Hawaii's marine life exists nowhere else on earth. Giant sea turtles, eagle rays, squid, the Hawaiian turkeyfish, dolphins, whales, crustaceans, octopi, large tiger cowries and tame morays abound in the crystal waters. Sunken tanks and jeeps, abandoned after World War II, lie motionless on the ocean floor, camouflaged with layers of coral, sponges and barnacles.

Oahu, the Big Island

Oahu, the undisputed vacation capital of Hawaii is home to Honolulu and Waikiki Beach. Miles of high rise-hotels create a luminescent skyline along its shoreline. Honolulu, the cultural center, entertains visitors with concerts, dance performances, live theater and fine restaurants. Outside Honolulu, small communities dot the coutryside. Nuuanu Pali Lookout provides a panoramic view of the windward side of the island. At Makapuu Point daring hang-gliders soar from towering cliffs while expert body-surfers ride the crashing waves. On the leeward side of Waianae Range, small towns and wide beaches line the coastline. North shore snorkeling is excellent during summer when the seas are calm.

Best Dives of Oahu

☆☆☆ **Hanauma Bay** on the southeast shore of Oahu is the most popular diving and snorkeling site in all of Hawaii. It is a state marine preserve hosting over a million visitors each year. Formed from an ancient volcanic crater, the bay is lined with a shallow inner reef that starts at 10 ft and slopes down to an outer reef at a depth of 70 ft.

Many snorkeling sites are accessible from the beach, but the outer reefs, which have superb visibility and feature dramatic coral seascapes, are reachable only by boat. Friendly fish.

☆☆ **Sea Cave**. Just west of Hanauma Bay, a large cavern at 60 ft hosts various sharks and occasional octopi.

☆☆☆ **Maunalua Bay**, west of Hanauma, offers a variety of dives. Green sea turtles of all sizes are commonly seen in Turtle Canyon. The bottom is var-

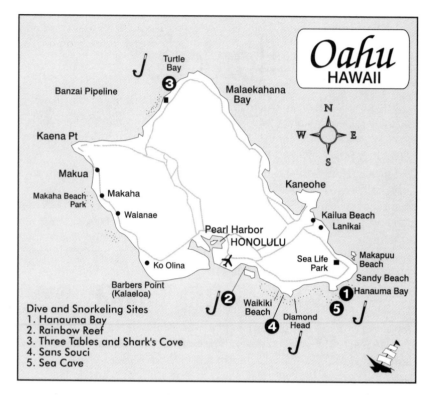

Oahu
HAWAII

Turtle Bay

Banzai Pipeline

Malaekahana Bay

Kaena Pt

N
W — E
S

Makua

Kaneohe

Makaha Beach Park

Makaha

Waianae

Kailua Beach
Lanikai

Pearl Harbor
HONOLULU

Ko Olina

Sea Life Park

Makapuu Beach

Barbers Point
(Kalaeloa)

Sandy Beach
Hanauma Bay

Waikiki Beach

Diamond Head

Dive and Snorkeling Sites
1. Hanauma Bay
2. Rainbow Reef
3. Three Tables and Shark's Cove
4. Sans Souci
5. Sea Cave

ied, with lava flow ridges and sandy canyons. **Big Eel Reef** shelters green and spotted moray eels and eagle rays. Dramatic lava ledges and archways form **Fantasy Reef**, on the western end of Maunalua Bay. Barracuda routinely drift by and big eels and lobsters live under the ledges. *Kahala Barge*, lying in 80 ft of water, is a 200-ft barge that was sunk to create an artificial reef. Still intact, pilothouse and all, it is frequented by large green sea turtles, amberjacks, butterflyfish, angelfish and Moorish idols. The top of the wreck is at 50 ft.

☆☆☆ **100 Ft Hole**, a lava formation creating a salt-water oasis a mile offshore. Marine life includes an eight-ft moray eel, lobsters, crabs, white-tip sharks, and tropicals. Depths range between 65 and 85 ft.

☆☆☆ **Shark Cove** on the northwest shore, is Oahu's most popular cavern dive. Light shimmering through openings in the tops of the caves resembles a stained-glass window. Depths range from 15 to 60 ft. Many arches and lava tubes. Only experienced divers accompanied by a professional guide should attempt Shark Cove. Diveable only during summer months. Extremely rough surf and strong currents from October through April.

☆☆ **Rainbow Reef**, just west of Waikiki Beach, is a favorite dive and snorkeling site for beginners. The reef begins at 10 ft and slopes to 30 ft. Also known as Magic Island, Rainbow Reef vibrates with hundreds of tame tropicals, including fantail file fish, parrot fish, triggerfish, surgeon fish, and porcupine puffers.

☆☆☆ **Three Tables**, part of Pupukea Marine Life Conservation District north of Waimea Bay, takes its name from a trio of flat rocks that break the surface close to the beach. Divers can explore large rock formations, caverns, arches, lava tubes and ledges. Beach access is easy. Depth 15 to 45 ft. Diveable only during summer months. Extremely rough surf and strong currents from October through April.

Oahu Dive Operators

Aaron's Dive Shop, 602 Kailua Road, Kailua HI 96734. ☎ 888-847-2822 or 808-262-2333. E-mail: aarons@aloha.com. Website: www.aloha.com/~aarons.

Dive Oahu offers dive trips that change with each season. Call for current locations. ☎ 808-235-9453. Website: diveoahu.com.

Reef Trekkers Hawaii-Scuba Diving Tours, 444 Lunalilo Home Road, Honolulu, HI 96825. Romulo Britto, Manager. In addition to English, staff are fluent in French, German, Portuguese and Spanish. ☎ 877-359-7333 or 808-943-0588. E-mail: dive@reeftrekkers.com. Website: www.reeftrekkers.com.

South Seas Aquatics, offers special tours for beginners as well as seasoned divers aboard a custom-built 44-ft dive vessel. This shop tries to avoid the crowds off the west shore. Owner, Masao Nakana. Rental, sales, repair and certification services. Located at 1050 Ala Moana Blvd., Honolulu, HI 96814. ☎ 808-538-3854. South Seas Aquatics' second location is 870 Kapahulu Avenue, No. 109, Honolulu, HI 96816. ☎ 800-252-6244 or 808-526-9550.

Oahu Accommodations

Oahu boasts tremendously diverse accommodations. For a complete list contact the Oahu Visitors Bureau at ☎ 800-624-8678 or 800-GO-HAWAII. Website: www.hawaii.gov/tourism/.

Nuhua Condominium Suites, 444 Nahua, Waikiki, are low-cost units with parking, pool, TV and kitchens. ☎ 800-446-6248, fax: 310-544-1643. Website: www.444nuhua.com.

Outrigger Waikiki, on Waikiki Beach. Five restaurants and nightly entertainment. Rooms $175-$530. ☎ 800-688-7444, fax 800-662-4852. Website: www.outrigger.com.

Hawaii

Maui, the Valley Isle

The West Maui mountains and the mountain of Haleakala cover most of Maui. Haleakala rises to 10,000 ft. Hiking here, especially at sunrise, is more of an "encounter" than a sport. Visitors enjoy wandering along the "road to Hana," a remote town on the windward side of Haleakala, passing bamboo forests, waterfalls and gardens of wild fruits and flowers. On the northwest side of Maui you can explore Lahaina, an old whaling village. Lahaina Harbor bustles with yachts from all over the world.

Maui County offers a variety of diving and snorkeling sites. It is also a jumping-off point for dive tours to the islands of Lanai, Molokai and Molokini Crater. At these out-island dive sites, you'll see creatures rarely seen elsewhere, docile 50-foot whale sharks and, during the winter months, humpback whales. Dive and snorkel operations are concentrated in the main resort areas of Wailea/Kihei and Lahaina. Side trips to Molokini and other nearby sites take 15 to 30 minutes; trips across the channel to Lanai and Molokai can take 1½ hours.

Best Dives of Maui

☆☆☆☆ **Molokini Crater**, a crescent-shaped island two miles from Maui, is Maui's most popular dive site. Expect to see as many as 30 or 40 dive boats anchored here at one time.

Formed by the top of an old volcanic crater, this unique site combines many ecosystems within a small area: deep water, shallow reef, flowing and still waters, with their natural complements of marine animals.

Marine life and sub-seascapes fascinate photographers and explorers alike. Dive or snorkel inside or outside the crater in the shallows or along the walls and drop-offs. Whales, porpoises and unusual marine animals are common. Armies of lemon butterfly fish, large ulua and surgeonfish greet divers. Depths range from 10 ft near the shore to about 80 ft. Drop-offs go as deep as 200 ft. Good visibility. Plan a morning trip, seas are rougher in the afternoon.

☆☆☆☆ **Moku Ho'oniki**, a small island off the eastern end of Molokai, is accessible only when the trade winds are not blowing. Eagle rays, jacks and scorpionfish. Many pelagics, including hammerheads and gray reef sharks. Depths from 40 to 100 ft and usually some current. Calmest in spring and fall.

☆☆☆ **Grand Canyon**, an enormous underwater canyon off Lanai's southern end, is bordered by towering walls of lava. Huge turtles and rays glide along the canyon's bottom. Parrot fish of all colors, triggerfish and surgeonfish hover near the ledges. Shrimp and squirrel fish peek from crevices. Depths from 20 to 100 ft.

☆☆☆ **First and Second Cathedrals**, also off Lanai, feature pinnacles rising from 60 ft to just below the surface. Far below, in spacious caverns that loom like cathedrals, there are lobsters, ghost shrimp, spotted moray eels, and eagle rays. Do not attempt to dive these caverns unless you're accompanied by a very experienced local guide. Morning is recommended since afternoon currents are sometimes treacherous. Visibility is excellent during periods of calm water and weather.

☆☆ **Tank and Landing Craft**, a 60-ft drift dive, starts at a US Army tank and drifts to a landing craft off the Southwest Mehena coastline of Maui. Numerous Army relics are strewn across the bottom. Once you near the site, large trumpet fish will dangle in front of your mask. Other denizens include schools of tropical fish tame enough for handfeeding, lemon butterfly fish, scorpion fish, goat fish, leaf fish and flounders. Usually calm seas.

☆☆☆ **Hawaiian Reef** sits between Maui and Molokini crater. The reef consists of numerous lava formations that rise 20 ft from the sandy bottom. Large antler coral trees line the base of the reef. Big schools of blue lined snappers, large shells and eagle rays are common residents. Pelagic fish are seen also. Seldom visited by divers. Depth 65-85 ft. The sea is usually calm, although an occasional current may be running.

☆☆ **Banyon Tree Reef** sits off Maui's southwest Makena shore. A number of patch reefs rise 15 ft off the bottom, with several large antler coral trees and lots of fish. Superb for invertebrate photos. Depth 50-65 ft.

Hawaii

Maui & Lanai
HAWAII

Molokai

Pailolo Channel

Honolua Bay · lighthouse

Black Rock

Kapalua

Kahului Bay

Hookipa Beach Park

Polihua Beach

Shipwreck Beach

Keomuku Village

Kaanaplai
Lahaina
Olowalu

Paia
Sprecklesville

Keanae Point
Wailua

Lanai

Lanai City

Kaumaiapau Harbor

Auau Channel

Maui

Kihei

Wailea

Hana

Sweetheart Rock

Maalaea

Molokini Island

Makena

Haleakala National Park

Kipahulu

Ahihi Bay

Alenuihaha Channel

Kahoolawe

Pacific Ocean

Dive and Snorkeling Sites
1. Black Rock
2. Molokini Crater
3. Sharfin Rock
4. Grand Canyon
5. First and Second Cathedrals
6. Moku Ho'oniki
7. Tank and Landing Craft
8. Hawaiin Reef
9. Banyon Tree Reef

Dive Operators of Maui

Ed Robinson's Diving Adventures. Ed Robinson has been diving and photographing the reefs off Maui since 1971. His photographs have appeared in over a hundred publications, including *National Geographic*, *Oceans* and *Islands* magazine. The shop caters to scuba divers, but welcomes snorkelers who are accompanying divers with a reduced rate. PO Box 616, Kihei HI 96753. ☎ 800-635-1273, fax 808-874-1939. E-mail: info@ mauiscuba.net. Website: www.maui.net/~robinson/erda.html.

Dive Maui/Offshore Adventures, owner Leslie Sternberg knows of many dive spots right off the beach where guests can join huge turtles and hundreds of different reef fish. They offer regular dive tours and dedicated snorkel trips. Snorkel trip depths range from 10 ft to 60 ft. Sites change based on weather and sea conditions. 900 Front St., Lahaina, HI 96761. ☎ 808-667-2080. E-mail: offshore@maui.net. Website: www.maui.net/~offshore.

Lahaina Divers, Inc., 143 Dickenson St., Lahaina, HI 96761. ☎ 800-998-3483 or 808-667-7496. E-mail: lahdivers@maui.net. Website: www.lahainadivers.com.

Other Activities

Train ride tours are available through "**The Sugar Cane Train**," ☎ 808-661-0089. A hiking permit must be obtained from the park concession for hikes around the volcano in Haleahala National Park. Board surfing is popular; check with **Extreme Sports**, ☎ 808-871-7954, for rentals and recommended locations. Extreme Sports also rents mountain bikes, body boards and snorkel gear. They have a climbing wall on premises. Maui has many historic museums and sites, as well as botanical gardens and plantations, a zoo in Kahului, and many beautiful beaches.

Maui Accommodations

Stouffer's Renaissance Wailea Beach is on the southwest coast, where beach snorkeling is great year-round. This luxury resort features five beautiful beaches, restaurants, tennis and golf. Expensive. Reserve through your travel agent or ☎ 808-879-4900. Website: renaissancehotels.com.

Sheraton Maui Hotel, on Kaanapali Beach in Lahaina, is near Black Rock, a favorite reef and wall dive for snorkelers and divers. The hotel features a lovely garden, restaurants, and a Polynesian show in the lounge. ☎ 800-325-3535 or 808-661-0031. Website: www.sheraton.com. Expensive.

The Westin Maui, a beautiful hotel on Kaanapali Beach. Standard rooms from $280 to $520 per night; suites $850 to $3,500. All rates for single or double occupancy. ☎ 808-526-4111, fax 808-523-3958. Website: www.westin.com.

Hawaii, the Big Island

Located 120 miles southeast of Oahu (40 minutes by air), Hawaii is the largest island of the archipelago. The birthplace of King Kamehameha, the best known ruler of the islands, it is also the location of the islands' only active volcanoes. Molten lava still flows to the sea. More than 20,000 varieties of orchids are grown. The entire west coast of Hawaii is a diving and snorkeling paradise. Over 50 miles of the shoreline are protected from high winds and swells, and many snorkeling areas can be reached easily from the beach. The most spectacular snorkeling is just offshore and all scuba and snorkeling sites are less than 30 minutes away by boat trip.

Best Dives of Hawaii

☆☆☆ **Casa Cave** lies north of Keauhou. Swim about 200 feet from the buoy toward shore to the wall. Descend to 50 feet, and you will see light coming from under a crack. The entrance to Casa Cave is eight feet high and 20 feet wide. Ten feet inside, the cave splits in two directions. Either path is 30 to 40 feet long and gets narrower as you swim through. Both exit in a small arena where you can turn around and return. After exiting, travel northward on the wall and use your light to explore overhangs for white tip sharks, which sometimes sleep in this area. The fish here are abundant in both number and variety. Expect to see numerous butterflyfish and angelfish.

☆☆☆ **Kaiwi**, also known as Fish Rock, is two miles from Kailua Baya. Depths range from 15 to 50 ft. Divers can swim through caves, around pinnacles and over coral-encrusted lava arches. Video and still photographers can capture graceful manta and eagle rays or large turtles. Triton and conch shells are found on the bottom as well as 7-11 crabs. Swarms of fish of all types are abundant. An occasional whale shark drifts by. Visibility is usually 75 to 100 ft and the seas are calm with a small south surge during the summer. Do not go too far north or west of this point as strong currents are not uncommon.

☆☆☆ **The Aquarium At Kealakekua Bay**, an underwater state park, is a beautiful reef inhabited by thousands of tame fish who enjoy following divers and snorkelers. The shallows can be reached from the beach, but the deeper reefs and drop-offs require a boat. Seas are flat calm, making this a popular site for novices. Divers can spot parrot fish, rudderfish , sergeant majors, bird wrasse, bronze tangs, trumpet fish, raccoon butterfly fish, tame moray eels and many more. The bottom is hard coral – lobe, finger, plate, cauliflower, octocorals – and patches of sand. Visibility is best on the outer reef. This is where Captain Cook was killed.

☆☆☆☆☆ **Manta Ray Madness**, one of the world's top 10 dive events, happens right off the Kona Surf Resort's beach. Just a couple of minutes by boat from Keauhou Bay, this nightly manta feeding ritual has become Kona's

Hawaii

favorite attraction. The mantas, ranging from four to 12 feet in wingspan, crowd this area to feed on plankton that thrives in the glow from the hotel floodlights. Depths of 20-40 ft.

☆☆☆☆ **Pine Tree Point**, just a 13-minute boat ride north of Honokohau Harbor, is a sensational lava flow area with many caves and arches. During the winter, whales are frequently sighted. Turtles, eels, manta rays, porpoises and armies of reef fish reside here. Finger and boulder corals cover the lava flows. Seas are usually calm with 75-100-ft visibility. Depths 15-60 ft.

☆☆☆ **Long Lava Tube** lies off the Red Hill area. At 120 feet in length, with shafts of sunlight coming through ceiling openings, these are the longest and most beautiful lava tubes on the Kona Coast. Schools of wrasse, butterfly fish, angelfish and snapper glide by. The crabs, coral shrimp and pipefish will keep photographers busy until they run out of air or film. Bring a dive light to see the creatures and lava formations inside the tubes. Depths run 25 to 45 ft. Occasional moderate surge.

Dive Operators of Hawaii

Jack's Diving Locker offers NAUI and PADI certifications and resort courses, with equipment provided at no charge. Guided tours to all the best sites on the coast and your portrait underwater if desired. Jack's doesn't offer scheduled, dedicated snorkeling trips, but will take snorkelers on normal dive trips and will charter boats for the day to snorkel or swim with dolphins. 75-5819 Alii Dr., Kailua-Kona, HI 96740. ☎ 800-345-4807. E-mail: divejdl@gte.net. Website: www.divejdl.com.

Kohala Divers, Ltd., a PADI five-star facility on the Kohala Coast, offers dive tours, certification courses and rentals. PO Box 44940, Kawaihae HI 96743. ☎ 808-882-7774, fax 808-882-1536. E-mail: theboss@kohaladivers.com. Website: www.kohaladivers.com.

Sea Paradise Scuba. Great diving and customer satisfaction are watchwords here. They will refund your money if you don't enjoy your dive. 78-7128 Kaleopapa Road, PO Box 5655, Kailua-Kona, HI 96745. ☎ 808-322-2500/4775. E-mail: spscuba@interpac.net. Website: www.seaparadise.com.

Kona Coast Divers offers complete vacation packages. Snorkeler rates include mask, fins and snorkel. The night manta ray trip includes an u/w light and chem-lite stick. Owners Julie and Jim Robinson operate a full-service shop with a well-equipped photography center. 75-5614 Palani Road, Kailua-Kona, HI 96740. ☎ 800-329-8802 or 808-329-8802. E-mail: divekona@ilhawaii. Website: http://konacoast divers.com

Manta Ray Dives Of Hawaii operates the *Rainbow Diver II*, a 28-foot, twin diesel powered, glass-bottom dive boat. They will take snorkeling and non-diving companions for a special rate. Night dives with mantas and day trips to the "Amphitheater" are favorites. PO Box 3457, Mililani, HI 96789. ☎ 800-982-6747. E-mail: rainbow@rainbowdiver.com. Website: www.rainbowdiver.com.

Offering a variety of dive trips, **Red Sail Sports** operates the *Noa Noa*, a 50-ft sailing catamaran for snorkelers. Captain Gary Hoover will not only take you to some wonderful sites, he can tell you of his experience as the captain of Kevin Costner's trimaran in the movie *Waterworld*. Red Sail Sports, 909 Montgomery St., San Francisco, CA 94133. ☎ 800-255-6425. E-mail: info@redsail.com. Website: www.redsail.com.

Live-Aboards

Kona Aggressor II takes you to offbeat, undiscovered reefs with unlimited diving and personalized service. Nitrox facilities, E-6 lab, battery charging stations on deck, light tables for viewing slides and video editing facilities. They also offer special charters with renowned photographers such as Stan Waterman and Jim Church. Luxury style and comfort. Live/Dive Pacific, Inc., 74-5588 Pawai Pl., Bldg. F, Kailua-Kona, HI 96740. ☎ 800-344-KONA or 808-329-8182, fax 329-2628. E-mail: 103162.2335@compuserve.com or diveboat@aol.com. Website: http://pac-agressor.com.

Hawaii Accommodations

For a complete list of accommodations on Hawaii, call the Hawaii Visitor and Convention Bureau, ☎ 800-464-2924 or 800-GO-HAWAII.

Kona Surf Resort is home to Manta Ray Divers and the *Rainbow Diver II*. Fifty yards off the point behind the hotel is Manta Ray Madness, one of the world's 10 best dives. Rooms $128-$215, suites $375-$550. The resort also offers wedding planning, from a simple ceremony to a lavish affair. Their chapel nestles in the palms by a romantic lagoon. ☎ 800-367-8011. E-mail: konasurf@ilhawaii.net. Website: www.ilhawaii. net/konasurf/index.html.

Royal Kona Resort, offers 441 rooms, health club, gym, fridges and tennis. Rooms $140-$250, suite $290. ☎ 800-919-8333. E-mail: craigd@royalkona.com. Website: www.royalkona.com.

Kauai, the Garden Isle

Kauai, a tropical oasis famed for its relaxed, rural atmosphere, features a wealth of dive and snorkeling adventures. The island's topside scenery delights visitors with postcard waterfalls, miles of beautiful beaches and swimming lagoons (featured as the dream world of Bali H'ai in the movie *South Pacific* and in the TV series *Fantasy Island*). There are exotic birds, rain forests, botanic gardens, deep canyons, and lush valleys. Kauai is also the oldest Hawaiian island and richest in folklore and history.

Because of Kauai's age, its marine life is more unusual and varied than any-where else in the state. South shore sites, accessible year-round, offer divers and snorkelers a wonderland of friendly fish and vibrant corals. On the north shore, huge surf pounds the beaches during winter, but summer offers oppor-tunities to explore networks of lava tubes and light-filled caverns.

Best Dive Sites of Kauai

☆☆☆☆ **Sheraton Caverns** are formed by three lava tubes intercon-nected with a small wall. Octopi, turtles, occasional lionfish, morays, frogfish and leaf scorpionfish live here. This is Kauai's most visited dive site. Depth 40-65 ft. No current.

☆☆☆☆☆ **Ni'ihau,** or *The Forbidden Island,* is a privately owned island 18 miles from Kauai. It is a preserve dedicated to the traditions and culture of old Hawaii. Residents lead a primitive lifestyle without electricity, medical fa-cilities or paved roads. Outsiders are forbidden to step on shore. Diving offers great visibility, depths from 15-130 ft, with vertical walls, lava tubes and tun-nels. Many fish, lobster, rays, monk seals, turtles, cowry shells, dolphins and sharks. Diveable only during the summer when the winds ease off. Diving and snorkeling areas.

☆☆☆☆ **Mana Crack**, an excellent 50-95-ft wall dive, sits off Kauai's west coast. Like the trip to Ni'ihau, it is weather-dependent, usually taking the whole day to complete. Both Mana and Ni'ihau diving are supreme. Pristine, near-virgin waters makes these dive sites awesome experiences.

☆☆☆The **Tunnels Beach** dive starts at the northeast corner of the large bay adjacent to Haena Beach Park. The bottom starts shallow then drops off to 70 feet at some spots. Once you go beyond the drop-off, you'll find tunnel entrances eroded into the reef. Be on the lookout for rafting company boats unloading their passengers in this area. To reach the site, travel .9 mile past Charo's Restaurant to the private driveway leading to Tunnels Beach. It's best to keep going to the park (after the next one-lane bridge and opposite the dry cave), then walk along the beach. The shallows are OK for snorkeling.

☆☆☆ **Ahukini Landing** features a nice wall dive on the west side with ea-gle rays and stingrays, turtles, leaf scorpion, frogfish, surgeonfish, octopi, cowry shells and ordnance from WWII. Lobsters too. Entry from shore. Al-though initial visibility in the harbor can be poor, this changes as you round the point of the harbor. A large ship dumped her cargo of World War II ord-nance over the reef, leaving artillery rounds, mortar shells and boxes upon boxes of bullets. (Look, but don't touch). Dive this site with a local guide. Depth 30-70 ft. The waters get extremely rough when an east wind is blowing.

☆☆☆ **Oasis Reef**, a lone seamount off Kauai's south shore, is protected and diveable all year. This coral-encrusted pinnacle rises from a sandy bot-tom at 35 ft to just below the ocean surface. Whirlwinds of false moorish idols, triggerfish, butterfly fish and porcupine pufferfish circle the mount. Octopi hide on the flats, lobsters and moray eels live under the ledges. Depths from four to 35 ft.

Snorkeling

☆☆ **Poipu Beach** offers ideal conditions for beginners. No current, depths from three to 20 ft and plenty of fish. Go south on Poipu Rd. from Koala town to Hoowili Rd. Turn right on Hoowili Rd. Parking and full facilities available.

☆☆☆☆ **Aquarium**, on the southeast side of Kauai, takes its name from the variety of colorful tropicals in residence. This shallow reef stretches into an expanse of lava ledges and small coral valleys. You'll see several cannons from an 18th-century wreck. Depths from 25 ft.

Dive Operators on Kauai

Dive Kauai Scuba Center, 576 Kuhio Hgwy., Kapa'a, HI 96746. ☎ 800-828-3483 or 808-822-0452. E-mail: email@divekauai.com. Website: www. divekauai.com.

Seasport Divers, ☎ 800-685-5889 or 808-742-9303. E-mail: seasport@ pixi.com. Website: www.aloha-hawaii.com/seasport.

Accommodations on Kauai

For a complete list of accommodations on Kauai, ☎ 800-245-2824.

The Holiday Inn Sunspree Kauai Resort, located in the town of Kapaa by Wailua Bay, features two pools, spa, fitness room, restaurant, mini-mart, room service, central laundry, tennis courts, and free parking. Rooms $150-$175, suites $195-$275. 3-5920 Kuhio Hwy, Kapaa, HI 96746. ☎ 888-823-5111, fax 808-823-6666. E-mail: info@holidayinn-kauai.com. Website: www.holidayinn-kauai.com.

Sheraton Kauai Resort has 413 rooms, two restaurants,, two pools, and three tennis courts. Rated three stars by AAA. Rooms $265-$425, suites $475-$740. 2440 Hoonani Road, Koloa, Kauai, HI 96756. ☎ 808-742-1661, fax 808-742 9777. E-mail: patty_alama@ittsheraton.com. Website: www.sheraton-kauai.com.

Offbeat & Adventure Tours

Midway Dive and Sport Fishing runs dive trips to Midway Island. Charter flights leave Honolulu for Midway on Monday and Wednesday. Midway, a remote coral atoll 1,250 miles west-northwest of Honolulu, is the site of the largest naval battle ever fought. Now a wildlife refuge, the island opened to the public for the first time in 1996. Midway rivals the Galapagos for the variety of wildlife and their lack of fear of humans. Accommodations are in restored military barracks. Rooms are double occupancy with private bath and cafeteria-style meals. A seven-night stay, including airfare, rooms, five days of diving (three dives per day), taxes and refuge fee, costs $2,700. ☎ 888-244-8582. E-mail: dglover@peachcity.com. Website: www.midwaydive.com.

Oceanic Society Expeditions offers year-round naturalist-led tours to Midway. You can walk among nesting seabirds, see monk seals, green turtles and spinner dolphins. Oceanic Society Expeditions, Fort Mason Center, Building E, San Francisco, CA 94123. ☎ 800-326-7491, fax 415-474-3395.

Facts

Recompression Chamber: Kuakini Hospital in Honolulu has a state-of-the-art hyperbaric facility with several chambers configured like an airliner. ☎ 808-587-3425. This is the only chamber in the islands for civilians. Pearl Harbor has one for active military members.

Medical Emergency: ☎ 911 (Kauai, Oahu, Maui), or "O" for operator. On Lanai, ☎ 565-6525 (police), 565-6411 (ambulance) or "O" for operator.

Getting There: All-expense packages including airfare can greatly simplify planning. Several major airlines fly into Honolulu International Airport from all mainland cities in the US. The largest carrier is Continental. Other flights are available from United, Northwest Orient, Western, American, Delta, Hawaiian Air, World. Frequent daily flights from Honolulu to the other main islands are offered by Aloha and Hawaiian Air.

Entry Requirements: Non-US citizens must have a passport and visa. Canadians must prove place of birth with either a birth certificate or passport.

Clothing: A lightweight wetsuit is suggested. Ocean temperatures range from 72° to 80°F. Topside is tropical with average air temperatures in the 80s. During winter when evening temperatures can dip as low as the upper 50s a light jacket or sweater is recommended. Light casual clothing is appropriate for most activities at sea level. Lower temperatures are found in the mountains.

Note: Divers and snorkelers should use a water-resistant sunscreen with a high sun protection factor (SPF) rating to prevent painful sunburn.

Export Restrictions: With the exception of pineapples and coconuts, no fruits, seeds, coffee, sugarcane, soils, or plants may be taken from the islands.

Currency: US $; credit cards widely accepted.

Marine Forecasts: Kauai, ☎ 245-3564; Oahu, ☎ 836-3921; Maui, ☎ 877-3477; Hawaii, ☎ 935-9883.

Additional Travel and Accommodation Information: ☎ 800-GO-HAWAII. Website: www.hawaii.gov/tourism/. See your travel agent or write to Hawaii Visitors Bureau, 2270 Kalakaua Avenue, Honolulu, HI 96815.

Index